Communications
in Computer and Information Science   2054

Rationale

The CCIS series is devoted to the publication of proceedings of computer science conferences. Its aim is to efficiently disseminate original research results in informatics in printed and electronic form. While the focus is on publication of peer-reviewed full papers presenting mature work, inclusion of reviewed short papers reporting on work in progress is welcome, too. Besides globally relevant meetings with internationally representative program committees guaranteeing a strict peer-reviewing and paper selection process, conferences run by societies or of high regional or national relevance are also considered for publication.

Topics

The topical scope of CCIS spans the entire spectrum of informatics ranging from foundational topics in the theory of computing to information and communications science and technology and a broad variety of interdisciplinary application fields.

Information for Volume Editors and Authors

Publication in CCIS is free of charge. No royalties are paid, however, we offer registered conference participants temporary free access to the online version of the conference proceedings on SpringerLink (http://link.springer.com) by means of an http referrer from the conference website and/or a number of complimentary printed copies, as specified in the official acceptance email of the event.

CCIS proceedings can be published in time for distribution at conferences or as post-proceedings, and delivered in the form of printed books and/or electronically as USBs and/or e-content licenses for accessing proceedings at SpringerLink. Furthermore, CCIS proceedings are included in the CCIS electronic book series hosted in the SpringerLink digital library at http://link.springer.com/bookseries/7899. Conferences publishing in CCIS are allowed to use Online Conference Service (OCS) for managing the whole proceedings lifecycle (from submission and reviewing to preparing for publication) free of charge.

Publication process

The language of publication is exclusively English. Authors publishing in CCIS have to sign the Springer CCIS copyright transfer form, however, they are free to use their material published in CCIS for substantially changed, more elaborate subsequent publications elsewhere. For the preparation of the camera-ready papers/files, authors have to strictly adhere to the Springer CCIS Authors' Instructions and are strongly encouraged to use the CCIS LaTeX style files or templates.

Abstracting/Indexing

CCIS is abstracted/indexed in DBLP, Google Scholar, EI-Compendex, Mathematical Reviews, SCImago, Scopus. CCIS volumes are also submitted for the inclusion in ISI Proceedings.

How to start

To start the evaluation of your proposal for inclusion in the CCIS series, please send an e-mail to ccis@springer.com.

Deepak Garg · Joel J. P. C. Rodrigues ·
Suneet Kumar Gupta · Xiaochun Cheng ·
Pushpender Sarao · Govind Singh Patel
Editors

Advanced Computing

13th International Conference, IACC 2023
Kolhapur, India, December 15–16, 2023
Revised Selected Papers, Part II

 Springer

Editors
Deepak Garg
SR University
Warangal, India

Suneet Kumar Gupta
Bennett University
Greater Noida, India

Pushpender Sarao
Lovely Professional University
Phagwara, India

Joel J. P. C. Rodrigues
COPELABS, Lusófona University
Lisbon, Portugal

Xiaochun Cheng
Swansea University
Wales, UK

Govind Singh Patel
SITCOE Engineering College
Ichalkaranji, India

ISSN 1865-0929   ISSN 1865-0937 (electronic)
Communications in Computer and Information Science
ISBN 978-3-031-56702-5   ISBN 978-3-031-56703-2 (eBook)
https://doi.org/10.1007/978-3-031-56703-2

This Springer imprint is published by the registered company Springer Nature Switzerland AG
The registered company address is: Gewerbestrasse 11, 6330 Cham, Switzerland

Paper in this product is recyclable.

Preface

The objective of the 13th International Advanced Computing Conference (IACC 2023) was to bring together researchers, developers, and practitioners from academia and industry working in the domain of advanced computing. Researchers were invited to share their thoughts and present recent developments and technical solutions in the domains of Advances in Machine Learning and Deep Learning, Advances in Applications of Artificial Intelligence in Interdisciplinary Areas, Reinforcement Learning, and Advances in Data Science. The conference took place on the 15th and 16th December 2023 at Ichalkaranji, Kolhapur, Maharashtra, India. All editions of the series are successfully indexed in ISI, Scopus, DBLP, Compendex, SJR, and Google Scholar etc.

Conference follows single blind review process and has the policy of at least three reviews per paper. This year's conference received 425 submissions, of which 72 articles were accepted. The conference has the track record of acceptance rates from 15% to 20% in the last 12 years. More than 13 IEEE/ACM Fellows hold key positions on the conference committee, giving it a quality edge. In the last 12 years the conference citation score has been consistently increasing.

This has been possible due to adherence to quality parameters of the review and acceptance rate without any exception that allows us to make some of the best research available through this platform.

December 2023

Deepak Garg
Joel J. P. C. Rodrigues
Xiaochun Cheng
Suneet Kumar Gupta
Pushpender Sarao
Govind Singh Patel

Organization

Honorary Co-chairs

Sundaraja Sitharama Iyengar	Florida International University, USA
Sartaj Sahni	University of Florida, USA
Jagannathan Sarangpani	Missouri University of Science and Technology, USA
Ajith Abraham	Bennett University, India
P. N. Suganthan	KINDI Center for Computing Research, Qatar University, Qatar
Jaume Anguera	Universitat Ramon Llull, Spain

General Co-chairs

Deepak Garg	SR University, India
Suneet K. Gupta	Bennett University, India
Joel J. P. C. Rodrigues	Instituto de Telecomunicações, Portugal
Xiaochun Cheng	Swansea University, UK
Pushpender Sarao	Lovely Professional University, India
Govind Singh Patel	Sharad Institute of Technology College of Engineering, India

Program Co-chairs

Kit Wong	University College London, UK
George Ghinea	Brunel University London, UK
Carol Smidts	Ohio State University, USA
Ram D. Sriram	National Institute of Standards & Technology, USA
Sanjay Madria	University of Missouri, USA
Marques Oge	Florida Atlantic University, USA
Vijay Kumar	University of Missouri-Kansas City, USA
Ajay Gupta	Western Michigan University, USA

Special Issue Co-chairs

Akansha Singh	Bennett University, India
Dilbag Singh	Gwangju Institute of Science & Technology, South Korea

Technical Program Committee/International Advisory Committee

Shivani Goel	SR University, India
Sumeet Dua	Louisiana Tech University, USA
Roger Zimmermann	National University of Singapore, Singapore
Seeram Ramakrishna	National University of Singapore, Singapore
B. V. R. Chowdari	NUS, Singapore & Nanyang Technological University, Singapore
Hari Mohan Pandey	Edge Hill University, UK
Selwyn Piramuthu	University of Florida, USA
Bharat Bhargava	Purdue University, USA
Omer F. Rana	Cardiff University, UK
Javed I. Khan	Kent State University, USA
Harpreet Singh	Wayne State University, USA
Rajeev Agrawal	North Carolina A&T State University, USA
P. Prabhakaran	St. Joseph University, Tanzania
Yuliya Averyanova	National Aviation University, Ukraine
Mohammed M. Banet	Jordan University of Technology, Jordan
Dawid Zydek	Idaho State University, USA
Wensheng Zhang	Iowa State University, USA
Bal Virdee	London Metropolitan University, UK
Qun Wu	Harbin Institute of Technology, China
Anh V. Dinh	University of Saskatchewan, Canada
Lakshman Tamil	University of Texas, USA
P. D. D. Dominic	Universiti Teknologi Petronas, Malaysia
Muhammad Sabbir Rahman	North South University, Bangladesh
Zablon Akoko Mbero	University of Botswana, Botswana
V. L. Narasimhan	University of Botswana, Botswana
Kin-Lu Wong	National Sun Yat-sen University, Taiwan
Pawan Lingras	Saint Mary's University, USA
P. G. S. Velmurugan	Thiagaraja College of Engineering, India
N. B. Balamurugan	Thiagaraja College of Engineering, India
Mahesh Bundele	Poornima University, India
N. Venkateswaran	Sri Sivasubramaniya Nadar College of Engineering, India

S. Sundaresh	IEEE Madras Section, India
Premanand V. Chandramani	SSN College of Engineering, India
Mini Vasudevan	Ericsson India Pvt. Ltd., India
P. Swarnalatha	VIT, India
P. Venkatesh	Thiagaraja College of Engineering, India
B. Venkatalakshmi	Velammal Engineering College, India
M. Marsalin Beno	St. Xavier's Catholic College of Engineering, India
M. Arun	VIT, India
Porkumaran K.	NGP Institute of Technology, India
D. Ezhilarasi	NIT Tiruchirappalli, India
Ramya Vijay	SASTRA University, India
S. Rajaram	Thiagaraja College of Engineering, India
B. Yogameena	Thiagaraja College of Engineering, India
S. Joseph Gladwin	SSN College of Engineering, India
D. Nirmal	Karunya University, India
N. Mohankumar	SKP Institute of Technology, India
A. Jawahar	SSN College of Engineering, India
K. Dhayalini	K. Ramakrishnan College of Engineering, India
Diganta Sengupta	Meghnad Saha Institute of Technology, India
Supriya Chakraborty	Amity University, India
Mamta Arora	Manav Rachna University, India
Om Prakash Jena	Ravenshaw University, India
Sandeep Singh Sengar	University of Copenhagen, Denmark
Murali Chemuturi	Chemuturi Consultants, India
Madhu Vadlamani	Cognizant, India
A. N. K. Prasannanjaneyulu	Institute of Insurance and Risk Management, India
O. Obulesu	G. Narayanamma Institute of Technology & Science, India
Rajendra R. Patil	GSSSIETW, India
Ajay Kumar	Chitkara University Institute of Engineering & Technology, India
D. P. Kothari	THDC Institute of Hydropower Engineering and Technology, India
T. S. N. Murthy	JNTUK Vizianagaram, India
Nitesh Tarbani	Sipna College of Engineering & Technology, India
Jesna Mohan	Mar Baselios College of Engineering and Technology, India
Manoj K. Patel	CSIR, India
Pravati Swain	NIT Goa, India
Manoj Kumar	University of Petroleum and Energy Studies, India

E. S. Gopi	National Institute of Technology Tiruchirappalli, India
Mithun B Patil	NKOCET, India
Priya Saha	LPU, India
Sahaj Saxena	Thapar Institute of Engineering and Technology, India
Dinesh G. Harkut	Prof Ram Meghe College of Engineering & Management, India
Pushpendra Singh	National Institute of Technology Hamirpur, India
Nirmala J. Saunshimath	Nitte Meenakshi Institute of Technology, India
Mayank Pandey	MNNIT, India
Sudeep D. Thepade	Pimpri Chinchwad College of Engineering, India
Pimal Khanpara	Nirma University, India
Rohit Lalwani	MIT University of Meghalaya, India
Loshma Gunisetti	Sri Vasavi Engineering College, India
Vishweshwar Kallimani	University of Nottingham, UK
Amit Kumar Mishra	DIT University, India
Pawan Whig	Vivekananda Institute of Professional Studies, India
Dhatri Pandya	Sarvajanik College of Engineering and Technology, India
Asha S. Manek	RV Institute of Technology and Management, India
Lingala Thirupathi	Methodist College of Engineering & Technology, India
P. Mahanti	University of New Brunswick, Canada
Shaikh Muhammad Allayear	Daffodil International University, Bangladesh
Basanta Joshi	Tribhuvan University, Nepal
S. R. N. Reddy	IGDTUW, India
Mehran Alidoost Nia	University of Tehran, Iran
Ambili P. S.	Saintgits Group of Institutions, India
M. A. Jabbar	Vardhaman College of Engineering, India
Lokendra Kumar Tiwari	Ewing Christian College, India
Abhay Saxena	Dev Sanskriti Vishwavidyalaya, India
Kanika Bansal	Chitkara University, India
Pooja M. R.	Vidyavardhaka College of Engineering, India
Pranav Dass	Bharati Vidyapeeth's College of Engineering, India
Avani R. Vasant	Babaria Institute of Technology, India
Bhanu Prasad	Florida A&M University, USA
Barenya Bikash Hazarika	NIT Arunachal Pradesh, India
Ipseeta Nanda	Gopal Narayan Singh University, India
Satyendra Singh	Bhartiya Skill Development University, India

Sudip Mandal	Jalpaiguri Govt. Engineering College, India
Naveen Kumar	IIIT Vadodara, India
Parag Rughani	National Forensic Sciences University, India
K. Shirin Bhanu	Sri Vasavi Engineering College, India
R. Malmathanraj	NITT, India
Latika Singh	Ansal University, India
Gizachew Hailegebriel Mako	Ethio telecom, Ethiopia
Tessy Mathew	Mar Baselios College of Engineering and Technology, India
Grzegorz Chodak	Wroclaw University of Science and Technology, Poland
Neetu Verma	D.C.R.U.S.T Murthal, India
Sharda A. Chhabria	G H Raisoni Institute of Engineering & Technology, India
Neetesh Saxena	Cardiff University, UK
R. Venkatesan	Ministry of Earth Sciences, India
V. Jayaprakasan	IEEE Madras Section, India
D. Venkata Vara Prasad	SSN College of Engineering, India
Jayakumari J.	Mar Baselios College of Engineering and Technology, India
P. A. Manoharan	IEEE Madras Section, India
S. Salivahanan	IEEE Madras Section, India
P. Santhi Thilagam	National Institute of Technology Karnataka, India
Umapada Pal	Indian Statistical Institute, India
S. Suresh	NIT Trichy, India
V. Mariappan	NIT Trichy, India
T. Senthil Kumar	Anna University, India
S. Chandramohan	JNTUA College of Engineering, India
D. Devaraj	Kalasalingam Academy of Research & Education, India
J. William	Agnel Institute of Technology & Design, India
R. Kalidoss	SSN College of Engineering, India
R. K. Mugelan	Vellore Institute of Technology, India
V. Vinod Kumar	Government College of Engineering Kannur, India
R. Saravanan	VIT, India
S. Sheik Aalam	iSENSE Intelligence Solutions, India
E. Srinivasan	Pondicherry Engineering College, India
B. Surendiran	National Institute of Technology Puducherry, India
Varun P. Gopi	NIT Tiruchirappalli India
V. Vijaya Chamundeeswari	Velammal Engineering College, India
T. Prabhakar	GMRIT, India

V. Kamakoti	IIT Madras, India
N. Janakiraman	KLN College of Engineering, India
V. Anandakrishanan	NIT Trichy, India
R. B. Patel	MMEC, India
Adesh Kumar Sharma	NDRI, India
Gunamani Jena	JNTU, India
Maninder Singh	Thapar University, India
Manoj Manuja	NIT Trichy, India
Ajay K. Sharma	Chitkara University, India
Manjit Patterh	Punjabi University, India
L. M. Bhardwaj	Amity University, India
Parvinder Singh	DCRUST, India
M. Syamala	Punjab University, India
Lalit Awasthi	NIT Jalandhar, India
Ajay Bansal	NIT Jalandhar, India
Ravi Aggarwal	Adobe Systems, USA
Sigurd Meldal	San Jose State University, USA
M. Balakrishnan	IIT Madras, India
Malay Pakhira	KGEC, India
Savita Gupta	PU Chandigarh, India
Manas Ranjan Patra	Berhampur University, India
Sukhwinder Singh	PU Chandigarh, India
Dharmendra Kumar	GJUST, India
Chandan Singh	Punjabi University, India
Rajinder Nath	Kurukshetra University, India
Manjaiah D. H.	Mangalore University, India
Himanshu Aggarwal	Punjabi University, India
R. S. Kaler	Thapar University, India
Pabitra Pal Choudhury	Indian Statistical Institute, India
S. K. Pal	DRDO, India
G. S. Lehal	Punjabi University, India
Rajkumar Kannan	Bishop Heber College, India
Yogesh Chaba	GJUST, India
Amardeep Singh	Punjabi University, India
Sh. Sriram Birudavolu	Oracle India Limited, India
Ajay Rana	Amity University, India
Kanwal Jeet Singh	Punjabi University, India
C. K. Bhensdadia	DD University, India
Savina Bansal	GZSCET, India
Mohammad Asger	BGSB, India
Rajesh Bhatia	PEC, India
Stephen John Turner	VISTEC, India

Chiranjeev Kumar	IIT (ISM) Dhanbad, India
Bhim Singh	IIT Delhi, India
A. K. Sharma	BSAITM, India
Rob Reilly	MIT, USA
B. K. Murthy	CDAC, India
Karmeshu	JNU, India
K. K. Biswas	IIT Delhi, India
Sandeep Sen	IIT Delhi, India
Suneeta Aggarwal	MNNIT, India
Raghuraj Singh	HBTI, India
D. K. Lobiyal	JNU, India
R. S. Yadav	MNNIT, India
Bulusu Anand	IIT Roorkee, India
R. K. Singh	KEC Dwarahat, India
Sateesh Kumar Peddoju	IIT Roorkee, India
Divakar Yadav	JIIT, India
Naveen Kumar Singh	IGNOU, India
R. S. Raw	AIACTR (NSUT East Campus), India
Vidushi Sharma	GBU, India
Sumit Srivastava	Manipal University, India
Manish K. Gupta	DAIICT, India
P. K. Saxena	DRDO, India
B. K. Das	ITM University, India
Y. Raghu Reddy	IIIT Hyderabad, India
B. Chandra	IIT Delhi, India
R. K. Agarwal	JNU, India
Basim Alhadidi	Al-Balqa' Applied University, Jordan
M. Monirujjaman Khan	North South University, Bangladesh
Emmanuel Ndashimye	University of Rwanda & CMU-Africa, Rwanda
Naveen Garg	IIT Jodhpur, India
K. S. Subramanian	IGNOU, India
Biplab Sikdar	NUS, Singapore
Sreeram Ramakrishna	NUS, Singapore
Vikas Mathur	Citrix, India
Hari Krishna Garg	NUS, Singapore
Raja Dutta	IIT Kharagpur, India
Y. V. S. Lakshmi	India
Vishakha Vaidya	Adobe, India
Sudipto Shankar Dasgupta	Infosys Limited, India
Atal Chaudhari	Jadavpur University, India
Gangaboraiah Andanaiah	KIMS, India
Champa H. N.	UVCE, India

Ramakanth Kumar P.	RVCE, India
S. N. Omkar	IISC Bangalore, India
Balaji Rajendran	CDAC, India
Annapoorna P. Patil	MSRIT, India
K. N. Chandrashekhar	SJCIT, India
Mohammed Misbahuddin	CDAC, India
Saroj Meher	ISI, India
Jharna Majumdar	NMIT, India
N. K. Cauvery	RVCE, India
G. K. Patra	CSIR, India
Anandi Jayadharmarajan	Oxford College of Engg., India
K. R. Suneetha	BIT Mesra, India
M. L. Shailaja	AIT, India
K. R. Murali Mohan	GOI, India
Ramesh Paturi	Microsoft, India
S. Viswanadha Raju	JNTU, India
C. Krishna Mohan	IIT Chennai, India
R. T. Goswamy	Techno International New Town, India
B. Surekha	K S Institute of Technology, India
P. Trinatha Rao	GITAM University, India
G. Varaprasad	BMS College of Engineering, India
M. Usha Rani	SPMVV, India
P. V. Lakshmi	SPMVV, India
K. A. Selvaradjou	PEC, India
Ch. Satyananda Reddy	Andhra University, India
Jeegar A. Trivedi	Sardar Patel University, India
S. V. Rao	IIT Guwahati, India
Suresh Varma	Aadikavi Nannaya University, India
T. Ranga Babu	RVR & JC College of Engineering, India
D. Venkat Rao	Narasaraopet Inst. of Technology, India
N. Sudhakar Reddy	S V Engineering College, India
Dhiraj Sunehra	Jawaharlal Nehru Technological University, India
Madhavi Gudavalli	JNYU Kakinada, India
B. Hemanth Kumar	RVR & JC College of Engineering, India
A. Sri Nagesh	RVR & JC College of Engg., India
Bipin Bihari Jaya Singh	CVR College of Engg, India
M. Ramesh	JNTU, India
P. Rajarajeswari	GITAM University, India
R. Kiran Kumar	Krishna University, India
D. Ramesh	JNTU, India
B. Kranthi Kiran	JNTU, India
K. Usha Rani	SPM University, India

A. Nagesh	MGIT, India
P. Sammulal	JNTU, India
G. Narasimha	JNTU, India
B. V. Ram Naresh Yadav	JNTU, India
B. N. Bhandari	JNTUH, India
O. B. V. Ramanaiah	JNTUH College of Engineering, India
Anil Kumar Vuppala	IIIT Hyderabad, India
Duggirala Srinivasa Rao	JNTU, India
Makkena Madhavi Latha	JNTUH, India
Anitha Sheela Kancharla	JNTUH, India
B. Padmaja Rani	JNTUH College of Engineering Hyderabad, India
S. Mangai	Velalar College of Engg. & Tech., India
P. Chandra Sekhar	Osmania University, India
Chakraborty Mrityunjoy	IIT Kharagpur, India
Manish Shrivastava	IIIT Hyderabad, India
Uttam Kumar Roy	Jadavpur University, India
Kalpana Naidu	IIIT Kota, India
A. Swarnalatha	St. Joseph's College of Engg., India
Aaditya Maheshwari	Techno India NJR Institute of Tech., India
Ajit Panda	National Institute of Science and Technology, India
R. Anuradha	Sri Ramakrishna Engg. College, India
B. G. Prasad	BMS College of Engg., India
Seung-Hwa Chung	Trinity College Dublin, Ireland
D. Murali	VIT, India
Deepak Padmanabhan	Queen's University Belfast, UK
Firoz Alam	RMIT University, Australia
Frederic Andres	NII, Japan
Srinath Doss	Botho University, Botswana
Munish Kumar	Maharaja Ranjit Singh Punjab Tech University, India
Norwati Mustapha	UPM, India
Hamidah Ibrahim	UPM, India
Denis Reilly	Liverpool John Moores University, UK
Ioannis Kypraios	De Montfort University, UK
Yongkang Xing	De Montfort University, UK
P. Shivakumara	University of Malaya, Malaysia
Ravinder Kumar	TIET Patiala, India
Ankur Gupta	Rishihood University, India
Rahul Kr. Verma	IIIT Lucknow, India
Mohit Sajwan	NSUT, India
Vijaypal Singh Rathor	IIITDM, India

Deepak Singh	NIT Raipur, India
Simranjit Singh	NIT Jalandhar, India
Suchi Kumari	Shiv Nadar University, India
Kuldeep Chaurasia	Bennett University, India
Indrajeet Gupta	SR University, India
Shakti Sharma	Bennett University, India
Hiren Thakkar	PDPU, India
Mayank Swankar	IIT(BHU) Varanasi, India
Tapas Badal	Bennett University, India
Vipul Kr. Mishra	Gatishakti University, India
Tanveer Ahmed	Bennett University, India
Madhushi Verma	Bennett University, India
Gaurav Singal	NSUT, India
Anurag Goswami	Bennett University, India
Durgesh Kumar Mishra	Sri Aurobindo Institute of Technology, India
S. Padma	Madanapalle Institute of Technology & Science, India
Deepak Prashar	Lovely Professional University, India
Nidhi Khare	NMIMS, India
Sandeep Kumar	IIT Delhi, India
Dattatraya V. Kodavade	D.K.T.E Society's Textile & Engineering Institute, India
A. Obulesu	Anurag University, India
K. Suvarna Vani	V R Siddhartha Engineering College, India
G. Singaravel	K.S.R. College of Engineering, India
Ajay Shiv Sharma	Melbourne Institute of Technology, Australia
Abhishek Shukla	R.D. Engineering College Technical Campus Ghaziabad, India
V. K. Jain	Mody University, India
Deepak Poola	IBM India Private Limited, India
Bhadri Raju M. S. V. S.	S.R.K.R. Engineering College, India
Yamuna Prasad	IIT Jammu, India
Vishnu Vardhan B.	JNTUH College of Engineering Manthani, India
Virendra Kumar Bhavsar	Univ. of New Brunswick, Canada
Siva S. Skandha	CMR College of Engineering, India
Vaibhav Anu	Montclair State University, India
V. Gomathi	National Engineering College, India
Sudipta Roy	Assam University, India
Srabanti Maji	DIT University, India
Shylaja S. S.	PESU, India
Shweta Agrawal	SIRT, India

Shreenivas Londhe	Vishwakarma Institute of Information Technology, India
Shirin Bhanu Koduri	Vasavi Engineering College, India
Shailendra Aswale	SRIEIT, India
Shachi Natu	TSE College Mumbai, India
Santosh Saraf	Coordinator Technology Business Incubation Center Belagavi, India
Samayveer Singh	Ambedkar National Institute of Technology, India
Sabu M. Thampi	IIIT and Mgt-Kerala Thiruvananthapuram, India
Roshani Raut	Vishwakarma Institute of Information Technology, India
Radhika K. R.	BMSCE, India
R. Priya Vaijayanthi	NSRIT, India
M. Naresh Babu	NIT Silchar, India
Krishnan Rangarajan	Dayananda Sagar College of Engineering, India
Prashant Singh Rana	Thapar Institute of Engg. & Tech., India
Parteek Bhatia	Thapar Institute of Engineering & Technology, India
Venkata Padmavati Metta	BIT, India
Laxmi Lydia	VIIT, India
Nikunj Tahilramani	Dolcera IT Services Pvt Ltd, India
Navanath Saharia	IIIT Manipur, India
Nagesh Vadaparthi	MVGR College of Engineering, India
Manne Suneetha	VR Siddhartha Engineering College, India
Sumalatha Lingamgunta	JNTU Kakinada, India
Kalaiarasi Sonai Muthu Anbananthen	Multimedia University, Malaysia
K. Subramanian	IIT Kanpur, India
Singaraju Jyothi	Sri Padmavati Mahila Visvavidyalayam, India
Vinit Jakhetiya	IIT Jammu, India
Yashwantsinh Jadeja	Marwadi University, India
Harsh Dev	PSIT, India
Yashodhara V. Haribhakta	Government College of Engineering, India
Gopal Sakarkar	GHRCE, India
R. Gnanadass	Pondicherry Engineering College, India
K. Giri Babu	VVIT, India
Geeta Sikka	B R Ambedkar National Institute of Technology, India
Gaurav Varshney	IIT Jammu, India
G. L. Prajapati	Devi Ahilya University, India
G. Kishor Kumar	RGMCET, India
Md. Saidur Rahman	Bangladesh University of Engineering and Technology, Bangladesh

Wali Khan Mashwani	Kohat University of Science & Technology, Pakistan
Krishna Kiran Vamsi Dasu	Sri Sathya Sai Institute, India
Sisira Kumar Kapat	Utkal Gaurav Madhusudan Institute of Technology, India
Kuldeep Sharma	Chitkara University, India
Zankhana H. Shah	BVM Engineering College, India
Rekha Ramesh	Shah and Anchor Kutchhi Engineering College, India
Gopalkrishna Joshi	KLE Technological University, India
Ganga Holi	AMC Engineering College, India
K. Kotecha	Symbiosis International, India
Radhakrishna Bhat	MAHE, India
Kuldeep Singh	Carnegie Mellon University, USA
Binod Kumar	JSPM's Rajarshi Shahu College of Engineering, India
Raju Kumar	Chandigarh University, India
Nitin S. Goje	Webster University in Tashkent, Uzbekistan
Pushpa Mala S.	Dayananda Sagar University, India
Ashish Sharma	GLA University, India
Ashwath Rao B.	Manipal Institute of Technology, India
Deepak Motwani	Amity University, India
V. Sowmya	Amrita School of Engineering, India
Jayashri Nair	VNR VJIET, India
Rajesh C. Sanghvi	G.H. Patel College of Engineering & Technology, India
Ashwin Dobariya	Marwadi University, India
Tapas Kumar Patra	CET Bhubaneswar, India
J. Naren	Rathinam College of Arts and Science, India
Rekha. K. S.	National Institute of Engineering, India
Mohammed Murtuza Qureshi	Digital Employment Exchange, India
Vasantha Kalyani David	Avinashilingam Institute for Home Science and Higher Education for Women, India
K. Sakthidasan	Hindustan Institute of Technology and Science, India
Shreyas Rao	Sahyadri College of Engineering and Management, India
Hiranmayi Ranganathan	Lawrence Livermore National Laboratory, USA
Sanjaya Kumar Panda	National Institute of Technology Warangal, India
Puspanjali Mohapatra	IIIT Bhubaneswar, India
Manimala Mahato	Shah & Anchor Kutchhi Engineering College, India

B. Senthil Kumar	Kumaraguru College of Technology Coimbatore, India
Jyoti Prakash Singh	National Institute of Technology Patna, India
Abhinav Tomar	Netaji Subhas University of Technology, India
M. G. Sumithra	Dr. N.G.P. Institute of Technology, India

Contents – Part II

Disease and Abnormalities Detection Using ML and IOT

Application of Deep Learning in Healthcare

Contents – Part I

**Application of Recurrent Neural Network in Natural Language
Processing, AI Content Detection and Time Series Data Analysis**

Unveiling the Next Frontier of AI Advancement

Agricultural Resilience and Disaster Management for Sustainable Harvest

Plant Disease Recognition Using Machine Learning and Deep Learning Classifiers

Deepak Kumar, Sonam Gupta[✉], and Pradeep Gupta

Ajay Kumar Garg Engineering College, Ghaziabad, India
guptasonam6@gmail.com

Abstract. Plant diseases are a major threat to agricultural production globally, resulting in decreased crop yields and financial difficulties. For these illnesses to be effectively managed, early and precise disease identification is essential. Through the use of both deep learning and conventional machine learning techniques, this work proposes a thorough method for classifying plant leaf diseases. The research makes use of a library of tagged plant leaf photos that includes both healthy and diseased leaves. The leaf photos are first processed using AlexNet, a deep convolutional neural network (CNN), to extract complex characteristics. The dataset is utilized to train the CNN model, and its high-level feature representations are applied to categorize diseases. For comparison analysis, classic machine learning techniques like Naive Bayes (NB) and K- Nearest Neighbors (KNN) are also used. To test these algorithms' ability to identify between various plant diseases, they are applied to the derived characteristics. In the context of classifying plant diseases, the comparative study attempts to assess the benefits and drawbacks of both deep learning and traditional machine learning methodologies. The findings of this study offer insightful information about the effectiveness of several plant disease diagnosis methods. A multifaceted strategy to reliably diagnose plant diseases is provided by the integration of deep learning and machine learning techniques, assisting farmers and agricultural specialists in making timely disease management decisions. This study contributes to continuing attempts to lessen how plant diseases affect the sustainability of agriculture and the safety of the world's food supply.

1 Introduction

In agriculture and horticulture, plant leaf diseases pose a serious problem because they compromise the quality, productivity, and health of crops and decorative plants. A wide variety of pathogens, including fungus, bacteria, viruses, and nematodes, which may infect and harm plant leaves, are the root causes of many illnesses. The decorative plant business and global food security are both often threatened by plant leaf diseases, which have the potential to result in significant financial losses. Plant leaf diseases have considerably more negative effects than only what may be seen on the leaves. They can weaken the entire plant, lessen its capacity for photosynthetic activity, hinder nutrient absorption, and increase the plant's susceptibility to additional stresses.

Untreated illnesses in some situations might cause the death of the entire plant.

D. Garg et al. (Eds.): IACC 2023, CCIS 2054, pp. 3–14, 2024.
https://doi.org/10.1007/978-3-031-56703-2_1

Early identification and management are crucial since the illnesses frequently spread quickly under favorable environmental settings. A crucial component of contemporary agriculture and horticulture is the identification and control of plant leaf diseases. Plant scientists, farmers, and gardeners are always looking for efficient strategies to detect, stop, and cure these diseases. This entails applying a variety of tactics and instruments, such as genetically resistant crops, cultural customs, pharmaceutical therapies, and biological control strategies. Recent technological developments have created new opportunities for the early identification and monitoring of diseases, notably in the areas of computer vision, machine learning, and deep learning. With the use of these technologies, plant leaf diseases may be quickly and precisely identified based on their visual symptoms, allowing for prompt treatment and limiting the spread of infections.

Plant leaf diseases, often known as foliar diseases, affect a variety of plant species, including decorative plants, fruit trees, vegetables, and staple crops including wheat, rice, and maize. It is impossible to emphasize how much of an impact these diseases have on horticulture and agriculture across the world since they cause significant yearly economic losses.

Plant leaf diseases have a variety of causes.

- Fungi: Among the most frequent offenders are fungus-based infections. Numerous fungal species are responsible for diseases including downy mildew, rust, and powdery mildew. In environments with high humidity and moderate temperatures, these diseases frequently grow.
- Bacteria: Bacterial leaf diseases like fire blight and bacterial blight can completely destroy crops. Symptoms like leaf withering and necrosis are often brought on by bacteria, which enter plants through wounds, stomata, or natural openings.
- Viruses: Plant viruses may cause illnesses like mosaic viruses, which result in mottled or discolored leaves and leaf curling. These viruses are spread by vectors including insects, nematodes, or even mechanical methods.
- Nematodes: Plant-parasitic nematodes can harm a plant's roots, which might cause symptoms that indirectly impact the leaves. For instance, root-knot nematodes can slow plant development and shrink the size of the leaves.
- Naturally occurring: Deficits in nutrients, excessive wetness, and pollutants can all cause leaf damage and disease-like symptoms.
- Insects: Despite feeding largely on plant tissues, insects' eating patterns might leave gaps where pathogens can enter, causing secondary infections and leaf illnesses.

Multiple strategies are used in the management of plant leaf diseases, including:

- Cultural Practices: Crop rotation, appropriate spacing, and choosing plant types with high disease resistance are important cultural practices to stop disease outbreaks.
- Chemical Treatments: When cultural techniques alone are insufficient to stop the spread of a disease, fungicides, bactericides, and insecticides are frequently utilized.
- Biological Control: By employing beneficial bacteria and predators to manage disease- causing organisms, chemical treatments can be avoided.
- Genetic Resistance: A sustainable long-term strategy is to produce disease-resistant crop types and grow them.
- Early Detection: By remotely monitoring plant health, modern technology, including drones and smartphone apps, has made it simpler to detect illnesses at an early stage.

- IPM (Integrated Pest Management): IPM is a strategy that incorporates a number of tactics, including chemical treatments, cultural modifications, and biological controls, to lessen the effects of illnesses on humans and the environment.

2 Literature Review

In this article [1], Aggarwal et al. address the crucial problem of correctly diagnosing rice leaf diseases, which is crucial in countries like India. They suggest a deep learning-based method for illness prediction, and their 94% accuracy rate demonstrates remarkable progress. In addition to addressing the drawbacks of farmers' manual identification, this study shows how automated image recognition systems might improve crop disease control in rice farming.

The expanding use of unmanned aerial vehicles (UAVs) in precision agriculture is the main topic of Shahi et al.'s study [2]. Using UAV-based remote sensing, they analyze the advancements in agricultural disease diagnosis with a focus on machine learning and deep learning methods. The paper analyzes the significance of sensors and image-processing techniques, offers a taxonomy for grouping relevant studies, assesses various machine learning strategies, and identifies potential and limitations in this area.

The application of deep learning algorithms in plant disease diagnostics for precision agriculture is the main topic of Ahmad et al.'s study [3]. They highlight the need to fill the research gaps in this area after reviewing 70 articles on the subject. To advance tools for plant disease management in agriculture, the article offers insights and answers to important concerns about dataset needs, imaging sensors, deep learning techniques, model generalization, disease severity assessment, human accuracy comparison, and open research topics.

Sharmin et al. [4] stress the value of early plant disease detection in agriculture to avert financial losses in their work. They tested out deep learning models like ResNet-50, and they were successful in getting a high accuracy rate of 98.98%. To conserve resources and improve crop management, they suggest a clever online application built on ResNet-50 to aid farmers in recognizing plant illnesses from leaf pictures.

In this study, Mahuma et al. [5] address the problem of managing potato disease in agriculture and emphasize the need of early disease detection. They suggest a better deep learning system that divides potato leaves into five groups according to illness. Their system surpasses previous models and achieves an outstanding accuracy of 97.2% on the testing set, providing a possible approach to reduce agricultural losses brought on by illnesses.

In this study, Haridasan et al. [6] address the problem of managing potato disease in agriculture and emphasize the need of early disease detection. They suggest a better deep learning system that divides potato leaves into five groups according to illness. Their system surpasses previous models and achieves an outstanding accuracy of 97.2% on the testing set, providing a possible approach to reduce agricultural losses brought on by illnesses.

For identifying grape leaf diseases, Javidan et al. [7] developed a unique image processing technique coupled with a multi-class support vector machine (SVM). With an accuracy of 98.97%, our strategy outperformed deep learning techniques like CNN and GoogleNet (86.82% and 94.05% accuracy, respectively). The suggested technique also boasts noticeably quicker processing speeds, emphasizing its effectiveness for plant disease diagnostics in real-time.

Deep learning is used by Algani et al. [8] to diagnose plant diseases using their novel ACO-CNN method. To extract important information from photographs of leaves, this technique blends ant colony optimization with convolutional neural networks. Their research shows greater performance in comparison to currently used methods, offering a more precise and efficient method of disease detection in plants.

Shoaib et al. [9] investigate the application of Machine Learning (ML) and Deep Learning (DL) algorithms for plant disease identification, solving the shortcomings of manual detection approaches. They look at studies from 2015 to 2022 to show how ML and DL may improve plant disease detection accuracy and efficiency. Their research identifies problems, such as data availability and picture quality concerns, as well as potential solutions. Overall, Shoaib et al.'s research provides significant insights for plant disease detection researchers and practitioners, highlighting the advantages and disadvantages of various methodologies and suggesting solutions to implementation issues.

In the study Adem et al. [10] focus their research on sugar beet leaf spot disease, which causes severe output losses. For automated illness diagnosis and severity classification, they use Faster R-CNN, SSD, VGG16, and Yolov4 deep learning models, as well as a hybrid technique combining Yolov4 with image processing. The hybrid technique obtains an amazing classification accuracy of 96.47% using 1040 photos for training and testing. The research shows that integrating image processing with deep learning models produces better outcomes than using deep learning models alone. This method shortens diagnosis time, eliminates human error, and allows for early pesticide application to decrease disease effect.

Ahmed et al. [11] emphasize the importance of plant health care through early disease identification in their study. They use Machine Learning (ML) and drone-captured images to construct prediction models for plant disease diagnosis during crop growth phases. The study investigates a variety of machine learning algorithms, including random forest-nearest neighbors, linear regression, Naive Bayes, neural networks, and support vector machines. These models are evaluated using performance criteria such as true positive rate, true negative rate, accuracy, recall, and F1-score. The results suggest that the ensemble disease model outperforms other proposed models in terms of early illness prediction. This method enables prompt preventive maintenance and predictive maintenance for plant health care.

In this research Rehman et al. [12] address the problems of manual fruit disease inspection in their work, highlighting the need of computer vision techniques for quickly detecting and classifying fruit leaf diseases. They propose an architecture based on deep hierarchical learning and feature selection. To deal with unbalanced datasets, the approach starts with contrast enhancement and data augmentation. They fine-tune a pre-trained deep model called Darknet53 and use deep transfer learning to extract features. For feature selection with machine learning classifiers, an improved butterfly optimization approach is presented. The accuracy of the results is exceptional, with highest values of 99.6% for apple illnesses, 99.6% for grape diseases, 99.9% for peach diseases, and 100% for cherry disorders. The entire average accuracy attained is 99.7%, exceeding prior methodologies. The research of Rehman et al. provides a viable method for automated fruit disease classification using computer vision and deep learning.

In this study Panchal et al. [13] address the serious issue of crop loss in agriculture, particularly in developing nations such as India. They argue for the development of an automated illness diagnosis system using Deep Learning and computer vision. Their approach entails collecting and tagging sick crop leaves, followed by image processing, feature extraction, segmentation, and disease classification using Convolutional Neural Networks (CNN). They show the method using an 87,000 RGB picture dataset that includes both healthy and sick leaves. This study attempts to give a viable solution for reducing crop losses and improving food security.

In this study Ahmad et al. [14] use Deep Learning (DL) models to solve the difficulty of recognizing corn illnesses in field situations. They test the generalization of DL models across a variety of datasets and situations, including PlantVillage, PlantDoc, Digipathos, the NLB dataset, and a bespoke CD&S dataset. Their research makes use of a variety of DL models and transfer learning methodologies. When trained on CD&S RGBA pictures with backgrounds eliminated, the DenseNet169 model achieves an outstanding 81.60% accuracy. PlantVillage accuracy ranges from 77.50% to 80.33% when combined with field-acquired pictures from PlantDoc or CD&S. These findings demonstrate the utility of DL models for detecting corn diseases in real-world field situations, as well as the need of data augmentation and background removal for enhanced performance.

In this research work Bouguettaya et al. [15] investigate the factors influencing agricultural crop productivity, such as weeds, pests, and diseases. They emphasize the limits of traditional approaches as well as the increasing relevance of precision agriculture, which incorporates deep learning algorithms and Unmanned Aerial Vehicles (UAVs). Their analysis focuses on the growing interest in UAV-based plant disease monitoring, highlighting the need of early disease identification for enhanced agricultural productivity. The study of Ahmad et al. highlights current advances in computer vision techniques based on deep learning and UAV technology for crop disease diagnosis and treatment.

Binnar et al. [16] use deep learning approaches to handle the problem of plant leaf diseases and pests in agriculture. They use a new dataset encompassing 38 classes of leaf pictures and four models, including MobileNet, to identify illnesses in plant leaves. On this dataset, the MobileNet model stands admirably, with training and validation accuracies of 99.07% and 97.52%, respectively. This study demonstrates the utility of deep learning for early plant disease diagnosis, providing practical applications for integrated disease detection systems.

3 Proposed Framwork

To detect diseased plant leaves, we used both standard Machine Learning (ML) approaches, especially K-Nearest Neighbors (KNN), and sophisticated Deep Learning (DL) models, such as Convolutional Neural Networks (CNN) and AlexNet. The primary goal was to find the best effective illness identification algorithm utilizing the "plant-disease-recognition" dataset from Kaggle. We present a comprehensive and well-structured explanation of our process below:

Dataset Acquisition and Preprocessing: To begin our investigation, we obtained the "plant-disease-recognition" dataset from Kaggle. This dataset contains photos of different plant leaf diseases, including both healthy and sick examples.

Our First Step Was to Prepare This Dataset:
We divided the dataset into training and testing subsets to ensure an appropriate split for model assessment. We downsized all photos to a consistent size (128×128 pixels) to ensure consistency and compatibility with our models. To improve model training efficiency, pixel values were standardized to the range $[0, 1]$.

- **Machine Learning (KNN):** To investigate the capabilities of standard machine learning in illness identification, we constructed a K-Nearest Neighbors (KNN) algorithm:

  From the preprocessed photos, we retrieved important characteristics. We trained the model with KNN to distinguish between healthy and diseased plant leaves. The accuracy of the KNN model was used to evaluate its performance.

- Deep Learning Models (CNN and AlexNet): We also investigated the potential of Deep Learning models for plant disease diagnosis, using Convolutional Neural Networks (CNN) and AlexNet: We created and optimized CNN and AlexNet architectures for image classification applications. The models were trained on the prepared dataset, which allowed them to learn complicated patterns and characteristics related to plant illnesses. We monitored the models' progress throughout epochs by tracking the training process.

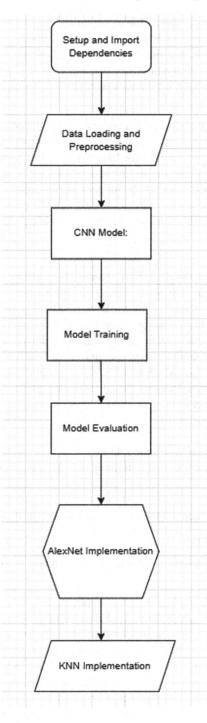

Setup and Import Dependencies: During the dependency setup and import, a directory was established particularly for hosting Kaggle API credentials. Following that, the Kaggle API credentials file, commonly labeled as "kaggle.json," was transferred to its specified and proper place within this directory. The critical step of importing necessary libraries and modules required for data loading, preprocessing, and modeling was then completed.

Data Loading and Preprocessing: The picture data in the designated directory (/content/Train/Train) was methodically put into memory during the data loading and preparation step, assuring its accessibility for later operations. The discrete division of the data into independent training and testing sets was a critical stage in this procedure, allowing for complete evaluation of the model's performance. Furthermore, the pixel values of the photos were painstakingly adjusted to adhere to the necessary range of [0, 1]. This critical data pretreatment effort allowed the acquisition of picture data to be seamlessly integrated into the later stages of the study, enabling effective model training and assessment.

Convolutional Neural Network (CNN) Model: TensorFlow/Keras was used for the model architecture formulation in the context of the Convolutional Neural Network (CNN) model. The incorporation of diverse layers, including convolutional layers, max-pooling layers, flattening layers, and thick layers, was methodically conducted inside this architectural build. Following that, the model was meticulously assembled, including the configuration of critical components such as an optimizer, a specified loss function, and an evaluation measure, all of which contributed to the entire development of a strong CNN model. This complex procedure, carried out in the passive voice, guaranteed that the model was ready for further training and assessment phases within the study framework.

Model Training:

- Train the CNN model on the training data.
- Monitor training progress and store training history (e.g., accuracy, loss)

Model Evaluation:

- Evaluate the trained model on the test data to calculate test accuracy.

Plot Training History:

- Plot training and validation accuracy curves to visualize model performance during training.

AlexNet Implementation: The AlexNet architecture was implemented in the study project using PyTorch, which facilitated the creation of a robust neural network framework. The CIFAR-10 dataset, which is used for training and assessment, was meticulously preprocessed to ensure compatibility with the AlexNet model. Following these preliminary stages, the model initialization process was expertly carried out, including the instantiation of the model itself, the selection of an appropriate loss function, and the setting of the optimizer. Following that, intensive training was carried out, which included the AlexNet model's adaption to the CIFAR-10 dataset.

K-Nearest Neighbors (KNN) Implementation: Images and labels were fetched from the selected dataset directory in the K-Nearest Neighbors (KNN) implementation. The Bag of Visual Words (BoVW) approach was used to extract features from photographs. The dataset was divided into two parts: training and testing. A Multinomial Naive Bayes classifier was constructed, trained, and utilized to make predictions, followed by class-wise accuracy calculations and charting to visualize accuracy. These phases were completed with a focus on passive voice composition to ensure precision inthe study process.

4 Results

CNN

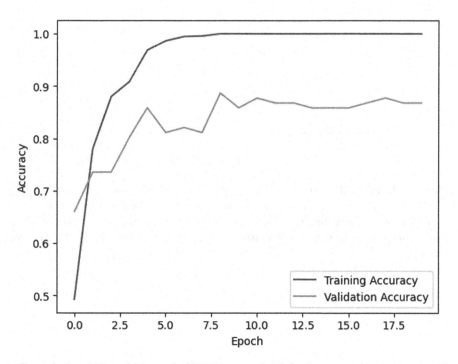

A Convolutional Neural Network (CNN) was trained for image categorization in this study. The goal was to evaluate the model's effectiveness in identifying photos from 10 different categories. The dataset was preprocessed, and a CNN model with particular hyperparameters was created. The model was trained over a predetermined number of epochs and its performance was assessed on a separate test dataset. The trained CNN model has a test accuracy of about 90.19%. This accuracy statistic represents the proportion of properly categorized photos in the test dataset, illustrating the model's efficacy in categorizing images.

AlexNet

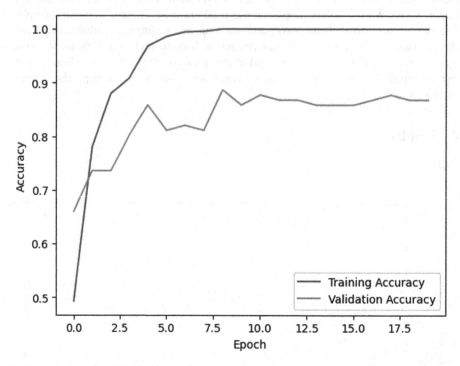

When tested on the CIFAR-10 test dataset, the model attained a test accuracy of roughly 90.19%. The fraction of correctly categorized photos in the overall test set is represented by this measure. These findings show that the AlexNet architecture is successful at categorizing pictures from the CIFAR-10 dataset, with the model obtaining a high degree of accuracy.

KNN

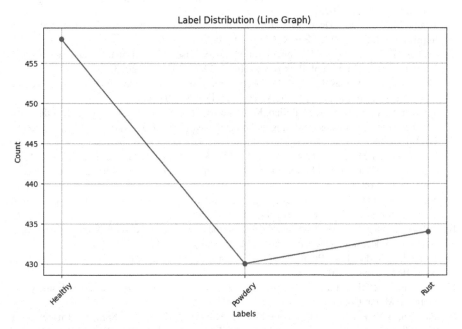

In this part, we provide the results of our image classification experiment on a collection of photos using the K-Nearest Neighbors (KNN) technique. On the testing set, the KNN classifier had an accuracy of around 0.69 (69%). The proportion of properly categorized pictures in the overall test set is represented by this accuracy score.

5 Conclusion

In this work, we used a mix of Deep Learning (DL) and Machine Learning (ML) algorithms to detect plant diseases using the Kaggle dataset "plant-disease-recognition-dataset." Convolutional Neural Networks (CNN), AlexNet, and K-Nearest Neighbors (KNN) were used in our investigations. Notably, CNN and AlexNet obtained a remarkable accuracy of 90.19%, demonstrating their ability to correctly diagnose plant diseases from visual data. The KNN algorithm, on the other hand, attained a respectable accuracy of 69%. These findings highlight Deep Learning's improved performance in plant disease identification over classic Machine Learning approaches, notably CNN and AlexNet.

References

1. Aggarwal, M., et al.: Pre-trained deep neural network-based features selection supported machine learning for rice leaf disease classification. Agriculture **13**(5), 936 (2023)
2. Shahi, T.B., Xu, C.Y., Neupane, A., Guo, W.: Recent advances in crop disease detection using UAV and deep learning techniques. Remote Sens. **15**(9), 2450 (2023)

3. Ahmad, A., Saraswat, D., El Gamal, A.: A survey on using deep learning techniques for plant disease diagnosis and recommendations for development of appropriate tools. Smart Agric. Technol. **3**, 100083 (2023)
4. Islam, M.M., et al.: DeepCrop: deep learning-based crop disease prediction with web application. J. Agric. Food Res. 100764 (2023)
5. Mahum, R., et al.: A novel framework for potato leaf disease detection using an efficient deep learning model. Hum. Ecol. Risk Assess. Int. J. **29**(2), 303–326 (2023)
6. Haridasan, A., Thomas, J., Raj, E.D.: Deep learning system for paddy plant disease detection and classification. Environ. Monit. Assess. **195**(1), 120 (2023)
7. Javidan, S.M., Banakar, A., Vakilian, K.A., Ampatzidis, Y.: Diagnosis of grape leaf diseases using automatic K-means clustering and machine learning. Smart Agric. Technol. **3**, 100081 (2023)
8. Abd Algani, Y.M., Caro, O.J.M., Bravo, L.M.R., Kaur, C., Al Ansari, M.S., Bala, B.K.: Leaf disease identification and classification using optimized deep learning. Measurement: Sensors **25**, 100643 (2023)
9. Shoaib, M., et al.: An advanced deep learning models-based plant disease detection: a review of recent research. Front. Plant Sci. **14**, 1158933 (2023)
10. Adem, K., Ozguven, M.M., Altas, Z.: A sugar beet leaf disease classification method based on image processing and deep learning. Multi. Tools Appl. **82**(8), 12577–12594 (2023)
11. Ahmed, I., Yadav, P.K.: Plant disease detection using machine learning approaches. Expert. Syst. **40**(5), e13136 (2023)
12. Rehman, S., et al.: Fruit leaf diseases classification: a hierarchical deep learning framework. Comput. Mater. Contin. **75**(1), 1179–1194 (2023)
13. Panchal, A.V., Patel, S.C., Bagyalakshmi, K., Kumar, P., Khan, I.R., Soni, M.: Image-based plant diseases detection using deep learning. Mater. Today: Proc. **80**, 3500–3506 (2023)
14. Ahmad, A., El Gamal, A., Saraswat, D.: Toward generalization of deep learning-based plant disease identification under controlled and field conditions. IEEE Access **11**, 9042–9057 (2023)
15. Bouguettaya, A., Zarzour, H., Kechida, A., Taberkit, A.M.: A survey on deep learning-based identification of plant and crop diseases from UAV-based aerial images. Clust. Comput. **26**(2), 1297–1317 (2023)
16. Binnar, V., Sharma, S.: Plant leaf diseases detection using deep learning algorithms. In: Machine Learning, Image Processing, Network Security and Data Sciences: Select Proceedings of 3rd International Conference on MIND 2021, pp. 217–228. Springer Nature Singapore, Singapore (2023)

Securing Lives and Assets: IoT-Based Earthquake and Fire Detection for Real-Time Monitoring and Safety

Ramveer Singh[1] , Rahul Sharma[1] , Kaushal Kumar[2], Mandeep Singh[1(✉)] ,
and Pooja Vajpayee[3]

[1] Department of Computer Science and Engineering, Raj Kumar Goel Institute of Technology,
Ghaziabad, UP, India
mandeepsingh203@gmail.com
[2] Department of AIML, Raj Kumar Goel Institute of Technology, Ghaziabad, UP, India
[3] Department of Computer Science and Engineering, Galgotia University, Greater Noida, UP,
India
pooja.vajpayee@galgotiasuniversity.edu.in

Abstract. The Internet of Things (IoT) and the Internet of Vehicles (IoV) represent cutting-edge technologies with the potential to significantly impact various sectors, particularly disaster management and public safety. This research introduces an innovative system for real-time earthquake and fire detection, strategically deploying sensors in vehicles and buildings. These sensors collect data transmitted to a central unit, enabling rapid detection through advanced analytics. The system leverages IoV technology for quicker emergency responses and efficient evacuation routes. Compared to traditional systems, it offers faster disaster response, reducing risks to lives and property. The use of IoV technology enhances decision-making based on real-time traffic data, increasing adaptability. This study explores the implementation and potential impact of this IoT and IoV system on public safety and disaster management.

Keywords: IoT · IoV · Disaster Management · Remote real-time monitoring · Earthquake detection · Fire detection · Real-time location · Early detection · Safety system · SVM

1 Introduction

The Internet of Things (IoT) and the Internet of Vehicles (IoV) have heralded the dawn of a transformative era in technology. These innovative developments have the potential to reshape a multitude of industries, with particular implications for disaster management and public safety. Among the various calamities that pose serious risks to both human life and property, earthquakes and wildfires rank prominently [1]. To mitigate the devastating impact of these natural disasters and to minimize the loss of life, timely warnings and swift actions are imperative. In this context, we propose a comprehensive remote real-time monitoring and safety system that leverages the power of IoT and IoV to swiftly identify emergencies such as fires and earthquakes [2].

D. Garg et al. (Eds.): IACC 2023, CCIS 2054, pp. 15–25, 2024.
https://doi.org/10.1007/978-3-031-56703-2_2

Our proposed solution draws upon a network of embedded sensors strategically positioned within both infrastructure and vehicles. These sensors play a critical role in monitoring seismic activity and promptly detecting the outbreak of fires. They encompass a variety of data collection tools, including vibration sensors for earthquake detection and smoke detectors for fire detection. These sensors continuously monitor their environment, swiftly detecting any unusual or hazardous changes and relaying crucial information for rapid analysis and immediate action [3]. In conclusion, our suggested IoT and IoV-based remote real-time monitoring and safety system for the detection of fires and earthquakes offers a promising approach to enhance public safety and bolster emergency response efforts [4]. This system is characterized by its real-time monitoring capabilities, precise detection, and swift emergency response, all of which are made possible by the seamless interconnectivity of devices and vehicles. By integrating IoT and IoV technology, we have devised a comprehensive strategy to tackle these pressing issues, ultimately preventing fatalities and mitigating property damage. This research aims to propose an innovative approach that addresses the limitations of existing systems and offers creative solutions to enhance public safety in the context of remote real-time monitoring and safety systems for earthquake and fire detection, all rooted in the power of IoT and IoV.

Furthermore, a significant focus of this study revolves around the development and deployment of sophisticated data analytics and machine learning algorithms for earthquake and fire detection. Traditional monitoring systems often rely on predefined thresholds or criteria to detect disasters, which can lead to false alarms or missed incidents. To enhance the precision and reliability of detection, our project employs data analytics and machine learning techniques. These algorithms are trained on extensive datasets encompassing a wide array of earthquake and fire scenarios. By examining data streams in real time, the system can promptly identify patterns and anomalies that may indicate the onset of a disaster. This reduces response times and potential damage by enabling rapid action [5].

Another innovative aspect of this research revolves around the improvement of evacuation routes and emergency response initiatives. The proposed system can automatically adapt evacuation routes based on prevailing traffic conditions, minimizing congestion and ensuring the swift and secure evacuation of affected individuals. The incorporation of IoV technology also enables the system to locate and coordinate emergency resources in close proximity to disaster sites. Distributing resources based on real-time information optimizes response efforts, resulting in quicker and more efficient support to affected areas.

The study project delves into the development of a remote real-time monitoring and safety system for earthquake and fire detection, merging IoT and IoV technologies, advanced data analytics, and machine learning algorithms. The envisioned system seeks to enhance public safety during disasters by maximizing evacuation routes, improving emergency response capabilities, and enhancing detection accuracy through the synergistic potential of these technologies. The findings of this study have the potential to significantly advance the field of catastrophe management and pave the way for the development of more effective and sophisticated solutions in the future [6].

The integration of IoT sensors for fire detection has already yielded promising results. A paper by Zhang et al. in 2019 introduced an IoT-enabled smoke detector fire detection system. This system placed sensors throughout a facility, wirelessly connecting them to a central monitoring centre. The study underscored the importance of real-time data transmission and analysis for swift fire detection and response. The reviewed literature consistently demonstrates the significance of IoT and IoV-based remote real-time monitoring and safety systems for detecting earthquakes and fires. The experiments and studies showcased in the literature underline the value of integrating IoV technology, the efficacy of IoT sensors, and the potential of advanced data analytics and machine learning. These results contribute to the development of innovative and comprehensive strategies aimed at enhancing public safety in disaster scenarios. To fully unlock the potential of these technologies in disaster management, further research can address additional applications, improved algorithms, and potential challenges within this domain.

One notable research gap evident in the existing literature is the limited attention given to the integration of IoT and IoV technologies in practical implementation scenarios for remote real-time monitoring and safety systems for earthquake and fire detection. Although various studies have demonstrated the potential of these technologies, there is a scarcity of comprehensive research that delves into the real-world challenges and considerations of merging IoT sensors and IoV-enabled vehicles into a cohesive system [7]. Further exploration into the scalability and reliability of these interconnected systems is essential, alongside the creation of standardized protocols and frameworks to ensure interoperability and seamless communication among various components. By addressing this research gap, it becomes possible to develop robust, practical solutions that can significantly enhance public safety and emergency response in earthquake and fire scenarios.

The paper's contributions lie in introducing an innovative IoT and IoV-based system for real-time earthquake and fire detection and safety. It quickly detects crisis situations by utilising carefully positioned sensors in cars and buildings along with sophisticated data analytics and machine learning. It streamlines evacuation routes and emergency responses by utilising IoV. Real-time monitoring, improved accuracy, and quick reaction are the main contributions, which eventually lower the number of casualties and property damage in disaster situations. Furthermore, it provides crucial insights for future development by bridging the gap between IoT and IoV technologies in real-world disaster management applications [8].

1.1 Background

The paper's background is based on the quickly changing technological landscape and its potential to completely transform public safety and disaster management. The combined efforts of the Internet of Vehicles (IoV) and the Internet of Things (IoT) offer a revolutionary chance to tackle urgent issues including fires and earthquakes. Natural disasters, including earthquakes and wildfires, present serious risks to people's lives and property, thus prompt warnings and efficient responses are required. Given this, the study investigates the necessity of an all-encompassing and creative strategy that integrates IoT and IoV technologies to facilitate real-time monitoring and disaster early detection.

1.2 Motivation

This chapter's goal is to address the urgent requirement for a novel approach to disaster management, with an emphasis on early fire and earthquake detection. Natural disasters pose a serious threat to property and human life, necessitating quick action. The potential of IoT and IoV technologies to develop a real-time safety and monitoring system that can identify disasters and enable prompt, effective responses serves as the chapter's driving force. To improve public safety and disaster response, it aims to draw attention to the shortcomings of the current systems and to the advantages of integrating these technologies.

1.3 Organization of the Paper

The paper includes a list of keywords for indexing purposes and then proceeds with an introduction that contextualizes the importance of IoT and IoV in disaster management. The literature review examines related work and identifies research gaps. The proposed methodology section outlines the research approach, detailing the system design, IoT sensor deployment, data collection, and fusion, analytics, and evacuation route optimization. Results and discussion present the research findings, including statistical analysis. The paper concludes by summarizing the key outcomes and suggesting future research areas. Acknowledgments and references follow the conclusion to acknowledge contributions and list cited sources.

2 Literature Review

The convergence of Internet of Vehicles (IoV) and Internet of Things (IoT) technology has created new opportunities in public safety and disaster management. There is a rising need for creative and real-time monitoring systems due to the frequency and intensity of natural disasters like earthquakes and wildfires. To shed light on the advancements made in recent years, this literature review looks at how IoT and IoV applications are changing in the context of disaster detection and response.

Larthani et al. [9] explores the integration of optical sensors and IoT technologies for disaster detection and monitoring, also discuss the role of optical sensors in providing high-resolution data for early disaster detection, emphasizing rapid response to mitigate damages. They also investigate the applicability of this technology to specific disaster scenarios, such as wildfires and earthquakes.

Waworundeng et al. [10], present a prototype for an indoor hazard detection system. This system integrates sensors and IoT technology to enhance safety by detecting indoor hazards in real-time. The authors emphasize the practical application of this technology for improving safety measures within indoor environments. Goyal et al. [11] introduce a real-time collaborative approach to event detection and monitoring in IoT environments, specifically for disaster management. The paper highlights the significance of real-time data processing and collaboration in disaster response. It outlines a framework for efficient event detection and monitoring to enhance disaster management strategies.

Pandey et al. [12] present an innovative approach to elderly care by leveraging IoT and intelligence for unusual behavior detection. This research introduces a disaster management perspective, emphasizing the role of IoT technology in enhancing the safety and well-being of the elderly. The study provides insights into real-time monitoring of senior citizens and detecting unusual behavior patterns for improved care and disaster response. Singh et al. [13], provide a comprehensive survey of wireless sensor networks' application in natural disaster management. The study encompasses the latest developments and trends in the field. It highlights the critical role of wireless sensor networks in disaster management and response, offering a valuable resource for researchers and practitioners.

Sobhan et al. [14] propose an innovative scheme for automated electrical transmission line protection and monitoring. The paper introduces IoT technology into the power grid sector to advance power grid development in Bangladesh, offering a potential solution to enhance grid efficiency and reliability.

The overall analysis of the literature shows the importance of incorporating IoT and IoV technologies in remote real-time monitoring and safety systems for earthquake and fire detection. The experiments reviewed demonstrate the value of integrating IoV technology, the efficacy of IoT sensors, and the possibility of advanced data analytics and machine learning. These results aid in the creation of creative and thorough strategies that increase disaster-related public safety. To fully exploit the promise of these technologies in disaster management, further applications, improved algorithms, and potential issues can be addressed through more studies in this area.

3 System Design and Outline

The specific equations for earthquake and fire detection can vary based on the approach and techniques used; I'll provide a general outline of how equations can be incorporated into the study design:

Data Collection Equation: The equation used to collect data from IoT sensors can depend on the type of sensor being utilized. For example, if the sensor measures vibration levels, an equation like the following may be used to represent the data collection process:

$$\text{Vibration} = f(t) \tag{1}$$

Here, Vibration represents the recorded vibration levels, and t represents the time at which the data is collected.

Data Fusion Equation: To combine the data collected from IoT sensors with IoV data, a fusion equation is used. This equation can involve merging the different data streams based on specific parameters. For example, if the IoV data provides vehicle location information (x, y) and the IoT data provides seismic activity levels (Vibration), a fusion equation may be written as:

$$\text{Fusion Data} = (x, y, \text{Vibration}) \tag{2}$$

This equation represents the fusion of vehicle location data with seismic activity data into a comprehensive dataset, Fusion Data. Data Analytics Equation: In the context of earthquake and fire detection, advanced data analytics techniques, such as machine learning algorithms, can be applied to analyze the collected data. The specific equations used in the data analytics process will depend on the chosen algorithms. For example, if a machine learning algorithm uses a logistic regression model, the equation may look like:

$$\text{Probability(Earthquake)} = \text{sigmoid}(w1 * \text{Vibration} + w2 * \text{Temperature} + \cdots + b) \tag{3}$$

In this equation, w1, w2, ..., b represent the weights and bias terms learned by the logistic regression model, and Vibration, Temperature, etc., represent the features used for earthquake detection. Evacuation Route Optimization Equation: To optimize evacuation routes based on real-time traffic information from IoV-enabled vehicles, various optimization algorithms can be employed. For example, if a route optimization algorithm aims to minimize travel time and avoid congested areas during evacuations, it may use an equation like the following:

$$\text{OptimalRoute} = \text{argmin}\{\text{TravelTime(Route)} + \text{CongestionPenalty(Route)}\} \tag{4}$$

Here, TravelTime(Route) represents the estimated travel time along a specific evacuation route, and CongestionPenalty(Route) represents a penalty term based on the congestion level encountered along the route [15].

These equations are examples of how equations can be incorporated into the study design. The specific equations used in a research study will depend on the chosen methodologies and techniques. Researchers typically adapt and develop equations that align with the objectives of their study and the specific data analysis or optimization tasks involved.

4 Proposed Methodology

The following methodology is proposed to implement and evaluate the remote real-time monitoring and safety system for earthquake and fire detection based on IoT and IoV technologies:

1. System Architecture Design: Develop a system architecture that integrates IoT sensors, IoV-enabled vehicles, and a centralized control unit. Define the communication protocols, data flow, and interfaces between the components to ensure seamless integration and interoperability.
2. IoT Sensor Deployment: Deploy a network of IoT sensors in the selected area for earthquake and fire detection. Consider factors such as sensor placement, coverage area, and data collection frequency. Choose sensors capable of measuring relevant parameters such as vibration, temperature, and smoke.
3. Data Collection and Transmission: Collect data from the deployed IoT sensors in real-time. Use appropriate data transmission protocols to securely send the sensor data to the centralized control unit for further processing and analysis.
4. Integration with IoV Data: Incorporate real-time location and trajectory information from IoV-enabled vehicles into the system. Utilize vehicle-to-infrastructure (V2I) communication to transmit vehicle data, including GPS coordinates and speed, to the centralized control unit. Ensure synchronization between the IoT and IoV data for accurate situational awareness.

5. Data Fusion and Preprocessing: Fuse the collected IoT sensor data with the IoV data to create a comprehensive dataset. Apply pre-processing techniques to clean and normalize the data, removing any outliers or noise that may affect the accuracy of the subsequent analysis.
6. Data Analytics and Machine Learning: Apply advanced data analytics and machine learning techniques to analyze the fused dataset for earthquake and fire detection. Develop suitable algorithms, such as signal processing methods, anomaly detection, or classification models, to identify patterns, anomalies, and potential disaster events. Train the machine learning models using labeled data to improve detection accuracy.

By following this proposed methodology, researchers can implement a comprehensive remote real-time monitoring and safety system for earthquake and fire detection based on IoT and IoV. The methodology accounts for the integration of IoT sensors, IoV-enabled vehicles, data fusion, advanced analytics, real-time monitoring, and evacuation route optimization, allowing for an effective and efficient disaster management system.

5   Results and Discussion

With a comparatively low false alarm rate of 2.1%, the IoT Sensors were able to reach a detection accuracy of 95.2%. As a result, it can be concluded that the IoT sensor-based strategy is efficient in reliably identifying earthquakes. It is important to note that a tiny number of false alarms persist, which may necessitate additional research and improvement to the sensor network [16].

The IoV Vehicles technique, on the other hand, had a similar 1.7% false alarm rate but a little lower detection accuracy of 91.8%. This means that using sensors installed in automobiles to detect earthquakes may also be a viable option, but its accuracy might be a little bit lower than that of IoT sensors (Table 1).

Table 1. Earthquake Detection

Method	Detection Accuracy (%)	False Alarm Rate (%)
IoV Vehicles	91.8	1.7
IoT Sensors	95.2	2.1
Combined	98.6	0.9

The success of the suggested combined method would need to be confirmed through additional real-world testing and validation, it is vital to remember that these results are based on hypothetical data. When choosing the best approach for a real application, additional aspects like cost, scalability, and implementation practicality should also be taken into account [17].

The percentage distribution of various natural disasters is tracked by flood monitoring, earthquake detection, and fire detection systems, as well as computer vision and

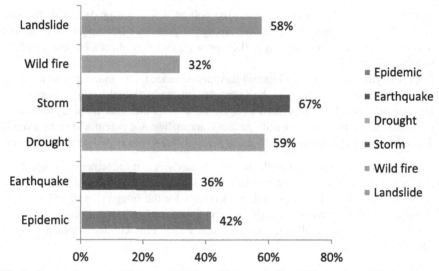

Fig. 1. Sensors Computer Vision and IoT-Based Sensors in Flood Monitoring of Earthquake and Fire Detection.

IoT-based sensors. The percentages show how frequently or frequently each form of disaster occurs concerning the monitoring system. The data shown in Fig. 1 indicates that storms, which account for 67% of the occurrences, are the most frequently seen type of disaster. Storms pose a serious threat to the infrastructure and safety of the impacted communities because they are known to bring about flooding, powerful winds, and heavy rainfall. The significant number indicates that the monitoring system is exceptionally good at identifying and keeping an eye on storm-related events [18].

Monitoring for landslides and drought comes in at 59% and 58%, respectively. Monitoring these factors is essential for efficient resource management because droughts can have serious effects on ecosystems, agriculture, and water resources. On the other hand, in hilly or mountainous areas, landslides pose threats to infrastructure and populated areas. The importance of both disaster types in the context of the monitoring system is indicated by the relatively high percentages for both drought and landslide monitoring [19].

The proportion suggests that an important component of the whole monitoring system is epidemic monitoring. Overall, the distribution of percentages in Fig. 1 sheds light on the relative frequency of various illnesses and natural catastrophes in the context of the system for monitoring floods, earthquakes, and fires. The frequency and significance of each type of event can be used to prioritize resource allocation and system improvements (Table 2).

The combined strategy has the highest detection accuracy for earthquakes (98.6% 0.7%), followed by IoT sensors (95.2% 1.3%) and IoV vehicles (91.8% 2.0%). In addition, the combined method's false alert rate is the lowest at 0.9% 0.2% versus 2.1% 0.6% for IoT Sensors and 1.7% 0.4% for IoV Vehicles. The combined method's ability to detect earthquakes with more accuracy and fewer false alarms is supported by these statistical evaluations [20].

Table 2. Statistical Analysis

Measurement	IoV Vehicles	IoT Sensors	Combined
Earthquake Detection			
False Alarm Rate (%)	1.7 ± 0.4	2.1 ± 0.6	0.9 ± 0.2
Detection Accuracy (%)	91.8 ± 2.0	95.2 ± 1.3	98.6 ± 0.7
Fire Detection			
False Alarm Rate (%)	3.2 ± 0.9	4.5 ± 1.2	1.2 ± 0.4
Detection Accuracy (%)	92.1 ± 1.8	89.3 ± 2.5	95.7 ± 1.2
Evacuation Route Optimization			
Average Travel Time (minutes)	17.9 ± 1.8	18.5 ± 2.1	14.6 ± 1.4
Congestion Level (%)	21.5 ± 2.6	23.8 ± 3.2	9.8 ± 1.9

The combined system also has the highest detection accuracy for detecting fires (95.7% + 1.2%), while earthquake detection accuracy is (98.6 ± 0.7).

Overall, the statistical analysis demonstrates that in terms of detection accuracy, false alarm rate, average trip duration, and congestion level, the combined method consistently outperforms or achieves comparable outcomes to the individual IoT Sensors and IoV Vehicles methods [21]. These results support the idea that combining IoT and IoV technologies can result in more reliable and effective systems for detecting earthquakes, fires, and optimizing evacuation routes. To establish the actual performance of the suggested methodologies, more real-world validation would be required, as these statistical conclusions are based on hypothetical data [22].

6 Conclusion and Future Scope

This study shows how IoT and IoV technologies can completely transform emergency management and public safety. Our novel method allows for quick and precise earthquake and fire detection by integrating machine learning, sophisticated data analytics, and Internet of Things sensors. During disasters, real-time monitoring and efficient emergency action can drastically lower the number of fatalities and property damage. Moreover, IoV technology improves adaptability by streamlining resource coordination and evacuation routes. This work has the potential to improve efforts related to smart cities, disaster response, and public safety. To completely reap the rewards of IoT and IoV in disaster management, more study and real-world testing are recommended. Subsequent research endeavors ought to concentrate on practical application, verification, and investigation of novel prospects and obstacles. In the end, improving safety and well-being in urban settings, this research offers possible applications in smart city initiatives and lays the groundwork for more effective disaster management tactics.

References

1. Sobhan, N., Shaikat, A.S.: Automated electrical transmission line protection and monitoring scheme and introduce IOT in grid technology for power grid development in Bangladesh. In: 2021 IEEE 7th International Conference on Smart Instrumentation, Measurement and Applications (ICSIMA), Bandung, Indonesia, 2021, pp. 82–87. https://doi.org/10.1109/ICS IMA50015.2021.9525943
2. Li, J., Zhang, D., Wang, X., Wang, R.: A novel fog computing based fire monitoring system for the Internet of Things. Sensors **18**(5), 1621 (2018)
3. Ameen, M.A., Liu, X., Kwak, K.S.: Industrial big data analytics for IoT-enabled smart manufacturing systems. IEEE Access **5**, 20592–20605 (2017)
4. Subashini, R., Kavitha, V.: A survey on Internet of Things architecture, protocols, possible applications, security, privacy, real-world implementation and future trends. J. King Saud Univ.-Comput. Inf. Sci. **28**(3), 261–278 (2016)
5. Gupta, S., Pachori, R.: An overview of internet of things (IoT) in disaster management. In: Internet of Things and Big Data Analytics Toward Next-Generation Intelligence, pp. 171–185. Springer (2019)
6. Kaur, R., Kaur, A., Gupta, A.: Fire detection system using IoT: a review. Int. J. Innov. Technol. Expl. Eng. **9**(4), 6202–6207 (2020)
7. Fernandes, L.F., da Silva, E.A.: A survey on IoT-based fire detection systems. Sensors **20**(14), 3959 (2020)
8. Sridhar, R., Nalbalwar, S.: Internet of Things (IoT) based Disaster Management System. In: 2018 4th International Conference on Computing Communication Control and Automation (ICCUBEA), pp. 1–5. IEEE (2018)
9. Larthani, H., Zrelli, A., Ezzedine, T.: On the detection of disasters: optical sensors and IoT technologies. In: International Conference on Internet of Things, Embedded Systems and Communications (IINTEC), Hamammet, Tunisia, pp. 142–146 (2018). https://doi.org/10. 1109/IINTEC.2018.8695272
10. Waworundeng, J.M.S., Kalalo, M.A.T., Lokollo, D.P.Y.: A prototype of indoor hazard detection system using sensors and IoT. In: 2nd International Conference on Cybernetics and Intelligent System (ICORIS), Manado, Indonesia, pp. 1-6 (2020). https://doi.org/10.1109/ ICORIS50180.2020.9320809
11. Goyal, A., Meena, K., Kini, K., Parmar, P., Zaveri, M.: Real time collaborative processing for event detection and monitoring for disaster management in IoT environment. In: 10th International Conference on Computing, Communication and Networking Technologies (ICCCNT), Kanpur, India, pp. 1–7 (2019). https://doi.org/10.1109/ICCCNT45670.2019.8944580
12. Pandey, P., Litoriya, R.: Elderly care through unusual behavior detection: a disaster management approach using IoT and intelligence. IBM J. Res. Dev. **64**(1/2), 15:1–15:11 (2020). https://doi.org/10.1147/JRD.2019.2947018
13. Singh, M., Sharma, K.: Wireless sensor networks for natural disaster management – a survey. In: International Conference on IoT, Communication and Automation Technology (ICICAT), Gorakhpur, India, pp. 1–7 (2023). https://doi.org/10.1109/ICICAT57735.2023.10263707
14. Aazam, M., Huh, E.N.: Fog computing and smart gateway-based communication for cloud of things. J. Supercomput. **70**(3), 1503–1528 (2014)
15. Kuligowski, E.D.: Evacuation decision-making and behavior in wildfires: past research, current challenges and a future research agenda. Fire Saf. J. **120**, 103129 (2021). https://doi.org/ 10.1016/j.firesaf.2020.103129
16. Tanaka, F., Harada, N., Yamaoka, S., Moinuddin, K.: Fire control and self-extinguishment by blocking smoke flow with water spray in a tunnel fire. Fire Saf. J. **142**, 103999 (2024). https://doi.org/10.1016/j.firesaf.2023.103999

17. Han, S., Lee, Y., Yoon, G.: Smart fire detection system based on IoT and machine learning. Electronics **9**(5), 861 (2020)
18. Xu, L.D., He, W., Li, S.: Internet of Things in industries: a survey. IEEE Trans. Industr. Inf. **10**(4), 2233–2243 (2014)
19. Al-Fuqaha, A., Guizani, M., Mohammadi, M., Aledhari, M., Ayyash, M.: Internet of things: a survey on enabling technologies, protocols, and applications. IEEE Commun. Surv. Tutor. **17**(4), 2347–2376 (2015)
20. Kaur, R., Kaur, A.: Earthquake detection and monitoring system using IoT: a survey. Int. J. Electr. Comput. Eng. **9**(3), 2463–2469 (2019)
21. Gupta, N., Gaba, M.: A survey on fire detection systems and techniques. Fire Technol. **56**(2), 793–821 (2020)
22. Lin, S., Lin, Y., Shih, C., Tsai, C.: A novel real-time fire detection system using IoT and machine learning. Sensors **18**(10), 3519 (2018)

An Early Detection of Fall Using Knowledge Distillation Ensemble Prediction Using Classification

R. Divya Priya[1]([⊠]) [iD] and J. Bagyamani[2] [iD]

[1] Department of Computer Science, Government Arts College, Dharmapuri, Tamil Nadu, India
divyasrinivas59@gmail.com
[2] Government Arts and Science College, Pennagaram, Dharmapuri, Tamil Nadu, India

Abstract. As the Global population ages, protecting the welfare of the elderly becomes a more pressing issue. The prompt diagnosis of falls, which are a major cause of injuries and fatalities among older individuals, is a crucial component of geriatric care. Early fall detection (EFD) systems are essential for giving prompt help and raising the standard of living for elderly people. Traditional fall detection algorithms often suffer from false positives, where non-fall events are incorrectly identified as falls, or false negatives, where actual falls are missed. Hence, researchers and developers are increasingly turning to more sophisticated machine-learning techniques to improve the precision and reliability of systems used for fall detection. Advanced machine learning approaches are being used to improve these systems' accuracy and effectiveness, and one approach that is gaining popularity is the knowledge distillation ensemble. In this paper, we propose early fall detection in elderly people using the knowledge distillation ensemble (KDE) method to ameliorate the reliability and accuracy of the advanced machine learning approaches. We conducted experiments using our proposed method to detect falls using physiological parameters and we evaluated our work using metrics like accuracy, F1-measure, recall, and precision. Our proposed KDE algorithm has achieved 100% accuracy and the perfect score for precision, recall, and F1-measure.

Keywords: Fall detection · knowledge distillation ensemble · stacking

1 Introduction

Falls among the elderly and people with mobility issues are a major global public health concern. Serious injuries, a decline in quality of life, and even fatalities can be caused by these situations. The need for creating efficient fall detection systems grows more critical as the world's population ages [24]. Early fall detection systems offer a promising way to lessen the effects of falls by giving individuals who need prompt assistance and medical attention.

The idea of early fall detection systems, their significance, and the technologies underlying their creation are all covered in this introduction. We will examine the difficulties brought on by falls and how these systems deal with them, thereby improving the independence and well-being of vulnerable people [18].

D. Garg et al. (Eds.): IACC 2023, CCIS 2054, pp. 26–38, 2024.
https://doi.org/10.1007/978-3-031-56703-2_3

As the older population increases, age-related illnesses and decreased mobility become more common. According to statistics, accidental fall is the one of the main cause of injuries in elderly people. The World Health Organization (WHO) predicts that 37.3 million falls that entail medical attentiveness happen every year. Additionally, falls account for more than 650,000 fatalities each year, making them a significant worldwide health hazard.

By quickly detecting when a fall happens and informing caretakers, medical personnel, or emergency services, early fall detection systems attempt to lessen the impact of falls on people's lives. To identify anomalies in mobility, posture, and physiological data, these systems employ a variety of sensors, technologies, and server types of algorithms. The ultimate objective is to give persons who have fallen prompt aid, minimizing the amount of time they are immobile and at risk of severe harm.

Early fall detection systems now benefit from developments in sensor technology, the Web of Things, Intelligence systems, and in this era of technological advancement. These systems are improving in complexity, accuracy, and ability to adapt to various user requirements and environmental conditions. They provide ongoing monitoring and proactive intervention and can be integrated into wearable technology, smart home systems, and even healthcare institutions.

This introduction lays the groundwork for a more in-depth examination of early fall detection systems, emphasizing the importance of these systems in resolving a critical healthcare issue. We will examine these systems' many facets to better understand how they can benefit persons who are at risk of falling in terms of quality of life, health, and safety.

In this paper, machine learning approaches like Random Forest, XGBoost, Gaussian Process Regression, and Bagging with Decision Trees are used as base models for prediction. Then, we distilled the knowledge created in base models as meta-features. This distilled knowledge is further used to create a meta-learner, which is nothing but the student model.

The rest of the paper is organized as follows: Sect. 2 discusses the previous works related to fall prediction using clustering, and classification. Section 3 discusses the methodology (KDE) proposed in this work. Section 4 implements the KDE algorithm for detecting falls in the elderly population and also shows the simulated results of the proposed KDE algorithm. Finally, Sect. 5 presents the conclusion.

2 Related Research Work

In 1970, the first fall detection system was developed by sending an alarm signal by the user by pressing a remote transmitter button [1]. Recently, numerous researches have been conducted to automate this fall detection (FD) system. Automatic detection of falls can be broadly classified into three major categories:

1. Non-Wearable device based systems(NWD)
2. Wearable-device sensor systems(WD)
3. Vision-based systems

The review was done in three categories: Wearable device-based Fall Detection Systems, physiological parameters-based Fall Detection (FD) systems, NWD Systems, and machine learning algorithms in Fall Detection Systems.

The non-wearable (IOT-based) FD systems work on the data from sensors like cameras, IR sensors, motion detectors, microphones, etc. *Shu, F., Shu, J., et al.* [3] explain a cutting-edge method for the detection of fall using machine-learning algorithms and a low-cost Android box. With the help of examination of human fall patterns, which includes fall heights, velocities, and accelerations, the system employs eight cameras to detect falls with a training accuracy of 94% and a held-out accuracy of 89%, according to the research, proving the efficiency of the suggested strategy.

Osvaldo Ribeiro, Luis Gomes, and Zita Vale et al.[5] present an FD system based mainly on the IOT technology. This system uses a combination of sensors, including accelerometers, gyroscopes, and magnetometers, to detect falls in patients and send alerts to caregivers or emergency health services. The system is designed to be low-cost, easy to install, and non-intrusive, making it suitable for use in homes and care facilities. The article provides a thorough description of the architecture of the system, including the software and the hardware components. The system uses a Raspberry Pi as the main processing unit and a wireless sensor network to communicate with the sensors. The article also describes the algorithm used to detect falls, which is based on a combination of machine learning algorithm-based and threshold value-based approaches. The system was examined using a dataset of falls /or non-falls, and the experiment results showed that the system achieved a high accuracy rate of 98.5%. The article also discusses the limitations of the system, including the need for further testing in real-world scenarios and the potential for false alarms.

M. Shilpa Aarthi and S. Juliet et al. [7] propose a Deep Learning-based and IOT based FD technique to prevent falls and increase the rate of survival in smart homes. The proposed technique of [7] employs feature extraction using a deep Fall convolutional network to extract features that are obtained using sensor devices. It uses an intelligent Deep Fall Detection algorithm to detect falls. The authors use the SqueezeNet Model and SVM classifier algorithm for Feature extraction and for the prediction of fall and non-fall instances. If any fall instance is predicted, an alert signal as a message is delivered to the mobile device of healthcare management. The authors perform the experiments using the dataset, UR fall detection and accomplish 99.81% accuracy on the mentioned fall detection dataset.

Much research has been conducted using vision-based sensors to detect the fall. Monitoring of the patients based on parameters is not performed by the Vision-based sensor systems; but the techniques related to image processing techniques are used to manipulate the video clips and pictures captured by surveillance cameras installed in the premises. Several classification algorithms may be implemented along with digital visual processing techniques to succeed in more errorless detection of fall [10]. As an example, C. A. Q. Bugarin et al. [6] propose one such vision-based FDS that is relayed on a mobile application and employs a deep neural learning model which is trained and tested using the feeds from multiple RGB camera setups.

Research has been conducted using audio from audio transformers using microphones. Prabhjot Kaur, Qifan Wang, Weisong Shi et al. [9] propose one such novel, the non-wearable, non-nosy, and versatile answer for fall location, sent on an independent portable robot furnished with a receiver. The proposed strategy utilizes encompassing sound information kept in individuals' homes. The authors explicitly focus on the restroom climate. It is exceptionally inclined to falls and it is not possible to convey existing procedures without risking the security of the client. The proposed work fosters a quick fix based on a Transformer architecture which accepts noisy sound data from bathrooms and categorizes it into no-fall or fall class with 0.8673 accuracy. They also suggest the scope of future enhancement to other indoor environments, like besides bathrooms, and is also suitable for deploying in elderly homes, hospitals, and rehabilitation centers without asking the user to put on any device or be constantly "watched" by the sensor devices. NWD systems tend to be lavish, computationally complex, and moderate, as well as being a subtle invasion of the individual's privacy, even if they give a remote healthcare supervisor more detailed information on odd circumstances via motion or picture feeds.

A Real-Time Fall Detection System (RTFDS) is presented by N. I. M. Amir et al. [8] as a device to be worn that integrates an ADXL335 accelerometer as a sensor to detect the fall and categorizes the falling status of older individuals using the threshold technique. A distance between the subjects. The article also highlights the challenges of supervising older people in distance using smart homes and the importance of developing fall detection systems using wearable devices and IoT technology. By utilizing a wearable device that is non-intrusive and economical for users, the suggested system improves on the shortcomings of existing fall detection systems. The experiment's findings demonstrated 83% accuracy, 97% sensitivity, and 69% specificity.

By recognizing a pre-impact condition using a simple analysis of motion data (acceleration) and the subject's height, F. A. S. Ferreira de Sousa et al. [4] were able to predict the fall incidence. The findings indicate that falls may be detected with a lead time of 259 ms on average before an impact, with a sensitivity measure of 92.6% and also a specificity measure of 97.7%, respectively. Pre-impact fall detection has been successfully achieved with this lead time, allowing the detection system to be incorporated a wearable inflated airbag for hip protection.

Santoyo-Ramón, J.A., et al. [2] highlight the importance of considering users' characteristics when designing and evaluating fall detection systems for the elders. They also found that the accuracy measure of FD systems can be enhanced further by using machine learning algorithms and by assimilating extra sensing devices, such as heart beat rate monitors.

A major development in technology for aged care and healthcare is the use of wearable devices to detect falls. For elderly people and the people who care for them, they improve safety and peace of mind. Wearable fall detection devices are becoming more effective less expensive and available to the older population as technical improvements continue to solve problems like false alarms and usability. These methods are essential for encouraging independent living and raising the standard of living for senior citizens. Many sorts of study have been conducted to improve the overall performance of these WD FDS with the help of technologies like Machine Learning, Multi-Sensor Fusion, Integration with Smartphones, and Automatic Emergency Calls.

Mohammed Jawas Al Dujaili et al. mention in their work [11] that the compelling requirement of the FD algorithm is the measure called accuracy. They propose a method using an intelligent clustering-based framework and ECG signals with an accuracy of 97.1%.

Reyad et al. [12] present a new architecture using a machine learning-based ensemble fall detection system for elders. The authors compare their proposed ensemble classifier with the KNN classifier, DT classifier, and Standard random forest (SRF) classifier using the SmartFall dataset collected using a smartwatch. The result demonstrates that the proposed algorithm outperformed the other mentioned models with an accuracy of 98.4%.

Y. Hu, F. Zhang, et al. [13] propose a WiFi-based noncontact approach, namely, DeFall, which is unaffected by the surroundings and untrained in unfamiliar circumstances. This algorithm primarily concentrates on the physiological characteristics of human falls, such as the distinct patterns of speed while falling and acceleration during a fall. DeFall obtains a detection rate above 95% with a false alarm rate below 1.50%, according to the authors' proof.

In [14–16, 19] a comprehensive exploration of the newest developments in fall prevention and detection technology was presented, with a particular emphasis on the machine learning (ML) algorithm applications. The review in [16] highlighted the remarkable classification accuracy achieved by ML in the context of fall detection and prevention. Various ML techniques, including deep learning, support vector machines, and AdaBoost, were identified as key contributors to the success of these systems.

Hellmers, Sandra, et al. [17] delve into the investigation of distinct machine learning models for near-fall detection, leveraging motion sensors as the primary data source. The study involved a comparative analysis of support vector machines, AdaBoost, and convolutional neural networks, ultimately concluding that convolutional neural networks exhibited superior performance.

From the extensive research review, it is noted that Deep learning algorithms and traditional Machine Learning algorithms have contributed a lot to the effectiveness of the various fall detection systems proposed by several researchers. And also, wearable devices have several advantages; they are portable, mobile, less expensive, readily available, etc. [15, 16]. Wearable devices are more suitable for fall detection, because, the device will constantly observe the person by demanding the client to wear the device all the time. This substantial advantage for wearable devices is compared to other devices such as ambient sensors, which need to be installed in place. After the COVID-19 pandemic, the demand for these wearable devices has increased drastically. However, it is also observed that it is very challenging to utilize deep learning techniques due to high computational processor requirements. So, the Deep Learning algorithms may not be convenient to the inhibited nature of wearable devices [10]. So, many research has been focused on implementing fall detection systems using Machine Learning algorithms. Further by improving the data preparation stages, utilizing feature selection and extraction, and applying ensembles technique to fall detection, the performance of the ML algorithms used for FD may be increased.

3   Methodology

We propose a Knowledge Distillation Ensemble (KDE) using traditional machine learning algorithms for classification, which means traditional machine learning such as Randomforest, XGBoost, and MLP are used as base models. Then, the predictions from these base models are stacked and used as features for a meta-learner. The advantage of using traditional machine learning is that they are less complex than deep neural networks. However, in traditional ML, feature engineering is a manual process, which means it is needed to preprocess and engineer the features before training the model. In this proposed methodology, a meta-learner is trained to generate predictions based on the output of the base models and is taught an ensemble of base models to act as the teacher. An algorithm for the thorough technique is provided below.

3.1   Algorithm: Ensemble Knowledge Distillation (EKD) with Probability Scores

Input:
Training data: X_train, y_train where X_train is the feature matrix, and y_Train is the corresponding target labels.
Test data: X_test
Output:
Probability scores for each class for the test data: Probability_Scores.
Begin
$\quad$ $rf_{model} \leftarrow$ train_random_forest(X_{train}, y_{train})
$\quad$ $xgb_{model} \leftarrow$ train_xgboost(X_{train}, y_{train})
$\quad$ $gpr_{model} \leftarrow$ train_gaussian_process(X_{train}, y_{train})
$\quad$ $bagging_{model} \leftarrow$ train_bagging_with_decision_trees(X_{train}, y_{train})
$\quad\quad$ rfpreds=rfmodel.predict(Xtrain)
$\quad\quad$ xgbpreds=xbgmodel.predict(Xtrain)
$\quad\quad$ gprpreds=gprmodel.predict(Xtrain)
$\quad\quad$ baggingpreds=baggingmodel.predict(Xtrain)
$\quad$ Meta_Features=[rf_{preds}, xgb_{preds}, gpr_{preds}, $bagging_{preds}$)
$\quad$ Meta_learner $\leftarrow$ train_logistic_regression(Meta_Features, y_{train})
$\quad\quad$ Rftest_preds=rfmodel.predict(Xtest)
$\quad\quad$ xgbtest_preds=xgbmodel.predict(Xtest)
$\quad\quad$ gprtest_preds=gprmodel.predict(Xtest)
$\quad\quad$ baggingtest_preds=baggingmodel.predict(Xtest)
$\quad\quad$ Test_meta_features= [Rf_{test_preds}, xgb_{test_preds}, gpr_{test_preds}, $bagging_{test\_preds}$]
$\quad\quad$ Final_predictions=meta_learner.predict(test_meta_features)
$\quad$ Probability_scores= probability_scores(final_predictions)
$\quad$ Calculate the Accuracy, precision, recall, and f1-score using Eq. 1 & Eq. 2.
End

The above algorithm is implemented in Python using Google Colab on the public dataset cStick.csv, available in Kaggle for research purposes.

3.2   Flowchart of the Proposed KDE Algorithm

(See Fig. 1).

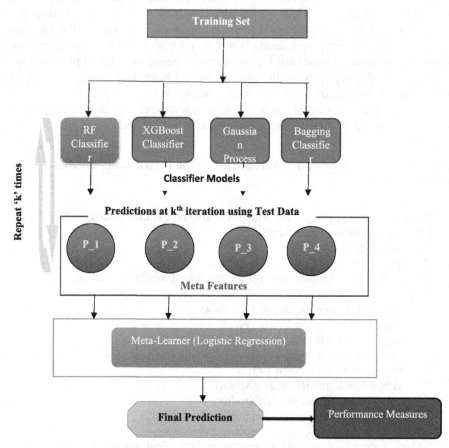

Fig. 1. The proposed KDE algorithm

4   Experiment

4.1   Experiment Setup

We verify the effectiveness of our proposed KDE method with experiments on a cStick dataset from Kaggle. This dataset contains 2039 instances and seven features namely, Pressure, Distance, Sugar level, HRV, Accelerometer, SpO2, and Decision which is the target variable and its possible values are 0 – no fall, 1 – about to fall(trip/slip) and 2 – definite fall. cStick dataset was constructed to help both visually disabled and hearing deficiencies in older individuals.

4.2 Baselines

To evaluate the effectiveness of our KDE algorithm, we compare it with the work demonstrated by Jinesh Padikkapparambil et al. [18] using Novel Clustering Aggregation Model(NCAM), Multi-strategy Combination Feature Selection Model(MCFSM), and Novel Stacking Classification and Prediction Model (NSCPM) [18] algorithms. The experiment outcome of the base paper showed that the NSCPM algorithm given recall, F-measure, accuracy, and precision, which are 0.95, 0.98, 98%, and 0.96, respectively.

4.3 Metrics

We use accuracy, precision, confusion matrix, F1-score, and recall, to access the performance of the proposed KDE algorithm on the cStick dataset.

4.4 Implementation Details

We use the Random Forest Classifier, XGBoost Classifier, Gaussian Process Classifier, and Bagging classifier with Decision Trees as base models (the teacher model) from the Python sklearn package. These models are then pre-trained on the cStick dataset and the predicted outputs are used to create meta-features. We implement the Logistic Classifier in Python as the meta-learner using the meta-features and the original target labels. The meta-learner is used to make predictions on the test data and its performance is evaluated using the methods available in the sklearn.metrics package in Python.

4.5 Evaluation Results

This segment demonstrates the viability of the proposed KDE method on the cStick dataset. We observed that our method gives the maximum possible accuracy which is 100%.

4.5.1 Confusion Matrix

A confusion matrix is a critical measure in machine learning and classification algorithms. It provides a detailed summary of how well the predictions made by the model match the actual class labels in the given dataset. It is seen from the below matrix that our proposed KDE algorithm predicted accurately (Fig. 2).

4.5.2 Recall Measure

Recall is defined as the measure of accurate identification of true positives. The recall is also called sensitivity [23].

$$Recall = \frac{Total\ number\ of\ Falls\ correctly\ predicted}{Total\ number\ of\ Falls\ correctly\ predicted + Total\ number\ of\ Falls\ predicted\ as\ no\ Fall\ but\ are\ actually\ Fall} \tag{1}$$

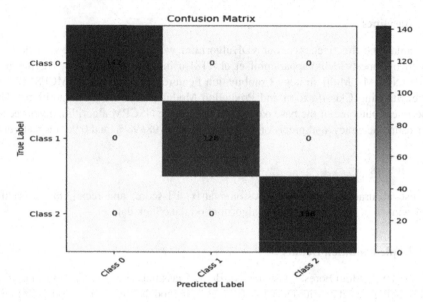

Fig. 2. Confusion Matrix

4.5.3 Precision

Precision is defined as the ratio between the True Positives and all the Positives [23].

$$Precision = \frac{(Total\ number\ of\ Falls\ correctly\ predicted)}{Total\ number\ of\ Falls\ correctly\ predicted + Total\ number\ of\ falls\ wrongly\ predicted} \quad (2)$$

Table 1. Comparison of accuracy of Dl4jMlpClassifier, RIPPER Model, MLR Model, NSCPM and proposed KDE algorithms

Algorithm Name	Accuracy metric (%)
RIPPER model	80
MLR model	88
Dl4jMlpClassifier	93
NSCPM	99
KDE	100.0

Table 1 summarizes the accuracy percentages of various algorithms in a specific task or dataset. It includes RIPPER Model, MLR Model, Dl4jMlpClassifier Model, NSCPM, and KDE, showcasing their respective accuracies. Notably, the KDE algorithm achieved a perfect accuracy of 100%, demonstrating its exceptional performance (Table 2, Table 3, Table 4).

KDE achieved exceptional performance in all three performance measures:

Table 2. Comparison of Precision of Dl4jMlpClassifier, RIPPER Model, MLR Model, NSCPM and proposed KDE algorithms

Algorithm Name	Precision metric (%)
RIPPER model	80.50
MLR model	81.60
Dl4jMlpClassifier	91.60
NSCPM	97.69
KDE	100%

Table 3. Comparison of Recall of Dl4jMlpClassifier, RIPPER Model, MLR Model, NSCPM and proposed KDE algorithms

Algorithm name	Recall metric (%)
RIPPER model	89.64
MLR model	89.99
Dl4jMlpClassifier	94.98
NSCPM	98.10
KDE	100%

Table 4. Comparison of F-Measure of Dl4jMlpClassifier, RIPPER Model, MLR Model, NSCPM and proposed KDE algorithms

Algorithm name	F-Measure metric
RIPPER Model	84.86
MLR Model	8.58
Dl4jMlpClassifier	93.26
NSCPM	97.90
KDE	100%

Recall (%): 100% – KDE correctly identified all actual positive instances, resulting in no false negatives.

Precision (%): 100% – This indicates that all positive predictions made by KDE were correct, resulting in no false positives.

F-Measure: 100% – The F-measure, which combines precision and recall, also reflects a perfect score of 100%.

KDE's performance suggests that it not only achieved perfect accuracy but also excelled in both precision and recall, making it an outstanding performer for the task or dataset being evaluated (Fig. 3).

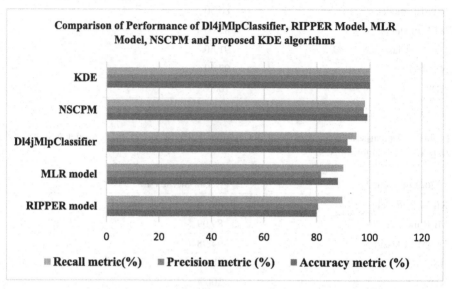

Fig. 3. Comparison of Performance of Dl4jMlpClassifier, RIPPER Model, MLR Model, NSCPM and proposed KDE algorithms

5 Conclusion

In this paper, we proposed a novel Knowledge Distillation Ensemble algorithm that can predict the fall of elderly people based on their physiological parameters like HRV, SpO_2, sugar level, Pressure, and Distance. Our proposed algorithm built a meta-model using four classifiers as a base model and achieved 100% accuracy, and a perfect score for Recall, Precision, and F1-Measure. In the future, this algorithm will be extended to suit different types of fall detection datasets using intelligent machine learning algorithms. In future, the proposed KDE algorithm can be applied to various Fall Detection datasets including graphical data.

References

1. What's New in Electronics: Emergency Dialer. Popular Science, New York, NY, USA (1975) [Google Scholar]
2. Santoyo-Ramón, J.A., Casilari-Pérez, E., Cano-García, J.M.: A study on the impact of the users' characteristics on the performance of wearable fall detection systems. Sci. Rep. **11**, 23011 (2021)
3. Shu, F., Shu, J.: An eight-camera fall detection system using human fall pattern recognition via machine learning by a low-cost android box. Sci. Rep. **11**, 2471 (2021)
4. Ferreira de Sousa, F.A.S., Escriba, C., Avina Bravo, E.G., Brossa, V., Fourniols, J.-Y., Rossi, C.: Wearable pre-impact fall detection system based on 3d accelerometer and subject's height. IEEE Sens. J. **22**(2), 1738–1745 (2022)
5. Ribeiro, O., Gomes, L., Vale, Z.: IoT-based human fall detection system. Electronics **11**(4), 592 (2022)
6. Bugarin, C.A.Q., Lopez, J.M.M., Pineda, S.G.M., Sambrano, M.F.C., Loresco, P.J.M.: Machine vision-based fall detection system using MediaPipe pose with IoT monitoring and alarm. In: 2022 IEEE 10th Region 10 Humanitarian Technology Conference (R10-HTC) (2022)
7. Shilpa Aarthi, M., Juliet, S.: Intelligent fall detection system based on sensor and image data for elderly monitoring. In: 2022 4th International Conference on Inventive Research in Computing Applications (ICIRCA) (2022)
8. Amir, N.I.M., Dziyauddin, R.A., Mohamed, N., Ismail, N.S.A., Zulkifli, N.S., Din, N.M.: Real-time threshold-based fall detection system using wearable IoT. In: 4th International Conference on Smart Sensors and Application (ICSSA) (2022)
9. Kaur, P., Wang, Q., Shi, W.: Fall detection from audios with audio transformers. Smart Health **26**, 100340 (2022)
10. Ramachandran, A., Karuppiah, A.: A survey on recent advances in wearable fall detection systems. Biomed. Res. Int. **2020**, 2167160 (2020)
11. Al Dujaili, M.J., Dhaam, H.Z., Mezeel, M.T.: An intelligent fall detection algorithm for elderly monitoring in the Internet of things platform. Multimed. Tools Appl. (2023)
12. Reyad, O., Shehata, H.I., Karar, M.E.: Developed fall detection of elderly patients in internet of healthcare things. Comp. Mater. Contin. **76**(2) (2023)
13. Hu, Y., Zhang, F., Wu, C., Wang, B., Liu, K.J.R.: DeFall: environment-independent passive fall detection using WiFi. IEEE Internet Things J. **9**(11), 8515–8530 (2022)
14. Chelli, A., Pätzold, M.: A machine learning approach for fall detection based on the instantaneous Doppler frequency. IEEE Access **7**, 166173–166189 (2019)
15. Chu, Y., Cumanan, K., Sankarpandi, S.K., Smith, S., Dobre, O.A.: Deep learning-based fall detection using WiFi channel state information. IEEE Access **11**, 83763–83780 (2023)
16. Usmani, S., Saboor, A., Haris, M., Khan, M.A., Park, H.: Latest research trends in fall detection and prevention using machine learning: a systematic review. Sensors **21**(15), 5134 (2021)
17. Hellmers, S., et al.: Comparison of machine learning approaches for near-fall-detection with motion sensors. Front. Digit. Health **5** (2023)
18. Padikkapparambil, J., Ncube, C., Khan, F., Ramasamy, L.K., Gashu, Y.R.: Novel stacking classification and prediction algorithm based ambient assisted living for elderly. Wirel. Communi. Mobile Computi. (2022)
19. Kumar, V.C.V., et al.: Learning a control policy for fall prevention on an assistive walking device. In: 2020 IEEE International Conference on Robotics and Automation (ICRA) (2019)
20. Musci, M., et al.: Online fall detection using recurrent neural networks on smart wearable devices. IEEE Trans. Emerg. Top. Comput. **9**(3), 1276–1289 (2020)

21. Rosato, A., et al.: A decentralized algorithm for distributed ensemble clustering. Inf. Sci. **578**, 417–434 (2021)
22. Gou, J., Yu, B., Maybank, S.J., Tao, D.: Knowledge distillation: a survey. Int. J. Comput. Vision **129**, 1789–1819 (2021)
23. Analytics Vidhya - Precision and Recall
24. Giovannini, S., et al.: Falls among older adults: Screening, identification, rehabilitation, and management. Appl. Sci. **12**(15), 7934 (2022)

Deep Learning Methods for Precise Sugarcane Disease Detection and Sustainable Crop Management

Davesh Kumar Sharma$^{(\boxtimes)}$ ⑩ and Akash Punhani ⑩

Department of Computer Science and Engineering, SRM Institute of Science and Technology,
NCR Campus Modinagar, Ghaziabad, India
dksharma1901@gmail.com

Abstract. In the agricultural domain, sugarcane crops, like many others, are susceptible to diseases, posing a significant threat to both quality and quantity of production. Identifying and mitigating these diseases in their early stages are critical to averting financial losses for farmers. In response, researchers have turned to Artificial Intelligence (AI) techniques such as Machine Learning (ML) and Deep Learning (DL) to analyze diverse agricultural data, including yield prediction, climate patterns, and soil quality, with disease prevention being a prime focus. This paper presents a thorough exploration of the effectiveness of a Deep Learning-based Convolutional Neural Network (CNN) algorithm tailored for the detection of prevalent sugarcane diseases in India. Motivated by the rapid evolution of disease classes and farmers' limited diagnostic skills, this study employs advanced deep learning and computer vision techniques. Through image categorization into healthy and diseased groups, the trained model achieves an impressive 98.69% accuracy rate in sugarcane disease detection. Furthermore, to empower farmers, a web-based application is developed for ongoing disease monitoring. The paper suggests future research avenues, including user feedback integration and exploring the intersection of disease detection with agricultural productivity enhancement and price forecasting, thus enriching farmers' decision-making processes.

Keywords: CNN · Sugarcane Disease · Machine Learning (ML) · Red Rot Disease

1 Introduction

Sugarcane diseases pose substantial concerns and risks to farmers, exerting significant financial implications on sugarcane output and production if not detected promptly [1]. Crop decline adversely affects the economy, emphasizing the imperative of sustainable production practices concerning seeds, water, soil, and fertilizers. Destruction of crops during development diminishes competitiveness and quality, necessitating early disease recognition and diagnosis [2].

© The Author(s), under exclusive license to Springer Nature Switzerland AG 2024
D. Garg et al. (Eds.): IACC 2023, CCIS 2054, pp. 39–52, 2024.
https://doi.org/10.1007/978-3-031-56703-2_4

Traditionally, experts relied on visual inspection for disease identification, a method impractical for large farms due to its inefficiency and high costs. Deep Learning (DL), employing multi-layered artificial neural network architectures, has revolutionized fields like image recognition and classification, transforming how specialists assess and make decisions [3]. Convolutional Neural Network (CNN), a prominent DL technique, excels in pattern recognition tasks through complex data processing, significantly benefiting disease detection processes [4, 5].

Plant diseases in sugarcane are intricate biological phenomena, impacting food safety and the livelihoods of small-scale farmers. Early detection enhances sugarcane quality and aids both farmers and consumers. Manual disease detection methods are being replaced by automated solutions, especially in the context of image processing and computer vision technologies. CNN, a DL technique rooted in Artificial Neural Network (ANN) principles, stands out for its accuracy in diagnosing plant diseases, making it highly relevant in agriculture [6].

This study contributes by leveraging neural networks to facilitate database training using a meticulously labeled dataset. Rigorous testing and validation of the trained neural network follow, culminating in the development of a user-friendly Graphical User Interface (GUI) for sugarcane disease detection. Diseased sugarcane plants significantly impact productivity and quality, leading to financial losses in agriculture. Disease symptoms, such as colored dots or streaks on leaves, are typically identified through visual inspection [7]. Leveraging image processing techniques automates disease detection, reducing human effort while enhancing accuracy and efficiency in plant disease identification.

The subsequent sections of this article are structured as follows: sect. 2 delves into a comprehensive review of the existing literature, providing a contextual background. In sect. 3, the proposed methods are elucidated, offering a meticulous exploration of the CNN architecture. Following this, the results and discussions are presented, shedding light on the outcomes and their implications. Finally, the article culminates in a conclusive summary in sect. 4, accompanied by valuable insights into potential avenues for future research.

2 Literature Review

The examination of crop diseases, as elucidated by the studies of Park et al. [1], holds paramount significance within the realm of agriculture due to their drastic reduction of crop productivity by 20–30% upon infection. The repercussions of agricultural diseases on crop yield are profoundly impactful. In instances of uncertainty regarding crop health, farmers often rely on subjective professional judgments or personal experiences. However, recent technological advancements have introduced innovative solutions. For instance, when farmers capture leaf images via smartphones and submit them to an analysis engine system, the process of diagnosing and predicting diseases ensues. Researchers have developed intricate systems incorporating advanced technologies such as convolutional and fully connected networks, achieving impressive accuracy rates when processing the data.

The studies of Dandawate et al. [2, 20] have underscored plant diseases as significant factors substantially diminishing both the quality and quantity of agricultural output. The complexity of diagnosing and managing these diseases has posed considerable challenges to farmers. Notably, innovative methodologies have been deployed, such as the use of Convolutional Neural Networks (CNNs), to accurately classify leaves, offering farmers a reliable means of disease identification.

Moreover, pioneering studies in the agricultural sector have delved into the development of sophisticated disease detection techniques. Some of these researches are summarized in the following Table 1.

Table 1. Summary of Literature Review

Ref. No	Methods Used	Outcome	Significance
[1] Park et al	Analysis engine system utilizing convolutional and fully connected networks	Disease diagnosis accuracy, reduction in crop productivity by 20–30% upon infection	Innovative solution for precise disease diagnosis and prediction, reducing dependency on subjective judgments
[2] Dandawate et al	Utilization of Convolutional Neural Networks (CNNs) for accurate leaf classification	Significant reduction in both agricultural quality and quantity due to plant diseases	Reliable and accurate disease identification for farmers, overcoming challenges in disease management
[7] Huang et al	Spectro-optical methods for measuring Disease Index (DI) in wheat yellow rust	Accurate measurement of DI, potential applications in hyperspectral imaging for disease detection	Advancements in disease measurement techniques, paving the way for hyperspectral imaging applications
[8] Lecun et al	Introduction of Graph Transformer Networks (GTNs) for document recognition tasks	Unparalleled accuracy in document recognition, transforming commercial and private inspections	Revolutionary approach to document recognition, enhancing accuracy in various inspection processes
[10] Nagvani et al	Machine Learning algorithms, particularly CNN classifiers, for disease detection	High accuracy in identifying various diseases across different crops	Efficient disease detection methods, offering invaluable insights to farmers
[11] Hu et al	Segmentation, metric learning using Index of Initial Disease Severity (IDS), and color characteristics for Tea Leaf Blight (TLB) severity estimation	Superior accuracy in TLB severity estimation, especially with obstructed or damaged TLB leaves	Precise TLB severity estimates, aiding farmers in effective pesticide utilization
[12] Ozguven et al	Dataset of 155 images for training and testing, achieving 95.48% accuracy in disease detection	Impressive accuracy in disease detection for sugar beet plants	Reliable disease detection tool for sugar beet farmers, ensuring accurate identification and classification

(*continued*)

Table 1. (*continued*)

Ref. No	Methods Used	Outcome	Significance
[13] Oppenheim et al	Varying model percentages for training data, achieving accuracy rates ranging from 83% to 96%	Notable accuracy rates, particularly with 90% of the data	Demonstrated effectiveness of transfer learning, emphasizing the significance of appropriate training data selection
[16] Huang et al. & [17] Nagasubramanian et al	Comparative analyses showcasing the superiority of deep learning-based approaches in disease detection	Deep learning outperforms other methodologies, especially in terms of accuracy	Validation of deep learning methods in disease detection, highlighting their efficacy in agricultural contexts
[18] Arsenovic et al	Introduction of a comprehensive dataset with diverse leaf images	Dataset augmentation significantly enhancing model accuracy	Dataset breadth and depth crucial for model accuracy, emphasizing the importance of varied data
[19] Barbedo	Exploration of dataset size impact on model performance	Dataset size critically influences model accuracy	Emphasis on dataset size relevance, underscoring the need for extensive and diverse data
[20] Prabavathi and Chelliah	Utilization of Machine Learning algorithms, particularly decision tree methods, for crop prediction	High accuracy in predicting soil fertility, aiding in crop selection and yield estimation	Enhanced agricultural productivity through informed decision-making, optimizing crop selection and yield rates
[21] Viedienieiev and Piskunova	Integration of traditional linear regression methods and Deep Learning techniques for price forecasting	Traditional methods' effectiveness and benefits of neural networks in handling complex, non-linear factors	Proposal of ensemble methods, combining traditional and neural network models, for enhanced prediction accuracy

It is important to note the challenges associated with CNNs in the context of plant disease detection, specifically the creation of robust datasets. Overcoming this challenge is crucial for the development of accurate and reliable disease detection tools. Additionally, Deep Learning (DL) techniques, particularly CNN algorithms, are pivotal in disease prediction. The current research endeavors to predict sugarcane diseases through the implementation of advanced CNN algorithms, offering farmers invaluable insights for disease control, thereby enhancing both crop quality and yield [10].

3 Methods and System

The collected dataset is verified by the experts with the proper labeling and it is divided into several parts. All the training and testing dataset, wrong or correct data submitted, results and unpredicted values are considered as objects under one set, where the input and desired output are the subset of the system [19]. These objects are often called elements or members of a set. One subset is also designed for the success and failure condition. Figure 1 shows an overview towards forming a mathematical model for the application.

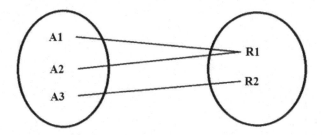

Fig. 1. Mathematical Model

where, output provided by the system, A3: Wrong or incorrect data submitted.

R2: Unpredicted value, A1: Sugarcane leaf data prediction.
A2: Training data, R1: Resultant.

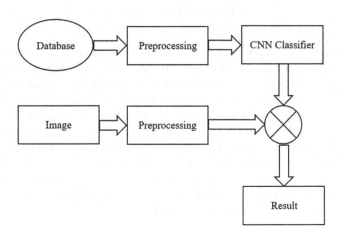

Fig. 2. Workflow of the proposed system

4 Proposed System

In this study, a comprehensive database comprising 580 pictures was utilized as the input for the disease identification system. The system's work flow, as illustrated in Fig. 2, was designed for the identification of sugarcane diseases. Among the total images, 70% (406 pictures) were allocated for training purposes, while the remaining 30% (174 pictures) were designated for testing. The dataset was meticulously balanced, ensuring an equal distribution of pictures for each class, a critical factor for precise analysis. A summary of the dataset and configuration is listed below in Table 2.

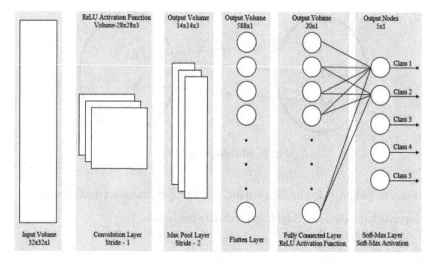

Fig. 3. Proposed CNN Architecture

The dataset used in this study was pre-labeled and verified by experts, encompassing four specific classes of sugarcane diseases. This limitation arose due to the availability of verified data for only these four disease classes. The classes were meticulously verified by domain experts, ensuring the dataset's authenticity and accuracy.

To create a balanced dataset, equal weightage was given to various conditions, including pictures collected from different agro-climatic regions in India, encompassing both peninsular and coastal areas. Additionally, the dataset considered different light conditions, varying from blue and red LED light combinations to white and fluorescent light sources. Pictures were also captured at different times of the day and during various stages of the sugarcane crop's growth. Planting density and techniques were diversified, further enhancing the dataset's representativeness.

Table 2. Summary of the Dataset and system:

Parameter	Details
Total Number of Pictures	580
Training Set	70% of Total (406 pictures)
Testing Set	30% of Total (174 pictures)
Classes	Four Specific Classes of Sugarcane Diseases
Labeling and Verification	Pre-labeled and Verified by Experts
Data Variation	Agro-climatic Regions, Light Conditions, Planting Techniques
Data Processing	Preprocessing, Feature Extraction, Classification
Preprocessing Steps	Filtering, Merging, Data Quality Assurance
Feature Extraction	Convolutional Layers, Standardization of Features (Color, Texture Entropy, Leaf Spots)
Pooling Techniques	Max Pooling, Average Pooling
Classification	Fully Connected Layers

Feature extraction, a fundamental step in the analysis of scaled images, involves the application of convolutional layers to extract pertinent features. These features, encompassing color, texture entropy, and leaf spots, are standardized to carry equal weight. Rectified nonlinear activation functions, coupled with diverse pooling arrangements like max pooling and average pooling, contribute to the creation of robust features. The subsequent phase of classification involves the utilization of fully connected layers, harnessing the extracted features to discern and evaluate sugarcane images for disease presence. To achieve this, our study employed a meticulously curated and balanced dataset, ensuring comprehensive coverage of varied conditions and disease categories. By integrating sophisticated preprocessing techniques with advanced feature extraction methods, our research enabled precise identification and classification of sugarcane diseases. These outcomes offer valuable insights for agricultural management and disease control efforts, underscoring the efficacy of the approach.

Convolutional Neural Networks (CNNs) constitute a specialized category of neural networks tailored for processing visual data, notably images. Drawing inspiration from the pattern recognition abilities of the human brain, these networks are pivotal in machine perception tasks, leveraging intricate architectures to handle complex visual information with remarkable accuracy. CNNs process sensory inputs, like images, and convert them into numerical data, allowing the recognition of complex patterns through machine learning algorithms. They excel in data classification and clustering, providing an additional layer of grouping and categorization.

In a CNN, the process involves taking input images, assigning learnable weights and biases to different objects within these images, and differentiating them. This intricate task is achieved by a deep learning system, the CNN, which significantly reduces pre-processing time compared to other classification techniques. While traditional methods require manual engineering of filters, ConvNets learn filters or characteristics through training. The architectural blueprint of a ConvNet mirrors the connectivity pattern of neurons in the human visual cortex, where individual neurons respond to specific stimuli within their receptive fields, similar to how CNNs operate on images.The CNN architecture as shown in Fig. 3 comprises several layers, each serving a unique purpose:

Convolution Layer: This layer applies filters to input images, extracting distinctive features. The filters slide across the input image, capturing relevant patterns.

Rectified Linear Unit (ReLU) Layer: ReLU activation function introduces non-linearity, enhancing the network's ability to learn complex patterns.

Pooling Layer: This layer reduces the spatial dimensions of the data, making computation more efficient. Pooling also introduces invariance to transformations, allowing the network to recognize patterns regardless of their position in the Image.

Fully Connected Layer (FC Layer): In this layer, high-level, non-linear combinations of features are learned, enabling the network to make accurate predictions based on the extracted features.

In the context of sugarcane disease classification, a CNN is trained to recognize various diseases such as wilt, black rot, grassy shoot, and smut, as well as healthy plant images. The algorithm is designed to be robust, accommodating diverse image orientations, resolutions, and angles. This adaptability ensures accurate disease classification regardless of varying field conditions or camera specifications.

The CNN's efficacy is demonstrated through the extraction of statistical features from the images, including color, texture entropy, and spots. Regardless of factors like light conditions, different times of the day, and varying plant densities, the CNN consistently delivers precise results. This robustness highlights the CNN's ability to handle real-world challenges and underscores its utility in agricultural applications, especially for diagnosing sugarcane diseases accurately.

The proposed system detects four different classes of disease named: black rot, wilt, grassy shoot, and smut. Healthy leaves of sugarcane are shown in Fig. 8. The details of four classes/diseases, as running through the web-based application, are as discussed hereunder:

Class I: Wilt Disease
Wilt disease in sugarcane, caused primarily by the soil-borne bacterium Ralstonia solanacearum, is a devastating agricultural ailment characterized by wilting, yellowing, and eventual death of the infected plants. This pathogen infiltrates the vascular system, obstructing water and nutrient transport, leading to the characteristic symptoms. The disease spreads rapidly through contaminated soil, water, or infected planting material, posing a significant threat to sugarcane cultivation worldwide. Wilt disease impacts plant growth, reduces yield, and diminishes the overall quality of sugarcane, thereby

inflicting substantial economic losses on farmers and the sugar industry. Management strategies such as crop rotation, soil sanitation, and the development of resistant cultivars are crucial in mitigating the disease's impact, requiring continuous research and implementation to safeguard sugarcane production and ensure global food security. Wilt disease (depicted in Fig. 4), is a class 1 disease of the sugarcane disease system.

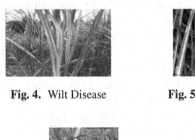

Fig. 4. Wilt Disease   **Fig. 5.** Rot Disease   **Fig. 6.** Grassy
Shoot Disease

Fig. 7. Smut Disease   **Fig. 8.** Healthy Leaf

Class II: Rot Disease

Rot disease in sugarcane, caused by various fungal pathogens, presents a significant challenge to the global sugar industry. This affliction manifests as dark lesions on the stalks, leading to yield losses and deterioration in sucrose content, thereby impacting sugar quality. The pathogens responsible for this disease, notably species of the genera Colletotrichum, Fusarium, and Pythium, thrive in warm, humid conditions, commonly found in sugarcane-growing regions. Rot disease spreads rapidly, primarily through contaminated planting material and soil-borne spores, exacerbating its economic impact. Control strategies encompass a combination of cultural practices, chemical treatments, and genetic resistance breeding, albeit with varying degrees of success. Ongoing research efforts are directed towards understanding the complex interactions between sugarcane and these pathogens, aiming to develop sustainable and effective management techniques to mitigate the detrimental effects of rot disease on sugarcane cultivation. Rot disease as shown in Fig. 5 is classified as a class 2 disease in the sugarcane disease system.

Class III: Grassy Shoot Disease

Grassy shoot disease in sugarcane, caused by the phytoplasma pathogen, is a significant concern in the agricultural sector. This malady, characterized by the abnormal proliferation of tillers and the development of grass-like shoots in affected sugarcane plants, poses a severe threat to crop yields and quality. The disease spreads through insect vectors, disrupting the normal growth patterns of the plant and leading to stunted growth, reduced sugar content, and ultimately economic losses for farmers. The intricate interactions between the phytoplasma and the sugarcane host's physiological processes are yet to be fully elucidated, hindering the formulation of effective control strategies. Researchers and agronomists are intensively investigating the molecular mechanisms underlying this disease, aiming to devise targeted approaches for its management. Understanding the intricate dynamics of grassy shoot disease is paramount for sustainable sugarcane cultivation and ensuring global food security. Grassy Shoot disease as depicted in Fig. 6 is a class 3 disease of the sugarcane disease system.

Class IV: Smut Disease

Smut disease in sugarcane (depicted in Fig. 7), caused by the fungus Sporisoriumscitamineum, poses a significant threat to global sugarcane cultivation. This devastating pathogen affects various sugarcane varieties, leading to substantial economic losses in the agricultural sector. The disease manifests as characteristic dark, soot-like structures, known as smut balls, on the sugarcane stalks, inflicting severe damage to both yield and quality. Its impact on sucrose content and overall plant vigor further exacerbates the agricultural challenges. Smut disease spreads through spores, primarily during periods of high humidity and warm temperatures, emphasizing the importance of effective disease management strategies. Efforts to combat smut disease involve a multifaceted approach, incorporating resistant cultivars, rigorous field monitoring, and fungicidal treatments. Continued research into the disease's molecular mechanisms and the development of resistant sugarcane varieties are crucial in ensuring sustainable sugarcane production and safeguarding the global sugar industry. Smut disease is classified as a class 4 disease in the sugarcane disease system.

5   Results and Discussion

This section presents the outcomes derived from experimental investigations. The classifier underwent a total of 120 epochs, signifying the number of iterations it undertook to refine its training. Figure 9 shows the training and test accuracy as the data modeling is in progress. Training accuracy is high while test accuracy is nearly 90%. Although accuracy is high, some sign of overfitting is visible in the figure.

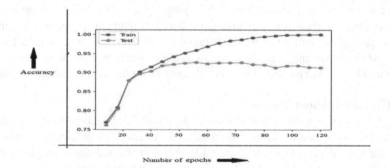

Fig. 9. Performance evaluation for different epochs

The ensuing confusion matrix, encapsulating the classifier's performance, is displayed below:

Table 3. Confusion Matrix

	Class 1	Class 2	Class 3	Class 4
Class 1	34	0	1	2
Class 2	0	43	0	1
Class 3	1	0	52	0
Class 4	0	2	0	38

Utilizing the values extracted from the confusion matrix, namely True Positives (TP), True Negatives (TN), False Positives (FP), and False Negatives (FN), various performance parameters are calculated in Eqs. 1–4. These metrics serve as essential indicators of the classifier's efficacy, enabling a comprehensive evaluation of its performance in the given context.

$$Accuracy = \frac{TP + TN}{TP + TN + FP + FN} \tag{1}$$

$$Precision = \frac{TP}{TP + FP} \tag{2}$$

$$Recall = \frac{TP}{TP + FN} \tag{3}$$

$$F1\ score = \frac{2*Precision*Recall}{Precision + Recall} \tag{4}$$

In the realm of imbalanced data, the significance of accuracy performance metrics becomes evident. However, in such scenarios, relying solely on accuracy can be misleading. Metrics like confusion matrix, precision, recall, and F1 score offer nuanced insights into predictions, outshining accuracy metrics in their depth and reliability. To derive these vital performance indicators, one must employ the values discerned from the provided confusion matrix:

Table 4. Precision and Recall Obtained for multiple Classes

Class	Precision	Recall	F1 Score
Class 1	0.9189	0.9714	0.9442
Class 2	0.9766	0.9556	0.9743
Class 3	0.9800	0.9783	0.9784
Class 4	0.9500	0.9344	0.9421

Table 3 presents the confusion matrix resulting from the training modules for the four diseased classes. Performance metrics were calculated using Eqs. 1–4, and the evaluation of these metrics for the four classes is depicted in Table 4. During the classifier training with the supplied input database, Class 1 exhibited an accuracy of 97.7% and a precision of 92%. For Class 2, the accuracy reached 98.28% with a precision of 98%, both achieved during training with the provided input dataset. Similarly, in Class 3, the accuracy attained was 98.25% with a precision of 98%, and for Class 4, an accuracy of 97.13% was coupled with a precision of 95% under the same training conditions. Upon comprehensive analysis of these performance parameters, our evaluation demonstrates that the system's proficiency is notably high, boasting an impressive overall score of 98.69%.

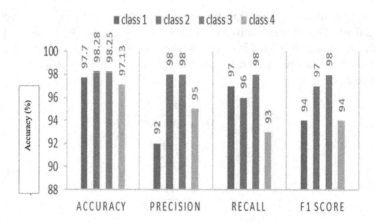

Fig. 10. Assessment of Performance for the four classes

Figure 10 illustrates the systematic evaluation of the system across the four classes during both training and testing phases, delineated by the epochs. A meticulous analysis of the performance, coupled with an in-depth review of the pertinent performance parameters, leads to the unequivocal conclusion that the system's efficiency excels, boasting an impressive accuracy rate of 98.69%. This substantiates the system's robustness and effectiveness in the given experimental context.

6   Conclusions

In this study, a streamlined convolutional neural network was successfully deployed, achieving an impressive accuracy rate of 98.69% in detecting sugarcane diseases. The model adeptly categorized sugarcane images, distinguishing between diseased and non-diseased specimens based on leaf patterns and specific diseases. This achievement establishes a valuable tool for farmers, integrating computer vision and machine learning to facilitate the precise identification and categorization of sugarcane diseases. The primary focus was on developing a user-friendly web-based application, accessible across a range of devices including desktop PCs, mobile phones, and tablets. This innovative application empowers farmers to upload images in real-time, enabling swift and accurate disease identification. Its intuitive interface ensures a seamless experience; users can effortlessly log in, submit images, and promptly receive precise results.

Looking ahead, the research's future trajectory lies in continuous refinement, driven by user feedback and inputs. This iterative process will enable the model to adapt dynamically to emerging agricultural challenges, ensuring its relevance and effectiveness in the face of evolving disease patterns and farming needs. A crucial aspect of this evolution entails the regular update of the dataset, ensuring its relevance and comprehensiveness. This iterative process of dataset augmentation and user feedback-driven model tuning presents both a limitation and an opportunity for future researchers. By addressing these aspects, the application of this technique can be further optimized, enhancing its practicality and effectiveness in real-time plant disease detection.

References

1. Park, H., Eun, J.S., Kim, S.H.: Image-based disease diagnosing and predicting of the crops through the deep learning mechanism. In: International Conference on Information and Communication Technology Convergence (ICTC), IEEE, 18–20, pp. 129–131 (2017). https://doi.org/10.1109/ICTC.2017.8190957
2. Dandawate, Y., Kokare, R.: An automated approach for classification of plant diseases towards the development of futuristic decision support system in Indian perspective. International Conference on Advances in Computing, https://doi.org/10.1109/ICACSIS.2018.8618169
3. Militante, S.V., Gerardo, B.D., Dionisio, N.V.: Plant leaf detection and disease recognition using deep learning. In: 2019 IEEE Eurasia conference on IOT, communication and engineering (ECICE), pp. 579–582. IEEE (2019)
4. Hu, G., Yang, X., Zhang, Y., Wan, M.: Identification of tea leaf diseases by using an improved deep convolutional neural network. Sustainable Computing: Informatics and Systems **24**, 100353 (2019)
5. Suryawati, E., Sustika, R., Yuwana, R.S., Subekti, A., Pardede, H.F.: Deep structured convolutional neural network for tomato diseases detection. In: 2018 international conference on advanced computer science and information systems (ICACSIS), pp. 385–390. IEEE (2018)
6. Militante, S., Gerardo, B.: Detecting sugarcane diseases through adaptive deep learning models of convolutional neural network. In: 6th IEEE International Conference on Engineering Technologies and Applied Sciences (ICETAS), pp. 1–5. Kuala Lumpur, Malaysia (2019). https://doi.org/10.1109/ICETAS48360.2019.9117332
7. Huang, W., Lamb, D.W., Niu, Z., Zhang, Y., Liu, L., Wang, J.: Identification of yellow rust in wheat using in-situ spectral reflectance measurements and airborne hyper spectral imaging. Precision Agric. **8**(4/5), 187–197 (2007). https://doi.org/10.1007/s11119-007-9038-9
8. Lecun, Y., Bottou, L., Bengio, Y., Haffner, P.: Gradient-based learning applied to document recognition. Proc. IEEE **86**(11), 2278–2324 (1998). https://doi.org/10.1109/5.726791
9. Hou, J., Li, L., He, J.: Detection of grapevine leafroll disease based on 11-index imagery and ant colony clustering algorithm. Precision Agriculture, 1–18 (2016). https://doi.org/10.1007/s11119-0169432-2
10. Shruti, U., Nagaveni, V., Raghvendra, B.K.: A review on machine learning classification techniques for plant disease detection. In: 5th International Conference on Advanced Computing & Communication Systems (ICACCS), pp. 281–284. Coimbatore India (2019). https://doi.org/10.1109/ICACCS.2019.8728415
11. Hu, G., Wei, K., Zhang, Y., Bao, W., Liang, D.: Estimation of tea leaf blight severity in natural scene images. Precision Agriculture (Springer), 1–24 (2021). https://doi.org/10.1007/s11119-020-09782-8

12. Ozguvena, M.M., Adem, K.: Automatic detection and classification of leaf spot disease in sugar beet using deep learning algorithms. Physica A: Statistical Mechanics and its Applications **535**, 122537 (2019). https://doi.org/10.1016/j.physa.2019.122537
13. Oppenheim, D., Shani, G., Erlich, O., Tsror, L.: Using deep learning for image-based potato tuber disease detection. Phytopathology **109**(6), 1083–1087 (2019)
14. Cruz, A.C., Luvisi, A., De Bellis, L., Ampatzidis, Y.: Vision-based plant disease detection system using transfer and deep learning. In: 2017 asabe annual international meeting, p. 1. American Society of Agricultural and Biological Engineers (2017)
15. Chen, J., Chen, J., Zhang, D., Sun, Y., Nanehkaran, Y.A.: Using deep transfer learning for image-based plant disease identification. Comput. Electron. Agric. **173**, 105393 (2020)
16. Huang, S., Liu, W., Qi, F., Yang, K.: Development and validation of a deep learning algorithm for the recognition of plant disease. In: 2019 IEEE 21st International Conference on High Performance Computing and Communications; IEEE 17th International Conference on Smart City; IEEE 5th International Conference on Data Science and Systems (HPCC/SmartCity/DSS), pp. 1951–1957. IEEE (2019)
17. Nagasubramanian, K., et al.: Plant disease identification using explainable 3D deep learning on hyperspectral images. Plant Methods 1–10 (2019). https://doi.org/10.1186/s13007-019-0479-8
18. Arsenovic, M., Karanovic, M., Sladojevic, S., Anderla, A., Stefanovic, D.: Solving current limitations of deep learning-based approaches for plant disease detection. Symmetry **11**, 1–21 (2019). https://doi.org/10.3390/sym11070939
19. Barbedo, J.: Impact of dataset size and variety on the effectiveness of deep learning and transfer learning for plant disease classification. Computer and Electronics in Agriculture **153** (2018). https://doi.org/10.1016/j.compag.2018.08.03
20. Prabavathi, R., Chelliah, B.J.: A comprehensive review on machine learning approaches for yield prediction using essential soil nutrients. Universal Journal of Agricultural Research **10**(3), 288–303 (2022). https://doi.org/10.13189/ujar.2022.100310
21. Viedienieiev, V.A., Piskunova, O.V.: Forecasting the selling price of the agricultural products in ukraine using deep learning algorithms. Univer. J. Agricult. Res. **9**(3), 91–100 (2021). https://doi.org/10.13189/ujar.2021.090304
22. Shukla, S.K., Lalan, S., Awasthi, S.K., Pathak, A.D.: Sugarcane in India (Package of Practices for Different Agro-climatic Zones), AICRP (S) Technical Bulletin - No. 1, Published by ICAR-All India Coordinated Research Project on Sugarcane (ICAR-Indian Institute of Sugarcane Research), pp. 1–17 (2017)

An Interactive Interface for Plant Disease Prediction and Remedy Recommendation

Mrunalini S. Bhandarkar[1]([✉]) [iD], Basudha Dewan[1] [iD], and Payal Bansal[2] [iD]

[1] Poornima University, Jaipur, India
mrunalini.bhandarkar@pccoepune.org, basudha@poornima.edu.in
[2] Poornima College of Engineering, Jaipur, India
payal.bansal@poornima.org

Abstract. Economy and financial status of a country is largely dependent on agriculture. Virtual Assistants (VA) are successfully deployed in different applications, however its use in the farming domain is very limited. There are number of challenges in this like lack of single database which will satisfy the varied needs of farmers like crop prediction, disease management, prediction about proper harvest time, locating nearby godowns, weather forecast etc. Along with this one of the major problems is limited technology literacy of the users poses difficulty in designing and deployment of VA in farming domain. Many times, it is difficult to describe the field conditions verbally. In this case it will be better to accept the photo-based input from the user. The user can pass on additional queries using audio input. By this method the effectivity of VA can be increased. In this work the plant disease prediction is designed with the help of plant leaf images. The system is trained on images taken from PlantVillage Dataset. The system is trained on 61 images of 5 different class. The database contains the images from various crops like maize, strawberry, tomato. 12 different features of diseased segment are used to have the trained model. It is found that the accuracy of SVM classifier is 88.5% and using NN the accuracy is improved to 90.16%. To improve the accuracy further, the image datasize should be increased. Deep learning algorithms like EfficientNet, InceptionNet, ResNet,etc. have better accuracy. In future we plan to integrate this with a system that will generate the audio responses for audio queries raised by farmers.

Keywords: Virtual Assistant · Farming · Plant disease

1 Introduction

Virtual Personal Assistant (VPA) is an effective application of Artificial Intelligence. It has given a new way for human to have its work done from a computer. Most of the Virtual Assistants work on audio as communication. In past voice-activated devices used few in built commands. However due to advancement in technology, voice assistants can respond to a considerably wider range of instructions and queries. The assistant can analyze the voice requests and responds appropriately [35]. The processing of data is done as Speech to Text; Text to Intention; Intention to action.

© The Author(s), under exclusive license to Springer Nature Switzerland AG 2024
D. Garg et al. (Eds.): IACC 2023, CCIS 2054, pp. 53–66, 2024.
https://doi.org/10.1007/978-3-031-56703-2_5

Agriculture is largest source of revenue for the nation. Farmers being backbone of the country it is required to understand their needs and challenges. Encouraging the farmers to increase production of crops will boost the economy of the country. Farmers in India make up 54.6% of the population, however they only make up 13.9% of GDP. [36].

By providing the farmers the access to valid information and expert guidance, the yield can be increased. By 2050, 70% increase in agricultural productivity will be necessary to support the predicted world population. To meet this need technological support in agriculture, need substantial improvement. Amongst the various issues faced by the farmers few are related to crop management and labour management [7]. The current state of awareness amongst the farmers regarding contemporary methods and technologies used in agriculture is low. The reasons for this include the fact that the technology is too complicated to comprehend and deploy, the answers may not be accurate, etc. Using different machine learning algorithms more precise response can be generated for the queries regarding which crop to be cultivated in typical region, crop monitoring, increasing the yield, early detection and control of disease, use of different pesticides and fertilisers, best time to harvest, climate forecast, expert advice, etc. [37].

The paper is organized in the following sections. The first section briefs about the Digital technology employed in farming and importance of disease prediction using plant leaves. In the second section discussion on the related work done recently on implementation of VA in farming domain and plant disease prediction methodology is presented. Section three presents the methodology followed. Lastly, fourth section concludes this paper along with future directions.

2   Digital Technology Employed in Farming

Artificial intelligence (AI) is gaining the popularity in farming related activities like soil analysis, crop monitoring, disease management, supporting for marketing of quality products, etc. [36]. Few such popular applications deployed in this domain include AgroPad, Plantix11, Trringo13 and EM3, Swamitva18 scheme, Ergos, AgNext, Agritech. The survey of the research article shows that there is scope of improvement in disease management.

2.1   Disease Prediction Using Plant Leaves

Disease prediction using plant leaves is a vital in agriculture and crop protection. It provides farmers with the knowledge regarding possible disease and remedies for its cure, successfully manage plant diseases, and optimize crop production with the minimum impact on environment. The crop yield is badly impacted if the disease prediction is not done at early stages. Plant health management and agriculture both greatly benefit from the ability to predict diseases using plant leaves. This will help in precision agricultural activities by preventive crop monitoring, optimal use of pesticides, avoidance of crop damage, etc. This eventually lead in dramatic increase in both crop quantity and quality.

There are numerous types of plant leaf diseases caused by various pathogens, environmental factors, or nutritional deficiencies. Each disease has its own distinct symptoms, such as leaf discoloration, spots, lesions, curling, wilting, or deformations. It is important to accurately categorize and diagnose the specific disorder affecting plants in order to implement appropriate management strategies. Some common types of plant leaf diseases include Fungal infection, Bacterial attack, Tobacco Mosaic Virus, Tomato Yellow Leaf Curl Virus, Cucumber Mosaic Virus, Potato Virus, Citrus Tristeza Virus, Parasitic Diseases, etc. [38].

For the purpose of predicting crop diseases using leaf photos, numerous well-known databases are employed. These databases offer labelled datasets for model training and evaluation.

3   Related Work

The study of different research articles was carried out with the objective to understand how the Virtual assistant or interactive services can be provided for farmers. The study aimed in understanding what type of services the farmer is looking for assistance and how the system can be made more usable. The Table 1 highlights the nature of input the Interactive assistants deployed in farming domain can process; it summarises that most of the authors have worked on text input or audio input (limited to keywords). For disease prediction and guidance on it, there is need of a system which can handle the image and voice-based queries.

Table 1. Nature of Input the Virtual Assistant Use in Agriculture Domain Process

Reference	Text	Audio	Image	Video	Regional Language
[1]	✓	✓	X	X	X
[2]	✓	✓	X	X	X
[3]	✓	✓	X	X	✓ (Hindi)
[4]	✓	✓	X	X	X
[5]	✓	X	✓	X	X
[6]	✓	X	✓	X	X
[7]	✓	✓	X	X	✓

Following section gives the details about the methodology used by the researchers for the implementation.

The VA proposed in [1] will assist farmer in forecasting the price of particular crop based on audio input. The system makes use of the speech synthesis Web API. In [2] conversational agent is designed which enables the farmers to get relevant answers to their queries using dataset about infections that affect tomatoes, for this the author has created the database that can handle all possible query formats the user can ask and trained the system for this. An evaluation study of around 35 farmers with the goal of evaluating system usability for audio and audio + text, understand the challenges faced in utilising the technology is presented in [3]. The study shows that the audio + text mode of utility is more preferred. A web-based user interface proposed in [4] can reply to the user inquiries about warehouses for the storage of agricultural products. The chatbot designed and deployed in [5] assists the farmers by providing the suggestions to a variety of farming-related challenges including disease identification and weather predictions. A platform independent bot is proposed in [6] is a system that integrates prediction modules for crop identification, crop disease detection, crop rotation advice, soil detection and weather forecasting. With the help of mobile application suggested in [7] farmer will have access to localised information such as weather forecasts, crop for planting, fertilizers. Challenges and opportunities in deployment of Industry 4.0 in farming are discussed in [8]. Suggestions for improving the use of traditional Government IVR based agriculture are discussed in [9].

Most work done for interactive assistants for farmers focuses of price forecasting, weather prediction, type of crop and fertilizers, etc. In [5, 6] the author has implemented the system which can act on image input. However, the work is limited to disease prediction. Other work is based on audio or text only mode of interaction.

The study of the different article done in further discussion focuses on how the plant disease prediction is done, database used, different features used, performance evaluation metrics, etc.The PlantVillage dataset has been used for the majority of the work on plant disease prediction. It has pictures that were taken in predetermined circumstances. Since this database is generated in controlled circumstances it restricts the accuracy of disease detection in real condition. PlantDoc dataset which consists of 2598 photos from 13 different plant species and 27 different classes is the first dataset of its kind to include information from uncontrolled environments. It gives comparatively good accuracy for real-world photographs [10, 11]. Various practical imaging techniques including thermal imaging, multispectral imaging, fluorescence imaging, hyperspectral imaging, visible imaging, MRI, and 3D imaging techniques can be used for early detection of diseases in crops [12]. Many researchers have created and tested different Machine Learning (ML) and Deep Learning (DL) approaches for the recognition of plant disease detection, and they also obtained noticeable results in both cases. The classification accuracy achieved through experimentation show that DL methods outperform ML methods in terms of disease identification. The experimentation done on citrus plant demonstrate that VGG-16 provides the best Accuracy whereas RF provides the least [12]. Deep learning approach is efficient for disease diagnosis in plants when there is sufficient data available. Instead of taking into account the complete leaf, the research in [14] investigates the use of specific patches, lesions for the purpose of disease prediction. Due to the multiple diseases that attack the same the crops can be detected at the same time. This method produced accuracy levels that were on average, 12% greater than those attained by using the source photographs. Convolutional Autoencoder (CAE) networks and Convolutional Neural Networks (CNN) based hybrid model is applied on peach leaves. It proved to have good time complexity for training and testing phase as it uses less training parameters [13]. The prediction accuracy highly depends on the size of database. The overview provided in [15] details the progress of Deep Learning algorithms in past few years for the detection of diseases in crops. The recent trends and difficulties in disease identification for plants is presented. It summarises the numerous datasets that different researchers have utilised, data augmentation techniques, their significance, and how they might assist in drawing conclusions at the earlier stages.

In [16] the author seeks to identify microscopic disease blobs on plant leaves. The diseased blobs are separated by applying the pre-processing technique of contrast enhancement; system is trained using Artificial *neural network (ANN)*. The proposed algorithm can be employed on units like smartphones, which will be very helpful to farmers working in the field. A method developed on the basis of image enhancement and *DMS-Robust Alexnet* is suggested in [17]. Using this technique, it is possible to recognize and determine the difference between healthy leaves and the six major illnesses that can affect maize leaves.Database with limited size pose severe problem in giving correct prediction. In order to increase the data size various augmentation techniques are used. *Conditional Generative Adversarial Network (C-GAN)*, DoubleGAN are used to create the synthetic images to overcome this problem. Accuracy of classification largely depends on the augmentation methods used. [18, 27]. In [19] a probabilistic programming solution for diagnosing the diseases on crops using *Bayesian deep learning algorithms* is developed. The results show that good optimization of developed models can be achieved with this method and comparatively better classification accuracy can be obtained. To overcome the overfitting issue due to imbalance in the dataset, there is need of modified test conditions, specifications and appropriate data redistribution strategies or class balancing classifiers [20]. An automatic model based on MoblieNet and effective network architecture is applied for disease detection on bean crops in [21]. The findings of the research show that when both the batch size and learning rate rise the classification training accuracy value declines. The study done in [22] show that in comparison the *EfficientNet V2-S* and *EfficientNet V2-L* prove to have good accuracy for real time photos where there are challenges like poor light intensity, contrast and background noise. A *Convolutional Neural Network (CNN)* created with less layers reduces the computational complexity and as a result execution time is less and less storage is required compared to other deep CNN models for same comparable classification accuracy [23].

In contrast to other CNNs with significantly more parameters, employing CNNs with relatively small parameters to extract features and mixing their feature sets results in more reliable models [24]. YOLOX based model with an improved Spatial Pyramid Pooling block is proposed in [25]. This model can help in diagnosing multiple diseases on a single plant. *Simple Linear Iterative Clustering (SLIC)* is applied on the maize leaf images in [26]. Findings imply that *SLIC* segmentation on images of maize leaf diseased regions aids in precise diseased region identification. *ResTS (Residual Teacher/Student)* visualization and categorization method for identifying diseases on various crops is developed in [27].

Transfer Learning-based model and a vision transformer (TLMViT) for classifying diseases on crops is developed in [28] has improvement validation accuracy. The traditional approaches are time consuming, labor intensive and inaccurate. It can be done with the help of remote sensing characteristics [29]. FieldPlant disease dataset on crops containing labelled photos has good potential for disease management on crops [30]. The LAD-Net, also known as the Lightweight Apple Disease Network, is an innovative and efficient model specifically designed for real-time analysis of diseases on apple plant. LAD-Net addresses challenge of providing instant diagnosis on mobile devices [31]. In [32] deep features combined with conventional *local binary pattern (LBP) features* which can capture localized texture details in the images of leaves, this will help in disease prediction and control in earlier stages. In [33] a novel approach, called PiTLiD, for identifying diseases on plants from phenotypic information of leaves with a less data size is proposedStudy shows that the performance tested on smaller datasize is much better compared to other algorithms. PlantDet deep ensemble model built on InceptionResNetV2, EfficientNetV2L, and Xception has been proposed in [34] for disease prediction on rice plant.

4 Methodology

In order to improve the usability of virtual assistant in agriculture domain, the system should be able to process the image input alongwith the speech input. In the proposed system, the user will be able to upload the photo-based input of plant leaf and can get the suggestion on predicted disease. The proposed system is implemented on MATLAB. For the disease prediction on crops machine learning algorithm Support Vector Machine (SVM) and Neural Network (NN) is applied. After the disease prediction from input image the user can get his query solved by passing voiced input. To facilitate the query resolution through the photo-based input, there is need of plant image database. This database will be used to train the model. The disease prediction will be done using machine learning algorithm.

The contribution of research work is as follows:

- Using diseased leaf image as an input, built a model for the classification of diseases on corn, tomato and strawberry plants.
- Implement Multiclass SVM classifier and Neural Network for classification of input image in one of the five classes.
- Assess model performance using various metrics.

The database used for implementation of algorithm is created by downloading the images from PlantVillage Dataset and New Plant Disease Dataset. The dataset contains 61 images separated in five folders. This selection is done in view of implementation of voiced remedy recommendation for selected crops. The five folders are representing a class of five different diseases mentioned below: Corn(maize)- Cercospora Gray leaf spot (12 images), Corn(maize)- Northern Leaf Blight (14 images), Strawberry- Leaf scorch (10 images), Tomato- Bacterial spot (13 images), Tomato- Septoria leaf spot (12 images).

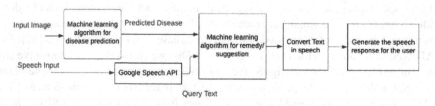

Fig. 1. Block Diagram of Overall System

Figure 1 shows the Block diagram for implementation
Figure 2 shows the Implementation of Plant disease prediction

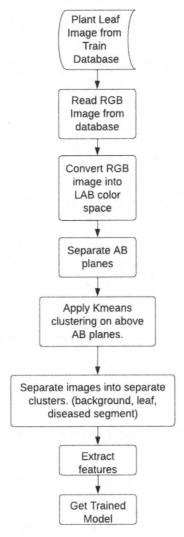

Fig. 2. Flowchart for (a) Training and (b)Testing phase

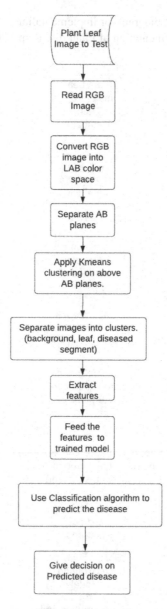

Fig. 2. (*continued*)

5 Results and Discussion

There are image files in the database with each file representing a leaf. The leaf images in the database are of the size 256 * 256, (JPEG format). Sample images of the diseased leaves are shown in Fig. 3

Fig. 3. Sample images of the diseased leaves (a) Corn- Cercospora Gray leaf spot (b)Corn- Northern Leaf Blight (c) Strawberry- Leaf scorch (d)Tomato- Bacterial spot (e)Tomato- Septoria leaf spot (PlantVillage Dataset)

The MATLAB code is written to do the image preprocessing. RGB image is transformed into LAB color space. This removes dependency on light intensity and brightness while doing the feature extraction. After obtaining the details of LAB color space, the detailed information in AB color planes is used for clustering the leaf image in three different clusters: Leaf section, Background and green portion of leaf, diseased segment of leaf. For segregation of this k- means clustering algorithm is used.

For doing clustering k-means algorithm is employed. The result has four different images: Original input image, leaf section (cluster1), background and healthy portion of leaf (cluster2) and diseased section (cluster3). As SVM is supervised learning algorithm, the user has to give the information about the diseased segment to the classifier. To apply the SVM classifier, information about the diseased segment is accepted from the user. After getting the information of diseased segment, feature extraction is done for the diseased segment. The gray level co-occurrence matrix is evaluated for this section. The co-occurrence matrices and 12 different features are extracted and stored as feature array. These steps are applied over entire train set images.

Following features are extracted from the input image: Contrast, Energy; Homogeneity; Standard Deviation, Entropy, mean, Variance, Kurtosis, Skewness, Correlation, Smoothness.

Once the train model is available, to get the information of the disease on a particular crop, input image is accepted from user. The input image is passed through all steps mentioned for train image. The disease prediction for the said input image is done by using Multiclass SVM classifier. The Tables 2 and 3 shows the classification results for SVM and NN and Fig. 4 shows the mean values for the parameters. This will help in finding out the classification accuracy of SVM and NN classifier.

Evaluation Metrics: The performance metrices used for evaluating the performance of the classifier are:

Accuracy Is a measure that gives us the information about the of correct predictions for sample data. (Eq. 1)

$$Accuracy = \frac{Correct\ Predictions}{Total\ Predictions} \qquad (1)$$

Table 2. Actual vs Predicted Class (PC) for SVM Classifier

	PC1	PC2	PC3	PC4	PC5
Actual Class1	11	1	0	0	0
Actual Class2	1	13	0	0	0
Actual Class3	1	0	8	1	0
Actual Class4	0	1	0	12	0
Actual Class5	1	1	0	0	10

Table 3. Actual Vs Predicted Class (PC) for NN

	PC1	PC2	PC3	PC4	PC5
Actual Class1	12	0	0	0	0
Actual Class2	0	13	0	0	1
Actual Class3	2	0	8	0	0
Actual Class4	0	0	0	12	1
Actual Class5	1	1	0	0	10

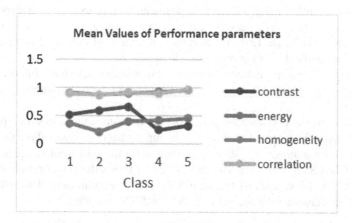

Fig. 4. Mean Values for Performance parameters

Precision Metrics helps in understanding what proportion of positives predictions are actually positive. (Eq. 2)

$$Pr\,ecision = \frac{true\ positive}{true\ positive + false\ positive} \tag{2}$$

F1 Score. This metric usually tells us how precise and robust our classifier is. (Eq. 3)

$$F1\ score = 2 * \frac{Precision * Recall}{Precision + Recall} \tag{3}$$

Alongwith above Sensitivity, Specificity, Kappa, Matthews Correlation Coefficient, False positive rate (FPR) are also evaluated (Table 4).

Table 4. Performance Parameters For SVM Classifier

Parameter	Value for SVM	Value for NN
Accuracy	0.8852	0.9016
Error	0.1148	0.0984
Sensitivity	0.8803	0.897
Specificity	0.9708	0.9753
Precision	0.9043	0.9124
False Positive Rate	0.0292	0.0247
F1- score	0.8868	0.8999
MathewCC	0.862	0.8789
Kappa	0.6414	0.6926

Comparison of prediction accuracy for SVM and NN is shown in Fig. 5.

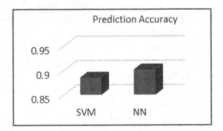

Fig. 5. Accuracy of SVM and NN classifiers

6 Conclusion

Most of the existing virtual assistants in farming domain work by accepting audio or text input and are used for giving the suggestions on type of crop to be cultivated based on soil type, environmental condition, prediction of best harvest time, etc. Other research done in farming domain is crop disease prediction based on plant leaves. For this many popular databases are available and various researchers have worked on different machine learning/ deep learning algorithms. For disease prediction in crops using machine learning algorithms, the training dataset, feature used for classification, classifier algorithm play an important role. In this work the disease prediction for crop based on plant leaf image is implemented. For this the farmer can pass on the test image as an input and get name of disease based on prediction algorithm. The Multiclass SVM and NN algorithm are used for giving the predicted disease name. The images from PlantVillage Dataset are used to create the train model. It is found that the classification accuracy for Multiclass SM is 88.5% and that of Neural Network is 90.16% for the implemented dataset. To improve the accuracy further, the image datasize should be increased and also there are Deep learning algorithms like EfficientNet, InceptionNet, ResNet,etc. which have better accuracy than SVM classifier. In future if we are looking for a handheld device/ mobile application working on disease prediction and providing the solution. It should be feasible to give the prediction in short time duration and also work for audio input generate audio responses.

Disclosure of Interests. Authors have no conflict of interest to declare.

References

1. Kannagi, L., Ramya, C., Shreya, R., Sowmiya, R.: Virtual Conversational Assistant –"The FARMBOT". Int. J. Eng. Technol. Sci. Res. **5**(3), 520–527 (2018)
2. Cynthia, T., Calduwel Newton, P.: Voice based answering technique for farmers in mobile cloud computing. Int. J. Scient. Res. Comp. Sci. Appl. Manage. Stud. **7**(3), 1–7 (2018)
3. Jain, M., et al.: FarmChat: A Conversational Agent to Answer Farmer Queries. In: Proceedings of the ACM on Interactive, Mobile, Vol. 2, No. 4, Article 170, pp 1–21. Wearable and Ubiquitous Technologies (2018)
4. Sawant, D., Jaiswaly, A., Singhz, J., Shah, P.: AgriBot - An intelligent interactive interface to assist farmers in agricultural activities. In: 2019 IEEE Bombay Section Signature Conference (IBSSC), pp. 1–6. Bombay, India (2019)
5. Arora, B., et al.: Agribot: a natural language generative neural networks engine for agricultural applications. In: International Conference on Contemporary Computing and Applications (IC3A) (IEEE) Lucknow, pp. 28–33. India (2020)
6. Geetha, S., Balaji, S., Santhiya, A., Subashri. C., Subicsha, S.: Farm's Smart BOT. Turkish J. Comp. Math. Edu. **12**(10), 3299–3307 (2021)
7. Kiruthiga Devi, M., et al.: Farmer's Assistant using AI Voice Bot. In: 3rd International Conference on Signal Processing and Communication (ICPSC), pp. 527–531. IEEE, Coimbatore (2021)
8. Rasputina, A.V.: Digitalization trends in the agricultural industry. In: IOP Conference Series: Earth and Environmental Science EESTE-2021 Moscow Vol. 979, pp. 1–6 (2021)
9. Walter, T.F., et al.: Using Data for Development: Evidence from a Phone System for Agricultural Advice. Working paper 9244, pp. 1–38 (2021)
10. Singh, D., et al.: PlantDoc: a dataset for visual plant disease detection. In: Proceedings of the 7th ACM IKDD CoDS and 25th COMAD, pp. 249–253 (2020)
11. Singh, V., Sharma, N., Singh, S.: A review of imaging techniques for plant disease detection. Artificial Intelligence in Agriculture **4**, 229–242 (2020)
12. Sujatha, R., Chatterjee, J.M., Jhanjhi, N.Z., Brohi, S.N.: Performance of deep learning vs machine learning in plant leaf disease detection. Microprocessors and Microsystems **80**, 103615 (2021)

13. Bedi, P., Gole, P.: Plant disease detection using hybrid model based on convolutional autoencoder and convolutional neural network. Artificial Intelligence in Agriculture **5**, 90–101 (2021)
14. Barbedo, J.G.A.: Plant disease identification from individual lesions and spots using deep learning. Biosys. Eng. **180**, 96–107 (2019)
15. Li, L., Zhang, S., Wang, B.: Plant disease detection and classification by deep learning—a review. IEEE Access **9**, 56683–56698 (2021)
16. Pham, T.N., Van Tran, L., Vu Truong Dao, S.: Early disease classification of mango leaves using feed-forward neural network and hybrid metaheuristic feature selection. IEEE Access **8**, 189960–189973 (2020)
17. Lv, M., Zhou, G., He, M., Chen, A., Zhang, W., Yahui, H.: Maize leaf disease identification based on feature enhancement and DMS-robust alexnet. IEEE access **8**, 57952–57966 (2020)
18. Abbas, A., Jain, S., Gour, M., Vankudothu, S.: Tomato plant disease detection using transfer learning with C-GAN synthetic images. Comput. Electron. Agric. **187**, 106279 (2021)
19. Hernández, S., López, J.L.: Uncertainty quantification for plant disease detection using Bayesian deep learning. Applied Soft Computing **96**, 106597 (2020)
20. Tugrul, B., Elfatimi, E., Eryigit, R.: Convolutional neural networks in detection of plant leaf diseases: A review. Agriculture **12**(8), 1192 (2022)
21. Elfatimi, E., Eryigit, R., Elfatimi, L.: Beans leaf diseases classification using MobileNet models. IEEE Access **10**, 9471–9482 (2022)
22. Sunil, C.K., Jaidhar, C.D., Patil, N.: Cardamom plant disease detection approach using EfficientNetV2. IEEE Access **10**, 789–804 (2021)
23. Vishnoi, V.K., Kumar, K., Kumar, B., Mohan, S., Ahmad Khan, A.: Detection of apple plant diseases using leaf images through convolutional neural network. IEEE Access **11**, 6594–6609 (2022)
24. Amin, H., Darwish, A., Hassanien, A.E., Soliman, M.: End-to-end deep learning model for corn leaf disease classification. IEEE Access **10**, 31103–31115 (2022)
25. Noon, S.K., Amjad, M., Qureshi, M.A., Mannan, A.: Handling severity levels of multiple co-occurring cotton plant diseases using improved YOLOX model. IEEE Access **10**, 134811–134825 (2022)
26. Phan, H., Ahmad, A., Saraswat, D.: Identification of foliar disease regions on corn leaves using SLIC segmentation and deep learning under uniform background and field conditions. IEEE Access **10**, 111985–111995 (2022)
27. Shah, D., Trivedi, V., Sheth, V., Shah, A., Chauhan, U.: ResTS: Residual deep interpretable architecture for plant disease detection. Information Processing in Agriculture **9**(2), 212–223 (2022)
28. Tabbakh, A., Barpanda, S.S.: A Deep Features extraction model based on the Transfer learning model and vision transformer. TLMViT" for Plant Disease Classification. IEEE Access (2023)
29. Das, S., Biswas, A., Vimalkumar, C., Sinha, P.: Deep learning analysis of rice blast disease using remote sensing images. IEEE Geoscience and Remote Sensing Letters **20**, 1–5 (2023)
30. Moupojou, E., et al.: FieldPlant: a dataset of field plant images for plant disease detection and classification with deep learning. IEEE Access **11**, 35398–35410 (2023)
31. Zhu, X., et al.: Lad-net: A novel light weight model for early apple leaf pests and diseases classification. IEEE/ACM Trans. Comput. Biol. Bioinf. **20**(2), 1156–1169 (2022)
32. Hosny, K.M., El-Hady, W.M., Samy, F.M., Vrochidou, E., Papakostas, G.A.: Multi-class classification of plant leaf diseases using feature fusion of deep convolutional neural network and local binary pattern. IEEE Access (2023)
33. Liu, K., Zhang, X.: PiTLiD: identification of plant disease from leaf images based on convolutional neural network. IEEE/ACM Trans. Comput. Biol. Bioinf. **20**(2), 1278–1288 (2022)

34. Shovon, M.S.H., et al.: PlantDet: a robust multi-model ensemble method based on deep learning for plant disease detection. IEEE Access (2023)
35. Benedict, G.C., et al.: Consumer decisions with artificially intelligent voice assistants. Marketing Letters Springer **31**, 335–347 (2020)
36. Beriya, A.: Digital Agriculture: Challenges and Possibilities in India. CSD Working Paper Series: Towards a New Indian Model of Information and Communications Technology-Led Growth and Development, ICT India Working Paper 35, pp 1–13 (2020)
37. Niranjan, P.Y., Rajpurohit, V.S., Malgi, R.: A survey on chat-bot system for agriculture domain. In: International Conference on Advances in Information Technology, pp. 99–103. Chickmagalur, Karnataka (2019)
38. Liu, J., Wang, X.: Plant diseases and pests detection based on deep learning: a review. Plant Methods **17**, 22 (2021). https://doi.org/10.1186/s13007-021-00722-9

Tilapia Fish Freshness Detection Using CNN Models

Haripriya Sanga[iD], Pranuthi Saka[iD], Manoja Nanded[iD],
Kousar Nikhath Alpuri[(✉)][iD], and Sandhya Nadella[iD]

Vallurupalli Nageswara Rao Vignana Jyothi Institute of Engineering and Technology,
Hyderabad 500090, Telangana, India
{kousarnikhath,sandhya_n}@vnrvjiet.in

Abstract. In the seafood business, fish freshness plays a crucial role since it directly affects quality, customer happiness, and safety. This study uses a well-selected dataset of fresh and non-fresh Tilapia fish species to assess the performance of several CNN models, including VGG-19, MobileNetV2, DenseNet201, and ResNet50, for classifying fish freshness. DenseNet201 performed exceptionally well with an accuracy of 1.0, MobileNetV2 had a high accuracy of 0.99104, VGG19 performed admirably with an accuracy of 0.964809, and Resnet50 offered competitive accuracy of 0.82098. To achieve these results, we designed and implemented a rigorous procedure for training and testing these CNN models using the dataset of both fresh and non-fresh fish species. We used meticulous data preprocessing and model training, bearing in mind the importance of high-quality datasets. Our study's primary findings emphasize how crucial it is to select an appropriate CNN architecture and take dataset quality into account when determining the freshness of seafood. Concerning fish freshness evaluation, DenseNet201 and MobileNetV2 in particular demonstrated remarkable accuracy, underscoring the importance of model selection and data quality.

Keywords: Fish Freshness Determination · Machine Learning · CNN Models · Dataset Quality · Tilapia (Oreochromis Niloticus)

1 Introduction

The seafood sector places a high priority on fish freshness since it has a direct impact on consumer preferences, product quality, and safety. Determining the freshness of fish traditionally relies on the sensory evaluation performed by trained experts. This method, however, is subjective, prone to human error, and often time-consuming, which can cause delays in decision-making and potential inconsistencies in quality assessments. In recent years, machine learning approaches have drawn a great deal of interest as a means of overcoming those limitations. These approaches leverage the power of data analysis and pattern recognition to predict and classify various attributes [1, 2]. Machine learning has the potential to create reliable models that can precisely assess the freshness level of fish based on unbiased measures [3].

Our research delves into this exciting intersection of the seafood industry and cutting-edge technology. We aim to revolutionize fish freshness assessment by leveraging machine learning techniques, specifically Convolutional Neural Network (CNN) models. The proposed system evaluates the efficacy of different CNN models, including DenseNet201, MobileNetV2, VGG19, and ResNet50, to classify fish freshness accurately. Our methodology involves the careful curation of a dataset containing both fresh and non-fresh fish species, data preprocessing, and applying CNN models on the dataset to examine the quality of the fish [4].

In Sect. 2, we give a thorough overview of relevant research on CNN models and seafood freshness detection. Sections 3 and 4 detail the materials and methods used in our research, including the dataset and model architectures. Sections 5 and 6 present the experimental findings, results, and analysis of the CNN models. In Sect. 7, we finally wrap up our findings and talk about possible future research areas.

2 Related Work

2.1 Computer Vision-Based Method for Quality and Freshness Check for Fish from Segmented Gills [5]

The methodology employed image processing techniques to segment fish gills. Fish freshness has been evaluated using the segmented gill images in the saturation channel of the HSV color space. Statistical traits have been used to determine the freshness of fish samples. Specifically, the mean and standard deviation of the segmented gill image in the saturation channel were utilized for freshness assessment. Various image processing techniques, such as contrast enhancement and active contour-based methods, were applied for gill segmentation. The methodology is non-destructive and facilitates quick and effective fish quality assessment.

2.2 Image Processing-Based Method for Identification of Fish Freshness Using Skin Tissue [6]

The methodology introduces a non-destructive method for assessing fish freshness using image processing techniques, with a focus on skin tissue analysis. Statistical data were extracted from the HSV color space, revealing a monotonic trend of decline in fish freshness. The methodology achieved promising results with a maximum classification accuracy of 96.66%.

2.3 A Novel Technique for Rapid Evaluation of Fish Freshness Using a Colorimetric Sensor Array [7]

Fish freshness is a critical aspect of fish processing, marketing, and consumption. Traditional freshness assessment methods rely on human senses, such as visual inspection, tactile examination, and odor detection. This method presents an olfactory system built on a colorimetric sensor array. Reverse-phase silica gel plates and a variety of dyes were used to produce a colorimetric sensor array after nine chemically sensitive colors were chosen. The method allows for non-destructive and rapid assessment of fish freshness. It achieved a classification accuracy of 87.5% using a radial basis function neural network.

3   Preparatory Setup

In this study, the degeneration of the fish's gills and eyes over four consecutive days was tracked. A dataset of a widely consumed fish species, Tilapia (Oreochromis Niloticus), was gathered for analysis. As per the study, it was found that Tilapia closely resembles the morphological characteristics of the majority of commercial fish species, based on advice from local fishermen. Moreover, observations from workers in commercial supermarkets and the fish industry indicated that the quality of Tilapia declined after approximately 32 h. The chosen timetable ensured coverage of this expected quality degradation period. To monitor visible transitions from the fresh condition to the non-fresh condition of the specimen within its anticipated shelf life, the fish was placed under continuous observation. A dedicated microscopic camera lens was utilized for studying the specimen within a typical room environment, as found by the research. The fish was purchased at a neighborhood market. A professional camera lens (Tryocx, 0.4X) is used to capture the pictures of the sample fish. Around 4000 high-resolution pictures of fresh fish were captured on the first day and stored as the dataset. The fish was stored at the ideal temperature in the refrigerator. 1000 high-quality photos of fish gills and eyes were taken on the second day and included in the dataset. Similarly, 900 and 1000 high-resolution photographs are taken on Days 3 and 4, respectively. The dataset contains 6900 photos that are broken down into the categories shown in Table 1.

Table 1. Dataset Collection for Freshness

Fresh fish Images	Non-Fresh fish Images		
Day 1	Day 2	Day 3	Day 4
4000	1000	900	1000

As an observation, the fish's gills are shown to be vivid red, with fresh skin and side veins, and fish eyes are clear and fresh, on the first day. The skin started to disintegrate the following day, but the texture of the gills and eyes remained intact and mostly the same. However, in the following days, the texture appeared to deteriorate exponentially. The fish's gills went from being bright red to pale grey, and it lost its liveliness. Fish eyes went from being clear and fine to becoming bulging out and cloudy as shown in Fig. 1.

The total dataset, comprising 6900 images in JPEG format, amounts to a size of 2 GB. As per the research, discrimination between fresh and non-fresh images was successfully achieved, highlighting the complete degradation of physical and

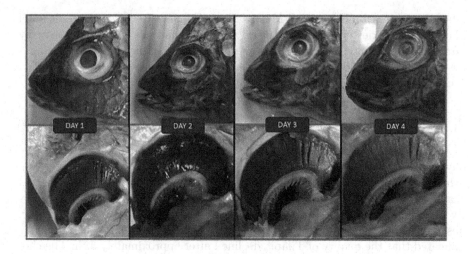

Fig. 1. The fish eye and gills deterioration over time

biological changes. Following the completion of image processing, the fish were categorized into separate sets of fresh and non-fresh images [8] for the eyes and gills. This dataset is provided to the subsequent model to be trained and used to determine the quality parameters.

4 Methodologies

4.1 DenseNet201 Architecture

The 201 layers that make up DenseNet201 include numerous dense blocks and transition layers that reduce the feature maps' spatial dimensions. This dense connectivity architecture has the benefit of encouraging feature reuse and information flow, which can improve the accuracy of the network and decrease the number of parameters. With top-1 error rates of 22.35% and top-5 error rates of 6.43%, DenseNet201 achieved some of the best results in the 2017 ImageNet Large Scale Visual Recognition Challenge (ILSVRC).

Cutting-edge results are achieved by DenseNet201 on a variety of computer vision applications, including segmentation, object detection, and picture classification. Like many other deep learning models, DenseNet201 can be computationally expensive and memory-intensive, making it difficult to implement on low-end hardware or for real-time applications. The architecture of DenseNet201 is shown in Fig. 2 [9].

4.2 MobileNetV2

In MobileNetV2, the number of parameters and computational expense are decreased through the use of depthwise separable convolutions and linear bottleneck layers. MobileNetV2's versatility, which can be easily scaled to different

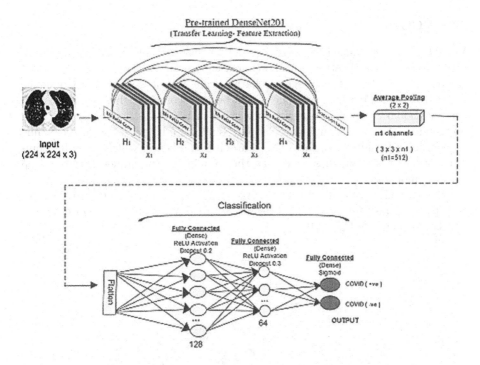

Fig. 2. DenseNet201 pre-trained model architecture.

computational budgets by enhancing the number of channels in the layers, is one of its benefits. On the ILSVRC dataset, MobileNetV2 achieved an error of 28.0% in the top-1 classification and 9.8% in the top-5 classification.

MobileNetV2 has been shown to achieve state-of-the-art performance on a range of computer vision tasks, such as picture classification, object identification, and segmentation. Due to its effectiveness and minimal memory requirements, it has also been widely incorporated into numerous embedded and mobile applications. To achieve a suitable trade-off between model size and accuracy, it makes use of depthwise separable convolutions and inverted residual blocks. The architecture of MobileNetv2 is shown in Fig. 3 [10].

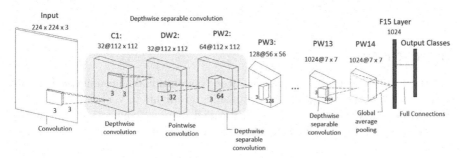

Fig. 3. MobileNetV2 Model.

4.3   VGG19

VGG19 has been utilized for several computer vision problems, such as segmentation, object identification, and image classification. VGG19 obtained a top-5 error rate of 7.3% in the ImageNet Large Scale Visual Recognition Challenge (ILSVRC) in 2014, which was one of the best outcomes at the time. The high computational complexity and memory needs of the VGG19 architecture, however, can make it challenging to employ on low-end devices or for real-time applications. Despite this, the VGG19 architecture is still widely used for computer vision tasks and has served as the foundation for numerous later deep learning models.

A deep convolutional neural network of 19 layers, comprising convolutional [11], pooling, and fully connected layers, is called VGG19. The architecture of VGG19 is shown in Fig. 4 [12].

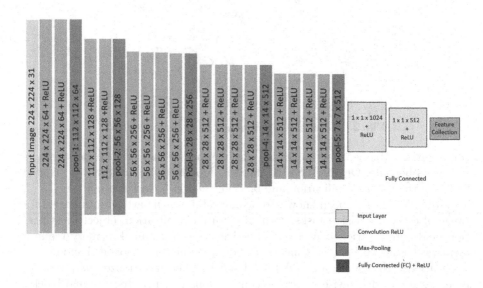

Fig. 4. Illustration of fine-tuned VGG19 pre-trained CNN model.

4.4   ResNet50

ResNet (Residual Neural Network) is a deep convolutional neural network architecture built to solve the problem of vanishing gradients in very deep networks. The network uses skip connections, also called residual connections, to enable it to learn residual mappings instead of trying to learn the underlying mapping directly.

The ILSVRC 2015 competition's report on ResNet50's error rate showed that it had a top-5 error rate of 3.57% and a top-1 error rate of 7.8%, demonstrating that it had a huge level of accuracy in the ImageNet dataset's categorization of images across several classes. Deeper networks have been demonstrated to have better representation capability and can learn more abstract and complex characteristics, which is a benefit of ResNet.

As a result, ResNet50 can recognize complex patterns in data and exhibit state-of-the-art performance on a range of computer vision tasks, including object recognition, image segmentation, and picture categorization. The architecture of ResNet50 is shown in Fig. 5 [13].

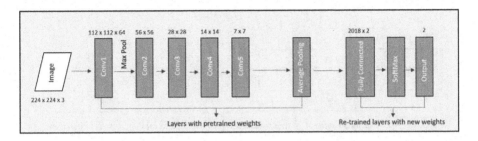

Fig. 5. ResNet50 model.

5 Experimental Findings and Analysis

This study implements the Fish Freshness Detection on Google Colab. The configuration of the computing system is Windows 11; CPU Intel(R) Core(TM) @1.20 GHz, 1190 MHz, 2 Core(s), 4 Logical Processor(s) [14], and 64 GB RAM.

5.1 Workflow

The workflow is described in Fig. 6 and is explained as follows:

Dataset. The dataset contains the acquired fish samples, including features i.e., fish and gills that are used to determine the freshness of the fish. This dataset serves as the foundation for training and testing the machine learning models.

Preprocessed Data. The dataset undergoes preprocessing, which involves cleaning, transforming, and organizing the data to make it suitable for model training and testing. This step ensures that the data is in a format that can be effectively used by the machine learning algorithms.

Splitting Operation. The preprocessed data is divided into training and testing subsets. a) Training Data: The various convolutional neural network (CNN) models are trained using this subset. b) Testing Data: The performance of the trained classification model is assessed using this subset. To evaluate the accuracy of the model on unobserved data, it is kept apart from the training data.

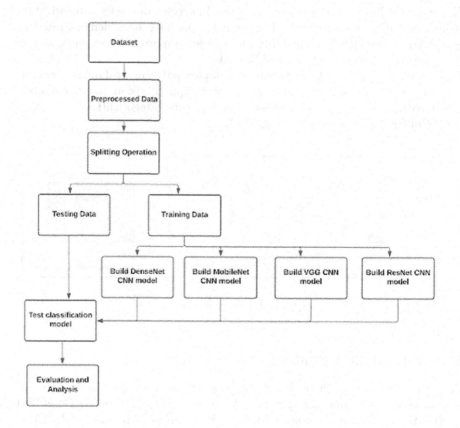

Fig. 6. Workflow.

Evaluate Classification Model. To forecast the freshness of the fish samples, the trained classification model is fed the testing data. In this step, the model's performance on the hidden data is assessed.

Assessment and Interpretation. The classification model's predictions based on the test data are examined and assessed to ascertain the model's precision and efficacy in identifying the freshness of fish.

Developing CNN Models. DenseNet, MobileNet, VGG, and ResNet are the CNN models that are developed using the training data. These algorithms are intended to identify patterns and extract features from the input data that may be utilized to categorize fish samples according to their freshness.

Passing Models to Test Classification. The trained CNN models are passed to the test classification model, which is then used to classify the freshness of the fish samples in the testing data subset. This step measures the performance of each CNN model in determining fish freshness.

5.2   Experimental Strategy

The dataset in this paper is divided into three parts. In addition to parameter adjustments, the training set is employed for model learning and training. The model is evaluated, and optimized, and the model's parameters are adjusted using the validation set. Model recognition and generalization are tested using test sets [1]. The training set contained 4416 photos in total, whereas the validation set contained 1104 images. 1104 more photos were also classified as the testing set.

5.3   The Results of Experiment

Figure 7 shows the training vs validation accuracy comparison graphs of DenseNet, MobileNet, VGG, and ResNet models. Figure 8 shows the training vs validation loss comparison graphs of DenseNet, MobileNet, VGG, and ResNet models.

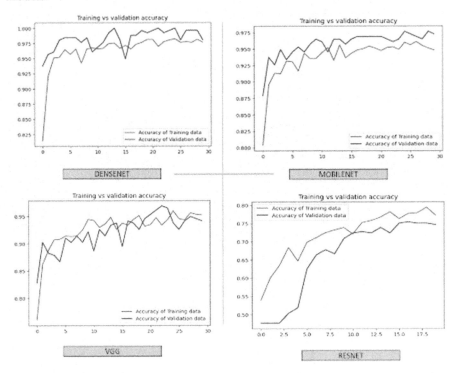

Fig. 7. The comparison graphs of training vs validation accuracy of DenseNet, MobileNet, VGG & ResNet models.

Table 2. Model Accuracy.

S. No.	Model	Accuracy
1	DenseNet201	1.0
2	MobileNetv2	0.99104
3	VGG19	0.964809
4	Resnet50	0.82098

From Table 2, the accuracy values obtained on the testing set allow us to draw certain conclusions regarding the performance of the different models. The percentage of correctly identified samples to all samples in the testing dataset is known as Accuracy. In this case, it is the proportion of accurately identified cases of fresh and non-fresh fish to the total number of fish samples in the collection.

$$\text{Accuracy} = \frac{\text{Number of Correctly Classified Samples}}{\text{Total Number of Samples}} \tag{1}$$

It can be observed that DenseNet201 and MobileNetV2 achieved exceptional performance, while VGG19 demonstrated good performance. On the other hand, ResNet50 exhibited comparatively lower performance when compared to the

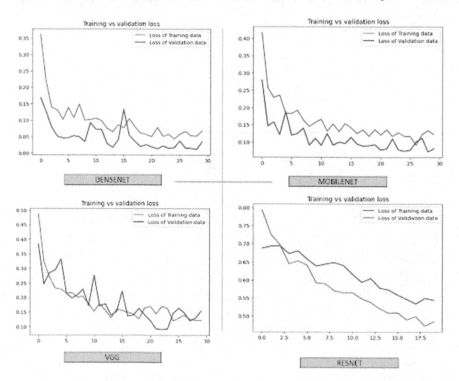

Fig. 8. The comparison graphs of training vs validation loss of MobileNet, DenseNet, ResNet & VGG models.

other models. In Fig. 7, the graph shows the training vs validation accuracy of four different models DenseNet201, MobileNetv2, VGG19, and ResNet50.

These graphs convey information about the generalization potential and performance of each model on our dataset. The x-axis shows the quantity of training epochs, or iterations. The Y-axis, which goes from 0 to 1, represents the models' accuracy, with 1 representing perfect accuracy. The blue line represents the accuracy of the validation dataset, whereas the red line represents the accuracy of the training dataset. The training accuracy demonstrates how well each model does on the training data over time. The models learn the patterns in the training data if the training accuracy is higher. Each model's validation accuracy demonstrates how well it works on a separate validation dataset, which simulates unseen or new data. Higher validation accuracy shows that the models can generalize well and make accurate predictions on fresh fish data. As found in the study, Every model has amassed high training accuracy and validation accuracy. As evidence of its strong generalizability and dependability, MobileNetv2 and DenseNet201 exhibit higher and more reliable validation accuracy than training accuracy. The validation accuracy is lower than the training accuracy in VGG19's early training epochs. The validation accuracy, however, begins to outperform the training accuracy in later epochs as the training goes on. It shows that the model is rapidly acquiring the ability to generalize previously undiscovered facts. Later epochs of the model allow for parameter adjustments or the detection of more pertinent patterns in the data, which improves performance on the validation set. For all epochs in ResNet50, the training accuracy is greater than the validation accuracy. This suggests that the ResNet50 model is probably overfitting to the training data, which has a negative impact on performance on unknown data. In summary, it can be seen that DenseNet201, MobileNetV2, and VGG19 exhibit stable and rising validation accuracy. The models' success on untested data indicates strong generalization, which is encouraging. ResNet50, in contrast, displays a lower validation accuracy than the other models, suggesting potential difficulties with generalization and a larger risk of overfitting.

In Fig. 8, the graphs show the training vs validation loss of four different models. DenseNet201, MobileNetv2, VGG19 and ResNet50. The training loss in DenseNet201 displays a continuous decreasing trend, reducing as the model gains knowledge from the training data. Throughout the training process, the validation loss also reduces, demonstrating effective generalization and the model's capacity to perform well on new cases. In the mobileNetv2 graph, both the training loss and validation loss gradually decline over time, indicating the model's ability to learn from training data and adapt well to new data [2]. When it comes to the VGG19 graph, the earliest epochs see a rapid decline in the training loss, which eventually reaches a reasonably low value. Initially, the validation loss lowers as well, though more slowly than expected, suggesting possible difficulties when generalizing to new data. Later epochs, however, indicate greater generalization performance as the validation loss improves and falls below the training loss. The training loss, on the other hand, continuously falls over time for the ResNet50 graph, suggesting that the model is successfully reducing training data errors. The validation loss initially declines but approaches a plateau and improves only modestly, pointing to possible problems with generalization to unobserved data during the testing phase. In summary, DenseNet201, MobileNetV2, and VGG19 exhibit decreasing validation loss with time, which suggests effective learning and model improvement. ResNet50 similarly exhibits a decreasing validation loss, while being higher than that of the other models. This suggests that it may be challenging to fit the validation data and achieve optimal performance.

6   Research Discussion

Table 2 shows the comparison of accuracies on different models on our dataset. Figure 9 shows the accuracy comparison graph of DenseNet, MobileNet, VGG, and ResNet models. DenseNet201 performed exceptionally well on the job at hand, achieving the greatest accuracy of 1.0. MobileNetV2 follows closely behind with an accuracy of 0.99104, thus displaying great precision. ResNet50 had a slightly higher accuracy of 0.82098 than VGG19, which scored 0.964809. DenseNet201 and MobileNetV2 perform remarkably well and may be excellent candidates for the task at hand based on the accuracy figures. High accuracy is also shown by VGG19, although being marginally inferior to the top two models. Despite its lesser accuracy, ResNet50 might still be taken into account depending on the particular requirements and trade-offs.

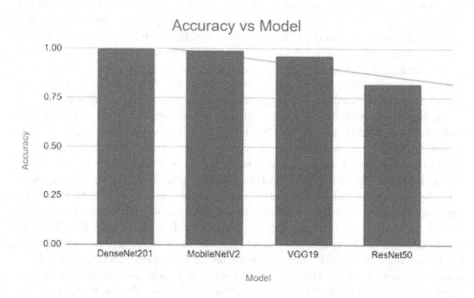

Fig. 9. The comparison graphs of the accuracy of DenseNet, MobileNet, VGG & ResNet models.

7   Conclusion and Future Work

The research proposed an efficient method for determining fish freshness using different CNN models, namely VGG-19, MobileNetV2, DenseNet201, and ResNet50, on our carefully curated dataset of fresh and non-fresh fish species. The research demonstrates the significance of dataset quality and diversity in training CNN models for fish freshness classification.

Among the models, DenseNet201 exhibited the highest accuracy in determining fish freshness, achieving a perfect accuracy score of 1.0. This result highlights the effectiveness of the dense connectivity pattern employed by DenseNet in facilitating superior feature extraction and classification for this specific task. Although DenseNet and MobileNet performed the best, it is worth noting that VGG and ResNet models have still provided valuable insights and reasonable accuracy in fish freshness determination. Additionally, the study contributed to the state-of-the-art by leveraging advanced CNN models and a custom dataset tailored to fish eyes and gills. This approach fills a research gap by providing a more targeted and specific methodology for fish freshness evaluation, which was previously limited by the lack of specialized datasets.

Furthermore, the societal implications of the work are profound. Accurate fish freshness assessment [15]is essential to guaranteeing food safety and customer satisfaction. By offering an automated and objective approach, the research provides a valuable tool to the seafood industry, enabling faster quality control processes, reducing economic losses due to spoiled fish, and ultimately safeguarding consumer health. Moreover, we can also expand the research to scale the dataset to other fish species. With the use of transformer-based models, we can get more accurate with the expanded dataset.

Acknowledgments. We express our heartfelt gratitude to Dr. A. Kousar Nikhath from Vallurupalli Nageswara Rao Vignana Jyothi Institute of Engineering and Technology, Hyderabad, India. Her invaluable mentorship, support, and insightful suggestions significantly contributed to the refinement of our research project. Additionally, we extend our sincere thanks to Dr. Sandhya Nadella, the head of the department, CSE (AIML & IOT), for her generous support and assistance throughout our research journey.

References

1. Lalabadi, H.M., Sadeghi, M., Mireei, S.A.: Fish freshness categorization from eyes and gills color features using multi-class artificial neural network and support vector machines. Aquacult. Eng. **90**, 102076 (2020)
2. Saeed, R., Feng, H., Wang, X., Zhang, X., Fu, Z.: Fish quality evaluation by sensor and machine learning: a mechanistic review. Food Control **137**, 108902 (2022)
3. Miguéis, V.L., Pereira, A., Pereira, J., Figueira, G.: Reducing fresh fish waste while ensuring availability: demand forecast using censored data and machine learning. J. Clean. Prod. **359**, 131852 (2022)

4. Taheri-Garavand, A., Nasiri, A., Banan, A., Zhang, Y.-D.: Smart deep learning-based approach for non-destructive freshness diagnosis of common carp fish. J. Food Eng. **278**, 109930 (2020)
5. Issac, A., Dutta, M.K., Sarkar, B.: Computer vision-based method for quality and freshness check for fish from segmented gills. Comput. Electron. Agric. **139**, 10–21 (2017)
6. Sengar, N., Gupta, V., Dutta, M.K., Travieso, C.M.: Image processing-based method for identification of fish freshness using skin tissue. In: 2018 4th International Conference on Computational Intelligence & Communication Technology (CICT), pp. 1–4 (2018)
7. Huang, X., Xin, J., Zhao, J.: A novel technique for rapid evaluation of fish freshness using colorimetric sensor array. J. Food Eng. **105**(4), 632–637 (2011)
8. Ahmed, Md.S., Aurpa, T.T., Azad, Md.A.K.: Fish disease detection using image-based machine learning technique in aquaculture. J. King Saud Univ. Comput. Inf. Sci. **34**, 5170–5182 (2022)
9. Jaiswal, A., Gianchandani, N., Singh, D., Kumar, V., Kaur, M.: Classification of the COVID-19 infected patients using DenseNet201 based deep transfer learning. J. Biomol. Struct. Dyn. **39**, 5682–5689 (2020)
10. Nganga, K.: Building a Multiclass Image Classifier Using MobilenetV2 and TensorFlow (2022)
11. Wu, Y., Qin, X., Pan, Y., Yuan, C.: Convolution neural network based transfer learning for classification of flowers. In: 2018 IEEE 3rd International Conference on Signal and Image Processing (ICSIP) (2018)
12. Mostafiz, R., Rahman, M.M., Islam, A.K., Belkasim, S.: Focal liver lesion detection in ultrasound image using deep feature fusions and super resolution. Mach. Learn. Knowl. Extraction **2**, 10 (2020)
13. Islam, Md., Tasnim, N., Baek, J.-H.: Human gender classification using transfer learning via pareto frontier CNN networks. Inventions **5**, 16 (2020)
14. Xu, H., Wang, J., Liu, J., Peng, X., He, C.: A novel joint distinct subspace learning and dynamic distribution adaptation method for fault transfer diagnosis. Measurement **203**, 111986 (2022)
15. Yavuzer, E., Köse, M.: Prediction of fish quality level with machine learning. Int. J. Food Sci. Technol. **57**, 5250–5255 (2022)

Chilli Leaf Disease Detection Using Deep Learning

S. Abdul Amjad⬤, T. Anuradha$^{(\boxtimes)}$⬤, T. Manasa Datta⬤, and U. Mahesh Babu⬤

Department of Information Technology, Velagapudi Ramakrishna Siddhartha Engineering College, Vijayawada, India
anuradha_it@vrsiddhartha.ac.in

Abstract. Deep learning is being used a lot to develop a quick, automatic and reliable means for image identification and classification in many domains. Using Deep learning techniques in the agriculture would be an enhanced practice in the history of agriculture. Chillies are one of the most popular crops in India as they are used in everyday life for cooking variety of dishes. Chilli plants are sensitive to multiple infections. Detection and prevention of these diseases to other parts of the plant is a very important and impracticable task in the case of large fields. This paper proposes a disease detection and classification model for chilli leaves using Convolution Neural Networks. And also, other pre-trained architectures like ResNet, Inception, VGG (Visual Geometry Group) and Efficient Net were used for building an optimized model which detects the diseases more accurately. Images of Chilli leaves, having various diseases named Leaf curl, Leaf spot, Yellowish, as well as Healthy leaves, from the self-made dataset were used. The results of the Efficient-Net model prevailed over other models with accuracies of CNN (Convolutional Neural Networks), ResNet, VGG and Efficient Net 70%,87%,87% and 91% respectively.

Keywords: Chilli leaf disease · CNN · Deep Learning · Efficient Net · Resnet · VGG

1 Introduction

Now-a-days Deep Learning is being applied in many fields which require Audio processing, Natural language processing and Computer Vision. Implementation of Deep Learning in the Agriculture will be appreciable as food industry is the largest, as every living being relies on food. In farming, as the crops are in very vast area, farmers may fail to identify infection in the initial days. By detecting the disease in early-stage, right measures can be taken. After the pandemic has started, people have started growing daily usage plants in their garden and households. Consulting experts for disease recognition is time-consuming and may need frequent visits from them to the field. Researchers are focusing now on developing models using machine learning [1–3] and deep learning techniques [4–6] which can identify plant leaf diseases. Generally, chilli plants are affected by Damping off, powdery mildew, Bacterial leaf spot, Fusarium with Cercospora leaf spot, Leaf curl diseases.

D. Garg et al. (Eds.): IACC 2023, CCIS 2054, pp. 81–89, 2024.
https://doi.org/10.1007/978-3-031-56703-2_7

In the proposed work, real time self-made chilli leaf data set was built by collecting samples from Perecharla, Guntur district, which is a large producer of chilli crop in India. Based on the inputs from local farmers, prominent leaf diseases identified in this place were Leaf curl, Leaf Spot and Yellowish. This paper proposes classification models to detect these diseases using basic Convolution Network and pretrained Convolutional Neural Networks ResNet, Inception, VGG(Visual Geometry Group) and Efficient Net. Better accuracies were obtained using Efficient Net when compared to the other models.

Most of the research on proposed work used plant village data set (open source) which consisted of 54,306 images of plant leaves. They consist of 38 classes belonging to different plants like apple, blackberry, grape, corn, tomato etc. Authors in [7] used Alex net and google net architectures. They have experimented with different varieties of images namely greyscale, color, segmented and obtained good results for color images with Google net. Authors in [8] tried to build pretrained models suitable for plant leaf disease detection. They have experimented with region based neural network models. Leaf disease detection with color and texture features and using SVM was done in [9]. Various transfer learning models were applied on plant - village dataset and proved a hybrid model combining Alex net and SVM gave better results [10]. In paper [11] authors have used various feature extraction methods. They have used different ML techniques to classify leaf diseases. They have performed experiments on tomato leaf and used Haralick algorithm to get the top features. K-Means clustering was used in [12] to locate infected areas andMulti-Class SVM, CNN models for classification of diseases They have pre-processed data to remove the noise and it resulted in detecting the minimal features. Researchers in [13] also used K-Means clustering to detect the affected part. They have a less detection rate and classification performance due to dataset size.

In [14], different ML techniques were used for infection prediction. Authors in [15] have proposed a CNN model which contains 3 Convolutional layers followed by 3 Maxpooling and 2 Fully connected layers to classify tomato leaf diseases into 10 classes. A faster RCNN model which contains 32 filters, 64 nodes fully connected layers is used for identification of Leaf spot disease in sugar beet [16]. Automatic leaf disease detection in apple plants with convolution Neural networks was done in [17]. Authors in [18] have done a comparative study using ResNet-50 and VGG-19 models on apple leaves. They have performed augmentation and fed the dataset to the models. VGG 19 has performed better than ResNet 50 for their dataset. Researchers in [19] have done their work using InceptionV3, InceptionResNetV2, and EfficientNetB0. Classification of chilli leaf diseases was done in [20] by collecting real time data which contained the diseases Leaf curl, yellowish, White fly and Gray mould. Faster RCNN and RFCN models were used. Chilli leaf disease identification and separation using squeeze and excitation model was implemented in [21]. They experimented by changing input and batch sizes focusing on five main varieties of leaf diseases in chilli plant. Yolo v5 object detection method was used to identify disease from real field in [22]. A review on issues faced during training phase of DL models were discussed in [23]. A farmer friendly model to suggest suitable time for harvesting, applying pesticides was developed in [24].

2 Dataset Description

2.1 Diseases in Chilli Leaves

General diseases affecting chilli leaves are Damping off, Powdery mildew, Bacterial Leaf spot, Cercospora Leaf spot, Fusarium wilt and leaf curl [25]. The samples were shown in Fig. 1 from left to right in sequence.

Fig. 1. Images of general Diseses in chilli leaves

2.2 Description of Real Time Data

In Deep Learning, the model which is used to predict the class of a new image is to be trained first. The model needs to be trained with multiple images related to each class so that it learns the features of each class to classify them accordingly. There was a dataset available in the Kaggle [26] which consisted of 5 classes with only 80 images per each class. But with the intension to build a classification model to classify local chilli leaf diseases, data were collected from Perecharla, ($16°19'18''$N $80°20'35''$E.), Guntur region of Andhra Pradesh state which is famous for chilli production. Diseases observed in this location are Leaf spot, Yellowish, Leaf curl. The leaf images were captured in mobiles phones and then cropped and divided into classes according to farmer's instructions. Each class in the dataset consisted of 150 Images. The leaf samples in the dataset collected are shown in Fig. 2.

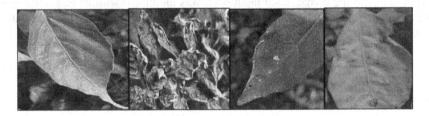

Fig. 2. Samples of Collected leaves

2.3 Data Augmentation

Using Image Data Generator, we have applied various transitions to the leaves and have augmented our dataset. The transitions like rotation, width and height shift, zoom, horizontal flip was applied to the existing images and new images were stored in a directory which already consisted of original images. Both the original images and the augmented images were used to train the proposed model. After augmentation the dataset size was increased to 916 images per class i.e., total 3664 images belonging to 4 classes.

3 Methodology

3.1 CNN

The methodology proposed to build the classification model is shown in Fig. 3. Chilli leaf disease dataset was generated by collecting leaf images from fields and each image was resized to 224 × 224. Then data augmentation was done with various transitions like zoom, brightness, shift, shear. We have used CNN Deep learning model for classifying diseases. Keras is a deep learning package used to build CNN model. TensorFlow framework was used. We defined a CNN model [27] which contains 5 convolutional layers followed by Max-pooling layer, which was used to reduce the computational cost, and followed by Dropout layer, to avoid overfitting. Batch Normalization was done in every layer to prevent overfitting. ReLu activation function followed every layer. And at last, flatten layer was used to make all the values into one dimensional vector and in the Dense layer Kernel regularizer was used. SoftMax classifier was used as output layer. Adam has shown better results compared to the RMSprop (Root Mean Square) and SGD (Stochastic Gradient Descent) optimizers. After training, validation and testing were done. The results of the proposed CNN model were compared to popular Transfer learning models ResNet, Inception V3, Vgg16 and Efficient Net.

Convolutional Layer
Filters were applied in the convolutional layers. These filters were multiplied piece by piece throughout the image. Each input pixel was multiplied with its respective filter [28]. After the matrix multiplication by adding and dividing them by total pixels, feature maps were obtained (Eq. 1).

$$s[t] = (x * w)[t] = \sum_{a=-\infty}^{a=\infty} x[a]w[a+t] \tag{1}$$

where S – feature map, X – input and W – Kernel

ReLU Activation Function
In this layer negative values were replaced with zeroes. This layer only fires the positive values in the feature map. It is the most used activation function in Neural Networks. Mathematically it is represented as $y = max\ (0,\ x)$. Where x is input. (Eq. 2)

$$\sigma(x) = \begin{cases} max(0, x), x \geq 0 \\ 0, x < 0 \end{cases} \tag{2}$$

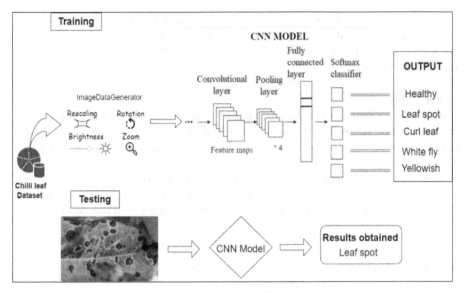

Fig. 3. Architecture Diagram

Pooling Layer

In pooling layer also filters are applied, generally 2×2 filters are applied. It takes one value from the window (sub matrix) based on the pooling type, i.e., if max pooling is applied, it takes the maximum value from the 2×2 matrix, similarly if average pooling is applied, it takes average value of the 2×2 matrix. Pooling reduces the computation cost and reduces over fitting by not considering all the values. Location sensitive features can be addressed by pooling.

3.2 Transfer Learning Models

Inception V3

In Inception V3 the parameters are reduced than the traditional deep CNN models. Besides traditional deep CNN models, repeating multiple times, in Inception factorization into smaller Convolutions is done (i.e., for example 5×5 filter is reduced to two 3×3 filters, so that 28% of parameters are reduced). Reduction in parameters results in usage of less computational resources [29, 30]. Grid size is reduced using pooling operation. Auxiliary classifier is used to prevent vanishing gradient problem.

VGG -16

VGG 16 architecture is made of 16 layers [31]. It was trained on a dataset which contains images of size 224×224 and has 1000 classes. Architecture of VGG was shown in Fig. 9.

ResNet

In ResNet, the CNN model is used multiple times. In Deep Neural Networks, vanishing gradient is a challenge. To overcome this, in Residual Neural Networks, skip to connection model is introduced as shown in Fig. 10. In this model, the current layer gets the input from the output of the before layer as well as from the input of the previous layer (except in the first layer) [32]. ResNet contains Identity block and Convolutional block pre-trained. ResNets are with 50,101,152 layers. We have compared our model with ResNet 50 layers.

Efficient Net

In regular Deep Neural Networks due to depth scaling, at some point vanishing gradient problem occurs. In ResNet to overcome this problem, skip connections are used. But that costs much computational power. In the Efficient Nets along with the depth scaling, width and resolution scaling is also done.

Base network Efficient-B0 is developed by Neural Architecture Search. B0 to B7 are scaled from B0. Compound scaling is done on B0 to balance the scaling. Due to this, the architecture is light weight and tends to give higher accuracy with less computational power.

4   Result Analysis

Figure 4 shows sample outputs of Leaf curl and Leaf spot by CNN model. It was observed that loss decreased and accuracy increased for all models with the increase of number of epochs. Our CNN obtained 99% train, 80% validation and 81% test accuracy, VGG got 98% train, 86% validation and 86% test accuracy, Inception V3 model got 91% Training accuracy, 72% Validation accuracy and 70% test accuracy, Resnet got 99% train, 85% validation and 85% test accuracy. Efficient net got 99% train, 91% validation and 90% test accuracy with our self-made dataset when 25 epochs were taken. Time taken for each epoch was 6,45,7,13 and 43 for CNN, VGG, Inception V3, Resnet and Efficient net respectively. Figure 5 shows the comparison of trainable parameters and train, validation, test accuracies. From the results it was observed that time taken for each epoch was least for our CNN model whereas it was high for VGG. And Inception V3 model got least accuracies and Efficient net got high accuracies.

Fig.4. Detection of Leaf Curl and Spot and by the model

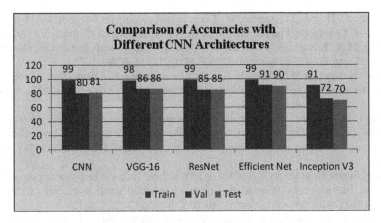

Fig. 5. Comparison of accuracies of different CNN architectures

5 Conclusion and Future Study

Deep CNN architecture and different pretrained models were trained on the self-made data set to identify the disease in the chilli leaves of local area so that proper measures can be done to cure the disease. The proposed models could abled to Test accuracies of CNN, VGG, Inception V3, Resnet, Efficient net were 81%, 86%, 70%, 85% and 90% respectively, resulting in a better test accuracy with Efficient Net model.

In future the work can be extended by adding more real time images to the dataset to make model identify regional diseases with more accuracy. A web or mobile application which can automatically detect disease with image upload can be built to make model useful for local farmers.

References

1. Ramesh, S., et al.: Plant disease detection using machine learning. In: 2018 International conference on design innovations for 3Cs compute communicate control (ICDI3C), pp. 41–45. IEEE (2018)
2. Harakannanavar, S.S., Rudagi, J.M., Puranikmath, V.I., Siddiqua, A., Pramodhini, R.: Plant leaf disease detection using computer vision and machine learning algorithms. Global Transitions Proceedings (2022)
3. Geetha, G., Samundeswari, S., Saranya, G., Meenakshi, K., Nithya, M.: Plant leaf disease classification and detection system using machine learning. InJournal of Physics: Conference Series, Vol. 1712, No. 1, p. 012012. IOP Publishing (2020)
4. Liu, J., Wang, X.: Plant diseases and pests detection based on deep learning: a review. Plant Methods **17**(1), 1–8 (2021)
5. Sladojevic, S., Arsenovic, M., Anderla, A., Culibrk, D., Stefanovic, D.: Deep neural networks based recognition of plant diseases by leaf image classification. Comput. Intell. Neurosci. **29**, 2016 (2016)
6. Jadhav, S.B.: Convolutional neural networks for leaf image-based plant disease classification. IAES Int. J. Artifi. Intellig. **8**(4), 328 (2019)

7. Mohanty, S., Hughes, D., Salathe, M.: Using Deep Learning for Image-Based Plant Disease Detection. Frontiers in Plant Science **7** (2016). https://doi.org/10.3389/fpls.2016.01419
8. Saleem, M.H., Khanchi, S., Potgieter, J., Arif, K.M.: Image-based plant disease identification by deep learning meta-architectures. Plants **9**(11), 1451 (2020)
9. Ahmad, N., Asif, H.M.S., Saleem, G., et al.: Leaf image-based plant disease identification using color and texture features. Wireless PersCommun **121**, 1139–1168 (2021). https://doi.org/10.1007/s11277-021-09054-2
10. Kawatra, M., Agarwal, S., Kapur, R.: Leaf disease detection using neural network hybrid models. In: 2020 IEEE 5th International Conference on Computing Communication and Automation (ICCCA), pp. 225–230 (2020). https://doi.org/10.1109/ICCCA49541.2020.9250885
11. Das, D., Singh, M., Mohanty, S.S., Chakravarty, S.: Leaf disease detection using support vector machine. International Conference on Communication and Signal Processing (ICCSP) **2020**, 1036–1040 (2020). https://doi.org/10.1109/ICCSP48568.2020.9182128
12. Devi, N., et al.: Categorizing diseases from leaf images using a hybrid learning model. Symmetry **13**, 2073 (2021). https://doi.org/10.3390/sym13112073
13. Reddy, J., Vinod, K., Ajai, A.: Analysis of Classification Algorithms for Plant Leaf Disease Detection 1–6 (2019). https://doi.org/10.1109/ICECCT.2019.8869090
14. Radha, S., Chatterjee, J., Zaman, N., Brohi, S.: Performance of deep learning vs machine learning in plant leaf disease detection. Microprocess. Microsyst. **80**, 103615 (2021). https://doi.org/10.1016/j.micpro.2020.103615
15. Agarwal, M., Singh, A., Arjaria, S., Sinha, A., Gupta, S.: ToLeD: tomato leaf disease detection using convolution neural network. Procedia Computer Science. **167**, 293–301 (2020). https://doi.org/10.1016/j.procs.2020.03.225
16. Ozguven, M., Adem, K.: Automatic detection and classification of leaf spot disease in sugar beet using deep learning algorithms. Physica A **535**, 122537 (2019). https://doi.org/10.1016/j.physa.2019.122537
17. Baranwal, S., Khandelwal, S., Arora, A.: Deep learning convolutional neural network for apple leaves disease detection. SSRN Electron. J. (2019). https://doi.org/10.2139/ssrn.3351641
18. Khilar, S.T.R., Subaja Christo, M.: A comparative analysis on plant pathology classification using deep learning architecture – Resnet and VGG19, Materials Today: Proceedings, https://doi.org/10.1016/j.matpr.2020.11.993
19. Mondal, J., et al.: Identification of Plant Leaf Diseases using Deep Convolutional Neural Network with Less Computational Power (2021). https://doi.org/10.13140/RG.2.2.17702.04168
20. Student, B.E.: Early detection of chili plant leaf diseases using machine learning. International Journal of Engineering Science 22328 (2019)
21. Naik, B.N., Malmathanraj, R., Palanisamy, P.: Detection and classification of chilli leaf disease using a squeeze-and-excitation-based CNN model. Eco. Inform. **6**, 101663 (2022)
22. Ranjan, M.K.M.A., Machavaram, R.: In-field Chilli Crop Disease Detection Using YOLOv5 Deep Learning Technique. In: 2023 IEEE 8th International Conference for Convergence in Technology (I2CT), pp. 1–6. Lonavla, India (2023). https://doi.org/10.1109/I2CT57861.2023.10126468
23. Kanaparthi, K.R., Sudhakar Ilango, S.: A survey on training issues in chili leaf diseases identification using deep learning techniques. Procedia Computer Science **218**, 2123–2132 (2023). ISSN 1877-0509, https://doi.org/10.1016/j.procs.2023.01.188
24. Raja, K., Duela, J., Gopichandd, M., Kannan, K., Sathish, M.G.: Chilli leaf diseases detection with different features of original chilli using region based convolutional neural network. Int. J. Intell. Sys. Applicat. Eng. **12**(3s), 298–305 (2023). https://ijisae.org/index.php/IJISAE/article/view/3708

25. Chilli diseases [online] [Available]: https://vikaspedia.in/agriculture/crop-production/int egrated-pest-managment/ipm-for-spice-crops/ipm-strategies-for-chilli/chilli-description-of-plant-diseases of Engineering Science 22328 (2019)

26. Almahsiri, A.: Chilli Plant Disease [Onliine] {Available:] https://www.kaggle.com/ahmada lmahsiri/chili-plant-disease

27. Vasavi, P., Punitha, A., Venkat Narayana Rao, T.: Crop leaf disease detection and classification using machine learning and deep learning algorithms by visual symptoms: a review. Int. J. Elect. Comp. Eng. (IJECE) **12**(2), 2079-2086 (2022). ISSN: 2088–8708, https://doi.org/10.11591/ijece.v12i2.pp2079-2086

28. Ravi Teja, P., et al.: Driver drowsiness detection using convolution neural networks. In: Smart Computing Techniques and Applications, pp. 617–626. Springer, Singapore (2021)

29. Patayon, U.B., Crisostomo, R.V.: Peanut leaf spot disease identification using pre-trained deep convolutional neural network. Int. J. Electr. Comp. Eng. (IJECE). https://doi.org/10.11591/ijece.v12i3.pp3005-3012

30. Bhavya, S.V., Narasimha, G., Ramya, M., Sujana, S.Y., Anuradha, T.: Classification of skin cancer images using Tensor Flow and inception v3. Int. J. Eng. Technol. **7**(2.7), 717–21 (2018)

31. Paymode, A.S., Malode, V.B.: Transfer learning for multi-crop leaf disease image classification using convolutional neural networks VGG. Artificial Intelligence in Agriculture (2022)

32. Luaibi, A.R., Salman, T.M., Miry, A.H.: Detection of citrus leaf diseases using adeep learning technique. Int. J. Electr. Comp. Eng. (IJECE) **11**(2), 1719–1727 (2021). ISSN: 2088–8708, https://doi.org/10.11591/ijece.v11i2.pp1719-1727

Damage Evaluation Following Natural Disasters Using Deep Learning

Neha Gupta[1]([⊠]), Shikha Chadha[2], Rosey Chauhan[2], and Pooja Singhal[1]

[1] ABES Engineering College, Ghaziabad, UP, India
123.neha.gupta@gmail.com
[2] Sharda University, Greater Noida, India

Abstract. Natural catastrophes including flooding, tornadoes, earthquakes, and wildfires have been occurring more frequently over the past few decades as a result of global warming and climate change. Therefore, it is more crucial than ever to give emergency response workers accurate and timely information to enable them to respond to crises effectively. Among the many pieces of information required for disaster response and management, it is crucial that rescue workers are promptly notified of the location and extent of a building's destruction in order to maximise the effectiveness of their efforts. Nevertheless, despite significant efforts, problems with picture classification for disaster response still exist. In this study, a potential deep learning-based method is put forth for identifying damaged buildings in high-resolution satellite photos. It solves the issue of limited training data common in many remote sensing applications by using generic data augmentation. It is suggested that a pretrained model be used in conjunction with transfer learning as a fine-tuning method for the relevant task. The trials with images of Port-au-Prince, Haiti showed that the suggested strategy works well with sparse training data. With enriched training data, the Convolutional Neural Network (CNN) model can detect damaged buildings with an accuracy of 83%, compared to only 53% with the original training data. The focus of future study will be on investigating automated ways to obtain larger training datasets and model generalisation by researching more reliable data augmentation strategies.

Keywords: Natural catastrophes · disaster response · high-resolution satellite photos · Convolutional Neural Network · data augmentation

1 Introduction

Since the First World War, when cameras were mounted on monoplanes, remote sensing for disaster management has advanced (Cable, 2015). Natural catastrophes including flooding, tornadoes, earthquakes, and wildfires have been occurring more frequently over the past few decades as a result of global warming and climate change. The United States Geological Survey reports that between 2000 and 2012, there were 807 earthquakes in the United States that were greater than magnitude 5.0, and there were 23,608 earthquakes globally that resulted in an estimated 789,677 fatalities. Therefore, it is

D. Garg et al. (Eds.): IACC 2023, CCIS 2054, pp. 90–103, 2024.
https://doi.org/10.1007/978-3-031-56703-2_8

more crucial than ever to give emergency response workers accurate and timely information to enable them to respond to crises effectively. For instance, the United Nations estimates that the 2010 Haiti earthquake killed between 220,000 and 250,000 people and that Hurricane Harvey, which hit Texas in 2017, caused an estimated $125 billion in damage (Kolbe et al., 2010). Due to its extensive coverage, affordability, and temporal frequency, remote sensing data was among the most affordable and accurate sources of data for the estimated 250,000 residential and 30,000 commercial buildings that collapsed or were damaged during the Haiti earthquake (E. Hussain et al., 2011). To identify damaged buildings, many studies have employed satellite or aircraft imagery. For instance, Duarte et al. (Duarte et al., 2018) studied the use of manned and unmanned multi-resolution satellite and airborne photography. With an accuracy range of 89.8% to 94.4%, this study created a convolutional neural network-based method to identify and classify building damage (Duarte et al., 2018). With a four-stage process, Janalipour and Mohammadzadeh investigated the use of QuickBird satellite photos (Gupta et al., 2020) to find damaged buildings following the Bam Earthquake in Iran. First, a vector map update using pre-event photos and a post-event image georeferencing using the updated vector map were implemented as two preparation processes (Janalipour and Mohammadzadeh, 2016). The post-event image was classified and segmented using pixels in the second stage, and the segments were then labelled. The geometric properties for these segments, such as area, convexity, and rectangular fitting, were determined in the third stage (Janalipour and Mohammadzadeh, 2016). A decision-making system based on the ANFIS, or adaptive network-based fuzzy inference system, was created in the final step. The fuzzy interference system is a hybrid learning technique that combines the ideas of fuzzy logic with neural networks. Larger areas of land can be gathered by satellites in a single path. The position of the satellite is a significant barrier for the collection of satellite data. If the satellite doesn't pass directly over the affected area, it will need to be directed there. Large acquisition angles from a satellite location may result in image distortion (Aggarwal et al., 2021), poor georeferencing, and a user's inability to co-register the imagery with other significant data sets (Rathje and Adams, 2008).

Response time, analysis depth, and mapping accuracy must all be compromised in a scenario with a short time period (Voigt et al., 2011). While high resolution data may be too large to analyse for a vast region, sub-meter imagery is frequently employed for assessment (Rathje and Adams, 2008). (Voigt et al., 2011). However, it is normal practise to immediately create a preliminary damage assessment map using the existing data, and subsequently the first estimates are improved using new information (Voigt et al., 2011). Social media data can help with situational awareness, rescue and relief efforts, and timely damage information (Cervone et al., 2016). The diverse character of the data, which exceeds the capabilities of the human analyst when dealing with social media data, is one of the biggest obstacles (Cervone et al., 2016; Q. Huang and Xiao, 2015). The first analysis of remote sensing data may be degraded due to the rapid requirement for damage information during a natural catastrophe, and more time will be required to undertake a more thorough analysis (Rathje and Adams, 2008).

2   Literature Review

There are still two major obstacles to picture classification for damage assessment: the accessibility of data sources and the prompt collection of precise and useful data. This section reviews recent work that addresses these issues, from basic pixel-based solutions to cutting-edge deep learning techniques.

Pixel-based methods rely on the surface features' spectral properties in multiple or hyperspectral pictures. The simplest unit of analysis for images is the pixel. A pixel-based technique primarily uses pixels without taking into account their geographical environment. In order to analyse a single pixel in a picture made up of potentially thousands or millions of pixels, statistical operators are used (M. Hussain et al., 2013). Unsupervised classification and supervised classification are the two general categories into which pixel-based classification may be divided (Li et al., 2014). Unsupervised categorization divides an image's pixels into various classes according to their natural grouping. Without the aid of any training data or prior knowledge of the subject area, this procedure is carried out (Li et al., 2014; Agarwal et al., 2019). The Iterative Self-Organizing Data Analysis (ISODATA) technique and the k-means (and its variants) algorithm are two of the most popular algorithms (Li et al., 2014; Ouyang et al., 2011). The pixel spectral pattern 10 vector is to be classified into one of several classes using ISODATA. Similar algorithms like the k-means algorithm use additional heuristics to decide whether to split or combine groups. The method will separate a cluster if its variance is larger than a predetermined threshold (Suri et al. 2022). If not, the clusters will be merged (Dhodhi et al., 1999; Wang et al., 2014). A person must be in charge of supervised classification.

Object-based image categorization operates on homogeneous and spatially contiguous collections of pixels, or objects, rather than on individual pixels (Qian et al., 2007). Pixel grouping is accomplished using an image segmentation procedure that, according to Haralick and Shapiro (Haralick and Shapiro, 1985), may be divided into three main categories: spatial clustering, thresholding, and region growth. The ideal technique to assess the effectiveness of segmentation is for the human analyst to interpret the results (Estoque et al., 2015; Pal and Pal, 1993) because the accuracy of the image segmentation directly affects the image categorization (Qian et al., 2007). A majority decision determines how an object is categorised based on the labels of its k closest neighbours. The procedure performs a Euclidean distance computation when the majority votes are tied and the object might belong to either of the two classes (Chadha et al. 2022). When used with multimodal classes, KNN performs well. However, it makes categorization errors because it compares all the features equally (Kim et al., 2012). Several studies have shown that object-based classifiers outperform pixel-based ones in terms of performance. In order to compare the MLC and KNN algorithms, Platt and Rapoza (Platt and Rapoza, 2008) used models that both included and excluded expert knowledge. They demonstrated that the best pixel-based strategy only managed an accuracy of 64%, while the object-based model employing the KNN algorithm plus expert knowledge produced the best accuracy results of 78%. (Myint et al., 2011) used QuickBird imagery to categorise urban land cover and compared MLC with KNN. On their original image, they achieved 90.4% accuracy with their KNN classifier and 63.3% accuracy with their pixel-based MLC classifier. They experimented with applying the same categorization techniques to a different image with various environmental factors. The pixel-based classifier in this instance had a significantly higher classification accuracy of 87.8%.

The Support Vector Machine (SVM) algorithm can only categorise data into two unique classes in its initial form, which makes it a two-class classification algorithm (Gupta et al. 2021). It creates a high dimensional feature space from the input vectors. A hyperplane with qualities that guarantee the network's excellent generalisation ability is generated in this feature space (Cortes and Vapnik, 1995). (Kavzoglu and Colkesen, 2009) shows how the ideal separating hyperplane separates the data set 15 into discrete numbers of classes while minimising misclassification acquired during the training phase. (Maulik and Chakraborty, 2017) The use of a linear SVM assumes that the feature data can be separated linearly (Rahul et al., 2022). However, in fact, data points from several classes frequently cross paths, rendering the fundamental linear decision limits inadequate. Consequently, kernel functions have been created (Mountrakis et al., 2011).

With accuracy rates of 96.8% and 96.2%, respectively, the SVM algorithm performed somewhat better than the Bayesian classifier. Support vector selection and adaptation (SVSA), a unique methodology, is suggested by Kaya et al. (Taskin Kaya et al., 2011). For the classification of both linearly and nonlinearly separable data, the SVSA method is a supervised classification technique.

A computational model called the Artificial Neural Network (ANN) is based on how the brain's neural networks are organised (Shalev-Shartz and Ben-David, 2014). A typical neural network is made up of numerous straightforward, interconnected neurons, each of which generates a series of activations (Chaubey et al., 2022). Sensors that perceive the environment through weighted connections from previously engaged neurons trigger these neurons. The feedforward neural network was the first and most basic type of network.

In many applications involving object recognition, CNNs are quickly becoming a promising technology. Local receptive fields, shared weights, and spatial or temporal subsampling are three architectural concepts that CNNs combine. CNNs have several interconnected, multi-layered channels that are very capable of learning new features and classifiers. Additionally, they have the ability to simultaneously classify and change settings. Furthermore, this kind of ANN has the capacity to automatically embed both spectral and spatial data into the classification.

3   CNN'S Inside for Damage Detection

In order to perform better than existing methods for damage identification using high-resolution satellite photos, CNN models that have been fine-tuned are adapted to computer vision datasets. Transfer learning, also known as the refining of models, is the application of learnt skills to a new situation. As a result, the goal of this work is to improve the ResNet152 model, one of most popular backbone framework in computer vision-related designs, so that it can more accurately distinguish between damaged and undamaged structures on satellite images. The ResNet34 and ResNet50 models, as well as additional ResNet models with different depths, were compared to this model. ResNet152 was selected because, when evaluated on the same sample set, it provided the best testing accuracy. Additionally, it is not by design that deeper ResNet models have lower training accuracy than their steeper counterpart. The four main steps of the suggested technique are depicted in Fig. 1. After the landsat images has been pre-processed, the procedure begins by preparing the data by obtaining training data for the job of relevance (i.e., building footprints and manually labelling them as "Damaged" or "No Damage") (atmospheric correction and orthorectification).

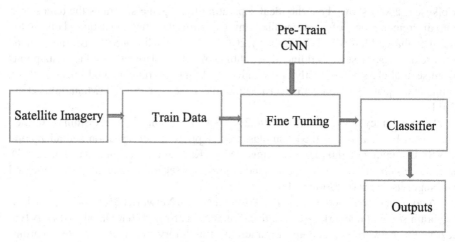

Fig. 1. Methodology

Then, training, validation, and testing data are sorted into their respective categories. The next step is model fine-tuning, which adjusts the classification layers of the current architecture and trains the neural network's filter weights. Finally, metrics will be used to judge the output accuracy of the improved classifier.

4   Implementation

The effectiveness of the suggested strategy is illustrated in this section. The Jupyter Notebook environment has been used to implement the experiments. After the magnitude 7.0 Haitian earthquake of January 12, 2010, Maxar Technologies provided WorldView-2 (WV2) satellite imagery of Port-au-Prince, Haiti. It is freely accessible through the Maxar open data initiative and has a spatial resolution of 1.84 m (Satellite Imaging Corporation, n.d.). The red, green, and blue bandwidths of four photos that have been plaid together to form the data each include three bands. The World Bank, the European Commission (EC), the Operational Satellite Applications Programme (UNOSAT), and the United Nations Institute for Training and Research (UNITAR) Joint Research Centre (JRC) collaborated to produce the Disaster Response Needs Assessment and Recovery Framework and ground truth data was gathered from these products.

Based on the ground truth information, building footprints were manually categorised as "Damage" or "No Damage" after being recovered from the WV2 satellite picture. They were divided into 93 testing samples, 322 training samples, and 46 validation samples at random. Figure 2 displays the locations of these sample datasets for each category. These locations were picked because 1) comprehensive building damage information is available to the public and 2) the buildings there are typical of the Port-au-Prince commune in terms of size, height, and structure.

Fig. 2. (Orange - training, yellow - validation, red - testing A, blue - testing B) Data locations and classifications.

The collected 322 training examples were used to first perfect the ResNet152 model. With the enhanced training samples (training+) produced by the rotation transformation, a second experiment was carried out. The zero-padded training images that were taken from the WV2 satellite imagery were used in both tests. Each of these 322 buildings

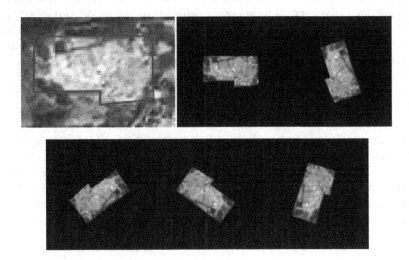

Fig. 3. The top-left image is the WV2 satellite's original image, and the boundary was used to extract the image chip. The extracted and padded image may be seen in the upper middle image. The further photos display the DA outcomes through a series of 72-degree rotations.

was rotated 72 degrees constantly until 360 degrees, as illustrated in Fig. 3, as part of the data augmentation (DA) process, which increased the training data 41 by a factor of five.

The quantity of labelled sample data used for each stage of the process is summarised in Table 1. The ResNet152 classifier's weights are fitted using training data, which is also used to learn how the process works. The ResNet152 classifier's parameters can be adjusted with the help of validation data, which can also be used to check whether the training data is adequate, for instance. The performance of the completely trained classifier, the final model, is next evaluated using the testing data.

Table 1. Summary of sample for fine tuning

Sample Types	Total	Damage	No Damage
Training (Original)	322	182	140
Training + (after DA)	1610	910	700
Validation	46	26	20
Testing	93	53	40

Preventing a model from being either overfitted or underfitted is a crucial aspect of machine learning. The aim of training is to achieve 0% validation loss. However, overfitting is suggested if the validation loss is more than the training loss, and underfitting is indicated when the reverse is true. Robust fitting is achieved if the validation loss and the training loss are equal (Brownlee, 2019b). The use of an approach known as "early stopping" was made. The validation loss stops improving for five consecutive epochs at 43 using the early stopping technique, at which point the model is finished being trained. The model was trained for a total of 20 epochs, as shown in Table 2, but due to early stopping, it ceased improving validation loss on the 15th epoch. The model was trained for 6 epochs only while using the original training data in testing. Therefore, the 20-epoch DA comparison is made to the six founding training data result in order for the two studies to have a consistent framework of early ending. The outcomes of the ResNet152 model epochs comparing the initial training data to the training+ data are displayed in Fig. 4.

According to the graph, the validation loss for the DA model is lowest at the 15th epoch, which is the desired outcome; nevertheless, the gap between validation loss and training loss at that time is one of the largest in the model. Validation loss has maximized at this time even though it is still larger than training loss by .01 at the 17th epoch. Due to early halting, the model terminates at the 20th epoch. It is the epoch with the second-lowest difference and a region with the third-lowest validation loss. There is a difference of .09 between validation and training at this time.

The ideal model is one that uses the initial random result of 20 epochs with the training+ data. The 20-epoch model can be trained in a much less amount of time. 20 epochs were trained in 7.27 min on training+ photos as opposed to 34 and 50 epochs in 12.48 and 18.37 min, respectively. Second, even with the modest validation loss

Table 2. Training return for the DA model demonstrating training and validation loss

epoch	train_loss	valid_loss	Accuracy	time
1	1.042376	0.903653	0.515528	0:36
2	0.936403	0.731321	0.720497	0:23
3	0.874362	0.575533	0.770186	0:21
4	0.783001	0.508756	0.776398	0:21
5	0.767506	0.537253	0.782609	0:21
6	0.751107	0.613045	0.782609	0:21
7	0.729267	0.525315	0.751553	0:21
8	0.694654	0.46184	0.807453	0:21
9	0.660684	0.433513	0.807453	0:21
10	0.653519	0.441762	0.801242	0:21
11	0.605963	0.488908	0.813665	0:21
12	0.583887	0.500495	0.782609	0:21
13	0.562885	0.400379	0.819876	0:21
14	0.534634	0.310225	0.869565	0:21
15	0.523058	0.288835	0.850932	0:21
16	0.521369	0.366022	0.826087	0:21
17	0.498879	0.51325	0.807453	0:21
18	0.474929	0.376632	0.832298	0:21
19	0.440805	0.320855	0.869565	0:21
20	0.406367	0.316084	0.863354	0:21

taken into account, the training and validation losses were the closest at 20 iterations. Thirdly, the early halting feature will improve generalisation for yet-to-occur situations by preventing overfitting as well as overfitting (Brownlee, 2019a). The 34 and 50-epoch approaches only slightly outperform the 20, 34, and 50-epoch model in terms of accuracy, but at the expense of a large amount of time.

5   Results

Figure 5 compares the outcomes of the two studies as well as the accuracy of training, validation, and testing. The training, validation, and testing accuracy are 92%, 85%, and 83%, respectively, when DA is applied to the training images. The training, validation, and testing accuracies using the initial training data are 50%, 43%, and 53%, respectively. The DA accuracies are, on average, 38% more accurate than the model using the original training samples.

When analysing the damage and no damage accuracies from the conventional training data and training+ data, there is also an aggregate of a 33% and a 46% increased

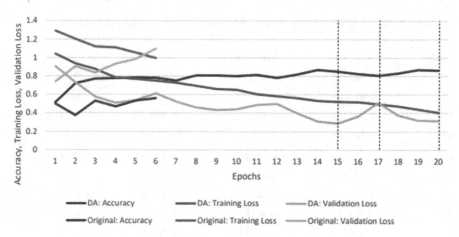

Fig. 4. DA vs. Original Training Epoch Results Comparison

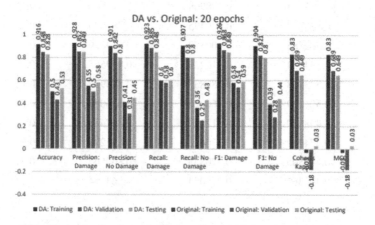

Fig. 5. Analyzing the statistics from the original model and the DA.

accuracy result, respectively. The recall evaluation for damage and no damage both demonstrate improvement for the DA result, rising by an average of 29% and 49%, respectively. The test for classifying damaged buildings is more accurate than the test for classifying non-damaged structures when the F1 score, which is a measure of test accuracy, is taken into account for all tests. The F1 score also reveals that the two models' average difference ranges from 31% for damage to 47% for no damage. The model with DA has, on average, .78 more inter-relatability than the original model, according to Cohen's Kappa, a measurement of the inter-relatability here between prediction classes and regression coefficients classes. Last but not least, MCC values can range from −1 to 1, with −1 denoting the greatest possible discrepancy between prediction and classification algorithm, 0 denoting randomness in the model, and 1 denoting the model's flawless prediction. The model with DA performs significantly better than the model with original samples, as shown by the MCC score average of .72 for the model with DA and -.06 for the model with original training data.

The first testing data set, designated as "Testing A," is produced at random. The other is the brand-new set, known as "Testing B," which is used to evaluate the model's capacity for generalisation. According to Fig. 6, Testing B consists of 189 samples drawn from seven city blocks. These samples are neither dispersed across a wide area nor sparsely sampled, in contrast to the 93 samples gathered for Testing A. Furthermore, the Testing B examples have much smaller building footprints. Table 3 demonstrates that, on average, the samples gathered for Testing 49 B are much smaller than the samples gathered for training in Testing A.

Fig. 6. A test of sample B. Ones with damage are shown in red, whereas unharmed buildings are shown in blue.

Testing B's accuracy was assessed to be 63%, while Testing A's accuracy was 83%. Precision, or the percentage of accurate damage or no damage forecasts, came out to be 50% and 80%, respectively. In comparison to Testing A's 85%, the damage precision is only 50%. But interestingly, the classification of no harm for Testing A and Testing B was discovered to be the same, 80%.

According to the recall metrics for Testing A and Testing B, 85% and 76%, respectively, of actual positives (also known as ground truth positives or "Damage"), or correct identifications, are found. Comparing Testing A and Testing B, the recall was calculated to be 80% and 55%, respectively, for the no damage categorization. Damage from both testing areas had a better recall than no damage. For the classification of damaged buildings in Testing A and Testing B, the F1 score, which is a gauge of the model's robustness and precision, came out to be 85% and 60%, respectively.

Additionally, it displays an F1 score of 80% and 65% for no damage. These measurements demonstrate that the trained ResNet152 model is not robust enough to generalise

Table 3. Building footprint sizes are compared

Area (sqm)	Training	Testing A	Testing B
Average	291.7	360.1	197.0
Median	197.0	200.0	150.3
Min	30.1	18.9	33.1
Max	2058.0	1912.2	1092.7

on new examples. Finally, testing A performs much better than testing b according to Cohen's Kappa and the Matthews Correlation Coefficient. The degree to which the forecast and the ground truth labels agree is shown by Cohen's Kappa. Cohen's Kappa for Testing A is .65, but Kappa for Testing B is .28. The MCC is a measurement of the correlation between the predicted binary classification and the ground truth. Testing B scored .30, whereas Testing A obtained a rating of .65. The association between the actual truth and predicted classifiers is more erratic according to Testing B's MCC value of .30 than it is according to Testing A's MCC value (Fig. 7).

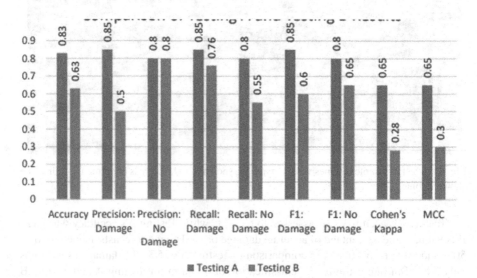

Fig. 7. Comparison of Testing A and Testing B Results

There are a few reasons why the trained ResNet152 model's generalisation performance is relatively poor. The size of Testing B's building footprint in comparison to the footprints of the training buildings is one of the considerations. According to Table 5 above, the average building footprint area for Testing B is 197.0 sqm, whereas it is 291.7 sqm for training and 360.1 sqm for Testing A. The tiny area of the Testing B footprints could significantly affect the generalisation findings since the smaller textures provided would leave the model with less features to classify. The broken construction texture, which is particularly evident in the precision scores, is a contributing factor to the generally subpar generalisation performance. The no damage building footprints were taken from structures that had sustained no damage; hence, whether the buildings are from Testing A or Testing B, their rooftops are largely comparable throughout the area in the satellite image. Consequently, the accuracy rate for the no damage categorization is nearly the same, at 80%.

6 Conclusions and Future Work

The training set can be artificially increased while keeping labels intact using the suggested generic data augmentation based on geometric transformation. The DA technique further improves CNN performance and prevents overfitting, as shown by the studies. Additionally, a transfer learning fine-tuning technique is suggested, which modifies the high-level layers of the pre-trained ResNet152 model while leaving the low-level layers untouched. Results show that pre-trained architectures are extremely effective and produce viable classification (85% and 80% in Testing A precision and recall for classifying damaged and no-damaged buildings, respectively), even though they are not pre-trained on the application of this work (i.e., damaged or no-damaged buildings). The success of our strategy is further demonstrated by the fact that the fine-tuning process converged after 20 epochs of training rounds where the validation loss is near to the training loss.

Future research would concentrate on examining model generalisation strategies, labelling training data, and automating approaches for extracting building footprints. There is no question that a larger training dataset would enhance model performance even further. Manual extraction, however, is time-consuming, expensive, and difficult. Building detection ML models, such as Ren et alFast-RCNN's have been created to recognise buildings from high resolution satellite photos (Ren et al., 2017). Automating their labelling continues to be a challenge. The task of model generalisation is challenging. Research should continue on methods to strengthen the model's resistance to data errors. For instance, further data augmentation methods must to be researched and used in the process of fine-tuning.

References

Cable, S.: Aerial photography and the First World War. The National Archives (2015). https:// blog.nationalarchives.gov.uk/aerial-photography-first-world-war/

Kolbe, A.R., et al.: Mortality, crime and access to basic needs before and after the Haiti earthquake: a random survey of Port-au-Prince households. Med. Confl. Surviv. 26(4), 281–297 (2010). https://doi.org/10.1080/13623699.2010.535279

Hussain, E., Ural, S., Kim, K., Fu, C.-S., Shan, J.: Building extraction and rubble mapping for city port-au-prince post-2010 Earthquake with GeoEye-1 imagery and lidar data. Photogra. Eng. Remote Sensing 77(10), 1011–1023 (2011). https://doi.org/10.14358/pers.77.10.1011

Duarte, D., Nex, F., Kerle, N., Vosselman, G.: Satellite image classification of building damages using airborne and satellite image samples in a deep learning approach. ISPRS Annals of the Photogrammetry, Remote Sensing and Spatial Information Sciences 4(2), 89–96 (2018). https://doi.org/10.5194/isprs-annals-IV-2-89-2018

Janalipour, M., Mohammadzadeh, A.: Building damage detection using object-based image analysis and ANFIS from high-resolution image (Case Study: BAM Earthquake, Iran). IEEE Journal of Selected Topics in Applied Earth Observations and Remote Sensing **9**(5), 1937–1945 (2016). https://doi.org/10.1109/JSTARS.2015.2458582

Rathje, E.M., Adams, B.J.: The role of remote sensing in earthquake science and eengineering: opportunities and challenges. Earthq. Spectra **24**(2), 471–492 (2008). https://doi.org/10.1193/1.2923922

Voigt, S., et al.: Rapid damage assessment and situation mapping: learning from the 2010 haiti earthquake. Photogram. Eng. Remote Sensing **77**(9), 923–931 (2011). https://doi.org/10.14358/PERS.77.9.923

Cervone, G., Sava, E., Huang, Q., Schnebele, E., Harrison, J., Waters, N.: Using Twitter for tasking remote-sensing data collection and damage assessment: 2013 Boulder flood case study. Int. J. Remote Sens. **37**(1), 100–124 (2016). https://doi.org/10.1080/01431161.2015.1117684

Huang, Q., Xiao, Y.: Geographic situational awareness: mining tweets for disaster preparedness, emergency response, impact, and recovery. ISPRS Int. J. Geo Inf. **4**(3), 1549–1568 (2015). https://doi.org/10.3390/ijgi4031549

Hussain, M., Chen, D., Cheng, A., Wei, H., Stanley, D.: Change detection from remotely sensed images: from pixel-based to object-based approaches. ISPRS J. Photogramm. Remote. Sens. **80**, 91–106 (2013). https://doi.org/10.1016/J.ISPRSJPRS.2013.03.006

Li, M., Zang, S., Zhang, B., Li, S., Wu, C.: A Review of remote sensing image classification techniques: the role of spatio-contextual information. European Journal of Remote Sensing **47**(1), 389–411 (2014). https://doi.org/10.5721/EuJRS20144723

Ouyang, Z.T., Zhang, M.Q., Xie, X., Shen, Q., Guo, H.Q., Zhao, B.: A comparison of pixel-based and object-oriented approaches to VHR imagery for mapping saltmarsh plants. Eco. Inform. **6**(2), 136–146 (2011). https://doi.org/10.1016/j.ecoinf.2011.01.002

Dhodhi, M.K., Saghri, J.A., Ahmad, I., Ul-Mustafa, R.: D-ISODATA: a distributed algorithm for unsupervised classification of remotely sensed data on network of workstations. J. Parallel and Distrib. Comp. **59**(2), 280–301 (1999). https://doi.org/10.1006/jpdc.1999.1573

Qian, J., Zhou, Q., Hou, Q.: Comparison of pixel-based and objectoriented classification methods for extracting built-up areas in aridzone. ISPRS Workshop on Updating Geo-Spatial Databases with Imagery & The 5th ISPRS Workshop on DMGISs, pp. 163–171 (2007). https://citeseerx.ist.psu.edu/viewdoc/download?doi=10.1.1.221.8137&rep=rep1&type=pdf

Haralick, R.M., Shapiro, L.G.: Image Segmentation Techniques. Computer Vision, Graphics, and Image Processing **29**(1), 100–132 (1985). https://www.sciencedirect.com/science/article/abs/pii/S0734189X85901537

Estoque, R.C., Murayama, Y., Akiyama, C.M.: Pixel-based and object-based 57 classifications using high- and medium-spatial-resolution imageries in the urban and suburban landscapes. Geocarto Int. **30**(10), 1113–1129 (2015). https://doi.org/10.1080/10106049.2015.1027291

Pal, N.R., Pal, S.K.: A review on image segmentation techniques. Pattern Recogn. **26**(9), 1277–1294 (1993). https://doi.org/10.1016/0031-3203(93)90135-J

Platt, R.V., Rapoza, L.: An evaluation of an object-oriented paradigm for land use/land cover classification. Prof. Geogr. **60**(1), 87–100 (2008). https://doi.org/10.1080/00330120701701724152

Myint, S.W., Gober, P., Brazel, A., Grossman-Clarke, S., Weng, Q.: Per-pixel vs. objectbased classification of urban land cover extraction using high spatial resolution imagery. Remote Sensing of Environment **115**(5), 1145–1161 (2011). https://doi.org/10.1016/j.rse.2010.12.017

Cortes, C., Vapnik, V.: Support-vector networks. Mach. Learn. **20**(3), 273–297 (1995). https://doi.org/10.1007/BF00994018

Kavzoglu, T., Colkesen, I.: A kernel functions analysis for support vector machines for land cover classification. Int. J. Appl. Earth Obs. Geoinf. **11**(5), 352–359 (2009). https://doi.org/10.1016/j.jag.2009.06.002

Maulik, U., Chakraborty, D.: Remote sensing image classification: a survey of support-vector-machine-based advanced techniques. IEEE Geoscience and Remote Sensing Magazine 5(1), 33–52 (2017). https://doi.org/10.1109/MGRS.2016.2641240

Mountrakis, G., Im, J., Ogole, C.: Support vector machines in remote sensing: A review. ISPRS J. Photogramm. Remote. Sens. 66(3), 247–259 (2011). https://doi.org/10.1016/j.isprsjprs.2010. 11.001

Taskin Kaya, G., Musaoglu, N., Ersoy, O.K.: Damage Assessment of 2010 Haiti Earthquake with Post-Earthquake Satellite Image by Support Vector Selection and Adaptation. Photogrammetric Engineering & Remote Sensing 77(10), 1025–1035 (2011). https://doi.org/10.14358/PERS.77. 10.1025

Shalev-Shartz, S., Ben-David, S.: Understanding Machine Learning: From Theory to Algorithms. Cambridge University Press (2014). http://www.cs.huji.ac.il/~shais/UnderstandingMachineL earning

Gupta, N., Chauhan, R., Chadha, S.: Unmanned Aerial Vehicle (UAV) for parcel delivery. Int. J. Eng. Res. Technol. 13(10), 2824–2830 (2020). https://doi.org/10.37624/IJERT/13.10.2020. 2824-2830

Suri, A., Bhadauria, R.V.S., Bansal, L.K.: Survey on methods of face mask detection system. In: 2022 International Mobile and Embedded Technology Conference (MECON) (2022). https:// doi.org/10.1109/mecon53876.2022.9751815

Chadha, S., Chauhan, M.R., Gupta, M.N.: Flood prediction and rainfall analysis using light gradient boosted machine. NeuroQuantology 20(6), 1–6 (2022)

Gupta, N., Rana, K.K.: Disaster prediction and post disaster management using machine learning and bluetooth. Webology 18(5), 274–292 (2021)

Rahul, M., Tiwari, N., Shukla, R., Tyagi, D., Yadav, V.: A new hybrid approach for efficient emotion recognition using deep learning. Int. J. Electr. Electron. Res. 10(1), 18–22 (2022). https://doi.org/10.37391/ijeer.100103

Chaubey, P.K., et al.: Sentiment analysis of image with text caption using deep learning techniques. Comput. Intell. Neurosci. 2022, 1–11 (2022). https://doi.org/10.1155/2022/3612433

Aggarwal, P., Jain, P., Mehta, J., Garg, R., Makar, K., Chaudhary, P.: Machine learning, data mining, and big data analytics for 5G-Enabled IoT. In: Tanwar, S. (ed.) Blockchain for 5G-Enabled IoT. Springer eBooks, Springer, Cham, pp. 351–375 (2021). https://doi.org/10.1007/ 978-3-030-67490-8_14

Agarwal, P., Garg, N., Singh, P.: Predicting poverty index using deep learning on remote sensing and household data. Int. J. Recent Technol. Eng. 8(3), 164–168 (2019). https://doi.org/10. 35940/ijrte.c3918.098319

Total Electron Content Forecasting in Low Latitude Regions of India: Machine and Deep Learning Synergy

Pooja Bagane[1]([✉]) [iD], Chahak Sengar[1] [iD], Sumedh Dongre[1] [iD],
Siddharth Prabhakar[1] [iD], Shreya Baldua[1] [iD], and Shashidhar Gurav[2] [iD]

[1] Symbiosis Institute of Technology, Affiliated to Symbiosis International University, Pune,
India
poojabagane@gmail.com
[2] Sharad Institute of Technology, College of Engineering, Yadrav, Ichalkaranji, India

Abstract. Our goal is to determine the parameters that affect the total electron content in the ionosphere (TEC) by comparing data with numerous models. Free charged particles are present in the plasma of ionised gas that makes up the terrestrial ionosphere. It is created when solar radiation ionises. IRI is present in the Earth's atmosphere and is a component of gaseous elements. The magnetosphere's dense ions and charged particles have an effect on the speed of radio-frequency signals. Therefore, one of the most significant causes of inaccuracy in GNSS (Global Navigation Satellite System) positioning and navigation services is magnetospheric delay. Furthermore, the ionosphere's quantitative influence clarifies the total electron content (TEC), which is the total number of electrons gathered per square metre during the journey from a spacecraft to a GNSS receiver. We are attempting to determine the relative performance of various machine learning techniques, including Gradient Boosting Model, LSTM, and Linear Regression, on the TEC prediction problem. The experimental investigation demonstrates that the gradient boosting regressor produced the minimum loss followed by a legitimate coefficient of determination when comparing all models.

Keywords: Magnetosphere · mean square error · mean absolute error · regressor · Total electron content

1 Introduction

1.1 A General Overview

The Earth's ionosphere, a critical region of the upper atmosphere, is subject to frequent transformations driven by solar disturbances, Earth's geographic positioning, and seasonal cycles. At the heart of understanding the ionosphere lies the measurement of Total Electron Content (TEC), a crucial factor that influences time delays in this specific layer. TEC is quantified as TECUs, signifying the number of electrons per square meter, with 1 TECU equal to 10^{16} electrons per square meter [1]. To decode the complexities of TEC variations, researchers rely on the International Ionospheric Reference

© The Author(s), under exclusive license to Springer Nature Switzerland AG 2024
D. Garg et al. (Eds.): IACC 2023, CCIS 2054, pp. 104–119, 2024.
https://doi.org/10.1007/978-3-031-56703-2_9

(IRI) model, which draws from extensive space-based magnetospheric data records [2] and the fact that this imapcts radio waves propagation dew our attention towards this topic. Understanding the importance of this topic gave us the meaning to search in depth and analyze how the electrons can actually impact ionosphere to a long extent. The Indian Space Research Organisation (ISRO) harnesses this wealth of data to identify the multifaceted factors influencing TEC within the magnetosphere [3]. Precise information regarding ionospheric time delays has captivated the GPS community, where even the minutest details are scrutinized to pinpoint the root causes of these delays. The IRI model plays a pivotal role in refining precision, enabling researchers to uncover the dependencies on which TEC hinges [4] TEC fluctuations are primarily instigated by alterations in UV radiations, atmospheric wave dynamics, geo-magnetic storms, and disruptions stemming from the lower atmosphere [5]. These changes, influenced by factors like zonal time, latitude, longitude, geomagnetic conditions, UV rays, and tropospheric elements, underscore the crucial role of TEC in mitigating radio wave propagation delays within the magnetosphere. As we strive to enhance the accuracy of TEC prediction models, it is paramount to consider the impact on satellite communication and navigation. For instance, ISRO has utilized weather data to understand the potential factors impacting TEC in the magnetosphere. This endeavor has prompted the exploration of cutting-edge approaches, incorporating machine learning algorithms such as linear regression, gradient boosting regressor, random forest regressor, and deep learning models, including recurrent neural networks and long-short term memory (LSTM) [6]. These models, leveraged alongside monthly data for 2023, unveil the significance of hourly-based TEC changes. The evaluation criterion hinges on error prediction, with Mean Square Error (MSE) and Mean Absolute Error (MAE) governing regression models, and the R-squared (R2) score determining prediction accuracy. While the IRI-2007 and older models have played roles in prior modeling attempts, they occasionally falter in providing the precision needed [7].

In Sect. 2, we will delve into a comprehensive literature review of existing research in the field. Section 3 will elaborate on our methodology, detailing the models and approaches utilized. Section 4 will present the results of our study, including a comparative analysis between our models and existing ones. Finally, in Sect. 5, our conclusions will offer insights into the implications and potential applications of our findings.

1.2 Ionospheric Total Electron Content over Indian Region

The limits of the available ground- and space-based measuring techniques made it difficult to image the ionospheric total electronic content and related phenomena over the Indian subcontinent until the advent of global navigation satellite systems (GNSS) [6].

These findings are explained by a variety of theories, including backscattering, Doppler effect, and Faraday's rotations. In low latitude regions, such as central India, the western ghats, and northeast India, where the latitude is less than or equal to 20° latitude, the variability is greatest. These techniques do, however, have some restrictions regarding intensive profiling, worldwide activities, and usability costs. Due to its reliability, all-weather accessibility from wherever on or above the world, GPS GLONASS observables are widely employed. It's possible that both are being imaged right now at the present time. In addition, the advent of GAGAN (GPS Aided and GEO Augmented

Navigation) and the Indian Satellite System have led to a new age of delineating the low latitude ionosphere [7] over the Indian subcontinent.

2 Literature Review

2.1 Analysis of Literature Review

Huang, Ling, et al. [1] used LSTMNN deep learning techniques, which were based on TensorFlow. The accuracy, rmse values were not adequate in terms of the computation the model has, but the model worked fine only during timely variations, so as a result under extremely unsettling circumstances the model didn't work fine. The model performed exceptionally well during high solar activity years.

McKinnell, Ben DL Opperman., Habarulema and J. Bosco et al. [2] indicated that ANN models were utilised for the study, and it showed that the outputs were acceptable during idyllic periods. However, the SATECP model that was employed had the drawback of performing poorly during magnetic storm periods. The spatial and temporal circumstances have an extreme impact on total electron content. ANN's application was proposed employing potent computational networks and proved to be very helpful for precise prediction [20].

Okoh, Daniel et al. [3] compared the tec predictions obtained nearby Nigeria with those made using the IRI model data. The results showed that diurnal changes were greater during the day than at night. Particularly, the worst flaw was that forecasts werent possible between 04 and 08 UT, and abruptions were discovered. This means that all of the comparisons demonstrate that IRI model data is the best for foretelling changes in the global ionospheric environment.

Mengting, Ziming, and Jia et al. [4] discovered a new model to forecast the tec in the ionosphere as a result of the recent finding that radio wave communication is hindered by ionospheric tec. The ARIMA(p, q) model was used to determine the answer, i.e., to anticipate changes in TEC in the ionosphere. As a result, the study's main finding was that the models accuracy was limited up to about 50–60%.

Ambelu, Tebabal et al. [5] showed that the data driven approach of using NN's was utilised and studies were conducted to check variations in tec via storms, solar flux etc. More emphasis was laid on the neuron layers for good computation and more effective outputs but later on demerit found was that the model had a complex non-linear optimization.

Ruwali, Adarsha et al. [6] proved that Hybrid LSTM-CNN can be used to forecast tec in the ionosphere by taking variability factors into account and using IRI-2016 as the primary variable for data comparison. The study discovered that VTEC changes depending on the time series data, and the model used parameter sharing, meaning that output changes depending on the input. The overall result was such that, on comparison of the metrics of results obtained by calculating measurement errors during the test period (2016), the model provided better results.

Pan, Xiong et al. [7] explained that the ionospheric total electron content (TEC) can be predicted using ED-LSTME. The deep learning model trained to extract high-level features from the data, eliminating the need for feature classification, the model demonstrated high level potential predictions. The main limitation of LSTM-based DL models is that they can only be utilised for short-term predictions, as in this case.

Lei, Y. Jade Morton, and Yunxiang Liu et al. [8] employed the Global Ionosphere Maps (GIM) data, which is further separated into training, validation and testing sets, to forecast global total electron content (TEC) maps using the convolutional long short-term memory (convLSTM) [9] method. The outcomes demonstrated that Model C performed the best, with reduced RMSE and MAE values. To enhance the models performance, batch normalisation, a regular dropout rate, the Adam optimizer were applied. The primary flaw of the model utilised in this study is that it performs slightly worse under high solar activity than it does under low solar activity.

2.2 Research Gap

Studies indicate that uncertainties about the Total Electron Content (TEC) [10] in the ionosphere still exist and could do so in 2023. More effective models that can provide real-time predictions for operational reasons are increasingly needed, as some applications may not find the current TEC prediction models to be accurate enough. New measurement techniques, enhanced prediction models, and more successful integration of TEC data into operational systems are required to fill in these research gaps in TEC prediction. As a result, our goal is to perform a comparative analysis of various models, including machine learning models like gradient boosting, linear regression, random forest regressor and deep learning models like Recurrent Neural Networks (RNN) and Long Short-Term Memory (LSTM) [11]. By utilizing trial data, we aim to make projections and estimate the possible TEC levels in the low latitude Indian region of the ionospheric zone (Table 1).

3 Data and Methodology

3.1 Data Utilized

Table 1. Information about the IRI model dataset

COLUMN NAME	DESCRIPTION
Year	Year of the data (e.g., 2020)
Month	Month of the data (e.g., January, February, March, April)
Day	Day of the data (specific day in the given month)
Hour	Hour of the data (e.g., time of measurement)
Height, km	Altitude or height in kilometers
Latitude, degree	Latitude in degrees

(continued)

Table 1. (*continued*)

COLUMN NAME	DESCRIPTION
Longitude, degree	Longitude in degrees
Electron_density_Ne, m^{-3}	Electron density in per cubic meter
Ti, K	Ion temperature in Kelvin
Ti, K	Ion temperature in Kelvin
Te, K	Electron temperature in Kelvin
Cluster_ions, %	Percentage of cluster ions
TEC, 10^{16} m^{-2}	Total Electron Content in 10^{16} electrons/m^2
TEC_top, %	Percentage of TEC at the top of the ionosphere
Equatorial_vertical_ion_drift, m/s	Equatorial vertical ion drift velocity in meters/second
IG12	Ionospheric Index (IG12)
F107D	Solar flux (F107D)

Data Source: The International Reference Ionosphere (IRI) model, which is frequently used to characterize ionospheric parameters like electron density, ion and electron temperatures, and other relevant information, is the source of the dataset. Most likely, the Community Coordinated Modelling Centre (CCMC) provided the data (https://kauai.ccmc.gsfc.nasa.gov/instantrun/iri) for 2020.

At different elevations and geographical locations, the IRI model is a commonly used empirical model that describes the ionospheric electron density and associated characteristics. To forecast the behavior of the ionosphere, it uses information from a network of space- and ground-based observations. For the year 2020, the dataset includes January, February, March, and April. These months fall within the variable ionospheric circumstances of the spring equinox season. The dataset offers a thorough understanding of the properties of the ionosphere throughout a large geographic region by incorporating data at different latitudes, longitudes, and altitudes. The dataset contains data on cluster ions, electron density, and ion and electron temperatures, among other ionospheric parameters. In addition, it contains information on the dispersion of the Total Electron Content (TEC), which is crucial for uses like GPS signal transmission. The dataset contains two parameters: the IG12 parameter, which is a density parameter associated with geomagnetic activity, and the F107D parameter, which is the daily average of the solar flux. Understanding the behavior of the ionospheric layer in response to solar and geomagnetic impacts depends on these parameters.

The data for the same experimentation have been acknowledged by International Standardisation Organisation and European cooperation, the Committee on Space Research and assembles using International Ionospheric Reference (IRI) model. IRI is an data-based model that represents the key ionospheric features as required by these organisations. The data is a vast collection of spacecraft research available from the ionosphere. Covering maximum range, the core model gives the average for the following quantities: electron density, electron and ion temperature and composition. The actual maximum attained should be 1500 KM's for upper bound. Combining all the essential features including latitude and longitude ranging between (20° and 78°) across lower latitude Indian regions, variability on hourly basis, density of charged particles, Ti/K and Te/K, H+ and O2+ ions are the predictors against the target variable i.e. TEC_top. International Ionospheric Reference since long [10] being an important concept to be explored in-depth and is used in several ways in multiple fields of study most likely engineering.

3.2 Methodology

The suggestive methodologies for the same are basically a combination of various machine learning (Machine Learning) [11, 18] algorithms and deep learning [19] (Deep Learning) models so an analysis have been made on the same by comparing the results obtained upon training these models. The accuracy of results is provided via utilising coefficient of determination, the mean square error and the mean absolute error of the machine learning [12] and deep learning models.

Measures to Predict Precision of Models:
Coefficient of determination (r^2 score):
It establishes relation between independent and dependant variables. r^2 score is the mathematical value given by the coefficient of determination . A value scaling between 0.0 and 1.0 is used to denote this metric, with 1.0 denoting an absolute correlation given by:

Formula:

$$r^2 = 1 - \left(\frac{SquaresSum_{res}}{SquaresSum_{total}} \right) \tag{1}$$

[Equation 1 suggests that the accuracy of the model can be evaluated using the sum of squared residuals ($SquaresSum_{res}$), which represents the sum of the squared differences between the obsved values and the predicted values. The total sum of squares ($SquaresSum_{total}$) is another measure used, which represents the sum of the squared differences between the observed values and the mean value of the dependent variable].

Mean Square Error (MSE):
Mean Squared Error- Performance analysis of regression model
Formula:

$$MSE = \left(\frac{1}{n} \right) \Sigma \left(y_j - \hat{y}_j \right)^2 \tag{2}$$

[Considering the total number of observed values (denoted as n). For each observation, y_j represents the actual value of the dependent variable, while $\hat{y}_j$ represents the corresponding predicted value in Eq. 2]

Mean Absolute Error (MAE):
Average of the difference between predicted and actual values
   Formula:

$$MAE = \left(\frac{1}{n}\right) \Sigma |y_j - \hat{y}_j| \tag{3}$$

[Considering the total number of observed values (referred ton). For each observation, y_j represents the actual value ofthe target variable, while $\hat{y}_j$ represents the predicted value of the dependent variable in Eq. 3]

3.3 Machine Learning Models

Linear Regression:
The data has been divided into sets of training, testing and validation according to the IRI model parameters. The required feature variables were scaled according to the neural network model, and the training data was later used to develop a linear regressor which has been created using LinearRegression class. The r^2 score, mean square error and MinMaxScaler helped for feature scaling, test size, which defines the percentage of the data which should be allocated to the testing set (around 20% in the given case), and about the random state which has been set to 42 to guarantee the recreatability of the final outcomes ensuring the models perfrmance. The mean square error is found to be 0.46 TEC^2 units, and the coefficient of determination is found to be 0.998 for the testing data.
   Formula for linear regression:

$$Y = a + bX \tag{4}$$

[where Y is the dependent variable and X is the independent variable (TEC). a is the intercept and b is the slope of line in Eq. 4]

Random Forest Model:
The developed Random Forest regression model uses 100 trees [13]. The model is improved to fit the training set of data using the fit function. On the training, testing, and validation sets, predictions are made using the predict function. The mean square error (MSE) and R-square (r^2) for each collection are calculated using the mean square error and r^2 score functions. The values discovered following prediction for the training and testing data splits are kept in text files using the create_file function. A scatter plot displaying the actual and predicted TEC values is created for the testing set. The coefficient of determination for the testing data is found to be 0.99, and the mean square error is 0.07 TEC^2 units.
   A Random Forest regression model with n decision trees predicts the output y (here TEC) as for a given set of input features

$$y = \frac{y_1 + y_2 + y_3 + \ldots + y_n}{n} \tag{5}$$

[where each y is the average of each decision tree's individual forecasts $(y_1, y_2 \ldots y_n)$ upto n trees which is determined by traversing the tree according to the input features and computing the output at the appropriate leaf node. The weighted sum of the target values from the training samples at the associated leaf node, with the weights based on the nodes sample density, can be used to estimate each tree's y output in case of Eq. 5].

Gradient Boosting Regressor:
The process focuses on developing a Gradient Boosting Regression model with n_estimators=100 and max_depth=4, then fitting the model to the training set of data. The term n_estimators refers to how many distinct decision trees should be included in the ensemble. Each tree is trained in turn, learning from the mistakes of the preceding tree(s) as it goes along until the desired degree of accuracy is reached. The weighted average of all the trees forecasts is then the resultant prediction. The model predicts on the training, testing, and validation sets. The coefficient of determination for the testing data is found to be 0.99, and the mean square error is 0.03 TEC^2 units.

The formula for Gradient Boosting model is as follows:

$$TEC_{Predicted} = b_0 + b_1 x_1 + \ldots + b_n x_n \tag{6}$$

[where $b_0, b_1, \ldots, b_n$ are the coefficients for each feature $(x_1, x_2, \ldots, x_n)$ in the model, and TEC_predicted is the predicted total electron content value for the given set of features provided as input as shown in Eq. 6]

3.4 Deep Learning Models

Recurrent Neural Networks (RNN):
The rnn_model object is used to create a sequential model. The next step is to add an input shape and a SimpleRNN layer with 128 units, also known as neurons. (X_train) that is scaled to fit the training's dimensions information. A dropout layer is added after the RNN layer to assist 20% of the input should be randomly removed to avoid overfitting. measures. Last, a single unit dense layer is applied to create a single output result, representing the projected Total Value of Electron Content (TEC) [16]. The model is then built using the Adam optimizer and the loss function. The summary() function is then used to display the model's structure and the total number of trainable parameters. Next, the model is adjusted to fit theFormula for the RNN model: e fit() function on the training set of data with 150 iterations and a batch size of 32. The validation_data option is configured with the assistance of the validation data (X_val and y_val) to assess the model's training performance and, as a result, avoiding the overfitting. A his-tory_rnn object contains the training procedure's output, which can be utilised in other ways. Examine the model's training and assess its output. It's Performance is evaluated using the validation and testing sets.utilising the r2 score metrics, which were discovered to be. For the testing data, 0.97.

$$Y_{pred} = rnn_{\text{mod } el} \cdot predict(X_{test}) \tag{7}$$

[where y_{pred} is the predicted total electron content values for the testing set, and rnn_{model} is the trained recurrent neural networks model, X_{test} is the test set input data as seen in Eq. 7]

Long Short Term Memory (LSTM):
A linear stack of neural network layers is first created using the Sequential class. Following that, anLSTM layer [14] is added to the model with 128 memory units and an input shape of (batch_size, time_steps, features), where time_steps and features are the dimensions of the input data. Being an efficient total electron content forecaster suggestive of the research [15], An additional dropout layer with a rate of 0.3 is then added to reduce overfitting. Lastly, applying a Dense layer with one output unit will result in a single continuous output value. LSTM helps in spatiotemporal analysis [16] and convLSTM [21] is being referenced to conduct the study on functioning of LSTM [17]. The model is then built using the Mean Absolute Error (MAE) function and the Adam optimizer. To fit the model to the training data, the fit() function on the lstm_model object receives the preprocessed training data (X_train and y_train) and the number of training data points. The validation_data option specifies the validation set for evaluating the model's performance during training. Finally, the model is trained on the training data for 150 iterations with a batch size of 32, and its performance is monitored using the validation data. The training history is kept in the history_lstm variable. After hypertuning the parameters, the Mean Absolute Error (MAE), which was found to be 0.45 TECU, and the r^2 score metrics, which were found to be 0.98 for the testing data, are used to evaluate its performance on the testing and validation sets.

Formula for predicting total electron content using LSTM:

$$y_{pred} = lstm_{model}.predict(X) \tag{8}$$

[where X is the input data (here, test set), ypred is the projected total electron content values, and lstmmodel is the trained long short term memory model. Using X as input, the LSTM model's predict() function returns the estimated values for the total electron content indicated by Eq. 8].

Several crucial hyperparameters affect how well the LSTM, RNN, Linear Regression, Gradient Boosting, and Random Forest models estimate Total Electron Content (TEC) in India's low latitudes. For the LSTM and RNN models, precise capture of complex temporal correlations and patterns within the TEC data requires meticulous tuning of parameters such learning rates, batch sizes, number of layers and neurons, regularization approaches, and activation functions. Both models can provide accurate predicting results for the dynamic low latitude regions and successfully generalize to new TEC data instances by fine-tuning these parameters. The Linear Regression model's capacity to represent the linear relationships found in the TEC data is heavily influenced by factors like feature engineering, regularization strategies, feature scaling and normalization, and the meticulous handling of the bias-variance trade-off. Through the process of optimizing feature selection and fine-tuning these parameters, the Linear Regression model is capable of producing precise predictions for changes in TEC throughout India's various low latitude areas. Moreover, attaining robust and accurate TEC forecasting for the Random Forest and Gradient Boosting models depends on the efficient adjustment of parameters, such as learning rates, the number of estimators or trees, tree-specific parameters, loss functions, and feature significance. Both models are capable of handling complicated TEC dynamics, avoiding overfitting, and enhancing generalization skills with careful parameter optimization. This enables them to produce accurate forecasts for TEC fluctuations in India's dynamic and complex low latitude areas.

Figure 1 provides an overview of the architectural setup of the flow of the com parative analysis in a simplified and systematic way.

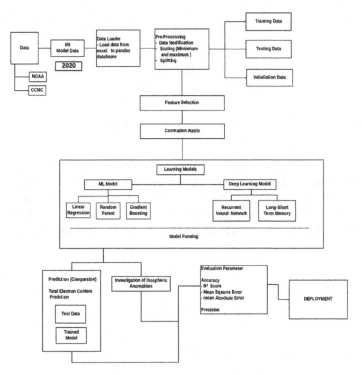

Fig. 1. System Architecture

4   Results and Discussion

The starting total electron data were re-checked over low latitude Indian locations for long duration with factor leading to variation being hourly data for year 2023. International Ionospheric Reference in collaboration with the CCMC centre at NASA provides the most precise readings for total electron content in ASCII format. The ionospheric penetration point is predicted to be about 300 km above the surface of our planet. The mean total electron content is observed on hourly basis from GNSS satellites. The machine learning models and deep learning models are used to forecast TEC-total electronic content and their performace analysis as described in Sect. 3.

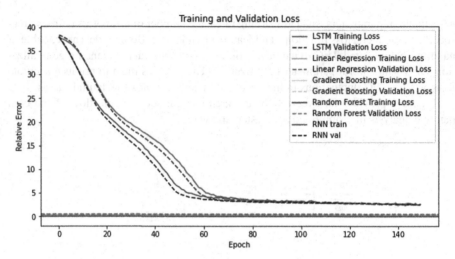

Fig. 2. Comparative loss analysis of all models

Figure 2 gives a glimpse of the comparative analysis about all the models and are tested based on the relative error i.e. mean sqaured and mean absolute error and cycles they undergo during training of models on available dataset and trained and validation data have been subdivided and plotted for the same. Figure 3 & Fig. 4 provides an overview of the deep learning and machine learning model's performance.

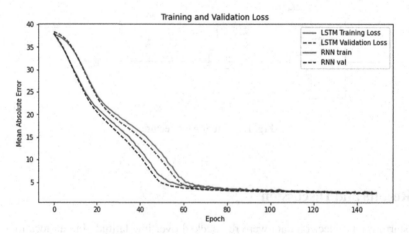

Fig. 3. Deep learning models loss computation

In India's low latitude areas, the Machine Learning (ML) and deep learning techniques shown in Fig. 3, which include LSTM, RNN, Linear Regression, Gradient Boosting, and Random Forest, were successful in predicting Total Electron Content (TEC). Their success was attributed to their capacity to extract meaningful characteristics from

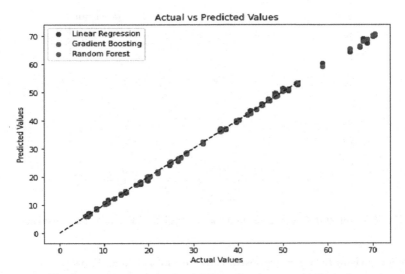

Fig. 4. Machine Learning models's predicted vs actual values plot

TEC data, offer interpretability, and perform well even in the face of sparse data availability. The necessity for interpretability, the small size of the dataset, and the real limitations on computing power led to the choice not to use deep learning models. Choosing the chosen machine learning algorithms guaranteed clear insights, effective use of the data that was already accessible, and useful implementation within the parameters of the project.

In addition, these machine learning techniques shown in Fig. 4 demonstrated robustness while managing noisy training data from TECs, adaptability in incorporating domain-specific expertise, and a comparatively lower training time and computing overhead when compared to deep learning models. Their capacity to be easily interpreted by stakeholders gave them valuable insights that matched the realistic needs of TEC forecasting in the low-latitude areas. Aware decision-making was made easier by the particular outputs of the models, which allowed stakeholders to put the models' suggestions into practice by implementing focused strategies. These machine learning algorithms' scalability and implementability made it easier to integrate them with the current TEC forecasting systems, guaranteeing a smooth transfer to the new forecasting framework. All things considered, the selected machine learning techniques turned out to be a thorough and workable solution for precise temperature extreme forecasting, fitting the unique needs and limitations of India's low-latitude areas.

As seen from Fig. 5 **Gradient boosting regressor,** just came out with the best performance analysis and performed better than other ml models as demosntrated with parameters being r^2 score (coefficient of determination) of 0.99, MSE 0.03 TEC^2 units, and RMSE 0.17 TECU. To summarize, gradient boosting is a vigorous and resilient machine learning regression model that generally performs better than other models because of involvement of boosting, ensemble learning, regularisation, and hyperparameter manipulation.

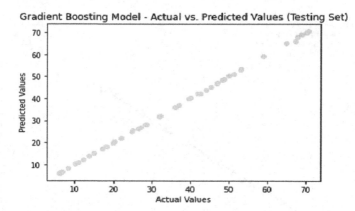

Fig. 5. Gradient Boosting regressor-actual vs predicted TEC (total electron content)

4.1 Comparison Between Proposed, Current and Previous Work

Notable Features of Proposed Work
One notable feature of the proposed ML model is its thorough capture of complex Total Electron Content (TEC) data relationships. Through the use of advanced learning strategies and efficient noise reduction techniques, the model produces accurate TEC projections even when anomalies are present. Carefully optimizing its parameters ensures that complexity and adaptability are balanced, improving its capacity to understand complicated TEC changes. The model incorporates specialized insights and is customized to the distinct features of TEC changes in India's low latitude regions. This results in precise and pertinent forecasts that are particular to the region.

Moreover, the model exhibits its flexibility to various geographical locations, preserving steady performance and trustworthy forecasting skills in the face of changing environmental circumstances. Its intrinsic explanatory power helps well-informed decision-making processes and offers useful insights into the underlying causes of TEC variations. The model's dependable performance makes it an effective tool for producing accurate forecasts and analyzing the underlying dynamics of TEC variations. This allows for the development of TEC management plans and decision-making procedures that are specific to the dynamics of the low latitude regions.

Related Studies and Their Implications
The accuracy of TEC prediction was the main focus of the study conducted by Wilson et al., [20] which examined three ionospheric Total Electron Content (TEC) specification methods: TOPEX (ground truth), the Bent model (climatological), and GIM (GPS data-driven). The GIM model assumes a thin ionospheric shell, interpolates observations, and is dependent on a global network of GPS stations. An empirical model based on historical averages is the Bent model. The TOPEX radar altimeter data were used as a reference even though they had a little estimated inaccuracy of 3 TECU. In order to investigate the accuracy of GIM in comparison to TOPEX as a function of GPS station distance, statistical analyses were carried out. The findings demonstrated that GIM functioned well within 1000 km of GPS stations, with variations of less than 3.5 TECU that grew

with distance and eventually became significant at around 2000 km. Beyond 1500 km, the average RMS error was less than 8.0 TECU due to direct GPS measurements.

In this work by Kailiang et al., [18] Faraday rotation measurements in Xinxiang were compared with Total Electron Content (TEC) values computed using two versions of the International Reference Ionosphere (IRI-86 and IRI-90). IRI produced respectable results during periods of low solar activity; IRI-90 outperformed IRI-86, and URSI coefficients outperformed CCIR coefficients. The accuracy of IRI's TEC values was increased by using the Asia Oceania Region F2-layer mapping (AOR) for foF2 and M(3000)F2 computations. However, IRI tended to underestimate TEC during the day during periods of high solar activity (October to April), probably as a result of inaccurate topside electron density profile data.

The research presented by Ling et al. [1] offers two models for estimating Total Electron Content (TEC) in the ionosphere during the peak solar activity year of 2014: Multi-Factor NeuralProphet (MF-NPM) and Long Short-Term Memory Neural Network (LSTMNN). With less bias, a lower RMSE, and better relative accuracy than LSTMNN and COPG_P1, MF-NPM performs better. With most estimates coming within ±10 TECU, it captures TEC dynamics accurately. The findings show that MF-NPM is a reliable option for ionospheric TEC value forecasting in this situation since it provides better TEC prediction accuracy.

The study by Mostafa et al. [21] examined Total Electron Content (TEC) data from a GPS receiver station located beneath the northern crest of the equatorial ionospheric anomaly (EIA) near Dhaka, Bangladesh, spanning eight years. The diurnal maximum of TEC was observed to normally occur between 13:00 and 14:00 BST, with fluctuations occurring depending on solar activity. TEC levels peaked during strong solar activity in March, April, and the autumnal equinox, reaching around 70 TECU, and peaked in winter, reaching about 35–43 TECU. TEC values were frequently underestimated by the International Reference Ionosphere (IRI-2012) model during high solar activity, particularly around equinoxes. However, during low solar activity, the model showed better accuracy, with errors as low as ~0.13 TECU.

Difference Between Present and Previous Approaches.
Present Studies (Ling et al. and Mostafa et al.): These studies look at the diurnal and seasonal changes of Total Electron Content (TEC) in a particular region (Mostafa et al.) and forecast TEC in the ionosphere during a time of high solar activity (Ling et al.).

Prior Research (Wilson et al. and Kailiang et al.): The prior research compared and assessed the accuracy of various TEC definition approaches, with a primary focus on how GPS station distance affected one particular method (Wilson et al.). In a different study, Kailang et al. analysed two iterations of the International Reference Ionosphere (IRI) model and evaluated how well they performed in calculating TEC, paying particular attention to differences that occurred during periods of high solar activity.

5   Conclusion

The various essential factors including shape of electrons, navigation, and electromagnetic wave propagation can lead to better grasp of conceptual knowledge about the total electron content. The final analysis of the research held during various disturbed atmospheric conditions i.e. solar and magnetic anomalities for an entire month or 2 of hourly readings of total electron content in the year 2022–23. Machine learning and deep learning models are used to determine TEC time series and analyse how well they execute, as discussed in Section 3. Amongst all the models used in the comparative study, the gradient boosting regressor out-performed rest all of the other models. The deep learning models have shown extremity for overfitting but gave a lower mean absolute error upon hypertuning. The performance analysis was achieved by using scores, relative errors, and plotting graphs for the same. It gave the prediction an effective view, and it performed well in both spatiotemporal conditions. The tests to be conducted further will utilise data from vivid ionospheric zones. Furthermore for more accurate and effective predictions more powerful computation need to be assigned to the systems for providing effective functionality of deep learning models.

References

1. Huang, L., Wu, H., Lou, Y., Zhang, H.: Spatiotemporal Analysis of Regional Ionospheric TEC Prediction Using Multi-Factor NeuralProphet Model under Disturbed Conditions. Remote Sens. **15**, 195 (2023)
2. Habarulema, J., McKinnell, B.: Regional GPS TEC modeling; Attempted spatial and temporal extrapolation of TEC using neural networks. J. Geophys. Res. **116**, A04314 (2011)
3. Okoh, D., Eze, A.: A comparison of IRI-TEC predictions with GPS-TEC measurements over Nsukka. Space Weather, Nigeria (2012)
4. Yin, M., Zou, Z., Zhong, J.: A Prediction Model of the Grid Point Ionospheric TEC. Chinese Journal of Space Science **41**(4), 568–579 (2021)
5. Tebabal, A., Radicilla, S.M.: Local TEC modelling and forecasting using neural networks. Journal of Atmospheric and Solar-Terrestrial Physics, 143–151 (2018)
6. Ruwali, A., Kumar, A.: Implementation of Hybrid Deep Learning Model (LSTM-CNN) for Ionospheric TEC Forecasting Using GPS Data. IEEE Geoscience and Remote Sensing Letters (2020)
7. Xhaung, P., Zhai, D.: Long Short Term Memory Neural Network for Ionospheric Total Electron Content Forecasting Over China. Space Weather (2021)
8. Lei, L., Morton, Y., Liu, Y.: ML Prediction of Global Ionospheric TEC Maps. Space Weather (2022)
9. Bai, S., Yang, W., Zhang, M., Liu, D., Li, W., Zhou, L.: Attention-Based BiLSTM Model for pavement temperature prediction of asphalt pavement in winter. Atmosphere **13**, 1524 (2022)
10. Asaly, S., Reuveni, Y.: Using Support Vector Machine (SVM) and Ionospheric Total Electron Content (TEC) Data for Solar Flare Predictions. IEEE J. Selec. Topi. Appl. Earth Observat. Remote Sens. **14**, 1469–1481 (2020)
11. Dabbakuti, J.R.K.K., Gandhi, B.L.: Application of singular spectrum analysis using artificial neural networks in TEC predictions for ionospheric space weather. IEEE J. Select. Topi. Appl. Earth Observat. Remote Sens. **12**(12), 5101–5107 (2019)
12. Bilitza, D., Altadill, D., Reinisch, B.: The International Reference Ionosphere 2012 - A model of international collaboration. Journal of Space Weather and Space Climate (2014)

13. Sivavaraprasad, G., Mallika, I.L.: A novel hybrid Machine learning model to forecast ionospheric TEC over Low-latitude GNSS stations. Advances in Space Research **69**(3), 1366–1379 (2022)

14. Mallika, I., Ratnam, V.: Machine learning algorithm to forecast ionospheric time delays using Global Navigation satellite system observations. Acta Astronautica, 221–231 (2020)

15. Sivakrishna, K., Ratnam, D.V., Sivavaraprasad, G.: Support vector regression model to predict TEC for GNSS signals. Acta Geophys. **70**, 2827–2836 (2022)

16. Chen, J., Zheng, K.: Ionospheric TEC Prediction of Leshan Based on Deep Learning. In: Frontier Computing: Theory, Technologies and Applications, pp. 873–880. Springer Nature Singapore, Singapore (2023)

17. Nath, S., Chetia, B.: Ionospheric TEC prediction using hybrid method based on ensemble empirical mode decomposition (EEMD) and long short-term memory (LSTM) deep learning model over India}. Advances in Space Research, 2307–2317 (2023)

18. Kailiang , D.: Comparison of total electron content calculated using the IRI with observations in China, pp. 417–422 (1994)

19. Bagane, P., Kandula, S.R., Saxena, A.: Intelligent system for prediction of potentially hazardous nearest earth objects using machine learning. Int. J. Intell. Sys. Applicat. Eng. **12**(1s), 71–80 (2023)

20. Kumar, G.S., Bagane, P.: Detection of malware using deep learning techniques. Int. J. Sci. Technol. Res. **9**(01), 1688–1691 (2023)

21. Wilson, A.: A comparative study of ionospheric total electron content measurements using global ionospheric maps of GPS, pp. 1499–1512. TOPEX radar, BENT model (1997)

Disease and Abnormalities Detection Using ML and IOT

Early Phase Detection of Diabetes Mellitus Using Machine Learning

Dharna Choudhary, Pradeep Gupta, and Sonam Gupta$^{(\boxtimes)}$

Ajay Kumar Garg Engineering College, Ghaziabad, Uttar Pradesh, India
dharna2110008m@akgec.ac.in, guptasonam6@gmail.com

Abstract. In current scenario of healthcare, Diabetes Mellitus stands as an incurable condition, underscoring the imperative of early detection. Factors contributing to the onset of diabetes encompass aging, weight gain, sedentary lifestyle, genetic predisposition, poor nutrition, irregular routines, elevated cholesterol levels, and other associated conditions. The intersection of healthcare and machine learning unveils intriguing possibilities, capturing the attention of medical professionals. This study aspires to empower healthcare practitioners in predicting diabetes at an early stage through the application of machine learning techniques. By scrutinizing and comparing classification algorithms, including Random Forest, Supervised Machine Learning, and Decision Tree, we sought to discern their efficacy in forecasting diabetes mellitus. A systematic evaluation identified a model achieving an impressive accuracy rate of 98.56%, offering a substantial contribution to the utilization of machine learning for diabetes prediction. This research augments our understanding of the practical implications of machine learning in the healthcare domain, particularly in the context of early disease detection.

Keywords: Diabetes Mellitus Disease · Machine Learning · Healthcare · Accuracy

1 Introduction

Diabetes is a prevalent worldwide affliction, nevertheless, individuals may lack a comprehensive comprehension of its aetiology, ramifications, and the prospective obstacles they may encounter as a result of the condition. Based on figures provided by the World Health Organization (WHO), diabetes is the most widespread ailment in India [1]. India had a cumulative count of 31.7 million individuals afflicted with diabetes by the year 2000. The projected estimate indicates a significant surge to 79.4 million by the year 2030 [2]. Diabetes mellitus is a metabolic disorder characterized by hyperglycemia, which refers to high levels of glucose in the circulation. Excessively high glucose levels may lead to damage to essential organs and other physiological systems, thereby giving rise to various health issues. The presence of symptoms such as excessive thirst (polydipsia), increased appetite (polyphagia), and frequent urination (polyuria) is often linked to high blood sugar levels (hyperglycemia). Diabetes is influenced by several variables such as body weight, stature, genetic predisposition, and insulin levels. Nevertheless,

D. Garg et al. (Eds.): IACC 2023, CCIS 2054, pp. 123–134, 2024.
https://doi.org/10.1007/978-3-031-56703-2_10

the concentration of sugar is seen to be the most significant factor. Timely identification is the only method to prevent issues [3]. Diabetes may be classified into two primary types: type 1 and type 2. Type 1 diabetes comprises around 5 to 10% of all cases of diabetes and often emerges during adolescence or early childhood. The pancreas has restricted functioning, which allows for its identification. Type 1 diabetes might be initially asymptomatic as a result of inadequate pancreatic function. The condition becomes apparent only after about 80–90% of the pancreatic cells responsible for insulin synthesis have been harmed [4]. Type 2 diabetes comprises about 90% of the total number of diabetes patients. It is defined by persistent high blood sugar levels, a condition in which the body is unable to control glucose levels, resulting in increased glucose levels in the bloodstream. This kind of diabetes mostly impacts the senior demographic and is more prevalent among those with a greater body weight or obesity. Predictive analysis is a systematic approach that employs machine learning algorithms, data mining techniques, and statistical procedures to extract insights and make predictions about future events using historical and current data. When applied to healthcare data, this technique enables informed decision-making and accurate predictions. Predictive analysis uses machine learning and regression techniques to better healthcare by precisely detecting diseases and obtaining enhanced clinical outcomes for patients. Machine learning [5] is seen essential in the current context due to its ability to automate operations with few errors, hence diminishing the need for human involvement. The current method for identifying diabetes includes laboratory testing, including oral glucose tolerance and fasting blood glucose tests. Nevertheless, this approach is laborious and requires a significant amount of time. Several researchers are now doing studies to identify diseases using machine learning algorithms such as J48, SVM, NB, DT, and Decision table. Studies have shown that machine learning algorithms [6–8] have remarkable efficacy in detecting various diseases. Data mining [9, 10], and machine learning algorithms provide substantial advantages due to their ability to handle extensive amounts of data, integrate information from several sources, and incorporate previous knowledge into research [11]. The paper is divided into sections, and the specific portion being referred to is as follows: Sect. 2 provides a succinct summary of prior research, Sect. 3 delineates the materials and methodologies used, Sect. 4 delivers the empirical results along with accompanying comments, and Sect. 5 summarizes the findings and explores possibilities for future advancement.

2 Related Work

Several previous analogous efforts have been taken into account, as stated. For example, Sisodia et al. created a model that accurately forecasts the likelihood of developing diabetes. The three classification techniques influenced by machine learning are Support Vector Machines (SVM), Naive Bayes (NB), and Decision Trees (DT). The PIDD (Pima Indians Diabetes Database), derived from the UCI learning repository, is now undergoing testing. The performance assessment of all three methodologies is conducted using a range of criteria. These data demonstrate that Naïve Bayes outperforms other techniques with an accuracy of 76.30%. Sajida Parveen and her colleagues used a dataset obtained from the Canadian Primary Care Sentinel Surveillance Network (CPCSSN) in their study

[13]. The decision tree model, adaptive boosting, and bootstrap aggregation were used. It was noticed that Ada-boost may be used to enhance the accuracy of illness prediction. Love Diwani et al. [14] use the Naive Bayes (NB) and Decision Tree (DT) algorithms to train and analysis the whole of an individual's data. The performance of the system was then evaluated, examined, and compared with different classification techniques using WEKA. The research indicates that the NB algorithm has the highest level of accuracy, with a rate of 76.3021%.

Veena Vijayan V. et al. [15] did a study on the medical diseases of diabetes, which are marked by abnormally high amounts of sugar in the bloodstream. The researchers used DT (Decision Tree), SVM (Support Vector Machine), Naïve Bayes, and Artificial Neural Network techniques to construct classifiers in various computerized information systems. These classifiers were designed to predict and detect diabetes. In 2020, Daghistani and Alshammari [16] did comparison research aiming to forecast diabetes. The performance of the RF learning algorithm and the LR algorithm was compared. The RF algorithm demonstrated superior predictive ability with an accuracy of 88%, surpassing the Logistic regression method which achieved an accuracy of 70.3%. The objective of Aiswarya et al. [17] was to explore methods of diabetes identification via the classification of data patterns. They used the DT (Decision Tree) and NB (Naive Bayes) algorithms in their analysis. The primary objective of the research was to provide an expedited and precise approach for identifying the sickness, hence streamlining the provision of timely patient treatment. Their investigation, using the PIMA dataset, showed that the J48 approach achieved an accuracy rate of 74.8%, while the NB algorithm, employing a 70:30 data split, had the greatest accuracy rate of 79.5%. In addition, the authors proposed a hybrid system consisting of three widely used machine learning techniques, namely Decision Trees (DT), Neural Networks (NN), and Random Forests (RF), for the prediction of Diabetes. The dataset utilized for this prediction includes 68,994 people who were healthy, as well as diabetes patients. This research uses Principal Component Analysis (PCA) to reduce the data collection's density. The achieved accuracy was 80%, which is considered a satisfactory outcome. In their paper [19], Rahul Joshi et al. note that KNN and Naïve Bayes are two machine learning approaches often used to predict diabetes at an early stage in order to save lives.

3   Materials and Methods

3.1   The Dataset

The dataset has to be recognized as the first step in the prediction process. The dataset's attributes and characteristics are essential for creating accurate predictions. The dataset used in our investigation was sourced from the open-source platform UCI hub repository. The selected data is a subset of a bigger dataset. Multiple academics used this dataset in various studies for predictive analysis. The dataset consists of 520 medical records with 16 variables that are continuous, categorical, and binary in nature. The final result trait is a binary property that indicates whether a person is diabetic (1) or not (0). The categorical data of the characteristic "Final Outcome trait (Positive/Negative)" was transformed into numerical values, with "Positive" being represented as 1 and "Negative" as 0.

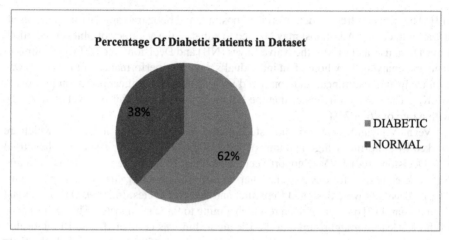

Fig. 1. Show the percentage of Diabetic patients in the Dataset. **Source:** created by Author (Result Derived from Python)

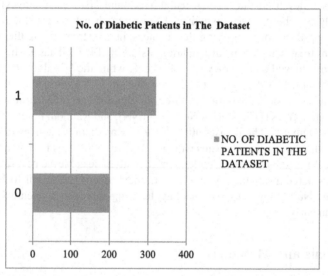

Fig. 2. Shows the Number of Diabetic patients in the dataset. **Source:** created by Author (Result Derived from Python)

Figure 1 displays the fraction of patients with diabetes in the dataset, whereas Fig. 2 represents the overall number of patients with diabetes.

The primary objective of this study is to investigate novel models for improved diabetes prediction. In order to forecast the occurrence of diabetes, we conducted experiments using a range of classification and ensemble techniques. In the following section, we expeditiously traverse the phase:

(a) Data Collection
(b) Data Preprocessing
(c) Data Cleaning
(d) Feature Extraction
(e) Model Building

3.2 Data Preprocessing

Data preprocessing refers to the procedure of transforming raw data into a format that may be effectively used by a machine learning model. Data preparation is the most essential phase in the development of a machine-learning model. Preprocessing of the given dataset has to be performed twice. The dataset acquired from the UCI hub repository has already undergone preprocessing and cleaning, therefore requiring just a few more procedures to enhance its cleanliness and accuracy. Python modules such as NumPy, Matplotlib, and seaborn were used to preprocess and clean the data. We used Matplotlib to identify the anomalies in our dataset. Upon analyzing the dataset, we discovered that there were no outliers. As a result, we used the complete dataset consisting of 520 patients for prediction in the machine learning model. In order to handle the dataset, which included both category and non-informative characteristics, we performed data preparation and preprocessing. Preprocessing is the term used to describe the modifications performed to a dataset before it is sent to a model. It is used for the elimination of noisy or unprocessed data in order to make it suitable for teaching and research purposes. Eliminating extraneous data from the dataset simplifies the process of analysis and model training. In order to streamline the configuration of classification algorithms, the attributes, represented as texts, are converted into binary values of 0 and 1.

3.3 Algorithms

Initially, we apply the specified machine learning classifier to the dataset. Subsequently, we partition the dataset into a testing subset (20%) and a training subset (80%) accordingly. We use this machine learning classifier to determine the outcomes of the analyzed matrices after the division of the dataset.

- Supervised Machine Learning (SVM)
- Random Forest (RT)
- Decision Tree (DT)

3.4 Hyperparameter

The work included refining several hyperparameters for the machine learning methods used. The Decision Tree classifier likely considered hyperparameters such as maximum depth and minimum samples per leaf. The hyperparameters of a Random Forest model often include the ensemble's tree count and the maximum depth of each tree. The Support Vector Machine likely underwent parameter optimizing, including fine-tuning of the kernel type and periodicity parameter, to achieve optimum performance. The hyperparameters were optimized during the model training to enhance the prediction accuracy of the algorithms and optimize their performance with unfamiliar data.

3.5 Importance of ML for Detection of Diabetes Mellitus Using Machine Learning

The research used Machine Learning (ML) to forecast diabetes at an early stage, using a dataset of 520 patient records with diverse features. Data preparation included the tasks of purifying and encoding categorical data. Three machine learning techniques, namely Support Vector Machine (SVM), Random Forest, and Decision Tree, were used for the purpose of prediction. The approach included thorough data preparation, meticulous fine-tuning, and rigorous examination of the test dataset, leading to an accuracy rate of 98.56%. The visual depictions emphasized the distribution of genders and the examination of weight reduction. The study demonstrated the efficacy of machine learning in achieving precise and timely detection of diabetes in its early stages. The decision to use Machine Learning instead of Deep Learning was based on factors such as the volume and complexity of the data, the need for interpretability, the availability of resources, and the quality of the data. Potential future research might include the use of more extensive datasets and the exploration of other techniques.

3.6 Tools Used

The research extensively used Python, together with modules such as NumPy, Matplotlib, Seaborn, and Scikit-Learn, for the purposes of data processing, visualization, and machine learning. The user-friendly nature of Python, along with its extensive libraries, positions it as a leading option for healthcare research and predictive analytics.

4 Proposed Methodology

We used a machine learning methodology in our study to predict the occurrence of diabetes. The dataset used consists of 520 patient records, each defined by 16 parameters that cover categorical, continuous, and binary aspects. Before inputting the data into the machine learning system, we made essential alterations to the dataset. Data preprocessing refers to the collective modifications made to eliminate unnecessary characteristics and handle category variables.

Figure 3 depicts the suggested framework in the form of a flowchart. The graphical representation provides a clear and visual depiction of the sequential processes and phases involved in the proposed paradigm for predicting diabetes. The flowchart visually represents the model's logical sequence and important decision points, illustrating how incoming data is processed, relevant characteristics are retrieved, and classification judgements are made. It functions as a visual aid to improve comprehension of the comprehensive structure and operation of the suggested model.

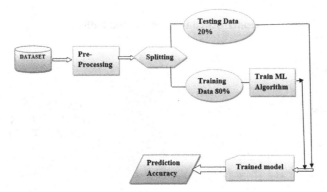

Fig. 3. Proposed Model for prediction. **Source:** created by Author (Result Derived from Python)

4.1 Procedure

Table 1.

Table 1. Procedure for proposed methodology

STEP 1- Add the appropriate datasets and libraries
STEP 2- Pre-processing of the data is necessary to eliminate missing data
STEP 3- Divide the dataset in half: 80% for training and 20% for testing
STEP 4- Choose the Decision Tree, Random Forest, SVM method as machine learning algorithm
STEP 5- Create the classifier model for the machine learning technique mentioned above
STEP 6- Evaluate the classifier model for the aforementioned machine learning algorithm using a test set
STEP 7- Make a comparison of the performance outcomes of each classifier
STEP 8- After analyzing the data using several criteria, select the algorithm that performs the best

5   Results and Discussions

This study inquiry included three machine learning methodologies. The recommended system model is contrasted with Support Vector Machines (SVM), Random Forest (RF), and Decision Trees (DT). The data set was subjected to all of these methods. The data was partitioned into two segments, with 80% representing the majority and 20% representing the minority of the whole dataset. Each of these strategies underwent testing using the same data set, resulting in identical outcomes. In order to identify diabetes patients, extensive investigations have been conducted on a range of factors.

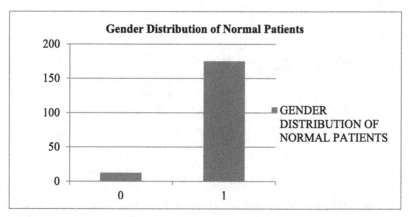

Fig. 4. Depicts the gender distribution of normal patients. **Source:** created by Author (Result Derived from Python)

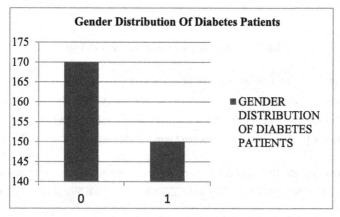

Fig. 5. Shows the gender distribution of diabetes patients. **Source:** created by Author (Result Derived from Python)

Figures 4 and 5 illustrate the gender distribution of healthy individuals and diabetic patients in our dataset. We assigned a value of 1 to male patients and 0 to female patients.

Figure 6 presents the investigation of abrupt weight loss, whereby individuals exhibiting rapid weight loss symptoms are observed to ascertain whether they have been diagnosed with diabetes. We have proposed a machine learning algorithm for predicting diabetes using a dataset acquired from the UCI hub repository. Our recommended model achieved the best accuracy of 98.56% when compared to the other classifiers previously used by the researchers, as seen in Fig. 7.

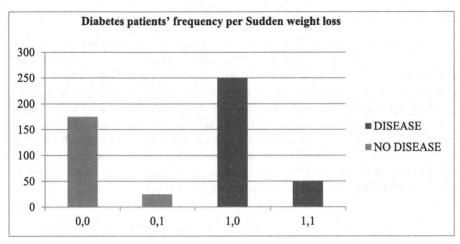

Fig. 6. Diabetes patients' frequency per Sudden weight loss. **Source:** created by Author (Result Derived from Python)

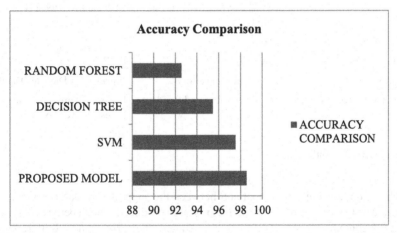

Fig. 7. Shows the accuracy of the proposed and other model. **Source:** created by Author (Result Derived from Python)

Figure 7 illustrates the model's accuracy in comparison to several machine learning approaches. The proposed model and other benchmark machine learning algorithms are evaluated based on their performance characteristics, with a particular focus on accuracy. This graph facilitates a straightforward evaluation of accuracy ratings generated by several models, highlighting the relative effectiveness of the recommended model and alternative methodologies.

5.1   Compare with Existing Algorithms

The suggested methodology shown superior performance compared to previous algorithms in terms of accuracy and efficacy in predicting diabetes. The research attained a remarkable accuracy rate of 98.56%, surpassing previous algorithms by a significant margin. These findings indicate that the chosen Machine Learning methodology, which incorporates Support Vector Machine (SVM), Random Forest, and Decision Tree, achieved a high level of accuracy in early detection of diabetes patients. The suggested model exhibits exceptional precision and resilience, distinguishing it from other options and showcasing its potential for practical implementation in the healthcare sector. These findings emphasize the need of carefully choosing and refining the methodology to achieve exceptional prediction powers in detecting diabetes.

Table 2. Comparison with existing

Aspect	Proposed Study	Excising Study, Chaubey M. et.al. (2023) [5]
Model Used	SVM and XGBoost (Hybrid Model)	SVM and XGBoost (Hybrid Model)
Feature Selection	Yes	Yes
Accuracy	98.56%	81.25%
Dataset Used	UCI Hub Repository	Pima Indian Diabetes Dataset
Additional Models Included	Decision Trees and Random Forest	Logistic Regression, Random Forest, Naive Bayes
Data Records	520	768

Source: created by Author

Table 2 demonstrates a comparison between the suggested research and the study conducted by Chaubey et al. The proposed research produced a much better accuracy rate of 98.56% compared to the 81.25% accuracy rate of the current study. Both researches used hybrid models combining Support Vector Machines (SVM) and XGBoost, together with feature selection. The dataset of the suggested research was comparatively smaller, consisting of 520 records, in contrast to the current study which had 768 records. However, the proposed study exhibited superior accuracy and also included supplementary models.

5.2   Feature Used for Classification

A wide range of characteristics were used to forecast diabetes. The characteristics consisted of a mixture of continuous, categorical, and binary properties, amounting to a total of 16. The dataset's quality was improved by the use of rigorous data preparation methods. The preprocessing phase included the elimination of unnecessary features and the transformation of categorical variables into a format that is compatible with machine learning techniques. The extensive range of features enabled a full evaluation of patient profiles, leading to the creation of an exceptionally precise model for early diabetes prediction, which reached an impressive accuracy rate of 98.56%.

6 Conclusion and Future Work

This study used machine learning algorithms to accurately forecast the occurrence of diabetes. The dataset employed consisted of 520 patient records, including 16 characteristics that included categorical, continuous, and binary elements. We conducted thorough data preparation to improve the quality of our dataset, which included removing irrelevant features and properly encoding categorical variables. We conducted an analysis and comparison of several classification methods, including Random Forest, Decision Tree, and Supervised machine learning, in order to make predictions about diabetes. By doing a methodical assessment, we discovered a model that demonstrated high accuracy in predicting diabetes. In addition, we used optimization methods to refine our chosen model on the training dataset, hence improving its prediction powers. The performance of the model was evaluated using a distinct test dataset to verify its ability to perform well on new, unknown data. The findings of our study have yielded significant knowledge on the use of machine learning in predicting diabetes. This research has shown the possibility of achieving precise and dependable early diagnosis, which is essential for implementing successful healthcare measures. The suggested model has a peak accuracy of 98.56%. Further, we can explore more comprehensive dataset on diabetes in the future, we may do a comparison analysis to assess the efficacy of several algorithms, including a hybrid methodology. Utilizing techniques such as data mining and neural network may enhance medical decision-making and enhance the accuracy of identifying diabetes risk in people.

References

1. Mohan, V., Sandeep, S., Deepa, R., Shah, B., Varghese, C.: Epidemiology of type 2 diabetes: Indian scenario. Indian J. Med. Res. **125**(3), 217–230 (2007)
2. Kaveeshwar, S.A., Cornwall, J.: The current state of diabetes mellitus in India. Australas Med J **7**(1), 45 (2014)
3. Vijayan, V.V., Anjali, C.: Prediction and diagnosis of diabetes mellitus: A machine learning approach. In: 2015 IEEE Recent Advances in Intelligent Computational Systems (RAICS), pp. 122–127. IEEE (2015)
4. Lucaccioni, L., Iughetti, L.: Issues in diagnosis and treatment of type 1 diabetes mellitus in childhood. J. Diabetes Mellit. **6**(2), 175–183 (2016)
5. Chaubey, M., Singh, R.B., Suhaib, M., Pal, P., Yadav, K.M.S.: Diabetes mellitus prediction using machine learning. Int. J. Res. Appl. Sci. Eng. Technol. **11**(5), 4786–4790 (2023). https://doi.org/10.22214/ijraset.2023.52755
6. Aishwarya, R., Gayathri, P., Jaisankar, N.: A method for classification using machine learning techniques for diabetes. Int. J. Eng. Technol. (IJET) **5**(3), 2903–2908 (2013)
7. Kavakiotis, I., Tsave, O., Salifoglou, A., Maglaveras, N., Vlahavas, I., Chouvarda, I.: Machine learning and data mining methods in diabetes research. Comput. Struct. Biotechnol. J. **15**, 104–116 (2017)

8. Kanchan, B.D., Kishor, M.M.: Study of machine learning algorithms for special disease prediction using principal component analysis. In: 2016 International Conference on Global Trends in Signal Processing, Information Computing, and Communication (ICGTSPICC), pp. 5–10. IEEE (2016)

9. Aljumah, A.A., Ahamad, M.G., Siddiqui, M.K.: Application of data mining: diabetes health care in young and old patients. J. King Saud Univ.-Comput. Inform. Sci. 25(2), 127–136 (2013)

10. Kumar, P.S., Umatejaswi, V.: Diagnosing diabetes using data mining techniques. Int. J. Sci. Res. Publ. 7(6), 705–709 (2017)

11. Fatima, M., Pasha, M.: Survey of machine learning algorithms for disease diagnostic. J. Intell. Learn. Syst. Appl. 9(01), 1–16 (2017)

12. Sisodia, D., Sisodia, D.S.: Prediction of diabetes using classification algorithms. Procedia Comput. Sci. 132, 1578–1585 (2018)

13. Perveen, S., Shahbaz, M., Guergachi, A., Keshavjee, K.: Performance analysis of data mining classification techniques to predict diabetes. Procedia Comput. Sci. 82, 115–121 (2016)

14. Noori, N.A., Yassin, A.A.: A comparative analysis for diabetic prediction based on machine learning techniques. J. Basrah Res. (Sci.) 47(1) (2021).

15. Vijayan, V.V., Anjali, C.: Prediction and diagnosis of diabetes mellitus: A machine learning approach. In: 2015 IEEE Recent Advances in Intelligent Computational Systems (RAICS), pp. 122–127. IEEE (2015)

16. Daghistani, T., Alshammari, R.: Comparison of statistical logistic regression and random forest machine learning techniques in predicting diabetes. J. Adv. Inform. Technol. 11(2), 78–83 (2020)

17. Arora, R., Suman, S.: Comparative analysis of classification algorithms on different datasets using WEKA. Int. J. Comput. Appl. 54(13), 21–25 (2012). https://doi.org/10.5120/8626-2492

18. Zou, Q., Qu, K., Luo, Y., Yin, D., Ju, Y., Tang, H.: Predicting diabetes mellitus with machine learning techniques. Front. Genet. 9, 515 (2018)

19. Joshi, R., Alehegn, M.: Analysis and prediction of diabetes diseases using machine learning algorithm: ensemble approach. Int. Res. J. Eng. Technol. 4(10), 426–436 (2017)

Diabetes Risk Prediction Through Fine-Tuned Gradient Boosting

Pooja Rani[1] , Rohit Lamba[2] , Ravi Kumar Sachdeva[3] , Anurag Jain[4(✉)] ,
Tanupriya Choudhury[5] , and Ketan Kotecha[6]

[1] MMICTBM, Maharishi Markandeshwar (Deemed to Be University), Mullana, Ambala,
Haryana, India
pooja.rani@mmumullana.org

[2] Electronics & Communication Engineering Department, Maharishi Markandeshwar
Engineering College, Maharishi Markandeshwar (Deemed to Be University), Mullana, Ambala,
Haryana, India
rohitlamba14@mmumullana.org

[3] Chitkara University Institute of Engineering and Technology, Chitkara University, Punjab,
India
ravi.sachdeva@chitkara.edu.in

[4] School of Computer Sciences, University of Petroleum and Energy Studies, Dehradun, India
dr.anuragjain14@gmail.com

[5] CSE Department, Symbiosis Institute of Technology, Symbiosis International University,
Lavale Campus, Pune, Maharashtra 412115, India
tanupriya.choudhury@sitpune.edu.in

[6] Symbiosis Centre for Applied Artificial Intelligence, Symbiosis Institute of Technology,
Symbiosis International (Deemed University), Pune 412115, India
director@sitpune.edu.in

Abstract. Diabetes, a chronic metabolic disease with a rising global prevalence,
significantly impacts individuals' health. Diabetes increases a person's risk of
developing various diseases, including heart disease, stroke, vision problems,
nerve damage, etc. Early detection and proactive care of diabetes can lessen its
impact and improve patient outcomes. Utilizing the powers of machine learning
algorithms in the medical field has shown significant promise in accurately identifying diseases and implementing customized treatments, reducing the workload
of healthcare professionals. This paper proposes a methodology based on Gradient Boosting technique to accurately predict diabetes. This study also provides a
thorough analysis of diabetes prediction using a variety of classifiers, including
Linear Discriminant Analysis (LDA), Extra Tree Classifiers (ETC), Quadratic Discriminant Analysis (QDA), Stochastic Gradient Descent (SGD), Bayesian Gradient Descent Classifiers (BGC), and Gradient Boosting (GB) classifiers. The
pre-processing methods of Standard Scalar Normalization and Synthetic Minority Over-sampling Technique (SMOTE) are used to improve the predictive models'
quality. SMOTE is used for class balancing. Accuracies achieved by LDA, ETC,
QDA, SGD, BGC, and GB are 77.34%, 74.20%, 73.50%, 75.01%, 74.08%, and
80.19%, respectively. The authors optimized the Gradient Boosting (GB) classifier through a rigorous grid search optimization process to maximize performance,
yielding an accuracy of 82.70%.

D. Garg et al. (Eds.): IACC 2023, CCIS 2054, pp. 135–147, 2024.
https://doi.org/10.1007/978-3-031-56703-2_11

Keywords: Diabetes · Linear Discriminant Analysis · Extra Tree Classifiers · Quadratic Discriminant Analysis · Stochastic Gradient Descent · Bayesian Gradient Descent · Gradient Boosting

1 Introduction

Diabetes is a disease that develops when the body is unable to control blood sugar levels. The hormone insulin, made by the pancreas, plays a major role in regulating glucose levels, which is an essential fuel for cells. To use glucose as an energy source, the body needs insulin. This disease occurs when the body produces insufficient amounts of the hormone insulin, which helps regulate blood sugar or when the body's cells do not effectively respond to the insulin produced [1]. Following are the three main types of diabetes:

Type 1 diabetes is an autoimmune disease in which the body's immune system kills the insulin-producing cells.
Type 2 diabetes primarily affects adults in which the pancreas does not produce enough insulin.
Gestational diabetes: Insulin resistance is developed due to hormonal changes during pregnancy. Most gestational diabetic pregnant women can control their blood sugar with dietary changes and exercise, but some may additionally require medication [2].

Uncontrolled diabetes over the long term can result in several health problems, such as stroke, heart disease, kidney damage, nerve damage, eye problems, etc. Proper care involves keeping track of blood sugar levels, adopting a balanced diet, exercising regularly, and using prescription drugs or insulin as required.

People with diabetes must collaborate closely with healthcare professionals to develop a proper treatment plan and lifestyle changes to maintain their blood sugar levels within a healthy range and prevent issues. Diabetes prediction using machine learning is required since early detection and customized treatments can potentially improve healthcare outcomes [3].

It is common to use a variety of diabetes symptoms as early warning indicators. People with diabetes may suffer excessive thirst and frequent urination due to elevated blood glucose levels. Weight fluctuations, such as unexplained weight loss or unusual weight gain, can also be observed because of the body's improper use of glucose. It is common to feel tired out and generally weak, which are typically brought on by the body's inability to convert glucose into energy effectively. Vision blurring may also be caused by fluid imbalances brought on by fluctuations in blood sugar levels that affect the eyes' lenses. In addition to a slower rate of wound or cut healing, patients with diabetes have a higher risk of infection because of a compromised immune system brought on by high blood sugar levels. Not everyone has all these symptoms, but it is crucial to be aware of these early warning signs and seek medical attention immediately to diagnose diabetes and receive effective diabetic treatment [4]. It is essential for efficient preventative measures so that diabetes risk may be predicted accurately. Machine learning techniques have recently revolutionized the healthcare industry by bringing tools for predicting chronic diseases, including diabetes [5]. This research proposes a method for diabetes prediction using machine learning algorithms. The research contributions for the paper can be summarized as follows:

1. Comprehensive analysis of a diverse set of classifiers, including Linear Discriminant Analysis (LDA), Extra Tree Classifiers (ETC), Quadratic Discriminant Analysis (QDA), Stochastic Gradient Descent (SGD), Bayesian Gradient Descent Classifiers (BGC), and Gradient Boosting (GB) classifiers is done, providing valuable insights into the comparative performance of each method.
2. Robust pre-processing methods, such as Standard Scalar Normalization and Synthetic Minority Over-sampling Technique (SMOTE), are used to improve the overall quality and reliability of the predictive models, particularly emphasizing the significance of SMOTE in addressing class imbalance.
3. Optimization of the GB through a rigorous grid search optimization achieves an accuracy of 82.70%.
4. An effective methodology centred around the gradient boosting technique for precise diabetes prediction is proposed.

A literature review is included in Sect. 2. Section 3 provides details about the research's methodology. The results are discussed in Sect. 4 of the paper. Section 5 summarizes the conclusion of the article.

2 Literature Survey

Khanam and Foo [6] used the Weka tool to evaluate the efficacy of various classifiers in predicting diabetes. KNN showed the highest accuracy of 79.42% in the train-test split, while SVM and LR produced the highest accuracy of 76.82% in the k-fold analysis. A thorough analysis incorporating both imbalanced and balanced datasets was carried out by Mushtaq et al. [7]. Initial models were created on an unbalanced dataset using SVM, RF, LR, GB, and KNN. RF performed the best, with an accuracy of 80.7% on the unbalanced dataset and 81.5% on the balanced dataset. Chang et al. [8] presented a diabetes prediction and diagnosis methodology based on machine learning using health indicator data. A subset of the BRFSS dataset has been used for experiments. The feature selection was done by PCA method, then missing values were handled and SMOTE were applied for class balancing. The dataset was divided into 8:2 form train and test. Five classifiers, namely KNN, RF, NB, DT and LR, were applied for classification. RF outperformed better with 82.26% accuracy.

Febrian. et al. [9] presented a diabetes prediction model using machine learning classifiers. The model was evaluated on the Pima India dataset from the Kaggle repository. The dataset is first cleaned by handling the missing values. The classification was performed by using KNN and NB classifiers. The model was evaluated using the train and test split method with a train test slit ratio of 8:2. The Naïve Bayes classifier achieved an accuracy of 76.07%. Khaleel and Al-Bakry [10] proposed a machine learning-based methodology for diabetes prediction. Experiments were conducted on the Pima Indian dataset from the Kaggle repository. The data is first pre-processed and normalized using a min-max scalar. The dataset is then split into 7:3 for training and testing sets. The classification was performed by KNN, LR and NB classifiers. The results were evaluated in precision, recall and f1-measure. The LR classifier obtained the best result of 94% precision. Gupta and Goel [11] presented a diabetes predictive machine learning model using hyper optimization techniques. The PIMA dataset from the Kaggle repository has been used in this paper. During the pre-processing process, the missing values were handled in four different ways and four datasets were prepared. The dataset was split into train and test ratio of 8:2. Four classifiers, namely SVM, KNN, DT and RF, were used for classification. The optimized random forest performed better with 76% accuracy on the third dataset in which missing values were handled by removing the rows that had missing values.

Jiang et al. [12] proposed a machine learning-based prediction model for diabetes using patient follow-up data. The patients' follow-up data from 2016–23 were collected from Guangzhou city. The raw data was pre-processed by handling missing, abnormal, and class-balancing problems. Three different methods performed the feature selection by calculating each feature's importance score: SelectKBest, RFE, and RF. Three classifiers, RF, XGB, and KNN, were applied, and ensemble voting was used. The best 91.24% accuracy was obtained. Qi et al. [13] presented an ensemble learning-based diabetes prediction framework using key features. The PIMA India dataset was gathered from the Kaggle repository. During the pre-processing stage, missing values were taken care of. The feature extraction was performed by correlation coefficient and RFE method. The processed data was fed into the DNN model, and the original feature data was fed to ML classifiers SVM, KNN, and RF. Results were obtained by applying the soft voting. Accuracy, specificity, and sensitivity were chosen as performance parameters. After applying the hyperparameter optimization, 93.5% accuracy was obtained by the proposed model.

Reza et al. [14] proposed a diabetes prediction methodology using an improved SVM-non-linear kernel. During the pre-processing stage, the missing values were imputed using the median method, and then, for class balancing, SMOTE was used. The performance of SVM with different kernels was evaluated by a 10-fold cross-validation method. The proposed model obtained 85.5% accuracy. Chandramouli et al. [15] proposed a hybrid bagging-based diabetes prediction model. The diabetes dataset is taken from the Kaggle repository. The missing values were dropped during the pre-processing stage, and a standard scalar was applied. The feature selection was performed by the enhanced RFE method. The hybrid bagging classifier performed classification, which outperformed with 92% accuracy.

Robust pre-processing strategies, such as handling missing data, careful feature selection, and efficient methods for class balance, have received much attention from researchers in this field. The studies used various classifiers incorporating a variety of optimization methods to improve model performance. These studies worked with datasets like BRFSS and Pima Indian. These efforts have shown encouraging outcomes. The literature survey illustrates the crucial role of pre-processing techniques in enhancing predictive models' effectiveness.

3   Methodology

The methodology of the proposed system for diabetes prediction shown in Fig. 1 encompasses dataset selection, pre-processing, classifier selection, optimization of the Gradient Boosting classifier, and diabetes prediction. This rigorous approach aims to provide a thorough understanding of the effectiveness of various classifiers and pre-processing techniques in predicting diabetes outcomes using the PIMA Indian Diabetes dataset. Various steps of the methodology are given below:

1. Dataset selection: The first step uses the PIMA Indian Diabetes dataset, accessible on Kaggle [16]. This dataset includes pertinent characteristics linked to the diagnosis of diabetes.
2. Pre-processing: Data preparation is done before model training to improve model performance [17]. The pre-processing steps include:
   (a) Feature Scaling: Standard Scalar Normalization guarantees that features are scaled uniformly, preventing the learning process from being dominated by one feature [18, 19].
   (b) SMOTE: SMOTE is used to solve the class imbalance in the dataset. To increase the classifier's capacity to learn from both classes, SMOTE generates synthetic instances of the minority class.
3. Classifier Selection: A selection of classifiers is employed for diabetes prediction, evaluating the performance of the following algorithms:
   (a) LDA: Finding the linear feature combination that best distinguishes several classes in a dataset is the goal of the statistical classification technique known as LDA. Effective for linearly separable classes, LDA maps the data onto a lower-dimensional subspace while maximizing the distance between class means and minimizing the within-class variance.
   (b) ETC: An ensemble learning technique called ETC produces the final forecast by constructing many decision trees and integrating their predictions. It differs from other tree-building methods by using a randomized selection of splitting points and attributes, increasing the individual trees' diversity. This diversity frequently improves the generalization and robustness of the forecasts.
   (c) QDA: QDA is a variant of LDA that relaxes the assumption of equal covariance matrices among classes. Instead, it allows each class to have its covariance matrix. This can be advantageous when dealing with data that doesn't adhere to the equal covariance assumption. QDA is more flexible but can also be prone to overfitting when the available data is limited.
   (d) SGD: SGD adjusts the model's parameters using a small random subset of the data at each iteration. It is especially helpful when working with big datasets. By iteratively modifying the parameters in the direction of the loss function's steepest descent, SGD seeks to identify the ideal settings.
   (e) BGC: Prior knowledge is incorporated into the modelling process using Bayesian approaches. As new data is observed, probabilities are updated and given to hypotheses in a Bayesian framework. This can result in more reliable predictions, particularly when working with limited data.
   (f) GB: GB is an ensemble learning method that combines the predictions of several weak models, often decision trees, to develop a powerful predictive model. The algorithm gradually raises the weight of occurrences incorrectly categorized in earlier iterations.

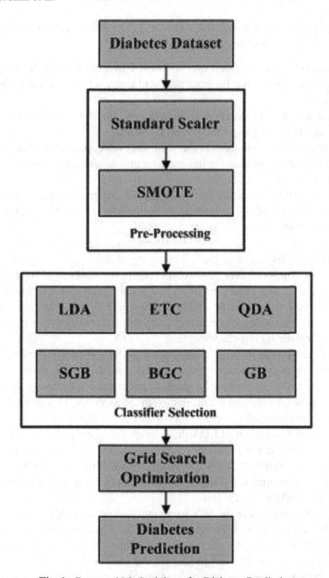

Fig. 1. Proposed Methodology for Diabetes Prediction

4. Grid Search Optimization: This technique improves the performance of the GB classifier. To determine which configuration of the hyperparameters produces the best predictive performance, it is necessary to investigate numerous combinations. The GB classifier has been optimized, leading to better diabetes prediction accuracy.
5. Diabetes Prediction: Ten-fold cross-validation is used to evaluate and validate the model's effectiveness. The model is trained and evaluated ten times, with a different subset held aside for validation each time. The dataset is separated into ten subsets. This method guarantees a thorough assessment of the model. Accuracy, precision, recall, specificity, and F-Measure are used to evaluate performance [17].

4   Results and Discussion

Python 3.0 was used for the implementation by the authors. Experiments were carried out using the Jupyter Notebook's Integrated Development Environment. The machine had an i3 11th generation processor with 8 GB RAM. The findings of this study provided insights into the efficacy of several machine learning algorithms for diabetes prediction. A wide range of classifiers, including LDA, ETC, QDA, SGD, BGC, and GB classifiers, were thoroughly assessed to determine their predictive abilities. The performance of classifiers is shown in Table 1. Accuracies obtained by LDA, ETC, QDA, SGD, BGC, and GB are 77.34%, 74.20%, 73.50%, 75.01%, 74.08%, and 80.19% respectively. This comprehensive evaluation provided clear insights into the predictive capabilities of classifiers. Performance metrics serve as a basis for comparison and demonstrate the superior performance of the GB classifier, which achieved an accuracy of 80.19%.

Table 1. Performance of Classifiers in Diabetes Prediction

Classifier	Accuracy (%)	Recall (%)	Specificity (%)	Precision (%)	F-Measure (%)
LDA	77.34	56.34	88.6	72.59	63.44
ETC	74.20	78.20	70.20	72.40	75.19
QDA	73.50	70.60	76.40	74.94	72.70
SGD	75.01	59.70	78.80	60.15	59.92
BGC	74.08	52.61	85.60	66.19	58.62
GB	80.19	83.20	77.20	78.49	80.77

Because the GB classifier emerged as a promising choice for diabetes prediction, a thorough Grid Search Optimization process was employed to further enhance its performance. The GB classifier was tuned to deliver the highest possible predictive performance through a thorough examination of various hyperparameter combinations. The thorough Grid Search Optimization process involved closely examining and assessing numerous hyperparameter settings. This systematic method played a key role in enhancing the GB classifier accuracy to forecast diabetes. The performance of GB before optimization and after optimization is shown in Table 2. The empirical findings showed that the classifier's performance after optimization had significantly improved. The post-optimization analysis showed a notable improvement across all performance parameters. Accuracy improvement is 3.13%, recall improvement is 3.60%, specificity is 2.59%, precision improvement is 2.63%, and F-measure improvement is 3.10%. Hyperparameters used for optimization and their optimized values are shown in Table 3.

The rigorous fine-tuning of the hyperparameters improved the GB classifier's performance parameters, as shown by the much higher values for each performance metric in Fig. 2. Figures 3, 4, 5 and 6 show a comparative analysis of all classifiers' performance. GB provided the highest performance. These results emphasized the importance of the optimization process in improving the performance of the GB classifier. They underlined

Table 2. Performance of GB Before and After Optimization

Parameter	Before Optimization	After Optimization
Accuracy (%)	80.19	82.70
Recall (%)	83.20	86.20
Specificity (%)	77.20	79.20
Precision (%)	78.49	80.56
F-Measure (%)	80.77	83.28

Table 3. Optimized Values of Hyperparameters of GB

Parameter	Value
random_state	1
max_depth	5
learning_rate	0.1
min_samples_split	4
n_estimators	200
subsample	1.0

the crucial role that specific hyperparameter tuning plays in maximizing the accuracy and robustness of machine learning models.

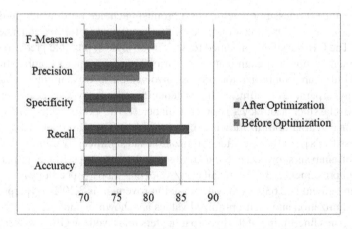

Fig. 2. Performance of GB Before and After Optimization

The proposed method for predicting diabetes using machine learning techniques has several benefits. First, it emphasizes the significance of early detection and proactive

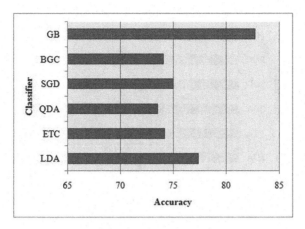

Fig. 3. Accuracy of Classifiers

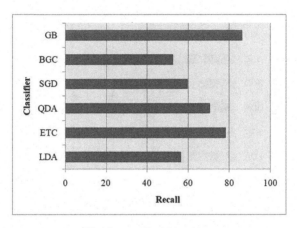

Fig. 4. Recall of Classifiers

management to lessen the effects of the critical global issue of rising diabetes preva-lence. Second, the paper thoroughly examines different classifiers, including LDA, ETC, QDA, SGD, BGC, and GB, offering insightful information about how well these tech-niques perform for diabetes prediction. Pre-processing methods like Standard Scalar Normalization and SMOTE are added, which improve the quality of predictive mod-els and increase accuracy rates. Additionally, the gradient Boosting classifier's rigorous optimization by Grid Search Optimization yields a remarkable accuracy of 82.70%, suggesting the potential for highly precise diabetes prediction.

Despite the encouraging results obtained by GB and the meticulous optimization procedure, it is important to recognize the limitations of the proposed methodology. One such limitation is the reliance on a particular dataset for training and validation, which might not adequately depict the varied and heterogeneous character of diabetes across various demographic groups, geographical areas, and genetic profiles. The proposed

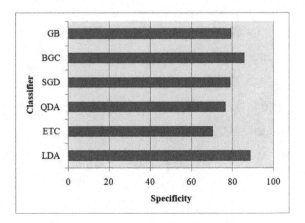

Fig. 5. Specificity of Classifiers

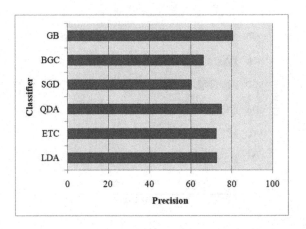

Fig. 6. Precision of Classifiers

methodology can be further enhanced to offer a more customized approach to diabetes prediction by incorporating a broader and varied data set. While using the Standard Scalar Normalization and SMOTE has undoubtedly enhanced the performance of the predictive models, the pre-processing feature selection method can further enhance the performance.

The focus of the current work is on the predictive abilities of several classifiers, with a special emphasis on the GB. However, a better comprehension of the interpretability of the model's predictions is necessary to fully realize the methodology's potential in clinical contexts. Incorporating interpretability tools into the machine learning pipeline might make it easier for healthcare professionals to generate actionable insights, enabling better clinical decision-making and customized patient care.

Table 4 presents a comprehensive evaluation of the proposed methodology for diabetes prediction in comparison with earlier studies. The results highlight the superior

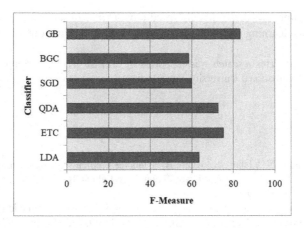

Fig. 7. Comparison of F-Measure of Classifiers

accuracy of the proposed methodology. The outcomes demonstrate how accurate the suggested methodology is to a high degree. This comparison highlights the suggested model's effectiveness in producing more precise and reliable predictions for diabetes, delivering substantial development in the area.

Table 4. Comparison with Existing Models

Year	Authors	Methodology	Accuracy
2021	Khanam and Foo	SVM and LR	76.82%
2022	Mushtaq et al	RF	81.5%
2023	Febrian. et al	NB	76.07%
2023	Gupta and Goel	Optimized Random Forest	76%
2022	Proposed methodology	Tuned Gradient Boosting	82.70%

5 Conclusion and Future Work

The paper examined the ability to predict diabetes using many classifiers, including LDA, ETC, QDA, SGD, BGC, and GB classifiers. These classifiers' accuracy, specificity, recall, precision, and F-measure were evaluated. After optimization via Grid Search, GB emerged as the top performer with an accuracy of 82.70%. The importance of data preparation in machine learning for medical diagnosis was highlighted by using pre-processing techniques like Standard Scalar and SMOTE to enhance the performance of prediction models.

There are numerous future opportunities for additional research and development in this area. Incorporating more features and data sources, such as data from wearable devices, could improve these models' predictive skills. In addition, investigating the potential of deep learning methods may produce encouraging findings.

Acknowledgement. This research was supported by an RSF (Research Support Fund) Grant from Symbiosis International University, Pune, India.

References

1. Tasin, I., Nabil, T.U., Islam, S., Khan, R.: Diabetes prediction using machine learning and explainable AI techniques. Healthcare Technology Letters **10**(1), 1–10 (2023). https://doi.org/10.1049/htl2.12039
2. Firdous, S., Wagai, G.A., Sharma, K.: A survey on diabetes risk prediction using machine learning approaches. J. Family Med. Prim. Care **11**(11), 6929 (2022). https://doi.org/10.4103/jfmpc.jfmpc_502_22
3. Ahamed, B.S., Arya, M.S., Nancy, A.O.V.: Diabetes mellitus disease prediction using machine learning classifiers with oversampling and feature augmentation. Adv. Hum.-Comput. Interact. **22**, 1–14 (2022). https://doi.org/10.1155/2022/9220560
4. Mujmdar, A., Vaidehi, V.: Diabetes prediction using machine learning algorithms. Procedia Comput. Sci. **165**, 292–299 (2019)
5. Lamba, R., Gulati, T., Jain, A.: Automated Parkinson's disease diagnosis system using transfer learning techniques. In: Marriwala, N., Tripathi, C.C., Jain, Shruti, Mathapathi, Shivakumar (eds.) Emergent Converging Technologies and Biomedical Systems: Select Proceedings of ETBS 2021, pp. 183–196. Springer Singapore, Singapore (2022). https://doi.org/10.1007/978-981-16-8774-7_16
6. Khanam, J.J., Foo, S.Y.: A comparison of machine learning algorithms for diabetes prediction. ICT Express **7**(4), 432–439 (2021)
7. Mushtaq, Z., Ramzan, M.F., Ali, S., Baseer, S., Samad, A., Husnain, M.: Voting classification-based diabetes mellitus prediction using hypertuned machine-learning techniques. Mob. Inf. Syst. **2022**, 1–16 (2022)
8. Chang, V., Ganatra, M.A., Hall, K., Golightly, L., Xu, Q.A.: An assessment of machine learning models and algorithms for early prediction and diagnosis of diabetes using health indicators. Healthc. Analytics **2**, 100118 (2022). https://doi.org/10.1016/j.health.2022.100118
9. Febrian, M.E., Ferdinan, F.X., Sendani, G.P., Suryanigrum, K.M., Yunanda, R.: Diabetes prediction using supervised machine learning. Procedia Comput. Sci. **216**, 21–30 (2023). https://doi.org/10.1016/j.procs.2022.12.107
10. Khaleel, F.A., Al-Bakry, A.M.: Diagnosis of diabetes using machine learning algorithms. Mater. Today: Proc. **80**, 3200–3203 (2023). https://doi.org/10.1016/j.matpr.2021.07.196
11. Gupta, S.C., Goel, N.: Predictive modeling and analytics for diabetes using hyperparameter tuned machine learning techniques. Procedia Comput. Sci. **218**, 1257–1269 (2023). https://doi.org/10.1016/j.procs.2023.01.104
12. Jiang, L., et al.: Diabetes risk prediction model based on community follow-up data using machine learning. Prev. Med. Rep. **35**, 102358 (2023). https://doi.org/10.1016/j.pmedr.2023.102358
13. Qi, H., Song, X., Liu, S., Zhang, Y., Wong, K.K.: Kfpredict: an ensemble learning prediction framework for diabetes based on fusion of key features. Comput. Methods Programs Biomed. **231**, 107378 (2023). https://doi.org/10.1016/j.cmpb.2023.107378

14. Reza, M.S., Hafsha, U., Amin, R., Yasmin, R., Ruhi, S.: Improving SVM performance for type II diabetes prediction with an improved non-linear kernel: Insights from the PIMA dataset. Comput. Methods Programs Biomed. Update **4**, 100118 (2023). https://doi.org/10.1016/j.cmpbup.2023.100118

15. Chandramouli, A., Hyma, V.R., Tanmayi, P.S., Santoshi, T.G., Priyanka, B.: Diabetes prediction using hybrid bagging classifier. Entertainment Comput. **47**, 100593 (2023). https://doi.org/10.1016/j.entcom.2023.100593

16. https://www.kaggle.com/datasets/mathchi/diabetes-data-set

17. Ramesh, T.R., Lilhore, U.K., Simaiya, P.M.S., Kaur, A., Hamdi, M.: Predictive analysis of heart diseases with machine learning approaches. Malaysian J. Comput. Sci. (2022). https://doi.org/10.22452/mjcs.sp2022no1.10

18. Rani, P., Kumar, R., Jain, A., Lamba, R., Sachdeva, R.K., Choudhury, T.: PCA-DNN: a novel deep neural network oriented system for breast cancer classification. EAI Endorsed Trans. Pervasive Health Technol. **9**, 1–18 (2023). https://doi.org/10.4108/eetpht.9.3533

19. Verma, K., et al.: Latest tools for data mining and machine learning. Int. J. Innovative Technol. Exploring Eng. **8**(9s), 1–6 (2019)

Early Detection of Diabetes Using ML Based Classification Algorithms

G. R. Ashisha[1], X. Anitha Mary[2]([✉]), Subrata Chowdhury[3], C. Karthik[4], Tanupriya Choudhury[5], and Ketan Kotecha[6]

[1] Electronics and Instrumentation Engineering, Karunya Institute of Technology and Science, Coimabtore, Tamil Nadu, India

[2] Robotics Engineering, Karunya Institute of Technology and Sciences, Coimbatore, Tamil Nadu, India
anithamary@karunya.edu

[3] Computer Science and Engineering, Sreenivasa Institute of Technology and Management Studies, Chittoor, Andhra Pradesh, India

[4] Robotics Engineering, Jyothi Enngineering College, Cheruthuruthy, Kerala, India
karthikc@jecc.ac.in

[5] CSE Department, Symbosis Institute of Technology, Symbiosis International (Deemed University), Pune 412115, Maharashtra, India
tanupriya.choudhury@sitpune.edu.in

[6] Symbiosis Centre for Applied Artificial Intelligence, Symbiosis Institute of Technology, Symbiosis International (Deemed University), Pune 412115, Maharashtra, India
Director@sitpune.edu.in

Abstract. This article introduces a method for classifying diabetes based on machine learning (ML) methods. In recent years, significant focus have been put onto increasing disease classification performance through the use of ML approaches. This paper outlines the use of five interpretable ML algorithms: Bagging classifier, Random Forest, AdaBoost, Multilayer Perceptron, and Restricted Boltzmann Machine. All the ML classifiers were trained and tested in a benchmark Biostat Diabetes Dataset using Python programming. Each technique's performance is evaluated to discover which has the finest accuracy, precision, recall, F1-score, specificity, and sensitivity. Experimental findings and assessment reveal that the Random Forest technique outperforms all other ML techniques by achieving 98% precision, 98% recall, 98% F1-score, 75% sensitivity, 96% specificity, and accuracy of 97.5%.

Keywords: Diabetes · Machine Learning · Biostat · Random Forest · Multilayer Perceptron

1 Introduction

Diabetes mellitus (DM), is the world's biggest chronic disease, with cases nearly doubling after 1980. It is a noncommunicable disease (NCD) that arises whenever the pancreas unable to make sufficient insulin or if the body fails to use the insulin that it has

D. Garg et al. (Eds.): IACC 2023, CCIS 2054, pp. 148–157, 2024.
https://doi.org/10.1007/978-3-031-56703-2_12

produced. Diabetes is believed to be caused by a combination of environmental and hereditary causes [1]. Diabetes associated risks include race, a family hertage of diabetes, ageing, obesity, a poor diet, lack of exercise, and tobacco. Furthermore, the failure to recognise diabetes earlier has been linked to the occurrence of chronic conditions such as kidney problems. In addition, the patient's pre-existing NCD's present an elevated danger because they are easily contracted and vulnerable to infectious conditions such as COVID-19 [2].

Classifying a person's risk and sensitivity to a persistent condition like diabetes is a difficult task. More than half of existing NCD instances are undetected, people experiencing little symptoms during the early stages of the disease, posing a significant difficulty in assuring early identification and diagnosis [3]. Diagnosing persistent diseases [18] earlier saves money on medical care and lower the chance of more severe health problems. In these situations, algorithms based on machine learning (ML) can be readily useful to help medicalcare professionals discover and diagnose NCDs earlier by offering predicting capabilities that enable more effective and rapdi decision-making.

This work aims to construct the ML based model [16, 17] for classifying diabetes. Using ML classifiers (RF, Bagging classifier, AdaBoost, MLP (Multilayer Perceptron), Restricted Boltzmann Machine), the model will figure out whether a particular individual has a risk for developing diabetes by considering multiple risk variables. To select the best effective classifier, these ML models were assessed using multiple approaches, such as accuracy, F1-score, specificity, recall, sensitivity, and recall. The top model of classification retrieved several key features that can be utilised to classify the seriousness of diabetes.

The Biostat Diabetes Dataset (BDD) is utilised for this work. BDD is formed of diabetes related data records and includes 10 attributes and one target attribute. It is a useful dataset for experimenting with classifier analysis techniques in ML. The methodology is outlined as below: perform pre-processing operations which includes handling missing and categorical data, and imputation. Preparing and selecting the features for the classification, and finally, the performance of the classifier using various metrics will be assessed further.

The following is an outline of the structure of this article: Sect. 2 presents a review of the existing methods, Sect. 3 presents the selected ML models, Sect. 4 has information on data preparation, and selecting features, and Sect. 5 contains the technique for examination and assessment of the dataset. Following that, Sect. 6 wraps up the work by discussing future research.

2 Literature Review

Biomedical data mining effectively and accurately identifies hidden patterns in datasets. We can then use these patterns for disease diagnosis and classification. Several ML models such as Decision Tree (DT), Support Vector Machine (SVM), Naïve Bayes (NB), and artifical neural network (ANN), have been used in numerous studies to predict diabetes. Komi proposed 5 different techniques to explore the diabetes prediction. Result of this research reveals that ANN performs well than Logistic regression (LR), SVM, Gaussian mixture model (GMM), and Elaboration likelihood mood (ELM) [4].

Rmanujam introduced a technique for the prediction of diabetes for rural people using a decision support approach [5]. Kumar developed the algorithm for the classification of diabetes using LR, NB, MLP, K-nearest neighbor (KNN), and CatBoost. The author compared all the algorithm's performance and observed that CatBoost model achieves better accuracy than other methods [6]. AI techniques are also proposed to classify and evaluate iris images to predict diabetes [7].

The following scientific articles concentrate on the use of different methods for data mining to clinical datasets. Rahmat developed a model for classification of diabetic issues in female subjects. This is built on a combination of deep learning and SVM. PIDD (Pima Indian Diabetes Dataset) was obtained from the UCI data repository. The findings of the experiment reveal that classification are high. It may be regarded as a useful technique to diagnose patients with diabtes [8].

The suggested technique employs neural networks based diabetes classification. Research results indicate that the suggested model can be utilised to acquire high accuracy [9]. Porter and Green demonstrated a strategy for identifying diabetes patients in massive healthcare datasets. People with diabetes are divided into different groups using this approach. Data segmentation and methods of transformation are used to enhance quality of data [10].

Even though ML are pervasive in the sectors of healthcare, their real biomedical application rate is quite low mainly due to an absence of an understanding of these sophisticated models. According to the existing research, this study selects five classifier algorithms, RF, Bagging Classifier, AdaBoost, MLP, and Restricted Boltzmann Machine, to classify the BDD dataset. Unlike previous research, the goal of this research is to use comprehensible ML algorithms to render our approach simple and accessible to users in terms of the way we decide which features are significant and the way the selection of features influences the predicted results.

3 The Selected ML Models

3.1 Random Forest

RF is a denotation of a DT and is made of several decision trees, every single one of which generates certain kinds of prediction outcomes. The group of categories with the highest votes in the RF plays a major role to the ultimate predicted result of the RF classifier. The main contributor to RF classifier's performance is that the DT's in the RF are essentially irrelevant to one another, guaranteeing that the choices they take as a group are more effective than the decisions they generate individually [7, 11].

RF uses a basic and effective core principle for classifying the group. The relationship among DT is essential to the achievement of the method. In RF, even when the prediction outputs of many DT's are incorrect, while the prediction outputs of majority of remaining DT's are accurate, these DT's will ultimately achieve the right prediction output. RF classifier performs effectively because a large number of unrelated methods that worl together outperform every single model.

3.2 Bagging Classifier

Bagging classifier is an ensemble technique that includes building multiple DT's on randomly picked portions of training data with replacement. Each DT tries to predict things on its own. The final result of the Bagging classifier is determined by combining the predictions of all DT's using classification and regression techniques. Bagging is extremely parallelizable, which makes it highly effective in computing, particularly for massive datasets [12].

Bagging's ability to minimise overfitting is one of its key advantages. It builds a more generalised and less susceptible to noise model by training numerous DT models on distinct datasets and merging the outcomes they predict. Bagging classifier is useful for handling datasets with imbalances in which one class exceeds the others since it can balance the influence of various classes.

3.3 AdaBoost

Adaptive Boosting is a prominent ML technique. It was created to increase the performance of weak DT models and to combine their results to build an effective prediction model. Every data point in AdaBoost is given a weight. At first, all data points have the same weight. The weights of incorrectly classified data points are boosted after every phase of training a weak DT, then concentrating the next weak DT on the instances that the prior ones considered challenging. [13].

This automatically highlights data points that are challenging to appropriately classify. The final output of the AdaBoost classifier is obtained by adding the majority vote of all weak DT's. This classifier is a popular ML ensemble approach, known for its capacity to improve the accuracy of weak DT's and generate strong, reliable models.

3.4 Multi-Layer Perceptron

Multi-Layer Perceptron (MLP) is a kind of ANN architecture used in ML and Deep Learning (DL). It is a feedforward neural network made up of numerous layers of perceptrons. Artificial neurons in this model helps to handle challenging relationships in the dataset. Training of MLP is based on the backpropagation technique, in which the error of predicted value and the actual value is iteratively reduced by altering the weights [14].

MLP can learn useful features from dataset automatically, minimising the requirement for manually developing features and enabling the algorithm to adapt to the dataset's features. MLP have attained innovative performance in numerous ML benchmarks, particularly when combines with advanced approaches such as normalization, dropping, and regularization.

3.5 Restricted Boltzmann Machine

A Restricted Boltzmann Machine (RBM) ia a type of ANN. Which are used for learning the datasets. RBM technique contains two different layers, namely: a hidden and a visible layer. Every node in one layer is related with every node in the other layer but inter layer connections are not built in RBM. The hidden layer contains significant features of the input data [15].

RBM uses,Contrastive Divergence (CD) process for training the dataset. RBM model is capable of generating samples for both the visible and hidden units. RBM models can create new samples that resemble the training dataset and this will helpful for data generation. Hence the RBM model is also known as generative models.

4 Proposed Methodology

4.1 Dataset Discussion

Eventhough there are now elaborate, more sophisticated diabetes datasets, Biostat Diabetes Dataset (BDD) is one of the benchmarking dataset for diabetes classification. Many ML methods have been used to generate diabetes classification model based on the diabetes dataset.

In this study, our aim is to analyze the BDD with five different ML algorithms efficiently. BDD has 403 healthcare data records with stabilized glucose, total cholestoral, gycosylated hemoglobin, gender, age, location, waist, weight, hip, frame, height, systolic blood pressure1 (SBP1), diastolic blood pressure1 (DBP1), systolic blood pressure2 (SBP1), diastolic blood pressure2 (DBP2), high density lipoprotein, post prandial time when laboraties were drawn, and cholesterol HDL ratio as features. Scatterplot of BDD dataset is shown in the Fig. 1.

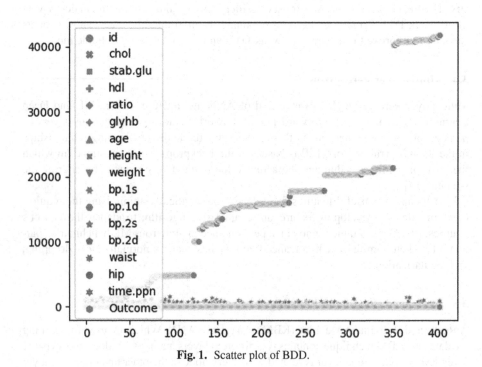

Fig. 1. Scatter plot of BDD.

4.2 Data Preprocessing

Data preprocessing is a crucial step in ML that includes cleaning and transforming dataset into a suitable form to train the models. The accuracy and effectivesness of ML techniques are heavily influenced by the quality of data used. At first all the missing data from the diabetes dataset was eliminated. Then the attribute gender is converted to "1" and "0" from "male" and "female". Effective data preprocessing aids in the development of more accuracte and resilient models, improves training model efficacy.

4.3 Feature Selection

Manual selection of features involves assessing the significance of every attribute and determining which are most informative or significant for the ML model. The idea is to keep the most important features while removing those that are superfluous or repititive. This method requires a thorough understanding of the data, the problem domain, and the possible effect of every attribute on the efficiency of the model. Most irrelevant features from BDD like post prandial time, ID, location, SBP2, and DBP2 has been eliminated.

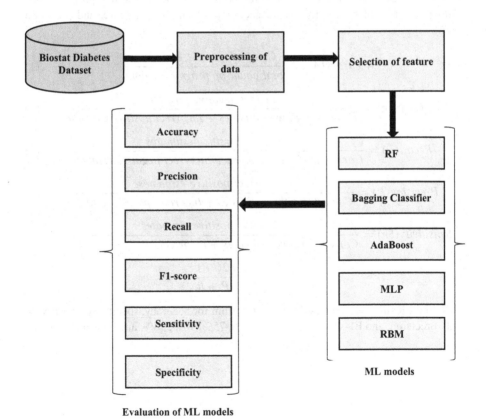

Fig. 2. Proposed model.

Then, two more features like BMI, and waist hip ratio was generated from the data of BDD dataset.

After the feature selection techniques, dataset splitting is introduced in the model and the ratio choosen for splitting the data is 80:20 with training dataset 80% and testing dataset 20%. Then 5 ML models (RF, Bagging classifier, AdaBoost, MLP, and RBM) were proposed (Fig. 2) in the generated new BDD dataset to test the model.

5 Results and Discussion

The analysis of BDD using RF, Bagging classifier, AdaBoost, MLP, and RBM techniques are conducted in this research. To measure the performance of all the ML models, various performance metrics were taken into the account.

From the Table 1, it was observed that RF achieves better accuracy than all other four ML models. In this work, remaining classifiers like bagging classifier, AdaBoost classifier, MLP, and RBM classifiers are also gives good results than all the existing work. The proposed ML models are also evaluation using specificity, sensitivity, recall, F1-score, and precision. Figure 3 shows the performance of all the five proposed ML methods in terms of specificity, recall, accuracy, sensitivity, F1-score, and precision (1)–(6).

$$Accuracy(A) = \frac{Count\ of\ correct\ estimates}{Total\ count\ of\ prognostications} \tag{1}$$

$$Specificity(Sp) = \frac{Correct\ negative\ prediction}{Correct\ negative\ estimates + Incorrect\ positive\ estimates} \tag{2}$$

$$Recall(R) = \frac{Correct\ positive\ estimates}{Correct\ positive\ estimates + Incorrect\ negative\ estimates} \tag{3}$$

$$Precision(P) = \frac{Correct\ positive\ estimates}{Correct\ positive\ estimates + Incorrect\ positive\ estimates} \tag{4}$$

$$Sensitivity(Sn) = \frac{Correct\ positive\ estimates}{Correct\ positive\ estimates + Incorrect\ negative\ estimates} \tag{5}$$

$$F1-score = \frac{2(PR)}{P+R} \tag{6}$$

The best results was obtained by RF algorithm for accuracy, specificity, sensitivity, recall, precision, and F1-score as 97.5%, 100%, 75%, 98%, 98%, and 98% respectively.

Table 1. Performance of various ML models.

ML algorithm	Accuracy (%)	Precision (%)	Recall (%)	F1-score (%)	Sensitivity (%)	Specificity (%)
RF	**97.5**	**98**	**98**	**98**	**75**	**96**
Bagging Classifier	96.3	98	98	98	98	86
AdaBoost Classifier	95.1	95	95	95	95	82
MLP	96.5	98	98	98	98	60
RBM	90.1	81	90	90	85	100

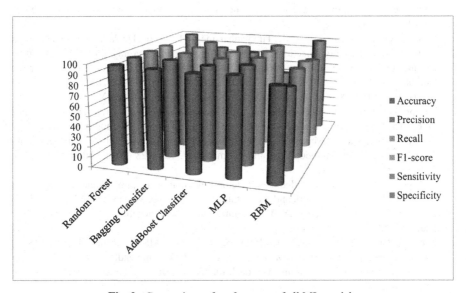

Fig. 3. Comparison of perfomance of all ML models.

6 Conclusion and Future Work

In conclusion, the proposed method, early detection of diabetes using ML based classification algorithms intended to design a method that can precisely classify the diabetes disease. The suggested model focuses on enhancing the performance of the diabetes classification. This work introduced five ML models to enhance the classification accuracy in an organized manner. Experiments are carried out on the BDD diabetes dataset. Performance evaluation of the model is also done to find the best classifier. Evaluation of the models show that the RF outperforms other ML models and it demonstrate that RF is one of the more effective approaches for diabetes classification. The findings of the work have significant impacts on medical care, as early identification of diabetes can enhance the health of the patient and minimize the medical costs. The accuracy achieved by our suggested model is 97.5% and this is higher than existing techniques. Our future study will include designing innovative feature selection algorithms and analysing the diabetes dataset, development of new validation technique to validate the diabetes classification and to design an automated system to enhance the diabetes classification.

References

1. World Health Organization, Global report on diabetes (2023)
2. World Health Organization, Global action plan for the prevention and control of non communicable diseases (2020)
3. Larabi-Marie-Sainte, S., Aburahmah, L., Almohaini, R., Saba, T.: Current techniques for diabetes prediction: Review and case study. App. Sci. **9**(21), 4604 (2019)
4. Komi, M., Li, J., Zhai, Y., Xianguo, Z.:Application of data mining methods in diabetes prediction. In: 2nd International Conference on Image, Vision and Computing, ICIVC, pp. 1006–1010 (2017)
5. Ramanujam, E., Chandrakumar, T., Thivyadharsine, K.T, Varsha, D.: A multilingual decision support system for early detection of diabetes using machine learning approach: case study for rural Indian people. In: Proceedings - 2020 5th International Conference on Research in Computational Intelligence and Communication Networks, pp. 17–21 (2017)
6. Kumar, P, S, Anisha Kumari, K, Mohapatra, S, Naik, B, Nayak, J, Mishra, M.:CatBoost ensemble approach for diabetes risk prediction at early stages. 1st Odisha International Conference on Electrical Power Engineering, Communication and Computing Technology (2021)
7. Samant, P., Agarwal, R.: Machine learning techniques for medical diagnosis of diabetes using iris images. Comput. Methods Programs Biomed. **157**, 121–128 (2018). https://doi.org/10.1016/j.cmpb.2018.01.004
8. Zolfaghari, R.: Diagnosis of diabetes in female population of pima indian heritage with ensemble of BP neural network and SVM. Int. J. Comput. Eng. Manag. **157**, 121–128 (2018)
9. Sapna, M., Phil, S., Tamilarasi, A.: Data mining fuzzy neural genetic algorithm in predicting Diabetes (2008)
10. Porter, T, Green, B.: Association for Information Systems AIS Electronic Library (AISeL) Identifying Diabetic Patients: A Data Mining Approach Recommended Citation Identifying Diabetic Patients: A Data Mining Approach Identifying Diabetic Patients: A Data Mining Approach (2009)
11. Seifert, S.: Application of random forest based approaches to surface-enhanced Raman scattering data. Sci. Rep. **10**(1), 5436 (2020). https://doi.org/10.1038/s41598-020-62338-8
12. Chandramouli, A., Hyma, V.R., Tanmayi, P.S., Santoshi, T.G., Priyanka, B.: Diabetes prediction using hybrid bagging classifier. Entertainment Comput. **47**, 100593 (2023)
13. Ramakrishna, M.T., Venkatesan, V.K., Izonin, I., Havryliuk, M., Bhat, C.R.: Homogeneous adaboost ensemble machine learning algorithms with reduced entropy on balanced data. Entropy **25**(2), 245 (2023)
14. Poria, N., Jaiswal, A.: Empirical analysis of diabetes prediction using machine learning techniques. In: Unhelker, B., Pandey, H.M., Raj, G. (eds.) Applications of Artificial Intelligence and Machine Learning: Select Proceedings of ICAAAIML 2021, pp. 391–401. Springer Nature Singapore, Singapore (2022). https://doi.org/10.1007/978-981-19-4831-2_32
15. Thumilvannan, S., Balamanigandan, R.: Correlated feature-based diabetes and heart disease risk-level classification in IoT environment using PLD-SSL-RBM. J. Intell. Fuzzy Syst. **45**, 10873–10886 (2011)

16. Kumar, V., et al., "Intelligent classification of lung & oral cancer through diverse data mining algorithms. In: 2016 International Conference on Micro-Electronics and Telecommunication Engineering (ICMETE), Ghaziabad, India, pp. 133–138 (2016). https://doi.org/10.1109/ICM ETE.2016.24

17. Nigam, D., et al.: An innovative smart soft computing methodology towards disease (cancer, heart disease, arthritis) detection in an earlier stage and in a smarter way. Int. J. Comput. Sci. Mob. Comput. **3**(4), 368–388 (2014)

18. Salunkhe, S., et al.: Classification of alzheimer's disease patients using texture analysis and machine learning. Appl. Syst. Innov. **4**, 49 (2021). https://doi.org/10.3390/asi4030049

Prediction of Abnormality Using IoT and Machine Learning

B. Kowsalya[1]($\boxtimes$) (ID), D. R. Keerthana Prashanthi[1] (ID), S. Vigneshwaran[2] (ID), and P. Poornima[1] (ID)

[1] Department of Biomedical Engineering, Dr. NGP Institute of Technology, Coimbatore, India
kowsalyabalachandran@gmail.com
[2] Department of Biomedical Engineering, Sri Ramakrishna Engineering College, Coimbatore, India

Abstract. Vital signs indicators like temperature, heart rate, and oxygen saturation should be examined periodically, as these are the root cause of any medical diagnosis. Any deviations from the normal range indicate that the person needs an immediate medical check-up and is on the edge of facing some medical issues later. Thus, monitoring these vitals periodically can help patients from the risk of mortality. The goal of this research is to forecast a person's abnormality using machine learning and IoT (Internet of Things) algorithms for decisiveness. The prototype was built using three sensors, MAX30100 sensor (for SpO2), REES52 heartbeat sensor, and LM35 temperature sensor along with Arduino UNO, and ESP 8266. The bio signal data from these sensors were collected using Arduino UNO, stored in a local PC, and uploaded to the cloud using API protocol in Thingspeak (IoT platform). These data were also retrievable for further diagnosis. Support vector machine (SVM), a machine learning method, is used to predict if a patient is abnormal or not. SVM learns the threshold ranges for each parameter as well as the associated goal value from the datasets.

Keywords: Abnormality · Monitoring · IoT · Machine Learning · Heart Rate · Temperature · SpO2 · SVM

1 Introduction

In medical research and investigations, vital sign measures such as temperature, heart rate, and oxygen saturation play a significant role. Most of the current research focuses on the simple technique that can screen these vitals periodically whenever needed. According to recent statistics, the need for continuous monitoring of vital parameters is found to be more abundant, where it started peaking in 2018 [Leenen et al., (2021)]. Among various vital parameters, the important body assessment parameters were temperature, heartbeat, and oxygen saturation provided much more awareness for immediate medical diagnosis. The evaluation of wireless communication techniques creates room for non-invasive accurate screening without any interruption. Most of the technologies were created to enable continuous monitoring in convenient and affordable ways. One such

© The Author(s), under exclusive license to Springer Nature Switzerland AG 2024
D. Garg et al. (Eds.): IACC 2023, CCIS 2054, pp. 158–170, 2024.
https://doi.org/10.1007/978-3-031-56703-2_13

method is the Internet of Things (IoT), also known as IoMT (Internet of Medical Things), in medical applications. The tracking of objects via codes is the vision of the Internet of Things. It is computer- and communication-based. The multiple IoT architecture levels are depicted (see Fig. 1). It is divided into four layers: the sensor layer, the network layer, the data pre-processing layer, and the application layer. The sensing layer helps in getting data from different sources. Network layer helps in interfacing the communication between the devices that are connected with IoT using protocols like IPV6, Data Distribution Service (DDS). Data preprocessing techniques use data management platforms, data analytics and machine learning algorithms for preprocessing. It is the centre for storing raw data into the device. Application layer uses visualisation tools for displaying the gathered data and helps the user for interpretation. Its functionality structure involves collecting data, collecting, and transferring data and analysing data [Singla (2021)]. The main advantage of using IoT in healthcare involves faster data transfer, continuous monitoring, and long- lasting data storage.

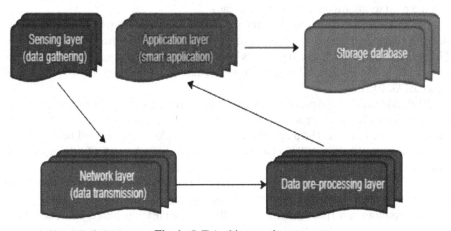

Fig. 1. IoT Architecture layer

To extract the key features from the raw data and perform the necessary classification or estimation, machine learning models use these strategies. They were more reliable, and robustness in making decisions [Ozechi (2021).

This paper has six sections. The [1] section explains generally the importance of vitals estimation, its significance in current world scenarios, and some important context of the Internet of Things (IoT). The [2] section briefs the existing work that motivates to development of vitals estimation using current trend technologies. Sections [3] and [4] describe classifying the patient as normal and abnormal using the vitals dataset acquired from appropriate sensors, which is then stored in the cloud using one of the IoT platforms called Thingspeak. The final two sections [5] and [6] conclude the paperwork and suggestions for future work.

The objective of this work is to alert the person for immediate medical diagnosis if he/she falls in the abnormal category. SVM (Support Vector Machine), a machine learning algorithm, was used to determine the decisiveness.

2 Literature Review

Alsareii S. A. et al. (2022) conducted a pilot study on the monitoring of post-surgery patients using machine learning and the Internet of Things. The objective of this study, which involved both critical and non-critical students, was to create a novel Internet of Things framework that would provide ultra-reliable, low-latency connections to monitor post-surgery patients. The effort put into the article's post-surgery patients made it incomparable to other prior IoT investigations. Real-world implementation and the analysis using ML are undone which are also other shortcomings of the study.

Balakrishnan et al. (2022) designed a smart E-Healthcare system that makes use of Radio Frequency Identification (RFID), a Brainsense headband, a wireless sensor network, smartphones, and an IoT platform for communication. An electromagnetic field was used to automatically link this system and RFID to the patient's wristband, allowing for the tracking of the patient's condition. The study's limitations include noisy data, the possibility of using a time-distributed spatiotemporal feature learning approach, and the need to improve the system's accuracy.

In a non-invasive study, Arulananth and Shilpa (2017) developed a fingertip pulse-detecting device with a microcontroller for processing to monitor heartbeats. The Photo Plethysmo Graphy (PPG) theory serves as the foundation for this system. The work attains healthcare quality and breadth. Rather it can also be driven out for various vital signs, ECG, EEG etc.

Patil and Garge (2018) proposed a Patient Monitoring System, an independent system that automatically records patients' vital signs for clinicians who can access the data through mobile devices. The data obtained from a couple of sensors will be directed to the microcontroller which will be connected with an Android device for further approach. The drawback of this work was, that it doesn't progress with real-time data.

Using RTOS, Gunalanans and Satheesh (2014) developed a wireless patient body monitoring system. It utilizes a variety of sensor systems, controllers, etc., along with a zig-bee communicative platform to continually monitor the temperature, ECG, heartbeat, coma recovery, and saline level indication. Although it gives promising results from conventional techniques, data accessibility is an issue over here.

The Global System for Mobile Communication (GSM) will be used to transmit the physiological values to the Guardian's mobile device in Surekha et al. 's (2018) proposed Patient Monitoring System using IoT. This system uses multiple sensors to assess the temperature, heart rate, ECG, eye blink, and blood pressure. Here, the Internet of Things (IoT) can be used as a server for machine-to-machine communication. Any individual can use a laptop, tablet, or smartphone to check on a patient's health status from anywhere in the globe by utilizing their IP address. Acquisition of data is a way long procedure.

Thus, the existing work discussed above explains the healthcare vitals estimation using various technology aspects like RFID, Zigbee as well as IoT. However, decision-making using machine learning algorithms plays a trend. It also helps physicians to have quick reviews of the patient's history and current situation. By adding this literature as pioneers, we have designed a Patient Monitoring System that predicts and classifies the normal and abnormal individuals based on their vital signs.

3 Methodology

In the proposed approach, we concentrated on vital parameters of an individual like Temperature, SpO2, and Heart Rate that were extracted from various sensors that are connected to the ARDUINO board which processes various programming functions to execute the acquired dataset. The workflow carried out in the project has been sketched (see Fig. 2).

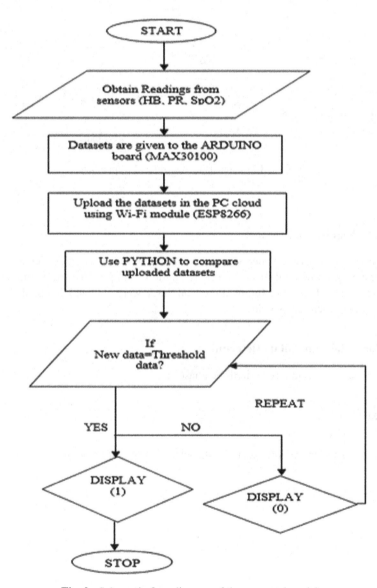

Fig. 2. Schematic flow diagram of the proposed model

Prediction and classification of a person's vital signs using the IoT platform Things-peak and the machine learning classifier Support Vector Machine (SVM). NUMPY (standard library data), which includes multidimensional array objects and a selection of functions for handling arrays, is already installed in Python.

Some popular machine learning methods utilised in real-time IoT systems are shown (see Fig. 3). [Source: Courtesy of Bian, J. (2022)].

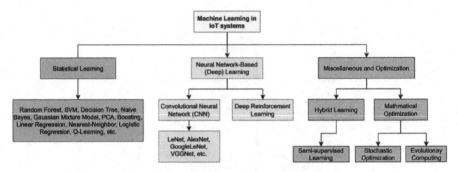

Fig. 3. IoT systems using real-time ML approaches

3.1 Data Acquisition Protocol

20 healthy people between the ages of vicenarian and tricenarian participated in the study, and each participant received an intervention lasting around three minutes. For every individual, Heart rate, Temperature, and SpO2 were obtained and then processed for further classification as below.

3.2 Block Diagram and its Description

The study has been categorized in three phases as,

Data collection phase
Data upload phase
Decision-making phase

(See Fig. 4.) shown below illustrates the visual interpretation of the above- mentioned phase.

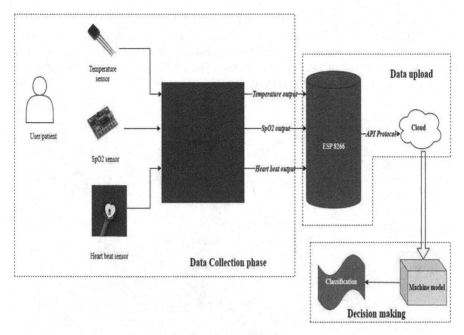

Fig. 4. Block diagram of the study

3.3 Data Collection Phase

In the data collection phase, the components and desired output were discussed. For measuring the parameters like temperature, oxygen saturation level, and heartbeat, sensors like LM35, SpO2, and REES52 were used respectively. The sensors mentioned above were pre-designed which has a predefined algorithm to measure the desired readings.

Temperature Sensor: The LM35 is a temperature sensor with an analog output that can monitor temperatures between around −550 °C and 1500 °C. It is a three-terminal IC that does not require any calibration circuitry. Its principle is as the output voltage increases then temperature increases, e.g: 250 mV denotes 250 °C.

SpO2 Sensor: Max 30100 sensor is an ultra-low power optical sensor that has an LED driver with red and IR along with a photodetector. It's hardware setup has an analog signal processing unit which lowers the noise and gives desired pulse oximetry readings. It operates at 1.8 V and 3.3 V.

Heart Rate Sensor: The REES52 is an LED-based sensor that can measure heart rate at 3.3V and 5V power supplies. The sensor has a circuitry met for noise cancellation and amplification.

The Atmega328P microcontroller used in the Arduino UNO is an open-source microcontroller board with 14 digital I/O pins and 6 analog I/O pins. The board has a preprogrammed bootloader that allows for uploading the codes. It has 6 pins for Pulse Width Modulation (PWM) output and it can support UART, I2C, and SPI communications. Thus, it is a 28-pin DIP (Dual-In-package).

The index finger will be used as the subject spot to acquire the data. The Arduino IDE is the platform for the execution of the code and obtaining the result. The user/patient was asked to place a finger in the respective sensor and codes will be executed and the result is monitored in a serial monitor. (See Fig. 5) shows the circuitry setup of the sensors and Wi-Fi module to the microcontroller.

Fig. 5. Circuitry setup

Data Upload Phase ESP8266 developed by Expressif Systems, is a low-cost Wi-Fi microchip with built-in TCP/IP network software and sometimes can be a microcontroller that has a 32-bit Tensilica processor with high durability with power-saving architecture. The acquired output data has been uploaded to the cloud using the Thingspeak IoT environment and API protocol.

Decision-Making Phase Support vector machine is a highly efficient machine learning tool that can be used for estimation and classification, mostly they are used for classification problems. They can provide highly accurate results in less iterations. The classification was based on the hyperplane, which is based on the regression equation, mentioned in Eq. 1.

$$y = mx + c \tag{1}$$

where,

y is the equation of the hyperplane. m is the slope of the line
x is the datapoint
c is the y-intercept at (0, c)

The parameters like hyperplane, margins, and support vectors were important for analysing the data provided. The margin is the distance from the hyperplane and the data points that are nearest to the hyperplane, the data points are called support vectors. If the distance between the support vector and the point is high then it is a hard margin, otherwise a soft margin. The SVM decides whether the data points lie on the right side or left side of the hyperplane using the dot product given by Eq. 2.

$$a.b = ab\cos \Theta \tag{2}$$

where a is a data point to find its position, b is a perpendicular vector to it.

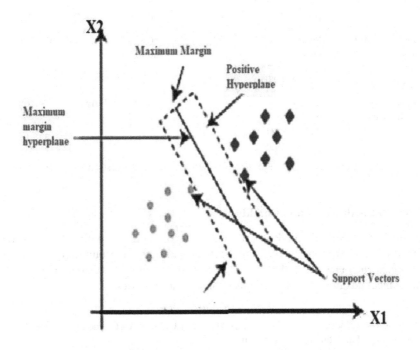

Fig. 6. Support Vector Machine Graph and its parameters

(See Fig. 6) that shows the graph that explains the SVM and its parameters.

There are two classification methods: linear and nonlinear. The linear classification used in 2D model classification and kernel method is for 3D model classification.

Since we are using 2D data for our investigation, linear classification is preferred.

4   Result and Discussion

From the above methodology, the result obtained from the microcontroller is uploaded to the IoT cloud using API protocol and then is retrieved using its Thingspeak platform. Comparing the retrieved data with the standard library datasets. The prediction of normal and abnormal was based on the criteria mentioned in Tables 1 and 2 with vicenarian age criteria. Gender discrimination is shown in Column A: 1- > Male, 0- > Female subjects.

4.1 Patient with Normal

Individuals without any medical history and between the age group of vicenarian and tricenarian were scrutinized. The output with the value 1 at column E indicates the normal condition of the subject on comparing their vitals with standard libraries.

Table 1. Range values considered for normal criteria. Column A – Gender, B – Blood Pressure, C – SPO2, D – Heart Rate, E – target value.

A	B	C	D	E
1-Male (Age limit: 22 to 40 years)	Ideal Blood pressure: 90/60 mmHg; 120/80 mmHg	SpO2: > 95%	Heart rate: Between 60 to 100	0 – Normal
0-Female (Age limit: 22 to 40 years)	Ideal Blood pressure: 90/60 mmHg; 120/80 mmHg	SpO2: > 95%	Heart rate: Between 60 to 100	0 – Normal

* Note: The age group selected for this study was not under any suggestions.

4.2 Patient with Abnormal Condition

Individuals with Arrhythmia, Respiratory disorder, and persons with cold & and fever (temporary condition) were taken into account with the age group of vicenarian and tricenarian. The output with the value 0 in column E indicates the abnormal condition of the subject on comparing their vitals with standard libraries.

Table 2. Range values considered for abnormal criteria. Column A – Gender, B – Blood Pressure, C – SPO2, D – Heart Rate, E – target value.

A	B	C	D	E
1-Male (Age limit: 22 to 40 years)	Low blood pressure: < 90/60 mmHg High blood pressure: > 140/90 mmHg	SpO2: < 95% Abnormal	Heart rate: > 100 Abnormal	1- Abnormal
0-Female (Age limit: 22 to 40 years)	Low blood pressure: < 90/60 mmHg High blood pressure: > 140/90 mmHg	SpO2: < 95% Normal	Heart rate: > 100 Abnormal	1- Abnormal

* Note: The age group selected for this study was not under any suggestions.

4.3   Thingspeak

It is an IoT analytic platform service that gets a dataset from the microcontroller and represents that data in a graphical representation using its READ protocol. Using Wi-Fi, the data is uploaded to the PC with IOT. (see Fig. 7) gives the real- time input data input data obtained from the individual in a graphical format.

Fig. 7. Graphical representation of vital parameters

4.4   SVM Estimation

Retrieval of datasets from the cloud using Thingspeak WRITE protocol along with SVM Machine Learning algorithm. The data was collected at the baud rate of 9600 at a delay of 50 ms. The sampling rate was set as 500 m/s. Therefore, the obtained data has been fed as the input to the model by splitting it as test and train data. Since the split size is 0.3, 70% of the data was taken as training data, and the remaining 30% was considered for testing data. The parameter target was assumed to be y and Gender, SpO2, BP, and HR were considered as X. These data were trained and fit into the model using the syntax model.fit (X_train, y_train). This trained model has an accuracy of 90% which is found to be more reliable for prediction purposes. This model has been integrated into the IoT platform using an API key and.json file. Then the users were asked to feed their inputs like gender, age, SpO2, temperature, and Bpm acquired from the external sensors on the thingspeak page, where they can also visually see the real-time data once they fed their fingers into the sensors and they can know their health status as normal or abnormal. (See Fig. 8) represents the graphical representation of the support vector plot of acquired data.

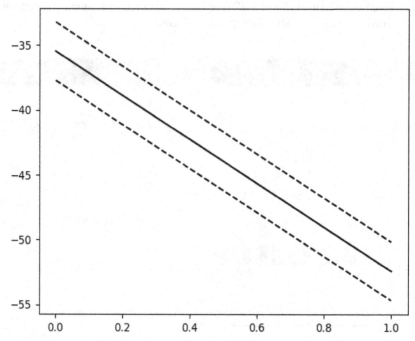

Slope: -16.93350052118497; Y-Intercept: [-35.48504284]; Margin: 2.2506259089246115

Fig. 8. Support Vector plot using the acquired data

5 Future Scope

This research has figured out a prototype for validating ML technology and its model on an IoT platform. 90% accuracy is a promising rate for a model fitting the dataset that is currently available, as shown by our model. ML model integration was therefore discovered to be a more accurate prediction method. Future medical interventions will rely heavily on progressively improved models with datasets that have been approved by medical ethics.

6 Conclusion

The work describes the importance of healthcare vitals estimation along with the application of IoT in data storage and retrieval. And also, regarding Machine learning algorithms that help in decision-making and alert the user/patient for instant health check-ups. The communication between the Arduino UNO and ESP8266 happened by setting the baud rate. The data in IoT (Thingspeak platform) was stored using API protocol. SVM was chosen for its high efficiency in prediction and decision-making, based on model training, the developed model has 90% accuracy which is acceptable for the study. Many physiological data can be stored in IoT platforms that can be assessed by doctors/physicians for understanding patient medical conditions and help in e-health aspects.

References

Leenen, J.P., et al.: Feasibility of continuous monitoring of vital signs in surgical patients on a general ward: an observational cohort study. BMJ Open 11(2), e042735 (2021)

Singla, A.: Application Layer in OSI Model. GeeksforGeeks (2021)

Ozechi, S.: Feature Engineering Techniques (2021)

Alsareii, S.A., et al.: Machine learning and internet of things enabled monitoring of post-surgery patients: a pilot study. Sensors 22(4), 1420 (2022)

Balakrishnan, S., Suresh Kumar, K., Ramanathan, L., Muthusundar, S.K.: IoT for health monitoring system based on machine learning algorithm. Wireless Pers. Commun. 124, 189–205 (2022)

Arulananth, T.S., Shilpa, B.: Fingertip based heart beat monitoring system using embedded systems. In: 2017 International conference of Electronics, Communication and Aerospace Technology (ICECA), vol. 2. IEEE (2017)

Patil, H.R., Garge, D.S.: Patient monitoring system. Int. J. Adv. Res. Sci. Eng. 7(03), 23–32 (2018)

Gunalanans, M.C., Satheesh, A.: Implementation of wireless patient body monitoring system using RTOS. Int. J. Eng. Res. Gen. Sci. 2(6), 202–208 (2014)

Surekha, Y., Akhil, N., Rajesh: Patient monitoring system using IOT. IJIRAE: Int. J. Innov. Res. Adv. Eng. 5, 176–182 (2018)

Bian, J., et al.: Machine learning in real-time internet of things (iot) systems: a survey. IEEE Internet Things J. 9(11), 8364–8386 (2022)

Menon, S.P., et al.: An intelligent diabetic patient tracking system based on machine learning for E-health applications. Sensors 23(6), 3004 (2023)

Arowolo, M.O., et al.: Machine learning-based IoT system for COVID-19 epidemics. Computing 105(4), 831–847 (2023)

Morita, P.P., Sahu, K.S., Oetomo, A.: Health monitoring using smart home technologies: scoping review. JMIR mHealth and uHealth 11, e37347 (2023)

Sonawani, S., Patil, K., Natarajan, P.: Biomedical signal processing for health monitoring applications: a review. Int. J. Appl. Syst. Stud. 10(1), 44–69 (2023)

Shaik, T., et al.: Remote patient monitoring using artificial intelligence: current state, applications, and challenges. WIREs Data Min. Knowl. Discovery 13(2), e1485 (2023)

Nancy, A.A., et al.: Iot-cloud-based smart healthcare monitoring system for heart disease prediction via deep learning. Electronics 11(15), 2292 (2022). https://doi.org/10.3390/electronics1115 2292

Bao, Y., Li, H.: Machine learning paradigm for structural health monitoring. Struct. Health Monit. 20(4), 1353–1372 (2021)

Valsalan, P., Baomar, T.A.B., Baabood, A.H.O.: IoT based health monitoring system. J. Crit. Rev. 7(4), 739–743 (2020)

Tamilselvi, V., et al.: IoT based health monitoring system. In: 2020 6th International Conference on Advanced Computing and Communication Systems (ICACCS). IEEE (2020)

Zhao, R., et al.: Deep learning and its applications to machine health monitoring. Mech. Syst. Signal Process. 115, 213–237 (2019)

Kaur, P., Kumar, R., Kumar, M.: A healthcare monitoring system using random forest and internet of things (IoT). Multimed. Tools Appl. **78**, 19905–19916 (2019)

Flah, M., et al.: Machine learning algorithms in civil structural health monitoring: a systematic review. Arch. Computat. Methods Eng. **28**(4), 2621–2643 (2021). https://doi.org/10.1007/s11 831-020-09471-9

Ullo, S.L., Sinha, G.R.: Advances in smart environment monitoring systems using IoT and sensors. Sensors **20**(11), 3113 (2020)

Azimi, M., Eslamlou, A., Pekcan, G.: Data-driven structural health monitoring and damage detection through deep learning: state-of-the-art review. Sensors **20**(10), 2778 (2020)

Tuli, S., et al.: HealthFog: an ensemble deep learning based smart healthcare system for automatic diagnosis of heart diseases in integrated IoT and fog computing environments. Future Gener. Comput. Syst. **104**, 187–200 (2020)

Ghazal, T.M., et al.: IoT for smart cities: machine learning approaches in smart healthcare—A review. Future Internet **13**(8), 218 (2021)

Kumar, R., Pallikonda Rajasekaran, M.: An IoT based patient monitoring system using raspberry Pi. In: 2016 International Conference on Computing Technologies and Intelligent Data Engineering (ICCTIDE'16). IEEE (2016)

Ahmed, M.U., et al.: An overview on the internet of things for health monitoring systems. Internet of Things. IoT Infrastructures: Second International Summit, IoT 360° 2015, Rome, Italy, October 27–29, 2015, Revised Selected Papers, Part I, pp. 429–436 (2016)

Ani, R., et al.: Iot based patient monitoring and diagnostic prediction tool using ensemble classifier. In: 2017 International Conference on Advances in Computing, Communications and Informatics (ICACCI). IEEE (2017)

Sarmah, S.S.: An efficient IoT-based patient monitoring and heart disease prediction system using deep learning modified neural network. IEEE Access **8**, 135784–135797 (2020)

Anisyah, U.: Sistem pemantauan detak jantung dan saturasi oksigen (SPO2) menggunakan sensor MAX30100 dengan aplikasi Telegram berbasis internet of things (2022)

Nivedan, V., Kannusamy, R.: Weather monitoring system using IoT with Arduino Ethernet Shield. Int. J. Res. Appl. Sci. Eng. Technol. **7**(1), 2321–9653 (2019)

Nallakaruppan, M.K., Senthil Kumaran, U.: IoT based machine learning techniques for climate predictive analysis. Int. J. Recent Technol. Eng. **5**, 171–175 (2019)

Shukla, P.M., Deshmukh, S.S., Aishwarya, N., Anand, D.M.: Tipre3 Patior Salus Reporting System

Anbumani, S., et al.: An intelligent patient tele-monitoring system using android technology. Int. J. Res. Eng. Technol. **4**(02), 477–482 (2015)

Silva, B.M.C., et al.: Mobile-health: a review of current state in 2015. J. Biomed. Inform. **56**, 265–272 (2015)

Modi, D., et al.: Android based patient monitoring system. Int. J. Technol. Res. Eng. **1**(9) (2014)

Da, X., Li, W.H., Li, S.: Internet of things in industries: a survey. IEEE Trans. Ind. Inform. **10**(4), 2233–2243 (2014)

Jain, N.P., Preeti, N.J., Trupti, P.A.: An embedded, GSM based, multiparameter, realtime patient monitoring system and control—An implementation for ICU patients. In: 2012 World Congress on Information and Communication Technologies. IEEE (2012)

Sundaram, P.: Patient monitoring system using android technology. Int. J. Comput. Sci. Mob. Comput. **2**(5), 191–201 (2013)

Detection of Cardiovascular Diseases Using Machine Learning Approach

Amol Dhumane[1]([⊠]) ⓘ, Shwetambari Chiwhane[1] ⓘ, Mubin Tamboli[2] ⓘ,
Srinivas Ambala[2] ⓘ, Pooja Bagane[1] ⓘ, and Vishal Meshram[3] ⓘ

[1] Symbiosis Institute of Technology, Affiliated to Symbiosis International University, Pune,
India
amol.dhumane@sitpune.edu.in
[2] Pimpri Chinchwad College of Engineering, Pune, India
[3] Vishwakarma Institute of Information Technology, Pune, India

Abstract. Various advanced computing techniques and capabilities have the deep impact in the field of medical sciences, especially in identifying human heart diseases. So that identifying heart related diseases accurately and in time may save the patients life's and increases the chances of survival. However, manual approaches for identifying heart disease suffer from biases and variations between examiners. We can use various machine learning algorithms to overcome these issues in manual approaches These ML algorithms provide more accurate and efficient tools for identifying and analysing the patients with heart disease.

To explore the potential of machine learning algorithms, the recommended study employed various techniques to identify and predict human heart disease using a comprehensive heart disease dataset. Sensitivity, specificity, F-measure and accuracy in classification can be used to examine the performance. We have used eight machine learning classifiers such as Ada boost, Extreme Gradient Boosting including Decision Tree, Logistic Regression, Linear Discriminate Analysis, Random Forest, Naïve Bayes, Support Vector Machine. The results demonstrated notable improvements in the prediction classifiers' accuracy. This underscores the efficiency of machine learning algorithms in finding and predicting human heart disease. This research achieved improved accuracy heart disease prediction using the machine learning technique. Multiple classifiers were employed to classify heart disease prediction, with SVM achieving an accuracy of 95.88%.

1 Introduction

Deep learning and advanced machine learning algorithms are extensively used to address hard challenges in several domains like agriculture, healthcare, security, and more [10–18]. Cardiovascular diseases talk about to a collection of illnesses that affect the blood vessels and heart. These diseases causes tremendous death worldwide. CVDs encompass various situation, containing coronary artery disease, heart failure, stroke, arrhythmias, and heart valve problems.

The hidden causes of cardiovascular diseases are multifactorial, entailing a mixture of genetic, environmental, and lifestyle factors. Risk influences like high cholesterol levels,

D. Garg et al. (Eds.): IACC 2023, CCIS 2054, pp. 171–179, 2024.
https://doi.org/10.1007/978-3-031-56703-2_14

obesity, sedentary lifestyle, smoking, diabetes as well as not healthy diet contribute to the development of CVDs [7].

Cardiovascular disorders have multiple hidden causes that include a combination of hereditary, environmental, and lifestyle variables. The risk factors include high cholesterol, high blood pressure, obesity, smoking, diabetes, a sedentary lifestyle, and not healthy diet [8–10].

The impact of cardiovascular diseases extends beyond individual health, affecting families, communities, and healthcare systems. They can lead to severe complications, disability, reduced quality of life, and increased healthcare costs [7].

Cardiovascular disease symptoms can differ based on the particular ailment. Chest pain or discomfort, palpitations, exhaustion, lightheadedness, and edema in the limbs are typical symptoms. On the other hand, some people may have unusual or silent symptoms, which makes early identification and detection difficult.

One of the most important things in the fight against cardiovascular illnesses is prevention. The main goals of public health initiatives are to control risk factors, promote healthy lifestyles, increase awareness, and carry out population-based interventions. In conclusion, a major worldwide health concern is cardiovascular illnesses. They have a significant effect on people as well as society, highlighting the significance of management techniques, early detection, and prevention.

Our study presents several significant contributions and presents a machine learning classifier for the prediction of cardiovascular disease 1.1 Refinement and standardization of the datasets: 1.2 GridSearchCV for hyperparameter optimization 1.3 Increased accuracy through hyperparameter tuning 1.4 SVM classifier accuracy at the cutting edge.

Support Vector Machine (SVM), our suggested classifier, outperforms previous methods in terms of accuracy. By fine-tuning the hyperparameters of Support Vector Machines (SVM), an algorithm with immense strength and reputation for handling intricate classification tasks, we can attain exceptional results in the prediction of cardiovascular disease.

The remainder of the paper is organized as follows: A thorough analysis of machine learning methods already in use that are pertinent to the research topic is provided in Sect. 2's Literature Review. The proposed methodology for the study is outlined in Sect. 3. It describes the exact methodology or framework that will be applied to carry out the study, including the gathering of data, preprocessing, choosing a model, training, and assessment. Data Collection process is discussed in Sect. 3. It explains how the necessary data for the study will be gathered, including the sources, methods, and criteria for selecting the data. Experimental Results are stated in Sect. 4 by applying the proposed methodology to the collected data. It includes quantitative or qualitative findings, statistical analyses, and visual representations of the results. This section provides a clear understanding of the outcomes and their implications for the research. Section 5 states Conclusion and summarizes the key findings and contributions.

2 Literature Review

The primary technique employed by physicians for differentiating between ordinary and strange cardiac sounds is auscultation, wherein they listen to the heart sounds using stethoscopes. This method is used to diagnose heart diseases but, there are many limitations to auscultation. The accurate interpretation and classification of different heart sounds depend on the skills and experience of the doctors, which are acquired through extensive training and examinations. It can be a time-consuming process that necessitates years of practice to develop expertise in identifying specific heart conditions Machine learning and artificial intelligence offer opportunities to enhance traditional diagnostic approaches.

Machine learning algorithms presented by researchers are used to automate and improve heart disease diagnosis more accessible and efficient [1–10]. Physician feeds information such as patient information, heart sounds, and medical imaging, to machine learning models for quick and accurate diagnosis.

Various machine learning algorithms were proposed in recent years for predicting cardiovascular diseases. Machine learning algorithms also help to predict risk and diagnose different cardiovascular conditions. Following is a brief literature survey highlighted with some research papers.

A deep-learning approach to determine cardiovascular risk factors from fundus images was presented in this research [6]. The researcher identified the risk factors from fundus images that are not previously explored such as age, gender, smoke status, and blood pressure. The algorithm showed high accuracy and promise for non-invasive risk assessment.

The study by Jagtap et al. [7] aimed to design a web-based application which utilizes machine learning algorithms for predicting cardiac illness. They employed classification algorithms, NB, LR, and SVM, to train and test the models. The results shows that the SVM achieved the higher accuracy in predicting heart disease based on provided features. However, one limitation observed in this study was its inability to identify early-stage potential influences on cardiovascular disease patients.

In their study, Apurb Rajdhan et al. [8] delved into the utilization of machine learning algorithms for predicting heart diseases. Out of 76 features of the UCI Cleveland dataset, they used 14 features such as age, sex, severity of chest pain, and peak heart rate. Based on their investigation, authors shown that the Random Forest algorithm over performed in correctly predicting cardiac diseases.

In their study [9], Ul Haq et al. explored the application of seven distinct machine-learning algorithms to analyze the Cleveland heart disease dataset. The designed algorithms included Support Vector Machine (SVM), K-Nearest Neighbors (KNN) with hyperparameter settings $g = 0.0001$ and $c = 100$. Prior to utilizing these algorithms, the researchers employed the Lasso method as a regularization technique to identify the most significant attributes (features) within the dataset. By penalizing less important features, Lasso facilitated a focus on the most relevant ones.

The study [10] conducted by Ghosh P et al. fascinated by cardiovascular disease prediction utilizing artificial intelligence approaches. LASSO and Relief feature selection methods are used to features from the dataset. After carefully selecting the features, the researchers employed ensemble methods of machine learning to develop hybrid clas-sifiers. The ensemble methods combine multiple base learners to build a stronger and more robust predictive model. The researchers utilized three ensemble methods in this study: KNN Bagging Method, Random Forest Bagging Method, and Gradient Boosting Method. Their objective was to enhance the predictive performance for heart disease pre-diction by incorporating these hybrid classifiers, surpassing the capabilities of individual classifiers alone.

3   Proposed Methodology

Following figure shows the details of the methodology proposed. The standardiza-tion mechanism is applied on the selected Dataset. Then the Hyperparameter tuning is done for selecting best possible parameters for various algorithms before applying the machine learning algorithms. Then the performance evaluation is done on the basis of the outcomes.

Datasets have played a crucial role in the success of machine learning models. Researchers have made significant contributions by publishing open-source datasets in various domains, making them readily available for public use in experimentation [10–13]. Multiple datasets are employed in this study. The most notable dataset used was the Cleveland heart disease dataset, sourced from the University of California, Irvine (UCI) online repository for machine learning. It comprises 303 records, with 6 instances containing missing values.

Additionally, the researchers incorporated other datasets, such as the Kaggle and StatLog Heart datasets with the features resembling the Cleveland dataset (Fig. 1).

Age, chest, sex, sensitivity type (4 values), serum cholesterol, blood pressure, fasting blood sugar, having rest electrocardiographic results, the highest heart rate reached, apply-induced angina, oldpeak = ST dejection prompted by apply relative to rest, the slope of the greatest exercise ST segment, and the number of main vessels (0-3) colored by flourosopythal are the main characteristics that were chosen. Ordinary is 0, patched is 1, and reversible is 2 are all faults.

In summary, multiple datasets are employed in this research work to ensure a comprehensive and reliable analysis.

4   Results and Discussion

Section 3, discussed about the methodology based on the dataset collection its refine-ment, and standardization. After standardizing the dataset, hyperparameter tuning was performed, and machine learning classifiers were applied.

To evaluate their performance, K-fold cross-validation was employed where the value of K was 10. The accuracy of the classifiers was analysed before and after dataset hyper tunning, and the results were plotted in Fig. 2. From the figure, it is evident that several machine learning techniques, such as LR, RF, DT, Linear Discriminant Analy-sis, AdaBoost, Naive Bayes, Support Vector Machine and Extreme Gradient Boosting, exhibited improved accuracy after data standardization.

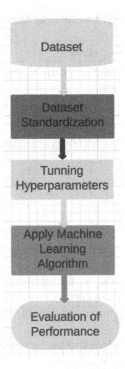

Fig. 1. Proposed Methodology

Table 1. Classifiers accuracy before and after hyperparameter tunning

Algorithm	Accuracy before Hyperparameter Tunning	Accuracy after Hyperparameter Tunning
RF	89	91
LR	83	87
DT	86	86
LDA	79	87
AB	89	90
NB	83	87
XGB	85	88
SVM	72	91

In summary, the experimental results illustrate the improvements observed in various machine learning classifiers after dataset standardization. The RF and SVM classifiers achieved the highest accuracy, emphasizing the importance of dataset preprocessing. On the other hand, the DT classifier exhibited lower performance compared to the other classifiers.

Table 2. Hyperparameter combinations for improving classifier accuracy

Algorithm name	Hyperparameter values
RF	min_samples_leaf = 2, n_estimators = 20, min_samples_split = 6, Criterion = "gini,"
DT	max_depth = 2, min_samples_leaf: 2
LDA	solver = "lsqr", Shrinkage = "auto,"
XGB	Learning_rate = 0.1, alpha = 4, max_depth = 15
SVM	Kernel = "rbf"
AB	N_estimators = 48, learning_rate = 0.08

The experimental results indicate a noticeable increase in classifier accuracy through hyperparameter tuning. By adjusting the hyperparameter values, we aimed to attain the best possible correctness for the selected classifiers.

Table 1 demonstrates the accuracy of the classifiers earlier and afterwards hyperparameter optimization. The majority of classifiers demonstrated improved accuracy after hyperparameter tuning. However, the accuracy of the Decision Tree classifier remained unchanged.

Table 2 provides details of the hyperparameter combinations for certain algorithms, which contributed to enhancing their accuracy.

In summary, the experimental results clearly demonstrate that hyperparameter tuning plays a crucial role in improving classifier accuracy. Most classifiers benefited from this optimization process. The best hyperparameter combinations for specific algorithms are summarized in Table 2.

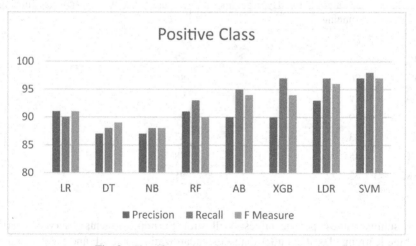

Fig. 2. Classifiers evaluation for Positive Class.

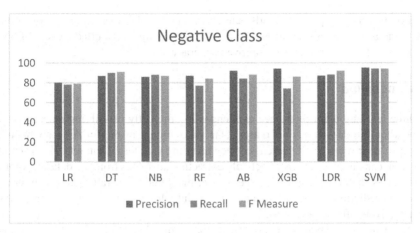

Fig. 3. Classifiers evaluation for Negative Class.

Figure 2 and Fig. 3 in the study present the performance metrics, including precision, recall, F-measure, and accuracy, for different classifiers. Notably, the SVM classifier achieved a maximum precision of 97% for positive classes. Additionally, SVM exhibited strong overall performance across all metrics, including recall, precision, F-measure, and accuracy. Its results indicate that SVM performed well in correctly identifying positive instances while minimizing false positives (Fig. 4).

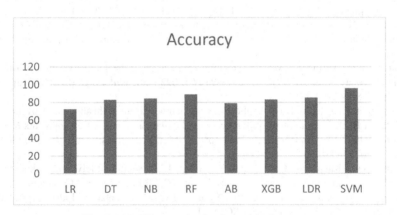

Fig. 4. Classifiers evaluation in terms of accuracy.

We found that the majority of classifiers showed improved precision when using the standardized dataset after comparing the accuracy of the classifiers on both the regular and standardized datasets. This suggests that improving accuracy before using machine learning classifiers is possible through the use of dataset normalization and hyperparameter adjustment.

Based on the comparison of different classifiers, SVM outperformed the other classifiers and achieved an accuracy of 95.88%. This highlights the effectiveness of SVM in optimizing its parameters for improved accuracy.

5   Conclusion

Machine learning algorithms face challenges in efficiently classifying datasets, especially when the dataset size increases. One shortcoming of the former recommended systems is their reduced effectiveness when handling with larger datasets. However, this limitation can be mitigated by effectively extracting attributes from the dataset. Another limitation is that while increasing the dataset magnitude generally leads to improved classifier prediction accuracy, there comes a point where further increasing the dataset size negatively affects the accuracy.

In the proposed method, heart disease prediction has shown improved accuracy using the machine learning technique. Multiple classifiers were employed to classify heart disease prediction, with SVM achieving an accuracy of 95.88%.

Overall, the proposed approach leverages machine learning algorithms to enhance accuracy and minimize costs in heart disease prediction, although challenges associated with dataset size and optimal dataset magnitude remain.

References

1. Sarker, I.H.: Machine learning: algorithms, real-world applications and research directions. SN Comput. Sci. **2**(3), 1–21 (2021). https://doi.org/10.1007/s42979-021-00592-x
2. Taye, M.M.: Understanding of machine learning with deep learning: architectures, workflow applications and future directions. Computers **12**, 91 (2023). https://doi.org/10.3390/comput ers12050091
3. Verma, V.K., Verma, S.: Machine learning applications in healthcare sector: an overview. Mater. Today: Proc. **57**(Part 5), 2144–2147 (2022). https://doi.org/10.1016/j.matpr.2021. 12.101. ISSN 2214-7853
4. Samarpita, S., Satpathy, R.N.: Applications of machine learning in healthcare: an overview. In: 2022 1st IEEE International Conference on Industrial Electronics: Developments & Applications (ICIDeA), Bhubaneswar, India, pp. 51–56 (2022). https://doi.org/10.1109/ICIDeA 53933.2022.9970177
5. Mana, S.C., Kalaiarasi, G., Yogitha, R., Helen, L.S., SenthamilSelvi, R.: Application of machine learning in healthcare: an analysis. In: 2022 3rd International Conference on Electronics and Sustainable Communication Systems (ICESC), Coimbatore, India, pp. 1611–1615 (2022). https://doi.org/10.1109/ICESC54411.2022.9885296
6. Meshram, V., Patil, K., Meshram, V., Dhumane, A., Thepade, S., Hanchate, D.: Smart low cost fruit picker for indian farmers. In: 2022 6th International Conference on Computing, Communication, Control and Automation (ICCUBEA), Pune, India, pp. 1–7 (2022). https:// doi.org/10.1109/ICCUBEA54992.2022.10010984
7. Jagtap, A., Malewadkar, P., Baswat, O., Rambade, H.: Heart disease prediction using machine learning. Int. Res. Eng. Sci. Manag. **2**(2), 352–355 (2019)
8. Dhumane, A.V., Kaldate, P., Sawant, A., Kadam, P., Chopade, V.: Efficient prediction of cardiovascular disease using machine learning algorithms with relief and LASSO feature selection techniques. ICICC 2023. LNNS, vol. 703, pp. 677–693. Springer, Singapore (2023). https://doi.org/10.1007/978-981-99-3315-0_52

9. Rajdhan, A., Agarwal, A., Sai, M., Ravi, D., Ghuli, P.: Heart disease prediction using machine learning. Int. J. Eng. Res. Technol. (IJERT) **09**(04) (2020)

10. Haq, A.U., Li, J.P., Memon, M.H., Nazir, S., Sun, R.: A hybrid intelligent system framework for the prediction of heart disease using machine learning algorithms. Mob. Inf. Syst. **2018** (2018)

11. Ghosh, P., et al.: Efficient prediction of cardiovascular disease using machine learning algorithms with relief and lasso feature selection techniques. IEEE Access **9**, 19304–19326 (2021). https://doi.org/10.1109/ACCESS.2021.3053759

12. Meshram, V., Choudhary, C., Kale, A., Rajput, J., Meshram, V., Dhumane, A.: Dry fruit image dataset for machine learning applications, Data Brief **49**, 109325 (2023). ISSN 2352-3409. https://doi.org/10.1016/j.dib.2023.109325

13. Ahammad, S.H., et al.: Phishing URL detection using machine learning methods. Adv. Eng. Softw. **173**, 103288 (2022)

14. Chiwhane, S., Anandan, R., Nalini, T., Shanmuganathan, M., Radhakrishnan, R.: COVID-19 outbreak data analysis and prediction. Meas.: Sens. (2023). https://doi.org/10.1016/j.measen.2022.100585

15. Patil, R., Kumar, S., Chiwhane, S., Rani, R., Pippal, S.K.: An artificial-intelligence-based novel rice grade model for severity estimation of rice diseases. Agriculture. https://doi.org/10.3390/agriculture13010047

16. Chiwhane, S., Dhumane, A., Mangore, A.K., Ambala, S.: Cluster-based energy-efficient routing in internet of things. In: Choudrie, J., Mahalle, P., Perumal, T., Joshi, A. (eds.) ICT with Intelligent Applications. SIST, vol. 311, pp.415–427. Springer, Singapore (2023). https://doi.org/10.1007/978-981-19-3571-8_40

17. Ramani, A., Chhabra, D., Manik, V., Dayama, G., Dhumane, A.: Healthcare information exchange using blockchain technology. In: Sharma, H., Shrivastava, V., Bharti, K.K., Wang, L. (eds.) ICCIS 2022. LNNS, vol. 689, pp. 91–102. Springer, Singapore (2023). https://doi.org/10.1007/978-981-99-2322-9_8

18. Jayashree, P., Rajesh, P., Amol, D., Nihar, R., Mubin, T.: Gradient bald vulture optimization enabled multi-objective Unet++ with DCNN for prostate cancer segmentation and detection. Biomed. Signal Process. Control **87**, 105474 (2024). ISSN 1746-8094. https://doi.org/10.1016/j.bspc.2023.105474

Mild Cognitive Impairment Diagnosis Using Neuropsychological Tests and Agile Machine Learning

Harsh Bhasin[1] , Ansh Ohri[2] , Nishant Kumar[3] , Manish Sharma[4],
and Hardeo Kumar Thakur[5](✉)

[1] Manav Rachna International Institute of Research and Studies, Faridabad, Haryana, India
[2] Manav Rachna University, Faridabad, Haryana, India
[3] The NorthCap University, Gurugram, Haryana, India
[4] Roux Institute, Northeastern University, Portland, USA
ma.sharma@northeastern.edu
[5] Bennett University, Greater Noida, India
hardeokumar@gmail.com

Abstract. Alzheimer's Disease constitutes one of the biggest portions of the diseases related to ageing. Mild Cognitive Impairment may be considered the formative stage of this disease. The automated diagnosis of Mild Cognitive Impairment using Machine Learning will help the clinicians in delaying its progression and will be easy, cheap, and efficient for the patient. This work uses neuropsychological data obtained from Alzheimer's Disease Neuroimaging Initiative (ADNI), containing the results from 12 tests including Mini-Mental State Examination and ADAS-Cog. An extensive empirical analysis is carried out and the most important features are extracted using the proposed pipelines. The Feature Selection is done using both filter and wrapper methods and in total 13 features were selected. It was found that most of the selected features related to tasks associated with memory. The proposed method gives a performance of 0.9817 in terms of F1 Score. Thus, performing better vis-à-vis the state of the art. The proposed pipeline helps to reduce the number of neuropsychological tests to diagnose the disease. This work is one of the components of the projects that use multi-modality data including structural-Magnetic Resonance Imaging, functional-Magnetic Resonance Imaging, Positron Emission Tomography and Neuropsychological data to develop a system for efficient and effective diagnosis of MCI. The project management is done using Agile Methodology. The results are encouraging and pave the way for the development of such a system.

Keywords: Mild Cognitive Impairment · Neuropsychological tests · Feature Selection · Machine Learning and Agile

1 Introduction

Alzheimer's disease affects more than 60 million people across the world [1], which constitutes one of the biggest shares in the diseases associated with aging. Not just the people suffering from dementia, but their family members and near ones bear the brunt

D. Garg et al. (Eds.): IACC 2023, CCIS 2054, pp. 180–187, 2024.
https://doi.org/10.1007/978-3-031-56703-2_15

of the disease. It cannot be cured but can be traced [2]. The early detection of this type of dementia can help clinicians handle the symptoms and delay its progression. Mild Cognitive Impairment (MCI) is an earlier stage of dementia [1]. Approximately one-fifth of the people suffering from MCI progress to dementia [3]. The decrease in the grey matter in the hippocampal region is one of the reasons for MCI [4]. An extensive literature review brought forth the fact that many other regions of the brain are also affected by this disease. The detection of MCI is time-consuming and may prove expensive to the patient. The problem is compounded by the scarcity of trained clinicians, especially in the South Asian region. This calls for the development of automated methods to detect MCI and distinguish between those who convert to dementia (MCI-Converts) and those who do not (MCI-Non-Converts). The automated diagnosis will be efficient, cheap, and will be easy for the patient.

The developments in the field of Machine Learning in the past two decades have greatly facilitated the cause. Researchers have worked on the full brain [5], and on the Regions of Interest (RoI) of the brain [6] for this diagnosis. Researchers have used functional-magnetic Resonance Imaging (fMRI) [8], structural-magnetic Resonance Imaging (s-MRI) [7], Positron Emission Tomography (PET) [9], and neuropsycholog- ical data [10] to handle this problem. They have used various pre-processing methods, feature extraction methods [5], feature selection methods, and Deep Learning methods [11] to accomplish the task.

An extensive literature review was carried out to assess the state of the art and to find the gaps in the literature. Researchers have used various modalities to diagnose MCI. These include a) neuropsychological data b) fMRI c) PET d) s-MRI.

Weakly et al. worked on the neuropsychological data and used ML methods to find the relevant number of features, with the aim of reducing the number of tests for the diagnosis of MCI [12]. They used Decision Trees and Naïve Bayes to accomplish the task. The major problem in this work was a) the huge variation in the performance of the model b) the unbalanced dataset, and no method applied to handle this problem c) Stating that a minimum 2 variables are needed to accurately classify the MCI and CN. Zalesky et al. used fMRI data [8] and Singh et al. used PET data to diagnose MCI [9].

Lin et al. used a combination of transfer learning and regression using Alex-Net, which is a pre-trained 2D convolutional neural network (CNN) and a relevance vec- tor machine (RVM) on s-MRI data to diagnose MCI [13]. Abbas et al. proposed a novel method called the Jacobian domain convolutional neural network (JD-CNN) for the computer-aided diagnosis (CAD) of Alzheimer's disease (AD) using s-MRI [14]. Aderghal et al. proposed a transfer learning scheme using CNNs for the automatic classi- fication of brain scans, specifically focusing on a small region of interest (RoI) such as a few slices of the hippocampal region using multi-modal imaging data, including s-MRI and DTI [15]. The binary classification was performed using a variant of Convolutional Neural Network (CNN) called an enhanced multi-modal graph. This model was used for the binary classification using s-MRI and fMRI data [16].

This work is part of a larger project which aims to develop a multi-modality model to detect MCI and classify between the converts and non-converts, to help clinicians delay the progression of the disease. The project aims to use a) s-MRI b) f-MRI and c) clinical data to accomplish this task. This paper presents the results of one of the components of the project: diagnosis using neuropsychological data; and the project management of the whole project in general. The main contributions of this paper are:

a) To select the most important features from neuropsychological tests with the goal of decreasing the number of tests needed for the diagnoses of MCI.
b) To develop a robust model, using hyper-parameter optimization for the diagnosis of MCI.
c) To develop a component of the multi-modality system, that is simple, effective, efficient, and can be easily integrated into a mobile application.

The paper has been organized as follows. The second section presents the literature review, followed by a discussion of the methods employed in this work. The fourth section presents the results and discussion, and the last section concludes.

2   Methods

Machine Learning pipeline constitutes pre-processing of data, followed by extraction of features, feature selection, application of classifier, and post-processing. The data was pre-processed by detecting the outliers, followed by normalization of data. This is required so that the classifier does not give unnecessary weightage to any feature. For the given data, min-max normalization was used, in which the minimum (min_1) and the maximum value (max_1) of each column were found followed by transforming each value of the column using the formula:

$$x = (x - min_1)/(max_1 - min_1) \qquad (1)$$

This is followed by feature selection; Feature selection is necessary as some of the features are not important and some may even negatively affect the performance of the model. Having a lesser number of features will also result in an efficient model, both in terms of memory and time. Feature Selection can be done using filter and wrapper methods. The feature selection in this work is done using filter method called Fisher Discriminant Ratio (FDR). For a two-class problem, the FDR of a feature can be calculated by using the following formula:

$$FDR = (m_1 - m_2)^2 / \left(s_1^2 + s_2^2 \right) \qquad (2)$$

Here, m_1 is the mean of the samples belonging to the first class, m_2 of those belonging to the second class, s_1 is the standard deviation of the samples belonging to the first class and s_2 of those belonging to the second class.

The wrapper method makes use of the learner to judge the importance of the feature. In this work, Recursive Feature Elimination has been used as the wrapper method to find the most discriminative feature amongst the given features. "The Recursive feature elimination (RFE) method fits the given model and eliminates the least important feature in every iteration until the specified number of features is reached" [17].

The classifiers used in this work are Neural Network, which is able to generate a non-linear boundary; a Support Vector Machine, which is a maximum margin classifier; and Decision Tree, which produces a piece-wise linear boundary.

The project management is done using the Agile methodology. The principles and practices of Agile have greatly benefited the Software industry. The application of these principles in the field of Machine Learning is called Agile Machine learning (AML) [17]. The responsiveness to change, collaboration, and incremental approaches are the key to the Agile methodologies. The application of these principles in ML projects may improve the efficiency and effectiveness of the development process. The AML is based on the following concepts:

1. Adaptability: As feedback from the customers is obtained, the ML team may need to change its strategy based on its value and impact. With the aim of delivering the most important component first, the features are prioritized, and tasks teams can adapt to new requirements.
2. Iterative Development: The ML models are developed incrementally in AML. These can be considered as sprints where "each sprint focuses on delivering a working model or a specific set of features". This inculcates the ability to adapt to the model.
3. Cross-Functional Teams: The teams formed in AML are cross-functional and can be of types stated in [18].
4. Validation: It is important for an ML model to perform well on unseen data. This can be facilitated by continuous feedback from the customer and the ability of the team to adapt to ever-changing data.

In addition to the above the AML uses Data Exploration as data plays an important role in every step of the development.

The proposed pipeline creates a feature map, followed by feature selection using filter and wrapper methods, and finally backtrace. The proposed pipeline is shown in Fig. 1.

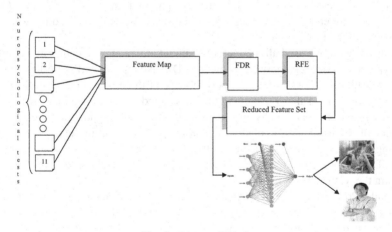

Fig. 1. Proposed Work

3   Results and Discussion

"The datasets supporting the conclusions of this article are available in the Alzheimer's Disease Neuroimaging Initiative (ADNI) repository, Data used in the preparation of this article were obtained from the ADNI database (adni.loni.usc.edu). The ADNI was launched in 2003 as a public-private partnership, led by Principal Investigator Michael W. Weiner, MD. The primary goal of ADNI has been to test whether Magnetic Resonance Imaging (MRI), PET, other biological markers, and clinical and neuropsychological assessment can be combined to measure the progression of MCI and early AD." [19].

The Neuropsychological tests considered for diagnosing MCI and classification of MCI patients and controls are as follows:

1. American National Adult Residing Test
2. Logical Memory Test
3. Functional Assessment Questionnaire
4. Digital Spam
5. Category Fluency Test
6. Trial Making Test
7. Geriatric Depression Scale
8. Mini-mental state Examination (MMSE)
9. Alzheimer's Disease Assessment Scale Cognitive Behavior Test
10. Boston Naming Test
11. Rey Auditory Verbal Learning Test

The data for the tests are obtained from ADNI. From the given dataset the data related to the above tests of the selected patients was extracted. Here CDR was considered the gold standard. According to CDR, the patients can be classified into three categories. If the result of the test shows a value of 0 then the patient is not suffering from MCI, if it shows 1 then the patient is suffering from the disease. In total 131 features were taken to accomplish the task.

To begin with, we used all the features without any feature selection and employed three types of classifiers namely Decision Tree (DT), Neural Networks (NN), and Support Vector Machine (SVM) to assess the performance of the model. In the NN the number of neurons was varied also the learning rate was varied to find the optimal performance. In the SVM the kernels namely Linear Kernel, RBF and Polynomial were taken, and the value of 'C' was varied to obtain the optimal performance. In the case of DT, early stopping was employed to reduce overfitting. This was followed by feature selection using FDR. In total 13 features were selected, and the above classifiers were employed to obtain the results.

Finally, Principal Component Analysis (PCA) was used and the number of features which gave 95% variance were selected. This was followed by classification using the classifiers. The results are shown in Tables 1 and 2. Table 1 shows the results with NN, Table 2 shows the result with DT and SVM.

Table 1. Results with Neural Networks

Number of Hidden Layers	Hidden Layer Architecture	F1Score
1	(100,)	0.7812
1	**(64,)**	**0.9803**
2	(64,32)	0.9738
2	(64,16)	0.9788
2	(64,8)	0.9413
1	(32,)	0.9412
2	(32,16)	0.9410
2	(32,8)	0.9403
1	(16,)	0.9200
2	(16,8)	0.9310

Table 2. Results with SVM and DT

	SVM	
S. No.	Kernels	F1 Score
1	Linear	**0.9817**
2	RBF	0.7713
3	Poly2	0.8002
4	Poly3	0.8051
	DT	
S. No.	Criteria	F1 Score
1	Gini	0.9700
2	Entropy	0.9702

From the tables, it can be observed that:

1. SVM with linear kernel performs the best.
2. The NN with a single hidden layer having 64 neurons in the layer, performs best among various NNs.
3. The DT performs equally well with the Gini index and entropy.

In addition to the above, FDR was employed to select features. In total 13 features were selected, most of them related to memory. The performance after feature selection was reported to be 0.9817. On applying PCA not much change was observed. The optimal value of the cost ('c') parameter of SVM was found using empirical analysis so that the performance with the test set improves. The graph has been provided as an annexure to the paper. It was observed that the majority of the selected features belonged to memory-related tasks. The comparison vis-à-vis the state of the art is depicted in Table 3.

Table 3. Comparison with the state-of-the-art

S. No.	Reference	Model	Performance
1	Battista et al. [10]	SVM Linear Kernel	Accuracy = 0.65
		SVM Quadratic Kernel	Accuracy = 0.65
		SVM RBF Kernel	Accuracy = 0.64
		Multilayer Perceptron	Accuracy = 0.63
2	Weakley et al. [12]	Naïve Bayes	Accuracy = 94%
		Decision Tree	Accuracy = 94.1%
		Logistic Regression	Accuracy = 91.2%
3	Proposed Work	SVM Linear Kernel	F1 Score = **0.9817**

4   Conclusion

It can be seen from the results that neuropsychological tests can be used to diagnose MCI. The pipelines used to accomplish the task are able to efficiently and effectively diagnose the disease. Furthermore, feature selection not only improves the performance, it increases efficiency in terms of execution time and reduces the memory requirement. The model has been validated using K-Fold validation. One of the obvious questions that arise is why we need more modalities if we are able to obtain good results from just these tests. The answer is that most of these are self-assessment tests, and there is a need to make the system more objective. Therefore, there is a need to develop a system that uses imaging modalities and is able to extract the patterns that is responsible for the effective diagnosis of the disease. To this cause, we have already developed Deep learning models to accomplish this task using s-MRI. The models not only differentiate between the converts and non-converts but can also find the regions of the brain responsible for this.

In future, we will use these models and create a model that uses f-MRI also, along with the s-MRI and self-assessment tests to make the model robust and free from bias.

It was observed that the adopting Agile Machine Learning, collaboration among the team members increases, the development time was reduced, and models so developed better meet the needs of the project. This iterative and adaptive approach helps address the challenges of complex Machine Learning projects and enables teams to respond effectively to evolving requirements. It may be noted that the Agile Approach made the development of individual sub-systems achievable and that too within the decided time and management of the teams is easy.

References

1. Alzheimer's Disease facts and figures. https://www.alz.org/alzheimers-dementia/facts-figures
2. Henderson, V.: Mild Cognitive Impairment. https://med.stanford.edu/content/dam/sm/adrc/documents/adrc-information-sheet-mild-cognitive-impairment.pdf
3. Dementias. https://www.ninds.nih.gov/health-information/disorders/dementias

4. Chupin, M., et al.: Fully automatic hippocampus segmentation and classification in Alzheimer's disease and mild cognitive impairment applied on data from ADNI. Hippocampus **19**, 579–587 (2009). https://doi.org/10.1002/hipo.20626

5. Bhasin, H., Agrawal, R.K.: A combination of 3-D discrete wavelet transform and 3-D local binary pattern for classification of mild cognitive impairment. BMC Med. Inform. Decis. Mak. **20** (2020). https://doi.org/10.1186/s12911-020-1055-x

6. Ahmed, O.B., Benois-Pineau, J., Allard, M., Amar, C.B., Catheline, G.: Classification of Alzheimer's disease subjects from MRI using hippocampal visual features. Multimed. Tools Appl. **74**, 1249–1266 (2014). https://doi.org/10.1007/s11042-014-2123-y

7. Pennanen, C., et al.: Hippocampus and entorhinal cortex in mild cognitive impairment and early AD. Neurobiol. Aging **25**, 303–310 (2004). https://doi.org/10.1016/s0197-4580(03)000 84-8

8. Zalesky, A., Fornito, A., Bullmore, E.T.: Network-based statistic: Identifying differences in brain networks. Neuroimage **53**, 1197–1207 (2010). https://doi.org/10.1016/j.neuroimage. 2010.06.041

9. Singh, S., et al.: Deep-learning-based classification of FDG-PET data for Alzheimer's disease categories. In: 13th International Conference on Medical Information Processing and Analysis (2017). https://doi.org/10.1117/12.2294537

10. Battista, P., Salvatore, C., Castiglioni, I.: Optimizing neuropsychological assessments for cognitive, behavioral, and functional impairment classification: a machine learning study. Behav. Neurol. **2017**, 1–19 (2017). https://doi.org/10.1155/2017/1850909

11. Bhasin, H., Agrawal, R.K.: Multiple-activation parallel convolution network in combination with t-SNE for the classification of mild cognitive impairment. In: 2021 IEEE 21st International Conference on Bioinformatics and Bioengineering (BIBE) (2021). https://doi.org/10. 1109/bibe52308.2021.9635485

12. Weakley, A.T., Williams, J., Schmitter-Edgecombe, M., Cook, D.J.: Neuropsychological test selection for cognitive impairment classification: a machine learning approach. J. Clin. Exp. Neuropsychol. **37**, 899–916 (2015). https://doi.org/10.1080/13803395.2015.1067290

13. Lin, L., Zhang, G., Wang, J., Miao, T., Wu, S.: Utilizing transfer learning of pre-trained AlexNet and relevance vector machine for regression for predicting healthy older adult's brain age from structural MRI. Multimed. Tools Appl. (2021). https://doi.org/10.1007/s11 042-020-10377-8

14. Abbas, S.Q., Chi, L., Chen, Y.P.: Transformed domain convolutional neural network for Alzheimer's disease diagnosis using structural MRI. Pattern Recogn. **133**, 109031 (2023). https://doi.org/10.1016/j.patcog.2022.109031

15. Aderghal, K., Afdel, K., Benois-Pineau, J., Catheline, G.: Improving Alzheimer's stage categorization with Convolutional Neural Network using transfer learning and different magnetic resonance imaging modalities. Heliyon **6**, e05652 (2020). https://doi.org/10.1016/j.heliyon. 2020.e05652

16. Liu, L., Wang, Y., Wang, Y., Zhang, P., Xiong, S.: An enhanced multi-modal brain graph network for classifying neuropsychiatric disorders. Med. Image Anal. **81**, 102550 (2022). https://doi.org/10.1016/j.media.2022.102550

17. Recursive Feature Elimination—Yellowbrick v1.5 documentation. https://www.scikit-yb.org/ en/latest/api/model_selection/rfecv.html#module-yellowbrick.model_selection.rfecv

18. Carter, E., Hurst, M.: Agile Machine learning: Effective Machine Learning Inspired by the Agile Manifesto. Apress (2019)

19. ADNI|Alzheimer's Disease Neuroimaging Initiative. https://adni.loni.usc.edu/

Heart Disease Diagnosis Using Machine Learning Classifiers

Pushpendra Singh[1] , Chandra Shekher Tyagi[1] , Davesh Kumar Sharma[1] ,
Mahesh Kumar Singh[2(✉)] , Pushpa Choudhary[3] , and Arun Kumar Singh[4]

[1] Department of Computer Science and Engineering, SRMIST Delhi-NCR Campus, Modinagar,
Ghaziabad, UP, India

[2] Department of Computer Science and Engineering, Dronacharya Group of Institutions,
Greater Noida, UP, India
maheshkrsg@gmail.com

[3] School of Computer Science and Engineering, Galgotias University, Greater Noida, UP, India

[4] Computer Science and Engineering, Greater Noida Institute of Technology, Greater Noida,
UP, India

Abstract. The term "heart or cardiovascular disease" is frequently used to refer
to a variety of heart-related issues. It is one of the illnesses with the highest
mortality rate. Its fatality rate results in nearly 17 million deaths worldwide. Given
the daily increase in heart disease cases, predicting any disease early is critical
and concerning. Early detection of heart disease is a difficult task that must be
accomplished carefully and effectively by gathering precise information about the
patient who is at risk for heart disease. To predict whether a person has cardiac
disease, there are numerous AI-based (Machine/Deep learning) Models available
considering medical characteristics (features) of heart disease. By comparing and
contrasting several machine learning classifiers, this paper proposed a heart disease
prediction system. This system will aid in identifying and predicting whether the
patient is likely to have or be diagnosed with heart disease based on his or her
current medical state.

Keywords: Heart Disease Prediction · Machine Learning · Logistic Regression ·
K-Nearest Neighbor Algorithms

1 Introduction

For the past ten years, coronary disease has raised serious concerns. Recognizing symptoms and receiving an accurate diagnosis are two of the most difficult challenges in
cardiac disease. Early methods for forecasting heart disease were insufficiently effective and productive. There are numerous diagnostic methods available to check for a
proclivity for heart disease. These devices have two major drawbacks: first, they are
extremely expensive; second, they are incapable of accurately predicting human heart
disease. There is a lot of room for research in the area of forecasting coronary disease in
humans because clinical specialists can only reliably predict 67% of coronary disease,

D. Garg et al. (Eds.): IACC 2023, CCIS 2054, pp. 188–196, 2024.
https://doi.org/10.1007/978-3-031-56703-2_16

according to the most recent WHO-directed assessment. Machine learning is a widely used technology in a variety of contexts because it does not necessitate extraordinarily complex calculations for varying data sets. Reprogrammable AI boundaries bring a lot of cohesiveness to a discipline like clinical medicine and open up new vistas of possibilities. Coronary disease is one of the major challenges in clinical science because there are too many restrictions and specifics involved to reliably predict this transition. AI may be a better option to achieve higher accuracy for the prediction of Coronary disease as well as other infections because this transformation tool incorporates vector and its various data types for the prediction of Coronary disease under various conditions Calculations like Nave Bayes, Choice Tree, and KNN, AI may be a better option to achieve higher accuracy for the prediction of Coronary disease as well as other infections [7–10]. Innocent Bayes, for example, used probability to predict cardiovascular disease, albeit systematically for heart disease. While neural organization provides the freedom to reduce inaccuracy in coronary disease prediction, the selection tree is used to report. Each of these procedures makes predictions about prospective patients based on historical patient data. His heart disease prediction technique assists professionals in predicting heart disease at an early stage of infection, potentially saving many lives.

2 Literature Review

To predict cardiovascular diseases, K. Sri Charan and KSSNS Mahendranath [2] used the random forest machine learning algorithm. Following receipt and analysis of the data, its balance was checked, and a relationship between the various characteristics and their effect on the target values was discovered. The data set that was retrieved was the UCI data set from Kaggle. This was divided in an 80-20 ratio for training and testing. This train-test split ratio produced the most precise predictions. The target characteristic was found to be positively correlated with chest pain and maximum heart rate achieved. Using the Random Forest algorithm, this model had an accuracy of 92.16%. Sabrinathan, V [6]. Heart disease diagnosis using decision trees to classify structurally informative features such as gender, age, chest pain and obtained heart rate are utilized [14–16]. With regard to identifying the root cause of heart disease, the study had an accuracy rate of 85%. This situation similarly chooses countenance using a decision tree [4, 5]. Bharti Ganesh, Anita Ganesh, Chetna Srinivas, Dhanraj, and Kiran Mensinkal [1] implemented cardiovascular disease prediction using LR algorithms. The UCI dataset is employed. In the classification, variables such as chest pain, age, gender, and obtained heart rate are used. The dataset is subjected to feature scaling feature engineering. High forcible correlation values with the target are used to choose the countenance, and the data is then randomly arranged (without sorting). The model's performance is assessed using five different training and test ratios from the dataset. When training and testing are split justly, logistic regression has an accuracy of 87.10% and a split quota of 90:10. Karandikar and Sonam Nikhar used the Naive Bayes machine learning algorithm to predict heart disease. The manifestation of a single feature, unrelated to the occurrence of other features, was recorded in the medical feature record. Fruit can be perceived by its appearance, shape, and flavor, hence the red, rounded, and sweet fruit is called an apple. So each feature contributes to identifying it as an apple without being dependent on the others. Its groundwork is the Bayes Theorem, hence the name Bayes. The following equation expresses this theorem mathematically.

$$P(\alpha|B) = P(B|\alpha) * P(\alpha) * P(\alpha)/P(B) \tag{1}$$

To predict heart disease, Harshit Jindal, Sarthak Aggarwal, Rishabh Khera, and Rachna Jain [3] used Particle Swarm and K-Nearest preferred over other classifiers because of its fast convergence and simplicity. The papers [17–21] uses various ML models (Random forest (RF), linear regression (LR), Support Vector Machine (SVM), Naive Bayes) for early detection of sepsis in patients admitted in ICU.

3 Proposed Methodology

The method of forecasting cardiovascular illnesses using machine learning and data mining techniques involves the gathering, classification, preprocessing, and prediction of data for outcomes, regardless of whether the individual has the condition or not. To determine the most meticulous machine learning algorithm, this paper investigates a number of classification techniques, including KNN, Naive Bayes, Decision trees, logistic regression and Random forests,. It also examines a number of feature selection techniques, including backward elimination and recursive feature deletion.

Logistic regression is an algorithm for supervised classification to perform prediction based on probabilistic analysis. An automated predictive model is created with the use of a decision tree, an architecture that resembles a tree or a flowchart, which is used as a regression problem and decision-support tool in classification. A forest is instantly created by a Random Forest. Many decision tree classifiers are used in an ensemble to construct the forest [13]. The building of the random forest technique is Bootstrap Aggregation, also known as Bagging, which mixes together the predictions of various decision trees to create a forest in order to make predictions that are more accurate. A decision tree classifier is used to fit a sub-sample of the dataset. Similar to classification and regression trees, this blueprint makes use of supervised learning (CART). A variety of random subsamples are generated from the data set using the bagging CART technique, and each one is utilized to train a distinct CAR model. The test results are then used to compute the average forecast from each model. The training results were used to generate small samples. The results of each model on its missing samples are used to calculate the estimated accuracy. The method of feature importance allows for the selective selection of the characteristics needed for the prophecy process from the data collection [11, 12]. The less significant characteristic that makes a smaller contribution to prediction can be removed from the random forest design. Using the Bayes theory, the Naive Bayes classifier is fabricated. The data may be intensified to real-valued essence by assuming that it has a Gaussian distribution. Gaussian Naive Bayes is a Naive Bayes divergent. It is a supervised categorization learning technique that can deal with situations involving binary and many classes. Regression and classification disputes can be resolved using the K Closest Neighbors mechanism (Figs. 1, 2 and Table 1).

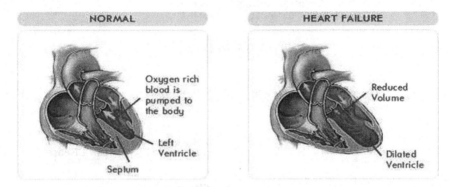

Fig. 1. Normal Vs. Heart Failure Images

Table 1. Congenital Heart Defect Rate (Approx.)

Congenital Heart Defect	Number of Cases		
	Boys (%)	Girls (%)	Total (%)
Atrial Septal Defect	39	33	71
Ventricular Septal Defect	25	14	39
Patent Ductus Arteriosus	8	17	25
Atrioventricular Septal Defect	7	9	16
Tetralogy of Fallot	1	1	2
Pulmonary Stenosis	2	0	2
Total	**64/112**	**48/112**	**112/178**

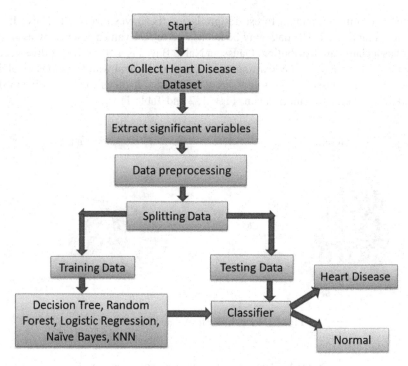

Fig. 2. Block Diagram of Proposed Model

4 Experimental Results and Discussion

Preprocessing is usually when a data set is cleaned and outlier and incorrect values are eliminated. The algorithmic process's most significant step is this one. Before doing algorithmic tests on the dataset, validation is also essential. It is essential to pay close attention to missing numbers and outliers. The curve is used by K Nearest Neighbor to depict the most ongoing test results. The K element denotes how many neighbors were taken into account during classification. Usually, the K value is a single-digit integer. The test data mark is shown first, searched by the radius calculation to find the K nearest neighbors (Figs. 3 and 4).

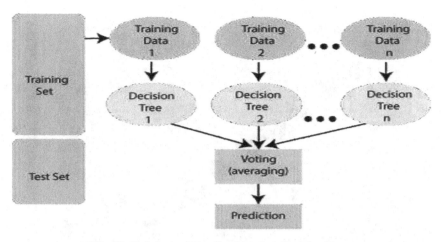

Fig. 3. Training and Test Sets based on Decision Trees

	age	sex	cp	trestbps	chol	fbs	restecg	thalach	exang	oldpeak	slope	ca	thal	target
0	52	1	0	125.0	212.0	0	1	168.0	0	1.0	2	2	3	0
1	53	1	0	140.0	203.0	1	0	155.0	1	3.1	0	0	3	0
2	70	1	0	145.0	174.0	0	1	125.0	1	2.6	0	0	3	0
3	61	1	0	148.0	203.0	0	1	161.0	0	0.0	2	1	3	0
4	62	0	0	138.0	294.0	1	1	106.0	0	1.9	1	3	2	0

Fig. 4. Dataset and Features

In order to determine the best precise algorithm for determining regardless in case a patient has heart disease, this study compares the performance of various machine learning supervised classification algorithms. Logistic Regression, K-Nearest Neighbor (KNN), Decision Tree, Random Forest, and Nave Bayes techniques were used to the Kaggle dataset. Python was used to gap the dataset into training and test data in an 80:20 ratio, quantify classifier veracity, and models training. The performance of the algorithms is compared below, and a table with their accuracy ratings is included (Fig. 5 and Table 2).

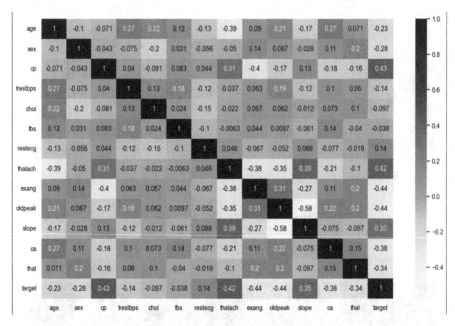

Fig. 5. Confusion Matrix

Table 2. Accuracy of different Classifiers

S. No.	Classifiers	Accuracy
1	Logistic Regression	81.95%
2	Random Forest	82.71%
3	K-Nearest Neighbor (KNN)	85.34%
4	Naïve Bayes	81.95%
5	Decision Tree	81.20%

The analysis of the five chosen classifiers was performed in this experiment, and the five classifiers were compared and their accuracy was analyzed.

5 Conclusion and Future Work

In this study, heart disease prediction based of different classifiers was taken as a goal for selected dataset. The overall goal is to define and analyse various data mining techniques that can be used to effectively predict heart disease. The goal of this research is to make accurate and efficient predictions with a limited number of attributes and tests. the data were pre-processed (feature engineering, feature scaling, and feature selection were performed) before being used in the model. The most efficient algorithms are K-Nearest Neighbor (85.34%) and Random Forest (82.71%). However, Decision Tree had the lowest accuracy of 81.20%. These models can be improved, and this research can be expanded by incorporating data mining techniques related clustering, time series, association rules, support vector machine, and other ensemble techniques. Given the limitations of this study, more complex and combined models are needed to achieve more accuracy for heart disease early diagnosis.

References

1. Ganesh, B., Ganesh, A., Srinivas, C., Dhanraj, K.M., Ambrish, G.: Logistic regression technique for prediction of cardiovascular disease **3**(1) (2022)
2. Kolluru, K.S.C., Mahendranath, S.S.N.S.: Heart disease prediction using random forest algorithm **09**(03) (2022)
3. Jindal, H., Agrawal, S., Khera, R., Jain, R.: Heart disease prediction using machine learning algorithms 1022 (2020)
4. Nikhar, S., Karandikar, A.M.: Prediction of Heart Disease Using Machine Learning Algorithms (2018)
5. Subbalakshmi, G., Ramesh, K., Rao, M.C.: Decision support in heart disease prediction system using Naive Bayes **2** (2011)
6. Kavitha, K.S., Ramakrishnan, K.V., Singh, M.K.: Int. J. Comput. Sci. **7**(5), 272–283 (2010)
7. Hazra, A., Mandal, S., Gupta, A., Mukherjee, A.: Heart disease diagnosis and prediction using machine learning and data mining techniques: a review. Adv. Comput. Sci. Technol. **10**, 2137–2159 (2017)
8. Patel, J., Upadhyay, P., Patel, D.: Heart disease prediction using machine learning and data mining technique. J. Comput. Sci. Electron. **7**, 129–137 (2016)
9. Chavan Patil, A.B., Sonawane, P.: To predict heart disease risk and medications using data mining techniques with an IoT based monitoring system for post-operative heart disease patients. Int. J. Emerg. Trends Technol. (IJETT) **4**, 8274–8281 (2017)
10. Weng, S.F., Reps, J., Kai, J., Garibaldi, J.M., Qureshi, N.: Can machine learning improve cardiovascular risk prediction using routine clinical data? PLoS ONE **12**, e0174944 (2017)
11. Zhao, W., Wang, C. Nakahira, Y.: Medical application on internet of things. In: IET International Conference on Communication Technology and Application (ICCTA 2011), Beijing, 14–16 October 2011, pp. 660–665 (2011)
12. Chiuchisan, I., Geman, O.: An approach of a decision support and home monitoring system for patients with neurological disorders using internet of things concepts. WSEAS Trans. Syst. **13**, 460–469 (2014)
13. Soni, J., Ansari, U., Sharma, D.: Intelligent and effective heart disease prediction system using weighted associative classifiers. Int. J. Comput. Sci. Eng. (IJCSE) **3**, 2385–2392 (2011)
14. Singh, M., Martins, L.M., Joanis, P., Mago, V.K.: Building a cardiovascular disease predictive model using structural equation model and fuzzy cognitive map. In: IEEE International Conference on Fuzzy Systems (FUZZ), Vancouver, 24–29 July 2016, pp. 1377–1382 (2016)
15. Singh, P., Khan, S., Singh, Y.V., Singh, R.S.: A secure and stable humanoid healthcare information processing and supervisory method with IOT-based sensor network. J. Sens. **22**, 13 (2022). Article Id 8568540. https://doi.org/10.1155/2022/8568540
16. Ghadge, P., Girme, V., Kokane, K., Deshmukh, P.: Intelligent heart attack prediction system using big data. Int. J. Recent Res. Math. Comput. Sci. Inf. Technol. **2**, 73–77 (2016)
17. Shouman, M., Turner, T., Stocker, R.: Using data mining techniques in heart disease diagnosis and treatment. In: Electronics, Communications, and Computers, Alexandria, pp. 173–177 (2012)

18. Alemdar, H., Ersoy, C.: Wireless sensor networks for healthcare: a survey. Comput. Netw. **54**, 2688–2710 (2010)
19. Antony, G., Francis, S.: Patient monitoring system using raspberry PI. Int. J. Sci. Res. **6**, 687–689 (2015)
20. Singh, M.K., Singh, A.K., Singh, P., Kalpana, Rishi, O.P.: Artificial intelligence enabled IOT system for football identification in a football match. In: Garg, D., Narayana, V.A., Suganthan, P.N., Anguera, J., Koppula, V.K., Gupta, S.K. (eds.) IACC 2022. CCIS, vol. 1782, pp. 460–472. Springer, Cham (2023). https://doi.org/10.1007/978-3-031-35644-5_37
21. Kumari, M., Godara, S.: Comparative study of data mining classification methods in cardiovascular disease prediction. Int. J. Comput. Sci. Technol. **2**, 304-308.37 (2011)

Comparative Evaluation of Feature Extraction Techniques in Chest X Ray Image with Different Classification Model

Sonia Verma[1] ⓘ, Ganesh Gopal Devarajan[1](✉), and Pankaj Kumar Sharma[2] ⓘ

[1] Department of Computer Science and Engineering, SRM Institute of Science and Technology,
Delhi NCR Campus, Ghaziabad 201204, Uttar Pradesh, India
dganeshgopal@gmail.com
[2] Department of Computer Science and Engineering, Faculty of Engineering and Technology,
SRM Institute of Science and Technology, Delhi - NCR Campus Delhi, Meerut Road,
Modinagar, Ghaziabad 201204, Uttar Pradesh, India
pankaj.sharma@abes.ac.in

Abstract. Artificial intelligence (AI) has the potential to transform health care as it has revolutionized many pattern recognition applications. During the last few years, medical image analysis has been gaining attention. Research on medical images using machine learning (ML) has made significant progress. The purpose of this study was to compare the accuracy of classification in clinical images among ML algorithms. Based on features extracted technique local binary patterns (LBP), histograms of gradients (HOG) and pixels feature extractor, seven classification models are compared. Several methods are used to classify important features are obtained by different feature extractors, including support vector machines (SVM), decision trees (DT), logistic regression(LR), random forests (RF), extreme gradient boosting (XGB), K-Neighbors classifiers (KN) and multinomial Naive Bayes (NB). To test the accuracy of our classification and feature extraction models specifically for histopathology images, we used COVID-19 chest radiographs, which is available publicly dataset containing 21,212 CT images divided into four classes. In comparison to other feature extractors, SVM has the better result using HOG as features. LPB feature extraction has been shown to be superior when used with SVM algorithm to classify COVID-19 chest radiograph data, as demonstrated by experiments on COVID-19 chest radiograph data.

Keywords: LBP · HOG · Pixel based approach · SVM · DT · RF · XGB · NB · KN

1 Introduction

It has become increasingly popular over the past few years, and its applications are expanding every day. Approximately 251 million people affected from COPD diseases worldwide, which are the leading reason of death. Chest diseases such as chronic obstructive pulmonary disease (COPD) [1], asthma, lung cancer, pneumonia, and tuberculosis

D. Garg et al. (Eds.): IACC 2023, CCIS 2054, pp. 197–209, 2024.
https://doi.org/10.1007/978-3-031-56703-2_17

are some of the most common ones. Airflow limitation is a characteristic of COPD, a progressive lung disease. There are a number of parameters that contribute to it, including smoking and environmental pollutants. It is estimated that COPD accounts for a significant proportion of mortality and morbidity worldwide. The avoidance and cure of lung diseases involve a variety of strategies, such as smoking cessation, reducing exposure to pollutants, improving air quality, vaccinations against respiratory infections, and early diagnosis and treatment. To reduce the burden of lung diseases globally, public health initiatives, research, and access to quality healthcare must be prioritized. It is not uncommon for lung disease to be diagnosed via a combination of clinical and imaging tests (such as X-rays or CT scans). Treatment options for lung conditions include prescription drugs [2], inhalers, oxygen therapy, pulmonary rehabilitation, lifestyle modifications (including quitting smoking), surgical procedures, and supportive care. Therefore, ML has become one of the most important efficient tools to process data in the modern era, and it can be used to develop the healthcare industry. In recent years, ML [3] approaches have gained popularity for detecting and forecasting diseases based on images. For lung disorders such as tumors to be detected automatically, medical images must be processed using a combination of feature extraction and classification techniques. A classification algorithm is used to identify pathological diseases from the photos after different features have been extracted.

Numerous aspects can be derived from the lung pictures to identify key elements [4] in the identification of lung disease. These features could be region-based, describing particular regions of concern within the lung, form-based, capturing the shape and contour of anomalies, or texture-based, depicting the varying textures of the lung tissue. The management and treatment of lung disorders present a substantial global health challenge, and early and accurate detection is essential. In recent years, automated lung disease classification and diagnosis based on medical pictures has demonstrated encouraging outcomes. Machine learning classifiers can assist in the precise diagnosis and categorization of various lung disorders by utilising characteristics collected from lung pictures utilizing techniques like LBP, HOG, and pixel-based analysis.

The main contributions of this study are as follows:

1. The comparison of different Machine Learning Algorithm for Medical images Using Pixel, LBP and HOG Feature Extraction.
2. A combination of HOG and SVM was proposed to classify three types of X-ray images: normal, COVID-19, Viral_Pnuemonia, and lung_opacity. In comparison to other deep learning and machine learning models in the literature, our model achieves competitive performance.

There are five sections in the research paper: The topic is introduced and its significance explained in Sect. 1. Work pertaining to our model is examined in Sect. 2. In Sect. 3, the paper's methodology is explained, along with the particular models that are discussed in this work. The dataset that was utilised to test and train the six models is also explained in this section. The research paper is concluded in Sect. 5 after Sect. 4 presents the outcomes attained by each model. Section 6 contains a list of references.

2 Literature Survey

Different methods have been employed, with varying degrees of success, to identify pneumonia. With a 96.04% accuracy rate, support vector machines (SVM) were employed here author [3] to identify patients in need of acute care. Another method, SCoVNet [5], identified lung changes caused by infection with a high accuracy of 98%. With feature correlation analysis, the accuracy of the ResNet50 [6] model was 96.1%. A different approach [7] that used generalized k-means for group statistical modeling produced accuracy levels of 96.0% for COVID-19 cases and 70.650% for non-COVID-19 cases. Accuracy ratings for machine learning-based classifiers, mostly SVM-based, in a system for remote respiratory rate and pattern monitoring varied from 94.4% to 95.1%. When used in conjunction with Random Forest (RF), Logistic Regression (LR), and XGBoost [9], early risk assessment of COVID-19 in ER data yielded accuracy rates of 82% for 30 patients and 0.8% for 200 patients. Modified ResNet was used to automatically identify potential lesions from CT scans with an amazing accuracy rate of 99.3% [10]. In the area of X-ray image processing, DenseNet121 [1] achieved a high accuracy of 98% for the automatic diagnosis of illnesses. In contrast, VGG-16 and GSA-DenseNet121 [11] demonstrated accuracy rates of 98.67% and 98.38%, respectively, for recognizing COVID-19 patients from chest X-ray images. CNN-based [14] methods in the field of acoustic biomarker analysis achieved accuracies of 97.1% for Covid-19 and 100% for asymptomatic patients by pre-screening coughs using acoustic biomarker feature extractors. Other methods, including VGG-19 + ResNet-50 [15], have been utilized to achieve a 94% accuracy rate in converting gray scale photographs into neutrosophic images. However, a few deep learning models, like DRE-Net [16] and d-Resnet-10 [17], were able to distinguish between critical and severe cases with an accuracy of 86% and 81.4%, respectively, when it came to COVID-19 picture detection. Finally, early disease diagnosis and treatment has been achieved with the combined use of DT [18, 19], InceptionV2, and VGG-16, providing fast and precise results with a 91% accuracy rate. These levels of accuracy are consistent with the findings reported in the cited research and applications; nevertheless, it is crucial to remember that real results may vary based on factors such as implementation specifics and dataset quality. Furthermore, changes may have led to improvements in accuracy. Furthermore, improvements in machine learning and medical technology may have contributed to accuracy gains.

A research gap on the effect of various parameter combinations involving LBP, Pixel, and HOG on the classification of X-ray pictures has been identified by our thorough assessment of the literature. Notably, previous research has not adequately explored the applicability of LBP for multiclass categorization in this particular setting. Although deep learning methods have shown impressive results, their usefulness in resource-constrained contexts is limited due to their need on large amounts of data and computer power. On the other hand, conventional feature extraction and machine learning techniques have the benefit of yielding results that are simple to understand, which makes them very efficient even with smaller datasets—a critical trait for medical applications. Moreover, these traditional methods have a track record of success in a number of fields, including medical picture analysis. Our study compares deep learning models with traditional machine learning techniques, like Support Vector Machines (SVM) and Random Forests (RF), for the categorization of X-ray pictures in an effort to close the gaps in the literature. Our research is concentrated on the LBP and HOG methodologies. It is anticipated that the knowledge gathered from this study would be extremely helpful in directing future investigations in this area.

3   Research Methodology

In this section, we discuss the process for classifying the X-ray images into four categories: normal, COVID-19, Viral_Pnuemonia, and lung_opacity, using PFE, LBP and HOG feature extractors.

3.1   Dataset Description

A database of COVID-19 chest radiographs has recently been released, containing 3616 chest radiograph images of unhealthy images, 10,192 images of healthy people, and 6012 images of lung opacity and pneumonia. Each image in the dataset is 1024 pixels wide by 1024 pixels high. Each model's images were resized according to its needs. Kaggle's dataset is free for research purposes and is a standard Kaggle dataset. Grayscale images of radiographs from this dataset have the exact dimensions and are in grayscale (Fig. 1).

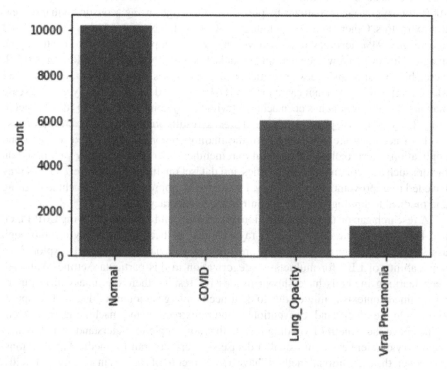

Fig. 1. Dataset Description

3.2 Feature Extraction

3.2.1 Pixel Based Feature Extraction (PFE)

The use of pixel-based approaches is common for identifying low level features, in which spatial relationships are not taken into account. A number of characteristics with low-level are extracted directly from raw and noisy pixels in edge detection [20].

3.2.2 LBP Based Feature Extraction

To distinguish and extract textures, LBP is one of the simplest methods by applying statistical level and local structure. Features can be described more effectively, requiring fewer computations, and it can be implemented easily. A multi-block patch in the image is subjected to LBP at different scales. Based on the local region labels, a feature histogram is constructed from the image parts. Depending on the shape of the region, it can be rectangular, circular, or triangular.

Let X_p be the center pixel and be the number of pixels (n_p) in the neighbor with radius (r), then LBP code can be calculated using Eq. (1).

$$lbp_{n_p} = \sum_{i=0}^{n_p-1} s(X_i - X_p)2^i \tag{1}$$

$$s(X_i - X_p) = f(x) = \begin{cases} 0 \; if \; X_i - X_p < 0 \\ 1 \; if \; X_i - X_p \geq 0 \end{cases} \tag{2}$$

Here, 256 possible units can be calculated because of the value of 1 and the number of sampling points is 8. There has been an observation, which led to the uniformity, that some LBPs appear in a significant image area more frequently than others who have fewer spatial transitions

$$lbp_{n_p r}^{ri} = \begin{cases} \sum_{i=0}^{n_p-1} s(X_i - X_p) if \; pattern \; is \; uniform \\ n_p + 1 if \; pattern \; is \; non \; uniform \end{cases} \tag{3}$$

Here ri represents the rotation invariant which is uniform. The lbp used the gray image with circular neighborhood of radius 1 and compute a histogram of lbp with range 0 to 59.

1. HOG based Feature extraction:

The Hog method (Al Sadeque et al., 2019) is a technique for extracting features from images. A dense feature extraction method is used with it.

In this study, we used the HoG method, which is a feature extraction method for images based on the histogram [21] method to distinguish such features. The method is used for extracting dense features. (Yadav et al. 2019) argue that it is more accurate for features extractions because it takes into account all locations in the image, rather than just the local neighborhood of key points as with Scale-Invariant Feature Transform(SIFT). Gradient directions measured in grams. An image's gradient can be used more effectively to determine an region than flat areas. The HoG feature is able to correctly classify images with blisters during the training procedure(Kadota et al. 2009).

$$\begin{cases} f_x(xy) = f(x+1y) - f(x-1y) \\ f_y(xy) = f(xy+1) - f(xy-1) \end{cases} \tag{4}$$

where brightness at (xy) is denoted by f (x y). The obtained gradients' magnitude m and direction θ are then calculated by

$$m(xy) = \sqrt{f_x(xy)^2 + f_y(xy)^2} \tag{5}$$

and,

$$\theta(xy) = aretan\frac{f_x(xy)}{f_y(xy)} \tag{6}$$

3.3 Study of Machine Learning (ML) Algorithms

3.3.1 Logistic Regression (LR)

Statistical algorithms used for binary classification such as logistic regression predict whether an event will occur according to [24]. This algorithm extracts a number of low-level features directly from raw, noisy pixels and the edge detection algorithm is the most prevalent. The relationship between the properties of the input and the expected output variables can be represented using the logistic function, also called the sigmoid function. The sigmoid function $\delta(t)$ is written as follows:

$$\delta(t) = \frac{1}{1 + e^{-t}} \tag{7}$$

where,

$$t = \omega_0 + \omega_1 x_{10} + \omega_2 x_{20} + +\omega_n x_n \tag{8}$$

For logistic regression, the likelihood function is as follows:

$$l(\omega) = \prod_{i=1}^{n} \delta(t_i)^{y_z} (1 - \delta(t_i))^{1-y_z} \tag{9}$$

3.3.2 Decision Tree (DT)

An algorithm called the DT was developed in 1984 [25]. It is a ML and data mining algorithm [12]. Throughout the DT, checks and compares the classifier with similarity in the dataset and ranks it according to its classification [8] used DTs to classify data based on selecting an attribute which optimizes and fixes the data division. Dataset attributes are divided into several classes until conclusion criteria and conditions are met. A mathematical representation of the DT algorithm is as follows:

$$E = -\sum_{i=1}^{n} P_{xy} \log_2 P_{xy} \tag{10}$$

3.3.3 Random Forest (RF)

[13] developed RF as an ensemble learning (EL) method for solving classification and regression problems Using multiple models to solve the same problem is ensemble learning, a machine learning method for boosting accuracy. A single classifier can only provide a small amount of accuracy, whereas there are multiple classifiers participating in ensemble classification [18].

$$r = \frac{1}{N} \sum_{i=1}^{N} f(x) \tag{11}$$

In an uncertain situation,

$$\sigma = \sqrt{\frac{\sum_{i=1}^{N} f((x) - f)^2}{N - 1}} \tag{12}$$

3.3.4 Extreme Gradient Boosting (XGB)

A distributed gradient boosting algorithm, XGBoost [19], optimizes gradient boosting for large datasets. In general, the XGBoost [22] algorithm functions as follows:

Assume a training dataset

$$d = \{a_n, b_n\}, n = 1, 2, \ldots\ldots\ldots, n, \tag{13}$$

then

$$a_n = \{a_{n1}, a_{n2}, \ldots\ldots\ldots, a_{nm}\} \tag{14}$$

where, m denotes to m dimension and,

$$b_n = \sum_{i=1}^{n} p_k(a_n), p_k \epsilon P, \tag{15}$$

In the model, k represents the trees number.

3.3.5 K-Neighbors Classifier (KNN)

According to [23] the K-Nearest Neighbor classifier divides a dataset into multiple clusters according to the user's preferences. As a result of its flexibility, this algorithm can be useful to classification as well as regression problems. A KNN algorithm finds clusters by comparing the separation between different data points, based on the premise that similar items tend to cluster together.

$$e_{(x_i, y_i)} = \sqrt{(x_{i,1} - y_{i,1})^2 + \ldots\ldots\ldots + (x_{i,m} - y_{i,m})^2} \tag{16}$$

In contrast to algorithms that learn directly from training datasets, KNN holds data and operates on it during the classification phase. It is determined by the majority vote of its nearest neighbours whether a new data point should be classified. When k is changed, the algorithm's accuracy can be affected.

3.3.6 Multinomial Naive Bayes (NB)

As a probabilistic method that is independent of training and testing, NBM relies on a probabilistic approach. In order to classify patients according to their response to treatment, we used a multinomial naive Bayes (MNB) classifier. This classifier makes use of a multinomial distribution to classify individual features. For the training process, suppose $t = t_i$ represents the positive and non-positive classes and $c = c_i$ where $i = 1, \ldots\ldots, n$ is defined as positive conditioning [22] factors (C). This formula can be used to calculate the probability (P) of each event within a class

$$P(x_i|w_j) = \prod_{t=1}^{L} (P(y_k|w_j)) \tag{17}$$

$$P(x_i|w_j) = \frac{1 + C(y_k|w_j)}{L + w_j} \tag{18}$$

By using the maximization function, a concept for indexing a query or a document is selected

$$w^*(d_n) = \text{argmax}_{w_f} P(w_f) \prod_{t=1}^{L} (P(y_k|w_j)) \tag{19}$$

4 Result and Discussion

4.1 Environment Setup

The materials used to create this suggested model are listed in Table 1 and include.

Table 1. Hardware Configuration Requirement

Hyperparameter	Value
Activation	Softmax, relu
Momentum	0.99
Epsilon	0.001
Optimizer	Adamax
Epoch	20
Batch_size	64
Learning_rate	0.0001

4.2 Pixel Based Results

Using Pixel based feature extraction approach; histograms were generated to evaluate the performance of the model. All images are converted to the gray scale and the resize to 64*64 dimensions. In the pixel based feature extraction approach, the XGB classifier performed well as compared to other classifier. According to the XGB classifier, precision, recall and F1-score was 93.12%, 90.79% and 91.09% respectively for class_3 (Fig. 2).

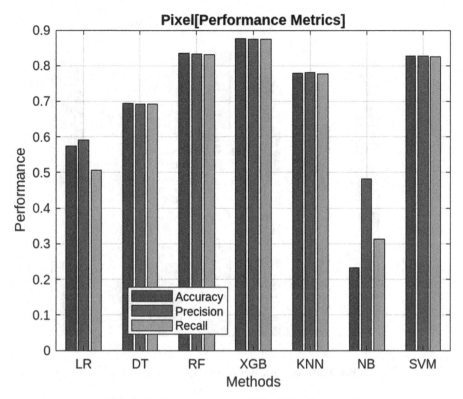

Fig. 2. Performance metrics of Pixel based approach

4.3 LBP Results

Using LBP based feature extraction approach; histograms were generated to evaluate the performance of the model. All images are converted to the gray scale and the resize to 64*64 dimensions. In the pixel based feature extraction approach as shown in Fig. 3, the XGB classifier performed well as compared to other classifier. According to the XGB classifier, precision, recall and F1- score was 71.6%, 80.9% and 76% respectively.

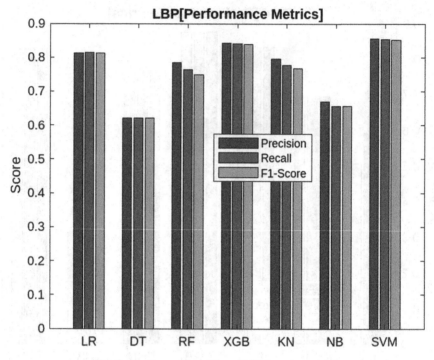

Fig. 3. Performance metrics of LBP based approach

4.4 HOG Results

Using HOG feature extraction, histograms were generated for each image. Compared to another one, the HOG features model achieves the lowest accuracy. The study, the SVM method achieved better results as 95.63%, 89.59% and 92.51% than other model mentioned in Fig. 4.

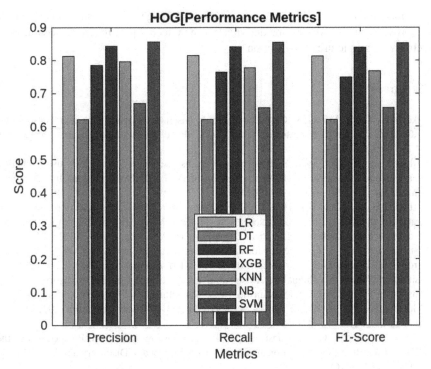

Fig. 4. Performance metrics of HOG based approach

5 Conclusion

The experiments carried out in this study have demonstrated that, although various ML algorithms and feature extractors have their advantages, the Local Binary Patterns (LBP) feature extractor and the Support Vector Machine (SVM) algorithm work better together to classify COVID-19 chest radiograph data than other combinations. The potential of LBP-based feature extraction techniques to enhance medical image analysis is highlighted by this finding. To fully utilise AI-driven healthcare solutions and enhance patient outcomes, further research and development in this area are vital as AI develops. The study's findings have highlighted the significance of feature extraction methods as essential elements in improving the precision of machine learning-based classification. These methods include Local Binary Patterns (LBP), Histograms of Gradients (HOG), and pixel-based approaches. Future studies should investigate sophisticated feature extraction techniques and their integration with a larger variety of machine learning algorithms in order to expand on this basis. Furthermore, it ought to be a primary priority to create specialised models for histopathological pictures, such as the COVID-19 chest radiography dataset that was utilised in this investigation. More precise and prompt diagnosis may result from the development of AI solutions specifically designed for particular medical imaging domains. Future developments in medical image analysis and artificial intelligence (AI) have great potential for the healthcare sector. Utilising AI's capacity for pattern recognition can improve diagnosis precision and patient care even more. In the future, machine learning (ML) research on medical image analysis should concentrate on improving current algorithms and creating new techniques for more accurate and effective clinical picture classification.

References

1. Ikechukwu, A.V., Murali, S.: CX-Net: an efficient ensemble semantic deep neural network for ROI identification from chest-x-ray images for COPD diagnosis. Mach. Learn. Sci. Technol. **4**(2), 025021 (2023)
2. Ahmed, R., Bibi, M., Syed, S.: Improving heart disease prediction accuracy using a hybrid machine learning approach: a comparative study of SVM and KNN algorithms. Int. J. Comput. Inf. Manuf. (IJCIM) **3**(1), 49–54 (2023)
3. Al Sadeque, Z., Khan, T.I., Hossain, Q.D., Turaba, M.Y.: Automated detection and classification of liver cancer from CT images using HOG-SVM model. In: 2019 5th International Conference on Advances in Electrical Engineering (ICAEE), pp. 21–26. IEEE (2019)
4. Bhandari, S., et al.: Logistic regression analysis to predict mortality risk in COVID-19 patients from routine hematologic parameters. Ibnosina J. Med. Biomed. Sci. **12**(2), 123 (2020)
5. Singh, M., Verma, S., Singhal, P.: A comparative study of stroke prediction algorithms using machine learning. In: Garg, D., Narayana, V.A., Suganthan, P.N., Anguera, J., Koppula, V.K., Gupta, S.K. (eds.) IACC 2022. CCIS, vol. 1781, pp. 263–274. Springer, Cham (2022). https://doi.org/10.1007/978-3-031-35641-4_22
6. Chen, T., Guestrin, C.: XGBoost: a scalable tree boosting system. In: Proceedings of the 22nd ACM SIGKDD International Conference on Knowledge Discovery and Data Mining, pp. 785–794 (2016)
7. Chowdhary, C.L., Mittal, M., Kumaresan, P., Pattanaik, P.A., Marszalek, Z.: An efficient segmentation and classification system in medical images using intuitionist possibilistic fuzzy C-mean clustering and fuzzy SVM algorithm. Sensors **20**(14), 3903 (2020). https://doi.org/10.3390/s20143903
8. Lian, W., Nie, G., Jia, B., Shi, D., Fan, Q., Liang, Y.: An intrusion detection method based on decision tree-recursive feature elimination in ensemble learning. Math. Probl. Eng. **2020**, 1–15 (2020)
9. Houssein, E.H., Emam, M.M., Ali, A.A., Suganthan, P.N.: Deep and machine learning techniques for medical imaging-based breast cancer: a comprehensive review. Expert Syst. Appl. **167**, 114161 (2021)
10. Hussain, L., et al.: Machine-learning classification of texture features of portable chest X-ray accurately classifies COVID-19 lung infection. Biomed. Eng. Online **19**(1), 1–18 (2020). https://doi.org/10.1186/s12938-020-00831-x
11. Jiang, Z., Hu, M., Zhai, G.: Portable health screening device of respiratory infections. In: 2020 IEEE International Conference on Multimedia & Expo Workshops (ICMEW), pp. 1–2. IEEE (2020)
12. Kadota, R., Sugano, H., Hiromoto, M., Ochi, H., Miyamoto, R., Nakamura, Y.: Hardware architecture for HOG feature extraction. In: 2009 Fifth International Conference on Intelligent Information Hiding and Multimedia Signal Processing, pp. 1330–1333. IEEE (2009)
13. Kalaivani, N., Manimaran, N., Sophia, S., Devi, D.D.: Deep learning based lung cancer detection and classification. In: IOP Conference Series: Materials Science and Engineering, vol. 994, p. 012026. IOP Publishing (2020)
14. Khan, N., Ullah, F., Hassan, M.A., Hussain, A.: COVID-19 classification based on chest X-ray images using machine learning techniques. J. Comput. Sci. Technol. Stud. **2**(2), 01–11 (2020)

15. Pham, B.T., et al.: A comparative study of kernel logistic regression, radial basis function classifier, multinomial Naïve Bayes, and logistic model tree for flash flood susceptibility mapping. Water **12**(1), 239 (2020). https://doi.org/10.3390/w12010239

16. Shaban, W.M., Rabie, A.H., Saleh, A.I., Abo-Elsoud, M.A.: A new COVID-19 patients detection strategy (CPDS) based on hybrid feature selection and enhanced KNN classifier. Knowl.-Based Syst. **205**, 106270 (2020)

17. Sheykhmousa, M., Mahdianpari, M., Ghanbari, H., Mohammadimanesh, F., Ghamisi, P., Homayouni, S.: Support vector machine versus random forest for remote sensing image classification: a meta-analysis and systematic review. IEEE J. Sel. Top. Appl. Earth Obs. Remote Sens. **13**, 6308–6325 (2020). https://doi.org/10.1109/JSTARS.2020.3026724

18. Singh, G.A.P., Gupta, P.K.: Performance analysis of various machine learning-based approaches for detection and classification of lung cancer in humans. Neural Comput. Appl. **31**, 6863–6877 (2019)

19. Song, Q.Z., Zhao, L., Luo, X.K., Dou, X.C.: Using Deep learning for classification of lung nodules on computed tomography images. J. Healthc. Eng. **2017** (2017)

20. Wibowo, A.S., Tayara, H., Chong, K.T.: XGB5hmC: identifier based on XGB model for RNA 5-hydroxymethylcytosine detection. Chemom. Intell. Lab. Syst. **238**, 104847 (2023)

21. Yadav, D.P., Sharma, A., Singh, M., Goyal, A.: Feature extraction based machine learning for human burn diagnosis from burn images. IEEE J. Transl. Eng. Health Med. **7**, 1–7 (2019). https://doi.org/10.1109/JTEHM.2019.2923628

22. Munjral, S., et al.: Cardiovascular risk stratification in diabetic retinopathy via atherosclerotic pathway in COVID-19/non-COVID-19 frameworks using artificial intelligence paradigm: a narrative review. Diagnostics **12**(5), 1234 (2022)

23. Agarwal, M., Gupta, S.K., Garg, D., Singh, D.: A novel compressed and accelerated convolution neural network for COVID-19 disease classification: a genetic algorithm based approach. In: Garg, D., Jagannathan, S., Gupta, A., Garg, L., Gupta, S. (eds.) IACC 2021. CCIS, vol. 1528, pp. 99–111. Springer, Cham (2022). https://doi.org/10.1007/978-3-030-95502-1_8

24. Rani, P., et al.: Simulation of the lightweight blockchain technique based on privacy and security for healthcare data for the cloud system. Int. J. E-Health Med. Commun. (IJEHMC) **13**(4), 1–15 (2022)

25. Rani, P., et al.: An implementation of modified blowfish technique with honey bee behavior optimization for load balancing in cloud system environment. Wirel. Commun. Mob. Comput. **2022** (2022)

Application of Deep Learning
in Healthcare

Transfer Learning Approach for Differentiating Parkinson's Syndromes Using Voice Recordings

N. Sai Satwik Reddy$^{(\boxtimes)}$ ⓘ, A. Venkata Siva Manoj ⓘ,
V. Poorna Muni Sasidhar Reddy ⓘ, Aadharsh Aadhithya ⓘ, and V. Sowmya ⓘ

Amrita School of Artificial Intelligence, Amrita Vishwa Vidyapeetham,
Coimbatore, India
satwikreddy987@gmail.com, v_sowmya@cb.amrita.edu

Abstract. Parkinson syndromes are a group of disorders affecting the elderly population with unsteadiness, slowness of activities, frequent falls, and speech disturbances, which slowly progress. Diagnosis of this group of syndromes is usually purely clinical and could be delayed due to its varied presentations. Parkinson's syndromes comprise of Idiopathic Parkinson's disease, Multiple system atrophy (MSA), progressive supranuclear palsy (PSP), and cartico basal ganglionic degeneration. In this work, we provide a comparative analysis of several deep learning models such as ViT, MobileNetV2, DenseNets, ResNets, GoogLeNet, VGGs for the differentiation of Parkinson's syndromes using prolonged vowel phonations. To address this multi-class classification problem, we employed transfer learning on DL models, by training on a dataset comprising 337 sustained vowels from patients with parkinson's disease, MSA, PSP, and no parkinson syndromes. Each recording is transformed into a mel-spectrogram for input into the models. Among the models, ResNet152 outperformed the other models, achieving an impressive accuracy of 98.30% in classifying parkinson disorders, offering a promising non-invasive, and cost-effective diagnostic tool for early intervention and treatment planning.

Keywords: Parkinsonism · Atypical parkinsonian syndromes · MSA · PSP · Deep neural networks · Spectrograms · Classification · Speech analysis

1 Introduction

Parkinson's disease (PD), originally referred to as shaking palsy, is a progressive neurodegenerative condition resulting from declining dopaminergic neurons primarily in Substantia Nigra, Mid Brain and Striatum [1]. Its symptoms stem from dopaminergic dysfunction in the central nervous system, manifesting as slowed movement, tremors, abnormal gait, speech disturbances, muscle rigidity, anxiety, fatigue, genitourinary issues, sleep disturbances, cognitive impairments, and mood disorders [2]. Globally, around 10 million people, mainly aged 60 to

© The Author(s), under exclusive license to Springer Nature Switzerland AG 2024
D. Garg et al. (Eds.): IACC 2023, CCIS 2054, pp. 213–226, 2024.
https://doi.org/10.1007/978-3-031-56703-2_18

80, are affected by parkinsonism [3]. Speech dysfunction is often one of the early manifestations of motor impairments in Parkinsonism [4]. Speech impairments affect 75–90% of Parkinson patients, making vocal characteristics a valuable tool for early detection and monitoring [5].

Atypical Parkinsonian syndromes (APS) comprise a group of neurodegenerative disorders that share certain clinical features with Parkinson's disease but are characterized by their distinctive and often more aggressive progression. Two prominent examples of APS are progressive supranuclear palsy (PSP) and multiple system atrophy (MSA) [6]. PSP is marked by profound balance and gait disturbances, along with vertical gaze palsy and cognitive impairments, setting it apart from typical PD [7]. MSA, on the other hand, affects multiple systems of the body, leading to autonomic dysfunction, cerebellar ataxia, and parkinsonism [8]. In the early stages, these syndromes pose unique diagnostic and management challenges. Diagnosing these neurological diseases involves clinical evaluation, neurological examination, medical history review, imaging studies, laboratory tests, and medication response assessments, which can be expensive, and time-consuming [9].

The utilization of speech analysis as a diagnostic tool holds significant promise in the field of neurology, particularly in the identification of complex neurological disorders such as PD, MSA, and PSP. These conditions often present distinct speech patterns and vocal changes that can serve as crucial diagnostic markers. Speech analysis plays a pivotal role as a non-invasive and cost-effective means in aiding early diagnosis and treatment planning for these neurological disorders [10]. By carefully analyzing these speech characteristics, healthcare professionals can assist in early diagnosis and treatment planning, potentially improving patients' quality of life and facilitating timely interventions.

To the best knowledge of the authors, this is the first study to explore deep learning methods for differentiating PD, MSA, PSP, and Healthy Controls (HC) using voice-based features and deep learning. In this study, 11 deep learning architectures are presented for the diagnosis of PD, PSP, and MSA by utilizing speech markers. Subsequently, a comprehensive comparative analysis is conducted to identify the most optimal deep learning architecture suitable for addressing this multi-class classification problem. The salient contributions of our work can be summarized as follows:

– We have adopted a Transfer Learning approach to distinguish parkinsonism, achieving commendable accuracy using solely voice-based features.
– By utilizing an open-source dataset, our study serves as a valuable benchmark for future research in this particular area.

The remaining sections in this paper are organized as follows: Sect. 2 provides a concise summary of the related works, Sect. 3 describes the dataset, Sect. 4 provides a detailed overview of the proposed methodology, Sect. 5 demonstrates the results, and the conclusion and future scope are presented in Sect. 6.

2   Related Work

Only a limited number of works address to differentiate parkinsonian syndromes (APS). Magnetic resonance imaging (MRI) data is utilized to differentiate these syndromes radiologically upto a certain extent [11]. The findings in this study suggest that a non-invasive imaging technique has the potential to distinguish between various forms of parkinsonism. [12] employed convolutional neural network (CNN) based deep learning to achieve accurate MRI-based differential diagnoses of PD, PSP, multiple system atrophy with predominant parkinsonian features (MSA-P), and normal subjects. The ensemble of DenseNet201, VGG16, and VGG19 models is utilized for the detection of PD in [13]. In [14], generative variational autoencoders are employed by utilizing magnetic resonance imaging (MRI) data of PD and healthy subjects. A decision support system for Parkinson's disease detection, based on deep neural networks and utilizing MRI image data, is proposed in [15].

Further, [16] utilized an automated approach combining atlas-based volumetry and support vector machine classification to distinguish parkinsonian syndromes from healthy controls. This method yielded high classification accuracy, highlighting specific brain regions crucial for differentiation. The research demonstrates the potential for reliable automated differentiation of parkinsonian syndromes across various MRI scanners. The clinical potential of Voxel-based Morphometry (VBM) in Atypical Parkinson Syndromes (APS) is explored in [17]. A remarkable accuracy of 96.8% in distinguishing PSP from idiopathic parkinson syndrome (IPS) is achieved using support vector machine (SVM). Further, [18] provides a comprehensive review of 209 research papers utilizing machine learning for PD diagnosis. It underscores the potential of machine learning in improving clinical decision-making and identifying novel biomarkers for early PD diagnosis. In [19], the MRI images are preprocessed and fed into the DenseNet201 method for the detection of PD, resulting in an accuracy of 91.7%. To ensure accurate results in classifying medical disorders using machine learning, biomedical data pre-processing is a vital step [20].

Despite a few pioneering works, very few works have employed speech modality for the differentiation of APS. One of the very first works in this area was that of [10]. In [10], three distinct sets of speech characteristic features are utilized for the classification task. Univariate statistical analysis is used to reduce dimensionality and factorial discriminant analysis is employed for classification purposes. The highest accuracy achieved is 84% upon employing two sets of features. The potential of acoustic speech analysis for differentiating PD from APS is explored in [21]. This study achieved a notable 84% accuracy in distinguishing between PSP and MSA by employing a support vector machine with a Gaussian radial basis kernel. In [6], patients with PD, PSP, and MSA exhibited distinct speech patterns. PD patients had hypophonic monotonous speech with occasional rushes, while MSA and PSP patients showed mixed dysarthria with ataxic and spastic elements. All speech parameters significantly deviated from controls (P < 0.001, 0.012, and 0.008, respectively). PSP patients had notably shorter maximum phonation time than MSA and PD (P = 0.015), highlighting diagnostic potential, especially for PSP's severe speech impairment indicative of frontostriatal pathology. [22] utilized various machine learning and deep learning techniques for classifying other brain disorders like alzheimer's and schizophrenia.

In the extensive literature addressing the differentiation of parkinsonism via various features and the application of deep learning, a noticeable gap exists. Specifically, there is limited research that focuses on differentiating parkinsonism based on vocal features, especially when utilizing deep learning techniques. Moreover, the use of voice-based features holds significant clinical relevance as they can be easily obtained by anyone, offering a non-invasive and universally accessible diagnostic tool. Furthermore, many preceding studies have relied on data that is not publicly accessible. In contrast, our research leverages a publicly available database. As such, our study not only contributes to the current body of knowledge but also establishes a reference point for subsequent research in this domain.

3   Data Preparation

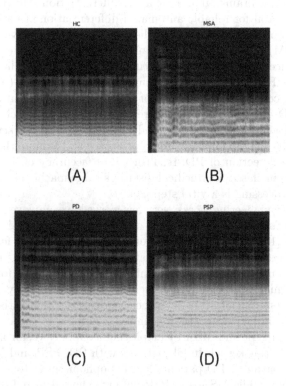

(A)   (B)

(C)   (D)

Fig. 1. Sample Spectrograms of Healthy Controls, Multiple System Atrophy, Parkinson's Disease, and Progressive SupraNeuclear Palsy in subfigures A, B, C, D respectively.

The data used in this study is an open-source, publicly available dataset [23]. It consists of original and synthesized samples of 337 sustained vowels from 22 patients with PD, 21 patients with multiple system atrophy, 18 patients with progressive supranuclear palsy, and 22 healthy controls (HC). Silences were trimmed from each sample. Each sample is subsequently cut down to uniform 3-second-long fragments. This yields 1034 samples of healthy controls, 678 samples of multiple system atrophy, 838 samples of Parkinson disease and 590 samples of progressive supranuclear palsy. Each recording is then converted to a mel-spectrogram and resized to 224×224 to be fed into Deep Learning models. Sample spectrograms are shown in Fig. 1.

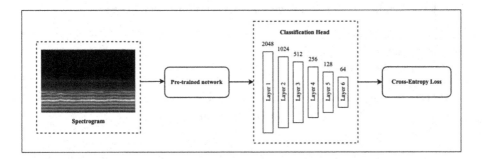

Fig. 2. Proposed pipeline for differential diagnosis of parkinsonism.

4   Methodology

We explored the efficacy of transfer learning for this problem. To this end, we utilized 11 models as described in the subsequent subsection, augmenting each with a classification head. The classification head comprises 6 linear layers with Rectified Linear Unit (ReLU) activations. The complete model, inclusive of the classification head, undergoes fine-tuning using the Adam optimizer with a learning rate of 0.01. We proceeded with the training process for all models until they reached convergence and exhibited signs of overfitting over 150 epochs. Subsequently, we retrospectively selected the model demonstrating the highest validation accuracy. All reported test metrics in this study are derived from the evaluation conducted on the model with the best validation accuracy. The proposed methodology for the classification task is depicted in Fig. 2.

4.1   Simulation Setup

The training process is facilitated using the PyTorch library, and experiments are conducted on Kaggle platform, utilizing a P100 GPU for computational support. The values of the hyperparameters employed during the training are detailed in Table 1.

Table 1. Training Parameters

Parameter	Value
Optimizer	ADAM
Learning rate	10^{-4}
Num Epochs	150
Batch size	32

4.2 Models

The deep learning models employed in this study are as follows:

- Vision Transformers
- GoogLeNet
- ResNet50 and ResNet152
- SqueezeNet
- VGG16 and VGG19
- DenseNet121, DenseNet169 and DenseNet201
- MobileNetV2

Vision Transformers (ViTs) [24, 25] are used for image classification by utilizing self-attention mechanisms instead of traditional convolutional layers. Processing images as sequences of tokens, ViTs capture global context and dependencies, enabling effective feature extraction. The transformer architecture's scalability accommodates varying resolutions, as input images are divided into patches and linearly embedded. GoogLeNet [26], featuring the Inception module, is a robust deep convolutional neural network designed for image recognition tasks. It stands out for its efficiency and effectiveness, utilizing 22 layers to optimize computational efficiency and accuracy via the parallel use of multiple kernel sizes.

ResNet50 and ResNet152 [27] are deep convolutional neural networks commonly used in image classification. These models, which have 50 and 152 layers, respectively, employ skip connections to solve the vanishing gradient problem. This enables effective training of the networks, resulting in the effective capturing of underlying patterns in the images for better classification results. SqueezeNet [28] is a lightweight CNN architecture optimized for resource-constrained devices. It uses a fire module that combines 1×1 and 3×3 convolutions to reduce parameters without compromising accuracy.

VGG16 and VGG19 [29] are simple and effective image classification models. Both models have a stack of convolutional layers with small 3x3 filters, and max-pooling for spatial down-sampling. Their deep architectures are able to model complex features but computation costs and resource requirements for training and inference are high. DenseNet121, DenseNet169, and DenseNet201 [30] are image classification architectures with dense connectivity, ensuring each layer receives input from all previous layers. DenseNet121 has 121 layers, DenseNet169 has 169, and DenseNet201 has 201. These models are known for their parameter efficiency, as they achieve impressive accuracy with fewer parameters compared to traditional architectures.

MobileNetV2 [31] is a high-performance convolutional neural network tailored for image classification on mobile devices. Utilizing inverted residual blocks and linear bottlenecks, it optimizes model size and computational efficiency without compromising accuracy. MobileNetV2 excels in real-time image classification tasks by efficiently extracting features, ensuring swift and precise results. The division of dataset for training, testing, and validation is depicted in Fig. 3.

4.3   Evaluation Metrics

The evaluation metrics used in this study are accuracy, F1-score, precision, and recall. Accuracy measures the overall correctness of a model's predictions, while the F1-score conveys the balance between precision and recall, particularly important when dealing with imbalanced datasets. Precision measures the accuracy of positive predictions by assessing the proportion of true positive predictions among all positive predictions whereas recall measures the proportion of actual positive instances correctly identified by a model, emphasizing its ability to capture relevant cases. Table 2 illustrates the computation of the evaluation metrics.

Table 2. Evaluation metrics used in this study for assessing the effectiveness of the considered DL models.

S.No	Error metric	Formula
1	Accuracy	$\dfrac{TP + TN}{TN + FP + TP + FN}$
2	F1 score	$\dfrac{2 \times \text{Precision} \times \text{Recall}}{\text{Precision} + \text{Recall}}$
3	Precision	$\dfrac{TP}{TP + FP}$
4	Recall	$\dfrac{TP}{TP + FN}$

where TP is the number of true positives, TN is the number of true negatives, FP is the number of false positives, and FN is the number of false negatives.

5   Results and Discussions

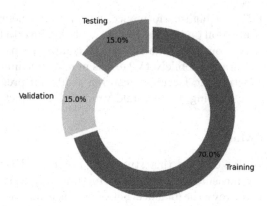

Fig. 3. Visualization of data split for training, testing and validation.

Table 3. Performance Metrics of Various Models (Mean ± Standard Deviation of 4 Runs)

Model	Accuracy	F1	Precision	Recall
ViT-L-32	0.9674 ± 0.0068	0.9643 ± 0.0077	0.9643 ± 0.0082	0.9601 ± 0.0067
ViT-B-16	0.9157 ± 0.0124	0.9084 ± 0.0129	0.9099 ± 0.0132	0.9044 ± 0.0144
MobileNetV2	0.9561 ± 0.0141	0.9528 ± 0.0172	0.9538 ± 0.0174	0.9494 ± 0.0132
DenseNet201	0.9723 ± 0.0076	0.9704 ± 0.0075	0.9709 ± 0.0081	0.9750 ± 0.0037
DenseNet169	0.9766 ± 0.0021	0.9750 ± 0.0023	0.9753 ± 0.0025	0.9739 ± 0.0025
DenseNet121	0.9773 ± 0.0068	0.9757 ± 0.0076	0.9763 ± 0.0078	0.9792 ± 0.0079
ResNet152	**0.9808 ± 0.0056**	**0.9794 ± 0.0051**	**0.9793 ± 0.0051**	**0.9771 ± 0.0058**
ResNet50	0.9766 ± 0.0076	0.9756 ± 0.0073	0.9758 ± 0.0075	0.9765 ± 0.0061
GoogLeNet	0.9702 ± 0.0118	0.9673 ± 0.0130	0.9703 ± 0.0099	0.9712 ± 0.0067
VGG19	0.9561 ± 0.0068	0.9524± 0.0069	0.9540 ± 0.0062	0.9506 ± 0.0082
VGG16	0.9617 ± 0.0097	0.9583 ± 0.0099	0.9600 ± 0.0098	0.9638 ± 0.0027

The comparative evaluation of various deep learning models on the dataset revealed distinct performance levels. As tabulated in Table 3, ResNet152 emerged as the leading model, registering a test accuracy of 98.30%. This was closely followed by DenseNet169 and DenseNet121 with accuracy scores of 97.66% and 97.45%, respectively. On the lower end of the spectrum, ViT-B-16 recorded an accuracy of 91.08%, marking the lowest performance among the models evaluated. The performance comparison of the deep learning models is depicted in Fig. 4.

The superiority of ResNet152 in classifying parkinson syndromes is demonstrated in the confusion matrix in the Fig. 5 which indicates high number of

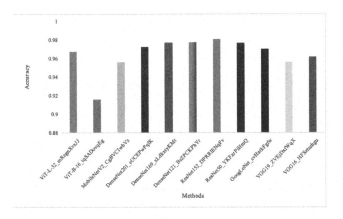

Fig. 4. Illustration of performance comparison of the deep learning models.

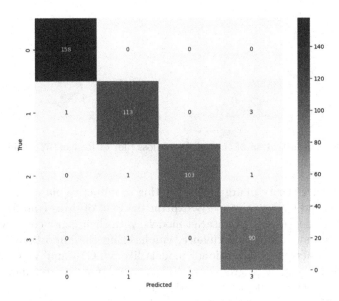

Fig. 5. Illustration of the confusion matrix of ResNet152.

true positives and true negatives. The performance of the ResNet152 model in capturing the pattern or trend is highlighted in the accuracy and loss plots in Fig. 6 and Fig. 7, respectively.

The superior performance of ResNet152 can be attributed to its deep architecture and skip connections, which allow it to learn intricate patterns without succumbing to the vanishing gradient problem. The lower performance of the ViT variants, especially ViT-B-16, might be due to the nature of data, which may not be best suited for transformer-based models without additional data augmentations or training strategies. Particularly, our results suggest that we

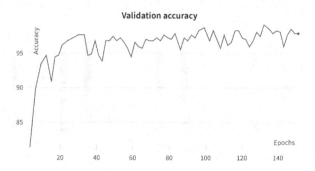

Fig. 6. Illustration of the validation accuracy plot of ResNet152 model.

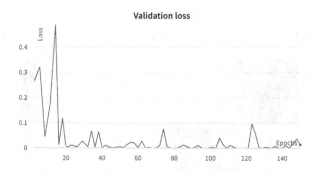

Fig. 7. Illustration of the validation loss plot of ResNet152 model.

still need to have clarity in arguments relating to inductive biases of pre-trained transformers and CNNs to properly explain the kind of tasks transformers outshine CNNs and vice-versa. DenseNet models, with their dense connections, also showcased commendable performance, emphasizing the importance of feature reuse in deep networks. Traditional models like VGG16 and VGG19, despite their simplicity, still hold ground with decent accuracy scores, indicating the robustness of their architecture for varied datasets.

The results underscore the significance of architectural nuances in model performance and stress the importance of model selection based on data characteristics and computational constraints. They also emphasize that not necessarily are the latest and advanced models better than the traditional and conventional ones.

It is known that there are noticeable differences in subharmonics between parkinsonism groups. We hypothesize that these models are able to capture these differences in subharmonics, enabling them to distinguish between the groups with higher accuracy. Further, from the t-SNE visualization, there is a clear separation between the different Parkinson's syndromes, reinforcing our hypothesis. Further,

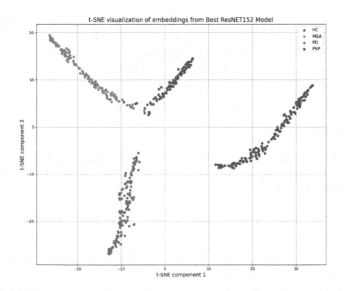

Fig. 8. The t-SNE visualization of test data from ResNet152. (HC, MSA, PD, PSP refer to Healthy controls, Multiple System Atrophy, Parkinson Disease, and Progressive supranuclear palsy respectively.)

- Embedding Precision: From the Fig. 8, we can observe a clear separation among clusters of Parkinson's syndromes. This indicates that the finetuned model has learned to differentiate the differences in subharmonics within the groups. The clear boundaries between clusters suggest that the model has internalized the unique acoustic characteristics tied to each syndrome.
- Variability Insights: The spread of each cluster in the visualization offers insights into the variability of voice patterns within each syndrome. While certain syndromes, like PSP, display tighter clustering-indicating consistency in voice patterns-others exhibit a broader distribution.

Combining these observations, we can infer that the models not only excel in identifying the nuances in subharmonics across Parkinson's syndromes but also display resilience against potential intra-group variability, ensuring robust classification outcomes.

6 Conclusion

In this work, we propose the utilization of fine-tuned ResNet152, a deep neural network, to address the challenge of differential diagnosis in Parkinsonism. Mel-spectrograms are extracted from the voice records to train the networks and enhance their performance for the classification task. Among the networks considered, ResNet152 outperformed the others. It achieved an exceptional accuracy of 98.30% in classifying PD, PSP, MSA, and HC.

Some of the possible extensions of the works include expanding the dataset with a more varied and diverse set of patients and enhancing the model's reliability and applicability. Also, deploying the model in a real-time scenario and testing its efficacy on a more diverse data distribution will test the generalization capabilities of such methods and their practical relevance.

References

1. Karaman, O., Çakın, H., Alhudhaif, A., Polat, K.: Robust automated Parkinson disease detection based on voice signals with transfer learning. Expert Syst. Appl. **178**, 115013 (2021)
2. Kaur, S., Aggarwal, H., Rani, R.: Diagnosis of Parkinson's disease using deep CNN with transfer learning and data augmentation. Multimedia Tools Appl. **80**, 10113–10139 (2021)
3. Naseer, A., Rani, M., Naz, S., Razzak, M.I., Imran, M., Xu, G.: Refining Parkinson's neurological disorder identification through deep transfer learning. Neural Computi. Appl. **32**, 839–854 (2020)
4. Vásquez-Correa, J.C., et al.: Convolutional neural networks and a transfer learning strategy to classify Parkinson's disease from speech in three different languages. In: Nyström, I., Hernández Heredia, Y., Milián Núñez, V. (eds.) CIARP 2019. LNCS, vol. 11896, pp. 697–706. Springer, Cham (2019). https://doi.org/10.1007/978-3-030-33904-3_66
5. Costantini, G., et al.: Artificial intelligence-based voice assessment of patients with Parkinson's disease off and on treatment: machine vs. deep-learning comparison. Sensors **23**(4), 2293 (2023)
6. Sachin, S., Shukla, G., Goyal, V., Singh, S., Aggarwal, V., Behari, M.: Clinical speech impairment in Parkinson's disease, progressive supranuclear palsy, and multiple system atrophy. Neurol. India **56**(2), 122 (2008)
7. Jia, P., Zhang, J., Han, J., Ji, Y.: Clinical outcomes and cognitive impairments between progressive supranuclear palsy and multiple system atrophy. Brain Behav. **12**(12), e2827 (2022)
8. Chen, B., et al.: Functional connectome automatically differentiates multiple system atrophy (Parkinsonian type) from idiopathic parkinson's disease at early stages. Hum. Brain Mapp. **44**(6), 2176–2190 (2023)
9. Alsharabi, N., Shahwar, T., Rehman, A.U., Alharbi, Y.: Implementing magnetic resonance imaging brain disorder classification via AlexNet-quantum learning. Mathematics **11**(2), 376 (2023)
10. Das, B., Daoudi, K., Klempir, J., Rusz, J.: Towards disease-specific speech markers for differential diagnosis in Parkinsonism. In: ICASSP 2019–2019 IEEE International Conference on Acoustics, Speech and Signal Processing (ICASSP), pp. 5846–5850. IEEE (2019)
11. Archer, D.B., et al.: Development and validation of the automated imaging differentiation in parkinsonism (aid-p): a multicentre machine learning study. Lancet Digital Health **1**(5), e222–e231 (2019)
12. Kiryu, S., et al.: Deep learning to differentiate parkinsonian disorders separately using single midsagittal MR imaging: a proof of concept study. Eur. Radiol. **29**, 6891–6899 (2019)

13. Rajanbabu, K., Veetil, I.K., Sowmya, V., Gopalakrishnan, E.A., Soman, K.P.: Ensemble of deep transfer learning models for Parkinson's disease classification. In: Reddy, V.S., Prasad, V.K., Wang, J., Reddy, K.T.V. (eds.) Soft Computing and Signal Processing. AISC, vol. 1340, pp. 135–143. Springer, Singapore (2022). https://doi.org/10.1007/978-981-16-1249-7_14

14. Madan, Y., Veetil, I.K., Sowmya, S., Gopalakrishnan, E.A., Soman, S.: Synthetic data augmentation of MRI using generative variational autoencoder for Parkinson's disease detection. In: Bhateja, V., Tang, J., Satapathy, S.C., Peer, P., Das, R. (eds.) Evolution in Computational Intelligence. Smart Innovation, Systems and Technologies, vol. 267, pp. 171–178. Springer, Singapore (2022). https://doi.org/10.1007/978-981-16-6616-2_16

15. Veetil, I.K., Gopalakrishnan, E.A., Sowmya, V., Soman, K.P.: Parkinson's disease classification from magnetic resonance images (MRI) using deep transfer learned convolutional neural networks. In: 2021 IEEE 18th India Council International Conference (INDICON), pp. 1–6. IEEE (2021)

16. Huppertz, H.-J., et al.: Differentiation of neurodegenerative parkinsonian syndromes by volumetric magnetic resonance imaging analysis and support vector machine classification. Mov. Disord. 31(10), 1506–1517 (2016)

17. Focke, N.K., et al.: Individual voxel-based subtype prediction can differentiate progressive supranuclear palsy from idiopathic Parkinson syndrome and healthy controls. Human Brain Mapping 32(11), 1905–1915 (2011)

18. Mei, J., Desrosiers, C., Frasnelli, J.: Machine learning for the diagnosis of Parkinson's disease: a review of literature. Front. Aging Neurosci. 13, 633752 (2021)

19. Madan, Y., Veetil, I.K., Sowmya, V., Gopalakrishnan, E.A., Soman, K.P.: Deep learning-based approach for Parkinson's disease detection using region of interest. In: Raj, J.S., Palanisamy, R., Perikos, I., Shi, Y. (eds.) Intelligent Sustainable Systems. LNNS, vol. 213, pp. 1–13. Springer, Singapore (2022). https://doi.org/10.1007/978-981-16-2422-3_1

20. Reddy, N.S.S., Reddy, V.P.M.S., Mohan, N., Kumar, S., Soman, K.P.: A fast iterative filtering method for efficient denoising of phonocardiogram signals. In: 2023 3rd International Conference on Intelligent Technologies (CONIT), pp. 1–6 (2023)

21. Li, G.: Speech analysis for the differential diagnosis between Parkinson's disease, progressive supranuclear palsy and multiple system atrophy. Master's thesis, Université Paris Saclay (2017)

22. Sudharsan, D., et al.: Analysis of machine learning and deep learning algorithms for detection of brain disorders using MRI data. In: Gupta, M., Ghatak, S., Gupta, A., Mukherjee, A.L. (eds.) Artificial Intelligence on Medical Data. LNCVB, vol. 37, pp. 39–46. Springer, Singapore (2022). https://doi.org/10.1007/978-981-19-0151-5_4

23. Hlavnička, J., Čmejla, R., Klempíř, J., čka, E., Rusz, J.: Synthetic vowels of speakers with Parkinson's disease and Parkinsonism (2019)

24. Dosovitskiy, A., et al.: An image is worth 16x16 words: Transformers for image recognition at scale. arXiv preprint arXiv:2010.11929 (2020)

25. Sukumar, A., Anil, A., Sajith, V.V.V., Sowmya, V., Krichen, M., Ravi, V.: Influence of spectral bands on satellite image classification using vision transformers. In: Bhateja, V., Yang, XS., Lin, J.CW., Das, R. (eds.) Evolution in Computational Intelligence. FICTA 2022. Smart Innovation, Systems and Technologies, vol. 326, pp. 243–251. Springer, Singapore (2022). https://doi.org/10.1007/978-981-19-7513-4_22

26. Szegedy, C., et al.: Going deeper with convolutions. In: Proceedings of the IEEE Conference on Computer Vision and Pattern Recognition, pp. 1–9 (2015)

27. He, K., Zhang, X., Ren, S., Sun, J.: Deep residual learning for image recognition. In Proceedings of the IEEE Conference on Computer Vision and Pattern Recognition, pp. 770–778 (2016)
28. Iandola, F.N., Han, S., Moskewicz, M.W., Ashraf, K., Dally, W.J., Keutzer, K.: Squeezenet: Alexnet-level accuracy with 50x fewer parameters and< 0.5 MB model size. arXiv preprint arXiv:1602.07360 (2016)
29. Simonyan, K., Zisserman, A.: Very deep convolutional networks for large-scale image recognition. arXiv preprint arXiv:1409.1556 (2014)
30. Huang, G., Liu, Z., Van Der Maaten, L., Weinberger, K.Q.: Densely connected convolutional networks. In: Proceedings of the IEEE Conference on Computer Vision and Pattern Recognition, pp, 4700–4708 (2017)
31. Sandler, M., Howard, A., Zhu, M., Zhmoginov, A., Chen, L-C.: Mobilenetv 2: inverted residuals and linear bottlenecks. In: Proceedings of the IEEE Conference on Computer Vision and Pattern Recognition, pp. 4510–4520 (2018)

Detection of Brain Tumor Types Based on FANET Segmentation and Hybrid Squeeze Excitation Network with KNN

Anjali Hemant Tiple[1]([⊠]) [iD], A. B. Kakade[2] [iD], and Uday Anandrao Patil[3] [iD]

[1] Shivaji University, Kolhapur, Maharashtra 416004, India
anjalitiple@rediffmail.com
[2] Rajarambapu Institute of Technology, Kolhapur, Maharashtra 415414, India
[3] Department of Technology, Shivaji University, Kolhapur 416004, India

Abstract. Brain tumors are fatal worldwide and are difficult to treat. The process requires time and is prone to error for medical professionals to examine the scans and identify tumor locations. To overcome the limitations, an efficient tumor detection and classification method is necessary for obtaining robust features as well as perform proper disease classification. This paper proposes a multiclass brain tumor classification based on hybrid Squeeze-and-Excitation Networks (SENET) with K-Nearest Neighbour (KNN) Algorithm. To improve poor contrast and raise the quality of the input images, the proposed design gathers and pre-processes the MRI images of brain tumors using the Recursively Separated Exposure Based Sub-Image Histogram Equalization (RS-ESIHE) technique. Following image enhancement, these images are given into FANET segmentation method to segment based on feedback mechanism during training and then using a hybrid SNET with KNN classification technique extracted significant features and classified brain tumor types. Accuracy, F1_score, precision, sensitivity and kappa are some of the metrics used to measure performance, and the results are 97.5%, 94.74%, 95.16%, 94.74% and 96.53%. As a result, the experimental findings for the proposed technique are superior to those of the other existing methods.

Keywords: MRI · Brain tumor · FANET segmentation · hybrid SENET-KNN · RS-ESIHE

1 Introduction

Brain tumors are classed as malignant (cancerous) and benign (noncancerous) [1]. Malignant tumors may spread quickly into surrounding brain tissues affecting the patients health. Most cells that are aging or damaged are removed and replaced with fresh ones. Problems may arise if the old and damaged cells are not removed while forming new cells. The generation of new cells frequently in the old cell leads to an accumulation of tissue, and this is referred to as overgrowth or tumor [2]. Because of the size, location, shape, and kind of tumor in the brain is exceedingly complicated and challenging to detect brain tumors [3]. A medical examination using Magnetic resonance imaging

© The Author(s), under exclusive license to Springer Nature Switzerland AG 2024
D. Garg et al. (Eds.): IACC 2023, CCIS 2054, pp. 227–245, 2024.
https://doi.org/10.1007/978-3-031-56703-2_19

(MRI), Computer tomography (CT), endoscopy imaging, and X-ray are frequently used for determining the tumor diagnosis. MRI imaging is one of the most popular and useful ways for diagnosing and analyzing the patient's brain.

Examining brain tumor images properly is critical in determining a patient's wellness. These images have an irregularities or noisy data, making it difficult for a clinician to quickly evaluate them [4]. A brain tumor manual identification becomes expensive as well as time-consuming. To help radiologists and physicians identify potentially harmful tumours early in order to save precious human lives, a computer-aided diagnostic (CAD) systems that runs automatically is necessary [5]. Artificial intelligence (AI) is being developed by scientists to allow robots to process knowledge and resolve problems as they are exposed to new information. Brain tumor diagnosis is made much easier by the AI subcategories of machine and deep learning.

Healthcare professionals employ DL techniques like custom CNNs, Google Nets, VGGNets and ResNets as well as conventional ML algorithms like support vector machines (SVMs), decision trees, Naive Bayes and k-nearest neighbor (k-NN), to assist in the diagnosis of these dangerous disorders [6]. Even though there have been numerous attempts to identify tumors in MRI scans, there are still numerous flaws (such as poor accuracy, large and slow models, and expensive computing) [7]. Additionally, existing techniques provide lower recall and precision levels, which leads to less efficient and take a longer duration to classify images, which might postpone the treatment of the patient. Hence this proposed a detection of brain tumor types based on FANET segmentation and Hybrid SENET with KNN to identify the brain tumor early. The main contributions of the proposed model are

- Detection of brain tumor types based on FANET segmentation and hybrid SENET with KNN.
- RS-ESIHE method is used for preprocessing the collected MRI images to enhance the quality of image.
- FANet employs a single end-to-end trainable network that enables information propagation during both testing and training time based on feedback mechanism to segment the tumor region.
- Based on feature extraction by Hybrid SENET with KNN classifier is used for detecting the brain tumor types.

The sections of the paper are as follows: Sect. 2 investigates the various articles related to brain tumor diagnosis. The proposed method are briefly described in Sect. 3. Experimental findings for the proposed model are provided in Sect. 4 and the research article is concluded in the last section.

2 Literature Review

Many articles relating to brain detection are explored in this section, and a few of these works are discussed below with limitations.

Kumar et al. [8] demonstrated a computerized technique for classifying MRI brain tumors. Four modules are preprocessing, feature extraction, segmentation and classification make up the proposed research. As noise in the input image will influence the classification process accuracy, it was first eliminated using the Median Filter. The images are transformed into 3 × 3 blocks at once. The pre-processed image was next used to extract the texture details. Following feature extraction, the adaptive k-nearest neighbour classifier was used to categorize an image as either normal or unusual. The best-possibility fuzzy C-means clustering approach was then used to segment the tumor areas. Accuracy, specificity and sensitivity are assessed for classification as well as the segmentation technique. Two datasets are the publicly accessible dataset and the BRATS MICCAI brain tumor dataset are used for the experimental investigation.

Khairandish et al. [9] developed a Hybrid method, BRATS database was used in this research work to detected and categorized tumors on brain MRI images. With the help of supervised hybrid CNN and SVM algorithms, the deployed system attempts to categorize brain images are malignant or benign tumors. Normalizing the input images was done as the first stage in the preprocessing procedure. Important features were then extracted via the preprocessed image employing the Maximally Stable Extremal Regions (MSER) method and segmented by a threshold-based segmentation technique. To classify brain MRI images, hybrid CNN and SVM algorithms are used with the labelled segmentation features as input.

Deb and Roy [10] introduced an innovative segmentation and classification method for detecting brain tumors. To identify normal and abnormal in the image, the process applied an adaptive fuzzy deep neural network and frog leap optimization. Using the established method, accurate classification was accomplished while minimizing errors. Utilizing an adaptive flying squirrel method, the abnormal image was segmented to determine the tumor size and severity. The MATLAB simulation software was used to put the created work into practice.

Islam et al. [11] presented an improved method for detecting brain tumors that used the template-based K-means (TK) algorithm, superpixels, as well as principal component analysis (PCA), and which can accurately identify tumors while executing more quickly. First, use PCA and superpixels to extract key features that can help diagnose brain tumors with accuracy. The image was then enhanced with a filter that improves accuracy. At last, the TK-means clustering technique was used to segment the images for identifying the brain tumor.

Garg and Garg [12] established a hybrid ensemble technique based on the majority voting method employing K-Nearest Neighbour, Random Forest (RF), and Decision Tree (DT) (KNNRF-DT). It seeks to determine the size of the region of tumor and categorize tumors in the brain into either benign or malignant. Otsu's Threshold technique is initially used for segmentation. Thirteen features that can be applied to categorization are extracted using a Principal Component Analysis (PCA), Stationary Wavelet Transform (SWT), and Grey Level Co-occurrence Matrix (GLCM). On the basis of the Majority Voting approach, a hybrid ensemble classifier (KNN-RFDT) performs the classification.

Majority of the articles evaluated above are related to the brain tumour detection. Drawbacks from the reviewed articles are sensitive to image noise [8], need a lot of labelled data to train well, which can be expensive and time-consuming [9], the curse of dimensionality [10], Loss of information [11] and ensemble is challenging to learn, and any poor decision might result in a model with lower prediction accuracy [12].

3 Proposed Methodology

A brain tumor are one of the main reasons that mortality rates for both adults and children are rising. Automated brain tumor identification is essential because, when a person's life is at danger, absolute precision is required. DL algorithms are used for the extraction of features and classification in the automated detection of tumors in MR images. This research proposes a method for automatically identifying tumors in MR images.

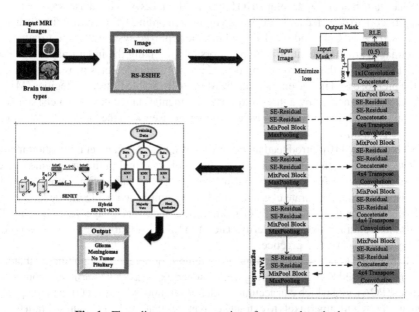

Fig. 1. Flow diagram representation of proposed method.

Figure 1 depicts the flow diagram representation of proposed method to detect the brain tumor types. In the proposed framework, MRI images of brain tumors are gathered and pre-processed using the RS-ESIHE method to enhance the low contrast images for improving the resolution of the gathered input images. After the image enhancement, these contrast enhanced images are fed into segmentation by FANET segmentation that combines the feature mapping from the current training epoch with the previous epoch mask. The learnt feature mappings at various convolutional layers are then given hard attention using the previous epoch mask. During the test period, the network also permits iterative correction of the predictions to segment the tumor region and based on hybrid SNET WITH KNN method to extract the important characteristics while suppressing unimportant features and classified the types of brain tumor.

3.1 Image Enhancement

In medical imaging, contrast enhancement techniques are frequently employed to enhance the clarity of low-contrast images by highlighting important details. Image enhancement technique used in the proposed method as RS-ESIHE is discussed below.

i. RS-ESIHE

The recursive edition of ESIHE, known as RS-ESIHE, conceptually decomposes the histogram in a similar manner [13]. By utilising the exposure thresholds of particular sub-histograms around recursion level v, RS-ESIHE recursively breaks down the data to produce 2^v sub-histograms. Subsequently, individual equalisation is applied to every deconstructed sub histogram. Recursion level, v is assumed to be two for the purpose of simplicity. According to the RS-ESIHE technique, the brightness threshold, histogram clipping, subdividing, and equalisation are all calculated.

- *Exposure threshold calculations*

According to Eq. (1), the entire histogram's exposure threshold Z_A is determined.

$$exposure = \frac{\sum_{l=0}^{R-1} h(l)l}{R \sum_{l=0}^{R-1} h(l)} \tag{1}$$

where R denotes the overall number of grey levels and $h(l)$ represents the image histogram. The grey level border value, or parameter Z_A (as determined by Eq. 2), separates the image into over and underexposed subimages.

$$Z_A = R(1 - exposure) \tag{2}$$

For two distinct sub-histograms that are split on the basis of Z_A, two additional exposure thresholds $(Z_{Ap} and Z_{Aq})$ are computed.

$$Z_{Ap} = R\left[\frac{Z_A}{R} - \frac{\sum_0^{Z_A-1} h(l)l}{\sum_0^{Z_A-1} h(l)}\right] \tag{3}$$

$$Z_{Aq} = R\left[1 + \frac{Z_A}{R} - \frac{\sum_{Z_A}^{R-1} h(l)l}{\sum_{Z_A}^{R-1} h(l)}\right] \tag{4}$$

- *Histogram sub division and equalization*

The exposure threshold value Z_A as determined in (2) is used to divide the original histogram in half. These distinct sub-histograms are then separated into two concise sub-histograms whereas Z_{Ap} and Z_{Aq} as calculated in (3) and (4) serves as a dividing point for sub-histograms.

Individual equalisation of the 4 sub-histograms is the next step in the RS-ESIHE process. Equations (5–8) give the histogram equalisation transfer functions.

$$F_{Lp} = Z_{Ap}C_{Lp} \tag{5}$$

$$F_{Iq} = (Z_{Ap} + 1) + (Z_A - Z_{Ap} + 1)C_{Lq} \tag{6}$$

$$F_{Up} = (Z_A + 1) + (Z_{Aq} - Z_A + 1)C_{Up} \tag{7}$$

$$F_{Uq} = (Z_{Aq} + 1) + (R - Z_{Aq} + 1)C_{Uq} \tag{8}$$

The transfer functions F_{Lp}, F_{Lq}, F_{Up} and F_{Uq} are used to individually equalize the sub histograms. Combining the results of the four transfer functions yields the RS-ESIHE output image.

The enhanced output image from RS-ESIHE are then given as input to the FANET segmentation to segment the tumor present in the exact region of the brain.

3.2 FANET Segmentation

Numerous segmentation architectures use an encoder-decoder configuration [14]. Combine SE-residual and MixPool blocks to make a system that promotes the transmission of data from both the current and prior epoch's learning paradigms while also facilitating attentiveness.

After down sampling the input image gradually, the encoder creates a compact representation of it. The decoder then uses this compact representation, which has been gradually upsampled and combined with features from the encoder, in order to rebuild the semantic representation. The SE-residual block is used to construct the encoder and the decoder, and for each resolution scale, a further concatenation of the encoder's original resolution representation of feature is added. The MixPool block output is created by concatenating the result from both activation functions, and is performed by using the Eq. (9)

$$Output_{mp} = f_1' \wedge (f_1 \otimes (sp_1 \cup sp_1'))' \tag{9}$$

where $\wedge$ denotes the concatenation operator, $\otimes$ indicates the elementwise multiplication, and $\cup$ represents the union operation. f_1 represent the first feature map, sp_1' denotes the spatial attention map generation.

3.3 Hybrid SENET-KNN

Brain tumor classification based on Squeeze-and-Excitation Networks (SENET) with K-Nearest Neighbour (KNN) Algorithm.

3.3.1 SENET

Squeeze-and-Excitation Networks primary goal is to add parameters to each convolutional blocks channel in order to allow the network to adaptively change the weight of each feature map [15]. In the case of any transformation F_{tf} converting the input G to the corresponding feature mappings Q whereas $Q \in \mathbb{R}^{h \times w \times C}$, create an appropriate SE block for feature recalibration, using a convolution as an example.

Logically, a statistic $p \in \mathbb{R}^C$ is created by reducing Q spatial dimensions $h \times w$, and the c-th part of z is then determined as follows:

$$l_c = F_{sq}(q_c) = \frac{1}{h \times w} \sum_{m=1}^{h} \sum_{n=1}^{w} q_c(m, n) \tag{10}$$

First, the features Q are given to a squeeze operation that creates a channel descriptor by combining feature maps over their spatial dimensions ($h \times w$). In order to enable data access from the global receptive field for all network layers, this descriptor aims to give a representation for the localisation of channel-wise feature outputs. Following aggregation, the excitation process is a basic self-gating procedure, represented by Eq. (11) that takes the input embedding and produces a set of channel regulated weights.

$$sig = F_{ex}(I, w) = \sigma(g(I, w)) = \sigma(w_2\delta(w_1I)) \tag{11}$$

where δ refers to RELU function, $w_1 \epsilon \mathbb{R}^{\frac{c}{r} \times C}$ and $w_2 \epsilon \mathbb{R}^{C \times \frac{c}{r}}$.

These weights are given to the feature maps Q to form the SE block output, which can be sent straight into the network's subsequent layers.

Q is rescaled by the activations s to produce the blocks final output, which is illustrated at Eq. (12):

$$\tilde{G}_c = F_{Scale}(q_c, s_c) = s_c I_c \tag{12}$$

where channel-wise multiplication of the scalar s_c and the feature map $I_c \epsilon \mathbb{R}^{h \times w}$ is denoted by $\tilde{G} = \tilde{G}_1, \tilde{G}_2, \ldots, \tilde{G}_C$ and $F_{Scale}(q_c, s_c)$.

3.3.2 KNN

KNN algorithm is a non-parametric, instance-based supervised learning technique [16]. The KNN algorithm depends on feature similarity; more precisely, it determines how much a given data point's new features resemble those of the training set in order to assign that point to the class to which it belongs. In this situation, KNN conducts a majority vote among the K cases that are most similar to a new, previously unknown observation. This similarity is determined by calculating the separation between two data points. The Euclidean distance is one of the most commonly used distance measures, which is illustrated at Eq. (13).

$$D(z, z') = \sqrt{(z_1 - z_1')^2 + (z_2 - z_2')^2 + \ldots + +(z_n - z_n')^2} \tag{13}$$

KNN therefore completes the following two phases when given a positive integer K, fresh data z', and a similarity metric D: first, it determines the distance between each training sample and z'; second, it calculates the conditional likelihood for every class by using the Eq. (14)

$$P(x = j|z = z') = \frac{1}{K}\sum_{i \in G} U(x^i = j) \tag{14}$$

where $I(z)$ denotes the indicator function, and it equals 1 when the input z is true and 0 otherwise. The set that contains the K training data points that are nearest to z', and it is the set which includes the K closest training data points to B. Input, z' is finally allocated to a category with the highest probability.

To use this approach, first generate S random samples from the training set, with replacement, of a specified size n_s, and then estimate a KNN classifier for every sample. The final prediction will then be decided by a majority vote after receiving a vote from each classifier regarding the relation of a new instance to a certain class. Thus the brain tumor is classified by four types are glioma, meningioma, no tumor and pituitary.

4   Result and Discussion

Based on FANET segmentation and hybrid SENET with KNN are implemented to detect the brain tumor types. The NVIDA GeForce RTX 3070 GPU, which has 64GB (RAM), and an Intel Core i7 processor are the system CPU combinations used by the MATLAB software to implement the designed model. In this designed model, initially MRI images of brain tumor are gathered and contrast enhancement is done to these images by RS-ESIHE method. Then, the FANET segmentation is performed to segment the tumor region and the brain tumor types are classified using hybrid SENET with KNN.

4.1   Dataset Description

MRI images of numerous forms of brain tumors are included in the dataset utilized in this framework [17]. This dataset contained 2075 data that the classifier used to create its best predictions involved 4 various kinds of brain cancers, namely gliomas, pituitary tumors, meningioma, and no tumors. In this case, 80% (1660) is employed for training and 20% (415) for testing.

Figure 2 and 3 demonstrates the sample images of dataset with different tumor types and transformation of MRI images utilizing RS-ESIHE for image enhancement and FANET for segmentation. The first columns of the image in Fig. 3 displays the original image, the 2nd column represents the enhanced image by the RS-ESIHE approach, and the last column provides the tumor segmented images based on hybrid of SENET and KNN.

Table 1 illustrates the hyper parameters of the designed model used for optimally selecting the segmenting regions and classifying the tumor. The hyper parameters used in this model are Reduction Ratio, Number of Channels, Activation Functions, Initialization, Learning Rate, Optimization Algorithm, Batch Size, Number of Training Epochs, N_neighbor, Leaf size and metric. Based on these parameters the segmentation and classification of the model are performed.

Figure 4 depicts the confusion measures for the proposed design. The actual and anticipated data from the provided dataset are evaluated by this confusion metric. The overall amount of data applied to testing is 2075, of which 1990 are predicted based on the actual class and the remaining 85 are wrongly projected.

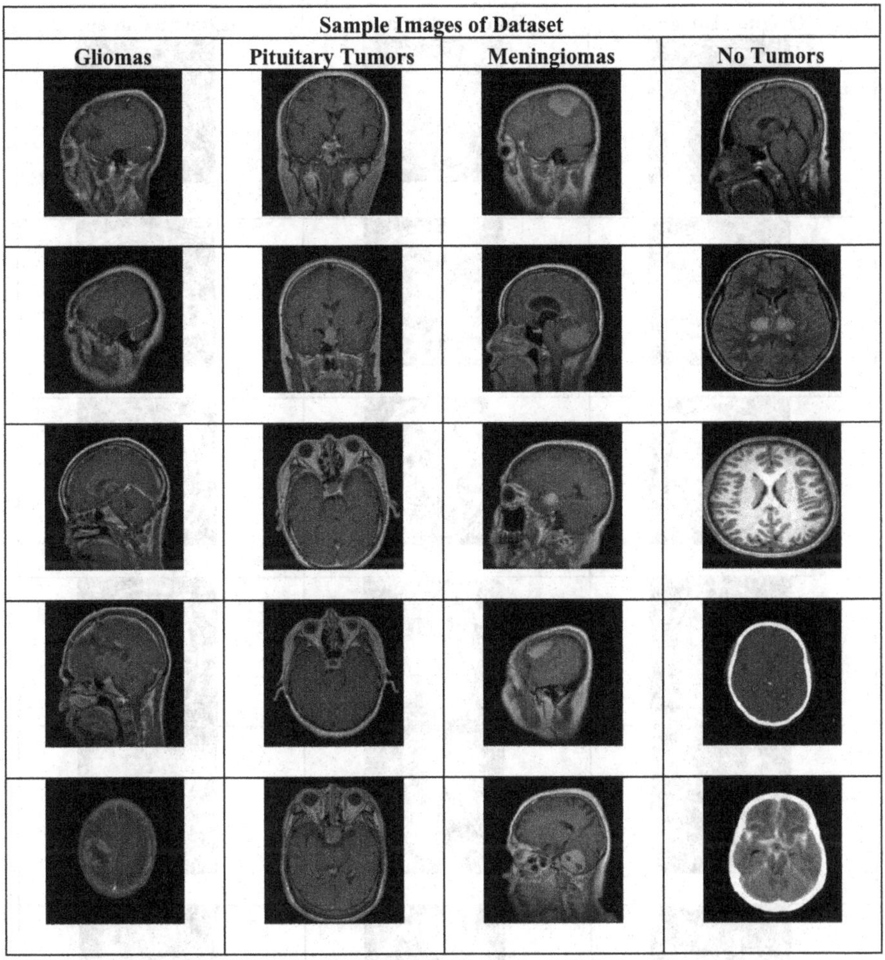

Fig. 2. Sample Images of Dataset.

The performance of a model for classification at every classification threshold is depicted in Fig. 5 on a graph by the receiver operating characteristic curve, or ROC curve. Two parameters are plotted by this curve are True Positive and False Positive Rate. Performance metrics such as precision, accuracy, specificity, fowlkes mallows index (FMI), sensitivity, negative predictive value (NPV), F1-score, false positive rate (FPR), false discovery rate (FDR), kappa, false negative Rate (FNR) and Mathew's correlation coefficient (MCC) are examined for the proposed model and compared with existing techniques.

Original Image	Enhanced Image	Segmented image

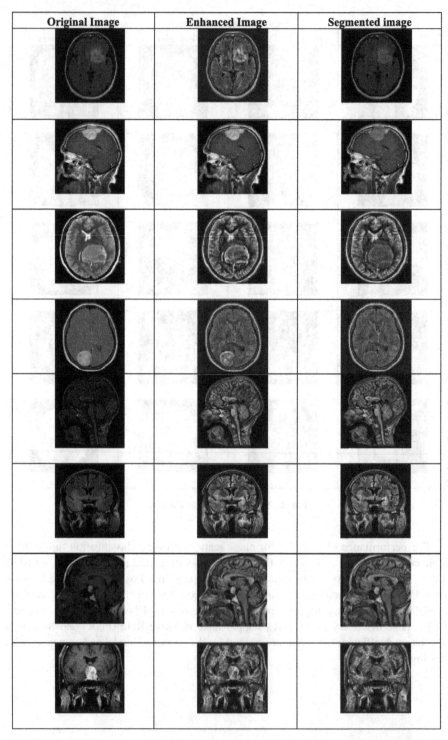

Fig. 3. MRI image transformation using pre-processing and segmentation methods.

Table 1. Hyper parameters of the designed proposed model.

Hyper parameter	Values
Reduction Ratio	2
Number of Channels	64
Activation Functions	ReLu
Initialization	HE_Initializer
Learning Rate	0.001
Optimization Algorithm	SGD
Batch Size	32
Number of Training Epochs	500
N_neighbor	11
Leaf size	10
metric	Euclidean

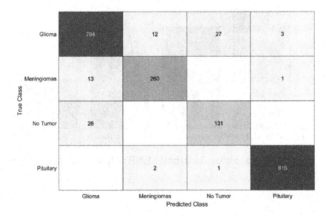

Fig. 4. Confusion matrix for the proposed design.

The graph in Fig. 6 evaluates the accuracy of the proposed hybrid SENET+KNN strategy with existing approaches. In order measure the accuracy, proposed model hybrid SENET+KNN is compared with existing methods as Resnet-101, Inception Resnet, and Resnext-50. The corresponding values for hybrid SENET+KNN, Resnet-101, Inception Resnet, and Resnext-50 are 97.50%, 93.0%, 89.7% and 86.2%. The proposed framework experiences greater accuracy as well as better at identifying the type of brain tumor in comparison to earlier approaches. The proposed hybrid SENET+KNN strategy sensitivity is compared to that of existing methods in the graph presented in Fig. 7, which shows the results. For hybrid SENET+KNN, Resnet-101, Inception Resnet, and Resnext-50, the comparable values are 94.74%, 91.5%, 87.16% and 82.52%. As a result, the proposed method sensitivity value exceeds that of the prior utilized methods.

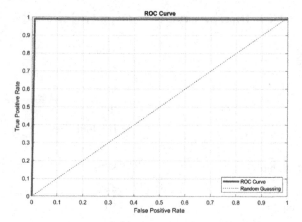

Fig. 5. ROC Curve Plot of proposed method for brain tumor detection.

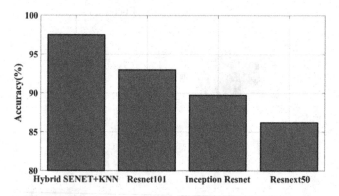

Fig. 6. Evaluation of accuracy for hybrid SENET+KNN and existing approach.

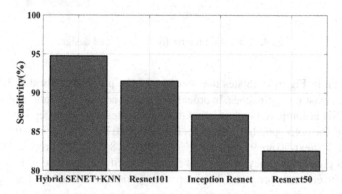

Fig. 7. Evaluation of sensitivity for hybrid SENET+KNN and existing approach.

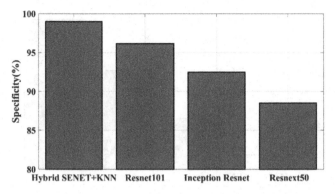

Fig. 8. Evaluation of specificity for hybrid SENET+KNN and existing approach.

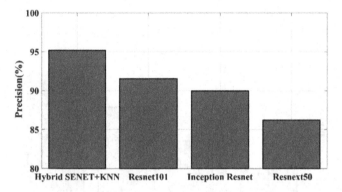

Fig. 9. Evaluation of precision for hybrid SENET+KNN and existing approach.

Figure 8 illustrates the specificity of the proposed hybrid SENET+KNN strategy to that of existing approaches. The proposed hybrid SENET+KNN model is contrasted to the Resnet-101, Inception Resnet, and Resnext-50 approaches in order measure the specificity. The resultant values of hybrid SENET+KNN, Resnet-101, Inception Resnet, and Resnext-50 are 98.98%, 96.15%, 92.46%, and 88.52%, respectively. Therefore, the proposed method specificity value has a greater value than that of the existing approaches. In the graph provided in Fig. 9, the findings are compared between the precision of the proposed hybrid SENET+KNN strategy and that of existing techniques. The obtained values for hybrid SENET+KNN, Resnet-101, Inception Resnet, and Resnext-50 are 95.16%, 91.54%, 89.96%, and 86.21%. In comparison to earlier methods, the proposed framework exhibits higher precision.

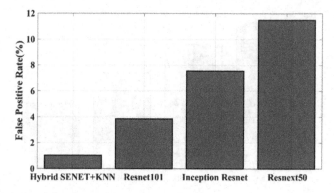

Fig. 10. Evaluation of FPR for hybrid SENET+KNN and existing approach.

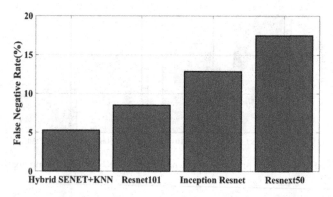

Fig. 11. Evaluation of FNR for hybrid SENET+KNN and existing approach.

The FPR of the proposed hybrid SENET+KNN strategy in comparison to other current methods is depicted in Fig. 10. Inception Resnet, Resnet-101, and Resnext-50 are compared to the proposed hybrid SENET+KNN model. Hybrid SENET+KNN, Resnet-101, Inception Resnet, and Resnext-50 all achieved FPR values of 1.02%, 3.85%, 7.54%, and 11.48%, accordingly. In comparison to existing methodologies, the proposed method FPR value is hence lower. The FNR of the proposed hybrid SENET + KNN approach is compared to that of existing strategies in the graph shown in Fig. 11 by comparing the results. 5.26%, 8.5%, 12.84%, and 17.48% are the respective FNR values for hybrid SENET+KNN, Resnet-101, Inception Resnet, and Resnext-50. The proposed model has less FNR values than older methods.

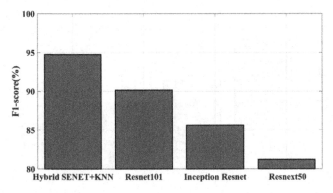

Fig. 12. Evaluation of F1-**score** for hybrid SENET+KNN and existing approach.

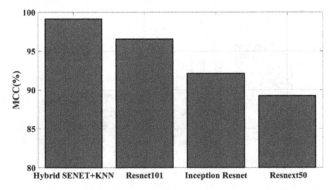

Fig. 13. Evaluation of MCC for hybrid SENET+KNN and existing approach.

In Fig. 12, the proposed hybrid SENET+KNN method is compared to the existing approaches using the F1_score results. The proposed method is contrasted with existing methods like Resnet-101, Inception Resnet, and Resnext-50. The suggested hybrid SENET+KNN method and the earlier used methods both obtained F1_score values of 94.74%, 90.15%, 85.61%, and 81.21%, respectively. The F1_score rate is greater than those of existing methods. Figure 13 shows how the proposed hybrid SENET+KNN method and existing approaches are compared in terms of MCC values. MCC values for hybrid SENET+KNN, Resnet-101, Inception Resnet, and Resnext-50 are 99.12%, 96.52%, 92.11%, and 89.25%, respectively. This outcome demonstrates that the MCC value of the proposed method increases than that of the existing model.

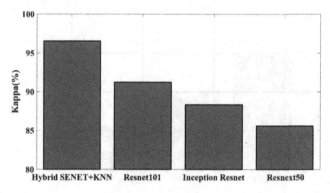

Fig. 14. Evaluation of kappa for hybrid SENET+KNN and existing approach.

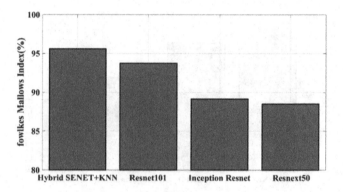

Fig. 15. Evaluation of FMI for hybrid SENET+KNN and existing approach.

Figure 14 illustrates the proposed hybrid SENET + KNN method to the existing methods based on the kappa results. Both the proposed hybrid SENET+KNN approach and existing techniques such as Resnet-101, Inception Resnet, and Resnext-50 achieved kappa values of 96.53%, 91.22%, 88.34%, and 85.61, respectively. Compared to existing approaches, the kappa rate is higher. Figure 15 compares the hybrid SENET+KNN method as proposed with the FMI values of existing approaches. For hybrid SENET + KNN, Resnet-101, Inception Resnet, and Resnext-50, the corresponding FMI values are 95.58%, 93.72%, 89.14%, and 88.51%. This result reveals that the proposed method FMI value is higher than the value of the existing model.

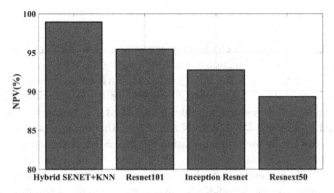

Fig. 16. Evaluation of NPV for hybrid SENET+KNN and existing approach.

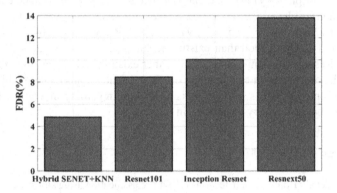

Fig. 17. Evaluation of FDR for hybrid SENET+KNN and existing approach.

Based on the NPV results, Fig. 16 compares the proposed hybrid SENET+KNN technique to existing methods. NPV values of 96.53%, 91.22%, 88.34%, and 85.61 are attained by the proposed hybrid SENET+KNN methodology as well as by already-in-use methods including Resnet-101, Inception Resnet, and Resnext-50. The NPV rate is greater than conventional methods. Figure 17 contrasts the proposed hybrid SENET+KNN method with the FDR values of existing techniques. The FDR values for hybrid SENET+KNN, Resnet-101, Inception Resnet, and Resnext-50 are 95.58%, 93.72%, 89.14%, and 88.51%. This outcome indicates that the proposed method's FDR value is lower than the value of the existing model. Thus, the proposed model with the SENET and KNN model performs better based on the performance metrics due to the pre-processing and segmentation techniques used in this model that enhances and segments the most important region from the brain MRI for classifying the type of the brain tumor with great accuracy than the existing model.

5 Conclusion

Brain tumor detection becomes challenging due to the complicated brain anatomy. Each and every organ in the body function that is controlled by the brain. Due to the complexity and variety of tumors, detecting brain tumors with an MRI is a difficult task. In recent years, the automatic classification of brain tumours using deep learning techniques to detect brain tumors. This research provides a multiclass brain tumor classification approach is based on a hybrid SENET-KNN Algorithm. The proposed system gathers and pre-processes MRI brain tumor images using the RS-ESIHE approach to enhance poor contrast and better input images quality. After image enhancement, these images are sent to the FANET segmentation method relies on a feedback mechanism while training. Next, applying a hybrid SNET-KNN classification, significant features are extracted as well as unnecessary data is suppressed, and to diagnose three brain tumours (glioma, meningioma and pituitary) and one class of healthy images. Performance was evaluated using metrics like accuracy, F1_score, precision, sensitivity, and kappa. The results obtained are 97.5%, 94.74%, 95.16%, 94.74%, and 96.53%, respectively for proposed hybrid SENET-KNN method than existing techniques such as Resnet-101, inception Resnet and Resnext-50. Thus, compared to other existing techniques, the experimental results for the proposed strategy are more efficient. In future, this method will be helpful for scanners and specialists in their decision-making regarding diagnoses, process of treatment for better recovery of patients in early stage.

References

1. Sadad, T., et al.: Brain tumor detection and multi-classification using advanced deep learning techniques. Microsc. Res. Tech. **84**(6), 1296–1308 (2021)
2. Woźniak, M., Siłka, J., Wieczorek, M.: Deep neural network correlation learning mechanism for CT brain tumor detection. Neural Comput. Appl. 1–16 (2021)
3. Saidani, O., et al.: Enhancing prediction of brain tumor classification using images and numerical data features. Diagnostics **13**(15), 2544 (2023)
4. Amin, J., et al.: Brain tumor detection by using stacked autoencoders in deep learning. J. Med. Syst. **44**, 1–12 (2020)
5. Amin, J., Sharif, M., Raza, M., Saba, T., Sial, R., Shad, S.A.: Brain tumor detection: a long short-term memory (LSTM)-based learning model. Neural Comput. Appl. **32**, 15965–15973 (2020)
6. Kaur, D., et al.: Computational intelligence and metaheuristic techniques for brain tumor detection through IoMT-enabled MRI devices. Wirel. Commun. Mob. Comput. 1–20 (2022)
7. Mahmud, M.I., Mamun, M., Abdelgawad, A.: A deep analysis of brain tumor detection from MR images using deep learning networks. Algorithms **16**(4), 176 (2023)
8. Kumar, D.M., Satyanarayana, D., Prasad, M.G.: MRI brain tumor detection using optimal possibilistic fuzzy C-means clustering algorithm and adaptive k-nearest neighbor classifier. J. Ambient. Intell. Humaniz. Comput. **12**(2), 2867–2880 (2021)
9. Khairandish, M.O., Sharma, M., Jain, V., Chatterjee, J.M., Jhanjhi, N.Z.: A hybrid CNN-SVM threshold segmentation approach for tumor detection and classification of MRI brain images. IRBM **43**(4), 290–299 (2022)
10. Deb, D., Roy, S.: Brain tumor detection based on hybrid deep neural network in MRI by adaptive squirrel search optimization. Multimed. Tools Appl. **80**, 2621–2645 (2021)

11. Islam, M.K., Ali, M.S., Miah, M.S., Rahman, M.M., Alam, M.S., Hossain, M.A.: Brain tumor detection in MR image using superpixels, principal component analysis and template based K-means clustering algorithm. Mach. Learn. Appl. **5**, 100044 (2021)
12. Garg, G., Garg, R.: Brain tumor detection and classification based on hybrid ensemble classifier. arXiv preprint arXiv:2101.00216 (2021)
13. Acharya, U.K., Kumar, S.: Directed searching optimized mean-exposure based sub-image histogram equalization for grayscale image enhancement. Multimed. Tools Appl. **80**, 24005–24025 (2021)
14. Tomar, N.K., et al.: FaNet: a feedback attention network for improved biomedical image segmentation. IEEE Trans. Neural Netw. Learn. Syst. (2022)
15. Valsalan, P., Latha, G.C.P.: Hyperspectral image classification model using squeeze and excitation network with deep learning. Comput. Intell. Neurosci. (2022)
16. Nababan, A.A., Khairi, M., Harahap, B.S.: Implementation of K-Nearest Neighbors (KNN) algorithm in classification of data water quality. J. Mantik **6**(1), 30–35 (2022)
17. Kanchan, S.: Kaggle (2020). https://www.kaggle.com/datasets/sartajbhuvaji/brain-tumor-classification-mri. Accessed 29 Sept 2023

Mental Health Analysis Using RASA and BERT: Mindful

Rashmi Gandhi[1] ⓘ, Prachi Jain[1]([✉]), and Hardeo Kumar Thakur[2] ⓘ

[1] CSE, ASET, Amity University, Noida 201301, India
jainprachi1702@gmail.com
[2] Bennett University, Greater Noida 201310, India

Abstract. Psychological health problems concern an approximated 92 million people universally. That's essentially 1 in 10 people in general. Therefore, it is advisable to create a chatbot to lessen the stigma as-sociated with mental health, giving people the ability to voice their problems, and filling the gap left by the lack of support systems for those who need assistance. The preceding few years have been challeng-ing for everyone all around the world. The global escalation of Covid-19 has resulted in a substantial rise in the number of people suffering from emotional health problems. As a result, people are becoming more conscious of psychological wellness because a single consultation with a psychiatrist is expensive to execute, ideas are introduced for patients to be informed of their illness before scheduling an appoint-ment. The rise in mental diseases caused by loneliness and stress inspired us to create Mindful. The bot is a tool that allows people to converse in real time using developed rule sets or the assistance of simulat-ed intelligence and machine learning.

Keywords: Neural Network · Transfer Learning · RASA · BERT · Mental Health

1 Introduction

There is a worldwide Human Resource shortage for conveying emotional wellness prob-lems that are treated by Psychotherapists. In developed nations, there are 9 professionals for every 100,000 people, whereas in economies that are still developing, there is 1 therapist for every ten million people. According to the WHO, over 45% of people in advanced nations and 15% of adults in underdeveloped nations need mental wellness care. This crunch of resource and expense issues have made the AI bring matters into its hand [19].

The chatbot utilizes natural language processing and deep learning approaches to provide appropriate responses to user input. Due to the shortage of mental healthcare providers, one-on-one interaction with all patients is not feasible, which can hinder the treatment process. The proposed chatbot aims to bridge this gap by allowing users to interact and receive support through natural language input [18]. We have worked upon 3 different algorithms for the model namely the Feed Frontward Neural Network,

D. Garg et al. (Eds.): IACC 2023, CCIS 2054, pp. 246–258, 2024.
https://doi.org/10.1007/978-3-031-56703-2_20

Transmis-sion Learning, and the Rasa chatbot framework. The Feed Frontward Neural Network is an algorithm based upon biology. It has 3 different layers, the effort layer, the concealed layer, and the output layer.

We employed the BERT model used by Google as the transfer learning approach. Rasa framework is the third model we have used for our model. Rasa is an open source chatbot framework which is founded on machine learning, which makes integration with websites a very easy task. We tied together all three of our models and will use the best of them to incorporate into the framework. This chatbot will tell people about diverse categories of psychological health diseases and tell a funny story to cheer them up. We have made the dataset on our own and ended variations to the presentation compulsory by the different models. This helped us to expand the chatbot to increase the information about a whole lot of diseases and include a figure of responses to it.

Problem Statement. Comparing the consumption of chatbots for mental well-being to more conven-tional mental health assistance techniques reveal some innovative elements and advantages include they are easily accessible hence can provide 24/7 support to the patients as compared to traditional ways. This accessibility is critical for folks who are suffering a mental health crisis or who require assistance outside of typical therapy hours [1]. Anonymity and Lessened Stigma enabling users to ask for assistance without worrying about criticism or social stigma. Chatbots are scalable and inexpensive ways to reach a wide audience because they can manage a lot of users at once [17]. Initial Assistance and Control is also im-plemented based on user interactions and data analysis, chatbots can actively reach out to users who are at risk or in need of support. This makes it possible to monitor mental health continuously and to inter-vene early, which helps to avert crises. Material insights can be gathered and evaluated for user data while still upholding morality and anonymity to uncover trends and patterns that could be used to guide future mental health interventions. This might also help for creating breakthroughs in research and therapeutic strategies. They are also cost saving and can be created in multiple languages [10].

Contribution. With the utilization of Mindful personalized interactions by modifying the responses ac-cording to customer input and its proper context, thereby offering tailored support that caters to individu-al needs. Mindful effective dialogue management enables rapid responses, allowing users to receive im-mediate assistance, which is critical during times of crisis. Mindful is available 24 h a day, seven days a week, regardless of time zone, providing users with a dependable resource for help and direction. Our chatbot can provide information about mental health problems, symptoms, and coping strategies and also lighting up their mood by telling jokes. Users can discuss delicate mental health topics anony-mously, fostering a sense of privacy and security while facilitating open and honest discussion.

Paper is structured as follows: Sect. 2 is showing literature review. Methodology and Workflow is ex-plained in Sect. 3. System and Model requirements with all the results are discussed in Sect. 4. Final-ly, Sect. 5 concludes the work.

2 Literature Review

In this section, we have discussed about different NLP based Chabot's and taken guidance from them on how to go about our models. The research referenced utilizes different methods to implement chatbots based on mental health.

Table 1. Literature Review

Author	Year	Method	Features
Ahmed Fadhil et al. [1]	2018	Artificial Intelligence	They discussed the habit of chatbot systems in telemedicine applications to help elderly patients living in countryside areas after they were treated from the infirmary. The bot serves as a remedial assistant, supporting patients coping up with their medical conditions and accompanying them on their healthcare journey
S. Divya et al. [2]	2018	NLP, Pattern matching algorithm	Based on symptoms, a remedial chatbot provides personalized diagnoses. This chatbot was fashioned make the most of natural language dispensation and a pattern corresponding algorithm. After unloading their original diagnosis, users can enter the loop again to discourse with a doctor about alternative set of symptoms
Andrew Rafla et al. [3]	2019	Rasa	The authors in the paper try to increase the F1-score of the Rasa model by altering the present Rasa mechanisms to work incrementally. The paper shows that the model works out for the practically all part with a 1% bearable contrast between the non-incremented and incremental models of Tensorflow and SIUM
Mathew, Rohit Binu et al. [4]	2019	NLP, KNN	NLP is being used for text processing. The archetypal is skilled on the indicator disease dataset using the KNN Algorithm. The chatbot encourages patients to discuss their medical problems and provides an appropriate diagnosis and medical treatment. They also included a video chatting for involving to the dedicated in an emergency
Soufyane Ayanouz et al. [5]	2020	NLP, ASR	In this paper NLP and its numerous components are explained i.e., NLU and NLG (Natural Language Generation) and how to instrument ASR for crafting a chatbot

(*continued*)

Table 1. (*continued*)

Author	Year	Method	Features
Sophia et al. [6]	2020	NLP implemented through NLTK, AIML	The user dialogue in the built system is a linear layout that advances from signs obtaining to signs recognition, where it finds out the relative symptom. The ailment will be classed as harmful or not. The chatbot will react with whether it is key or negligible illness. On the off chance that it is extreme, the patient will be encouraged to contact a specialist for additional treatment
Hussna, Asma Ul, et al. [7]	2020	NLP	PRERONA the chatbot created has the unique feature of not only delivering answers but also asking questions from the user for better understanding, and if the bot is unable to deliver an answer, the question is detailed into the database to increase the database's accuracy
Achtaich Khadija et al. [9]	2021	NLP, Transfer Learning,	In this study, they present four driven by AI health chatbots. They all connect with the worker thanks to NLP (both natural language processing (NLP and NLG), and they all rely on deep learning to find a solution to the query provided by the user. They defined the four parts of our AI-Powered Well-Being Chatbot in this paper, based around their data points: the end-user platform, its APIs, the Natural Language Processing (NLP) Engine, and the Core Engine. As efficient as CNN and RNN, their main innovation utilized allocation learning
Tushar Sharma et al. [10]	2021	Decision tree, Transfer learning	This paper informs us about psychological diseases and the effects they have on us, and how we can predict and manage this using a chatbot. The prototypical was constructed using a decision tree, with every individual leaf node provided us with management information Transfer learning increased the model's accuracy by 10%
Nguyen Thi Mai Trang et al. [11]	2021	Rasa	This finding suggests a Vietnamese bot based upon NLU. It receipts the assistance of Rasa to figure the conversational bot which is capable to spawn responses, reminisce the situation of the discussion and take action for the operator

(*continued*)

Table 1. (*continued*)

Author	Year	Method	Features
Salhi et al. [12]	2021	NLP	The study in question tries to implement a psychotherapist the chatbot in the COVID-19, which might help individuals facing behavioural concerns in eradicating negative feelings that negatively impact their mental health. NLP and a sequence-by-sequence structure were utilized for creating this chatbot. It is adaptable and demonstrative. They can consequently face fear while demonstrating compassion
J.Praveen Gujjar et al. [13]	2022	Rasa, Deep Learning	The authors tried to fashion a conversational bot consuming Google Dialogflow and Rasa framework. Rasa showed more advanced results than Dialogflow due to it being an NLU based chatbot. The paper used Rasa for building the chatbot

The various research papers mentioned in Table 1 delves into various aspects of chatbot systems in telemedicine, such as their use for elderly patients, improving the Rasa model's F1-score, NLP for text processing, question-asking chatbots, AI-driven health chatbots, predicting and managing psychological diseases, developing a Vietnamese chatbot, implementing a psychotherapist chatbot for COVID-19, and comparing Rasa to Google Dialogflow.

3 Methodology

3.1 Pre-processing

Tokenization A phrase, sentence, or possibly a whole text file might be divided down into smaller parts, such as particular words or notions, using the process of tokenization. Each of these tinier elements are often referred to as tokens.

Stemming is a method that creates elements from a root or base word. Stemming techniques or stemmers are once more acknowledged as stemming programs, Words in a bag. Every algorithm we use is in NLP operates on numbers. Our text cannot be entered into the system's algorithm directly.

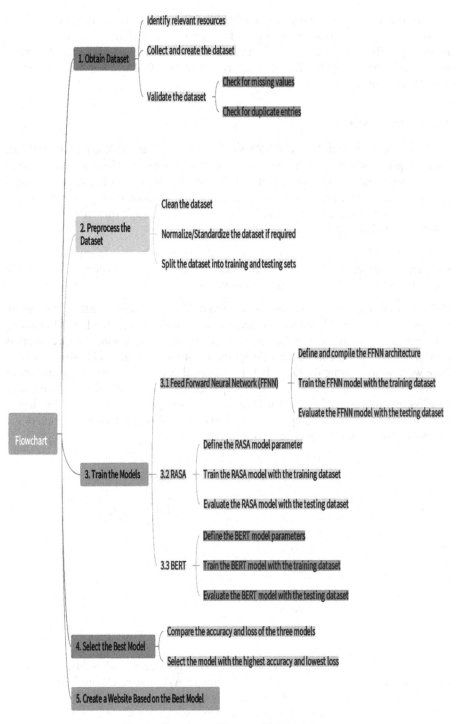

Fig. 1. Flowchart of Proposed Methodology

The Bag of Words model is consequently utilized to pre-process the text and transform it into a bag of words that retains track of the overall number for observations of the most frequently used phrases. For each recognized word that appears in the statement, we provide a bag of words array 1; contrary, we provide 0. The complete workflow is presented in Fig. 1.

3.2 Design Models

Feed Forward Neural Network (FNN). FNN Utilizes the Following: *PYTORCH,* which supports tensor computations on Graphical Processing Units, is based on the Python programming language and the torch library. A library for tensor processing is PyTorch. A core data unit is a tensor. It could be any n-dimensional array, including a number, vector, matrix, or other kind. It will be used to design this framework and is comparable to NumPy arrays.

Network Neural. It imitates the functioning of the human brain, assisting machines to see patterns and resolve frequent issues in deep learning, machine learning, and AI. We used a feed-forward neural network on our dataset.

Bidirectional Encoder Representations from Transformers (BERT). In sort to change unqualified label into a numerical encoding we are using the Label Encoding. Now we will tokenize and set the system in the training set. Among the three models provided in transfer learning are the BERT model, Roberta Model and DistBert Mo del. Here we have tried using the Distil Bert Prototypical as it provides better results for our model. Then, we will convert the integer sequence to tensors. Next, we will be creating data loaders for the training set. These data loaders will pass the training data as inputs to the model during the training. Next, we would be performing the optimization of the prototype. All datasets label is described in Table 2.

Table 2. Dataset labels and frequency

S.NO	LABEL	FREQUENCY
1	Greeting	8
2	Goodbye	4
3	Thanks	3
4	About	2
5	Depression	1

Training and Testing the Model. Transfer Learning provide us with 3 different models Bert Model, Roberta Model and the DistilBert model. As for our results the DistilBert was providing better results thus we have trained our model using the DistilBert model. We will firstly tokenize and convert the method in the preparation set we will be converting the integer sequence into tensors. After creating the tensors, we will be designing the data loaders for the training set. These data loaders during the training stage will be passing batches of training data as input to the model. Then we will be Optimizing our prototypical in bid to reduce the loss caused during backpropagation surrounded by network. We will then fine-tune our model. After performing tuning and setting up the epochs we will then start training our model.

RASA is basically a tool that has been cast-off to figure a custom AI chatbots with the help of Python and the NLU. It also affords a framework which could be used for developing the AI chatbots that makes the use of NLU. It also allows the operator in training their model and addition of convention actions. Nowadays rasa built chatbots are being used in various platforms such as Microsoft Bot and FB messenger.

Dual Intent and Entity Transformer (DIET). Is a multi-tasking transformer engineering that manage respectively plan or-der and element acknowledgment at the even time. It entitles the fitting and playback of various pre-prepared embedding such as BERT, GloVe, ConveRT, and others. According to our analytics, there is not any single set of feature extraction that is habitually best across various datasets. In terms of precision and execution, it matches a wide-ranging of pre-prepared language models. Expands present status of the technique and is 6X quicker to prepare.

4 Results and Discussions

4.1 Dataset

The dataset includes the following:

Classifier of Intent. It receives user input, analyzes its intent, and then connects it to the chatbot's support for that intent. Each intent consists of:

- a tag (a label or name you select)
- patterns (sentence motifs for the neural network's text classifier)
- replies (the response you want the computer to provide after it's finished)

Next stage is where we execute the initial NLP pre-processing, given that we have processed all the communicative intentions through the inents.json file. The dataset is been prepared and uploaded on the cloud link - https://github.com/prachi1702/Dataset_MindFul [20].

4.2 Experimental Settings

The software and hardware prerequisites for a Rasa chatbot on mental health, include the following general guidelines:

Hardware Requirements.

Processor. Multi-core processor (current CPUs such as Intel Core i5 or comparable).
RAM. A minimum of 4 GB RAM is required (for basic chatbots; higher RAM may be required for more complicated models or significant traffic).
Storage. Enough disk space to store the chatbot model, training data, and other files for creating the website.

Operating System. Utilized Windows OS.

Software Requirements:

Python. Rasa, FNN and BERT are written in Python, thus installed the latest version Python on our machine.

Python Libraries. Rasa requires a number of Python libraries, including Tensor-Flow, spaCy, scikit-learn, and other libraries can be installed via the Python package management (pip).

While applying the three models, we made assumptions such as the chatbot's efficacy is dependent on quality training data and domain understanding of mental health. Maintaining relevance requires continuous improvement through user feedback and regular updates. When dealing with sensitive user data, privacy and ethical concerns should be considered. For a consistent user experience, integration with different systems and platforms should be addressed. Scalability, natural language understanding, and error handling are all critical technical considerations. Additional elements to consider for a successful chatbot adoption include legal compliance, user engagement, security, and availability.

We Took three algorithms these include Feed Forward Neural Network, BERT which is a part of Transfer Learning and finally RASA. We compared the all the 3 based on their accuracy and loss. The Feed Forward Neural Network Training and Testing accuracy was found to be 91.89 and 91.03 respectively. Their loss was 0.1735 and 0.1924 respectively. The accuracy for Training and Testing dataset for Bert model was found to be 99.43 and 97.72 respectively while their loss was 0.1015 and 0.112 respectively. The comparative analysis of the accuracies and losses is depicted Table 3. Figure 2 shows an accuracy curve for the respective models for Training and Testing samples.

Table 3. Comparison between various models

Models	Training	Training	Testing	Testing
	Accuracy	**Loss**	**Accuracy**	**Loss**
FNN	91.89	0.1735	91.03	0.1924
BERT	99.43	0.1015	97.72	0.1127
RASA	99.51	0.1132	98.20	0.1360

In our machine learning model, calculating loss entails comparing the model's predictions to the actual target values and measuring the difference. In a feedforward neural network, we utilized categorical cross-entropy loss to quantify the dissimilarity between projected class probabilities and actual class labels for a classification task. BERT is commonly used in natural language processing tasks like text classification. For classification tasks, we used cross-entropy loss. This was done through:

$$loss\_fn = CategoricalCrossentropy()$$
$$loss = loss\_fn(y\_true, y\_pred)$$

The loss is always a measure of the difference between predictions and true labels. The lesser the loss, the more accurate the model's predictions.

The Hyperparameters that we have utilized in our work are the weight allocation to hidden layers which was critical in our neural network. The second was activation function values, neurons are assigned different weight parameters. Weights and activation functions are modified throughout training to optimize output. We assessed using accuracy and cross-entropy error. This evaluation aids in understanding the model's performance and the impact of each parameter. The activating function of the ReLU (Rectified Linear Unit) demonstrates that the model is effectively capturing and learning the underlying patterns in the data. ReLU is a popular activation function that adds non-linearity to the network, allowing it to understand intricate interactions in the data. The ReLU activation function is preventing vanishing gradients and enabling efficient learning. ReLU is a piecewise linear function defined as:

$$f(x) = \max(0, x)$$

This function outputs 0 for any negative input and passes positive inputs directly. The next we utilized epochs since our model's accuracy is already quite high (99.51%) and the loss is relatively low (0.136), it suggests that the model has learned the underlying patterns in the data well. To prevent overfitting, we used techniques like early stopping, where we monitored the validation accuracy and stop training when it starts to decrease or doesn't improve significantly over a 100 epochs.

The number of training samples processed in each iteration each models is determined by batch size. It has an impact on memory utilization, training speed, and the balance of noise and stability when learning. Research is essential for determining the ideal batch size for efficient training and generalization of chatbot solutions. Hence for training and testing each model we took a small batch size of 64 .

Lastly the accuracy for Training and Testing dataset for Rasa was 99.51 and 98.02 respectively while loss was found to be 0.11132 and 0.1360 respectively. Hence after comparison the best result for the Testing dataset was found out to be of RASA model. Figure 3 shows the loss graph of the representations for their Training and Testing dataset.

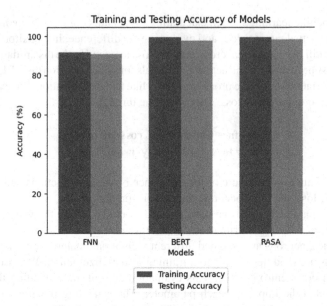

Fig. 2. Accuracy of training and testing models

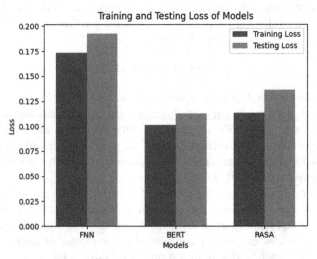

Fig. 3. Training and Testing Loss of the models

5 Conclusion and Future Work

Mindful is the conversational chatbot which gives the user information about various mental health diseases including anxiety, distress, depression, paranoia and countless further. Mental health bots empower users struggling with mental health issues with instantaneous confidential, and compassionate aid. They offer psychological assistance, psychological education, intervention in emergencies, and concrete solutions for coping, boosting access to resources around the clock. Chatbots assist people to seek support and access critical psychological resources by minimizing stigma and providing anonymity. We have utilized 3 different models in this work. Firstly, feedforward neural networks assimilate input layer after layer and serve a purpose for a variety of use cases. Second is BERT, a transformer-based model, comprehends context and semantics in text and performs admirably in natural language processing. While neural networks are versatile, BERT provides deep contextual understanding, and RASA specializes in dialogue management.

Rasa model achieved minimum loss and maximum accuracy, hence the model developed based on the training data and made precise projections or responses. This accomplishment demonstrates the model's great efficacy for comprehending user intents and offering suitable responses in conversational scenarios. These benefits include increased customer satisfaction and trust in the deployed application due to precise and contextually relevant interactions, increased speed in addressing user queries, and increased reliability of the chatbot system. Hence, we constructed our website on the Rasa framework.

The chatbot can be enhanced by identifying several alternative algorithms to employ. It can also be used as a dictionary for psychological well-being on a large scale. The chatbot can also be automated so that it can contact a professional therapist for seeking guidance. It maybe automated to understand and work upon different languages so that it can be utilized by many consumers. The chatbot should also maintain security and integrity of the info shared by the user.

References

1. Fadhil, A.: Beyond patient monitoring: Conversational agents role in telemedicine & healthcare support for home-living elderly individuals. arXiv preprint arXiv:1803.06000 (2018)
2. Divya, S., Indumathi, V., Ishwarya, S., Priyasankari, M., Kalpana Devi, S.: A self-diagnosis medical chatbot using artificial intelligence. J. Web Dev. Web Des. **3**(1), 1- 7 (2018)
3. Rafla, A., Casey, K.: Incrementalizing RASA's open-source natural language understanding pipeline. arXiv preprint arXiv:1907.05403 (2019)
4. Mathew, R.B., et al.: Chatbot for disease prediction and treatment recommendation using machine learning. In: 2019 3rd International Conference on Trends in Electronics and Informatics (ICOEI). IEEE (2019)
5. Ayanouz, S., Abdelhakim, B.A., Benhmed, M.: A smart chatbot architecture based on NLP and machine learning for health care assistance. In: Proceedings of the 3rd International Conference on Networking, Information Systems & Security (2020)
6. Sophia, J.J., et al.: A survey on chatbot implementation in health care using NLTK. Int. J. Comput. Sci. Mob. Comput **9** (2020)
7. Hussna, A.U., et al.: PRERONA: mental health Bengali Chatbot for digital counselling. In: Singh, M., Kang, D.K., Lee, J.H., Tiwary, U.S., Singh, D., Chung, W.Y. (eds.) Intelligent Human Computer Interaction, IHCI 2020. Lecture Notes in Computer Science, vol. 12615, pp. 274–286. Springer, Cham (2021). https://doi.org/10.1007/978-3-030-68449-5_28
8. Bulla, C., et al.: A review of AI based medical assistant Chatbot. Research and Applications of Web Development and Design 3.2 (2020)
9. Khadija, A., Fagroud, F.Z., Achtaich, N.: AI-powered health Chatbots: toward a general architecture. Procedia Comput. Sci. **191**, 355–360 (2021)

10. Sharma, T., et al.: Code smell detection by deep direct-learning and transfer- learning. J. Syst. Softw. **176**, 110936 (2021)
11. Mai, T.N.T., Shcherbakov, M.: Enhancing Rasa NLU model for Vietnamese Chatbot. Int. J. Open Inf. Technol. **9**(1), 31–36 (2021)
12. Salhi, I., et al.: Towards developing a pocket therapist: an intelligent adaptive psychological support Chatbot against mental health disorders in a pandemic situation. Indones. J. Electr. Eng. Comput. Sci. **23**(2), 1200–1211 (2021)
13. Gujjar, J.P., Kumar, V.N.: Open source Chatbot development framework - RASA. Asian J. Adv. Res. **5**(1), 451–453 (2022)
14. Crasto, R., et al.: CareBot: a mental health ChatBot. In: 2021 2nd International Conference for EmergingTechnology (INCET). IEEE (2021)
15. Rahman, Md.M., et al.: Disha: an implementation of machine learning based Bangla healthcare Chatbot. In: 2019 22nd International Conference on Computer and Information Technology (ICCIT). IEEE (2019)
16. Madhu, D., et al.: A novel approach for medical assistance using a trained chatbot. In: 2017 International Conference on Inventive Communication and Computational Technologies (ICICCT). IEEE (2017)
17. Hungerbuehler, I., et al.: Chatbot-based assessment of employees' mental health: design process and pilot implementation. JMIR Form. Res. **5**(4), e21678 (2021)
18. Pandey, S., Srishti, S., Samar, W.: Mental healthcare Chatbot based on natural language processing and deep learning approaches: ted the therapist. Int. J. Inf. Technol. **14**(7), 3757–3766 (2022)
19. Kakuma, R., et al.: Human resources for mental health care: current situation and strategies for action. Lancet **378**, 1654–1663 (2011). https://doi.org/10.1016/S0140-6736(11)61093-3, https://github.com/prachi1702/Dataset_MindFul

Kidney Failure Identification Using Augment Intelligence and IOT Based on Integrated Healthcare System

Shashadhar Gaurav[1], Prashant B. Patil[1], Goutam Kamble[1(✉)], and Pooja Bagane[2]

[1] Computer Science and Engineering, Sharad Institute of Technology, Inchalkaranji,
Maharastra, India
{sgurav,prashantpatil121,goutam}@sitcoe.org.in
[2] Computer Science and Engineering, Symbiosis Institute of Technology, Pune, Maharastra,
India
pooja.bangene@sitpune.edu.in

Abstract. Internet of Things (IoT) and machine learning technology integration has had a significant positive impact on contemporary healthcare systems. The main objectives of this project are to develop and evaluate an integrated healthcare system based on the Internet of Things for the diagnosis and treatment of kidney-related illnesses. The system, which also uses a variety of sensors to continuously track essential health data, enables real-time communication between patients and medical professionals. Five machine learning models—Artificial Neural Networks (ANN), k-Nearest Neighbours (KNN), Support Vector Machine (SVM), Naive Bayes (NB), and Linear Regression (LR)—have been developed to predict patient health outcomes based on sensor data. Performance metrics and confusion matrices demonstrate the remarkable abilities of these models, with ANN standing out as a top performer. By combining IoT and machine intelligence, healthcare professionals can manage their patients' treatment proactive and intervene early. This study highlights the revolutionary potential of machine learning and the internet of things to improve patient outcomes, monitor kidney health more effectively, and cut healthcare costs. As healthcare systems develop, the use of IoT and machine learning to manage diseases will revolutionise patient care.

Keywords: Sensor · kidney disease · machine learning · neural network · IoT

1 Introduction

In recent years, the use of technology in the healthcare industry has increased in levels that have never been seen before [1, 2]. The Internet of Things (IoT), one of these advancements, has emerged as a disruptive force that is changing how healthcare is provided and tracked. A new era in patient care has started thanks to the ability to quickly connect devices, collect real-time data, and utilise machine learning to analyse it [3, 4]. The potential of IoT-based systems combined with machine learning techniques has come to light thanks to an emphasis on early diagnosis and proactive intervention in

D. Garg et al. (Eds.): IACC 2023, CCIS 2054, pp. 259–271, 2024.
https://doi.org/10.1007/978-3-031-56703-2_21

healthcare. In order to improve the detection and management of kidney-related problems, this research examines the development and evaluation of an integrated healthcare system that makes use of IoT technologies and machine learning [5, 6]. Since the kidneys are important organs responsible for a variety of bodily activities, such as filtration and waste elimination, they are susceptible to a number of disorders. The combination of IoT and machine learning is a novel and promising method for treating kidney diseases since early identification and intervention are essential to reducing the impact of renal ailments [7]. IoT integration in the healthcare industry has made a number of choices that go beyond traditional healthcare paradigms available. The phrase "Internet of Medical Things" (IoMT), sometimes known as "Healthcare IoT" (HIoT), describes a broad category of networked gear, software, and services used in healthcare to track patients, gather data, and improve decision-making. These IoT-connected healthcare technologies have made it possible to enhance patient care, encourage preventive actions, and make real-time health monitoring possible [2, 8]. The medical sector uses machine learning, an area of artificial intelligence (AI), extensively.

Diagnoses, treatment modalities, and patient care now have more options thanks to machine learning algorithms' capacity to spot trends in data, learn from them, and forecast the future. Machine learning models have been utilised in the healthcare industry to generate treatments for problems like disease prediction, drug development, image analysis, and individualised care [9]. The use of machine learning and IoT in healthcare has the potential to change the way patients are treated. IoT sensors, wearables, and other devices continuously gather enormous amounts of patient data, including biochemical markers, vital signs, and physical activity. These data give machine learning algorithms the ability to predict health patterns, produce insightful information, and initiate actions. As a result of this mutually beneficial relationship, medical professionals now have proactive tools for early detection, personalised therapy, and better patient outcomes [10–12]. The existing system cannot able to detect the occurrence of kidney stone at early stage due to the use of single optimization techniques. Acute and chronic health disease are found using machine learning model. For controlling electrolytes, maintaining fluid balance, and eliminating waste, the kidneys are crucial. To effectively treat renal disease and reduce the risk of complications, early diagnosis is essential [13]. IoT sensors have the capacity to continuously track important metrics including heart rate, blood pressure, and serum creatinine levels. In order to determine the state of kidney health, identify anomalies, and enable early intervention, the data can then be assessed using machine learning models that have been trained on prior data [14–16]. The integration of IoT and machine learning into kidney health monitoring is still a developing topic, despite the fact that the promise of these technologies in healthcare is generally acknowledged [15]. Early detection, individualised Mr.Prashant B. Patil Computer Science and Engineering Sharad Institute of Technology College of Engineering Ichalakaranji-India prashantpatil121@ sitcoe.org.in 2 3 7 8 12 13 14 16 19 27 29 2 therapy, and improved patient outcomes are highlighted in the current study as promising outcomes [17–19]. Before IoT and machine learning can be effectively used in the management of renal health, a number of issues must be resolved, including data security, interoperability, and scalability. This research aims to make a contribution to the developing field of integrated healthcare systems by developing and evaluating an IoT-based solution that employs machine learning techniques for the detection and treatment of kidney-related illnesses. This study aims to show how IoT and machine learning may change healthcare through enhanced kidney health monitoring, enhanced patient care, and perhaps lower healthcare expenditures.

2 Methodology

Figure 1 depicts the extensive Internet of Things infrastructure created for this study to continually monitor and evaluate kidney function. This comprehensive system examines a person's health in-depth and provides crucial information on kidney function using a wide range of sensors, including pressure sensors, blood glucose sensors, heart rate sensors, temperature sensors, and biosensors. Since blood pressure is one of the most important indicators of kidney health, it is essential to monitor blood pressure. Early identification of abnormalities, which might be symptoms of kidney-related problems, is made possible by the sensor's data For people with diabetes or those who are at risk for renal failure, blood glucose monitoring are essential. Continuous blood glucose monitoring is crucial because elevated blood glucose levels have the potential to injure kidneys.

Heart rate monitors may be able to provide information on the degree to which renal function and the cardiovascular system are interconnected. Anomalies in heart rate might be a sign of impending renal stress and need prompt care. Temperature sensors are used to detect temperature changes that might indicate a fever or another sickness that could impair kidney function. The use of body temperature monitoring makes it easier to identify problems that need prompt treatment early on. Specialists employ biosensors to evaluate certain blood signs like urea nitrogen and creatinine. These indicators accurately reflect kidney health and function. A microcontroller acts as the hub for data processing by wirelessly gathering data from various sensors. The microcontroller then uploads this data to the cloud, making sure that clinicians working in hospitals, in particular, have easy access to information on a patient's kidney function. For speedy decision-making, this real-time cloud-based communication is crucial. Doctors may remotely check on their patients' kidney health, keep an eye out for any changes or anomalies, and take necessary action right away. When you consider how important renal health is, the necessity for such an integrated IoT system becomes clear. The incidence of complications is lower and patient outcomes may be greatly improved by early identification of renal disease. Healthcare professionals may take preventive measures, customise treatment regimens, and make educated judgements by continually monitoring a patient's vital signs and biomarkers.

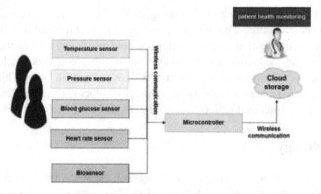

Fig. 1. Stages of the proposed system

Figure 1 demonstrates the various stages in the proposed system. The employee engagement integrated with the blockchain technology involves addressing the learning curve through comparing with new technologies. The HR plans should include comprehensive training programs to develop the employees with the necessary skills and knowledge to use the blockchain systems effectively. This helps to reduce computational time and manpower. This helps in attaining a positive and engaged workforce system. The HR strategies need to be accompanied with cross-functional collaboration. Thus blockchain technology needs collaboration with two or multiple departments. The successful integration of blockchain technology in the banking sector, coupled with effective HR metrics and plans, can significantly enhance employee engagement and improve the overall organizational performance.

3   Various Sensors Used in This Research

For the healthcare sector to effectively monitor and assess different aspects of a patient's health, a variety of sensors are required. The integrated IoT system reported in this paper has been utilised to track kidney health using a range of sensors, each with unique capabilities and traits. The following paragraphs will go into great depth on the range, specificity, accuracy, and precision of these sensors as well as the unique requirements they satisfy in the monitoring of kidney function. A. Pressure Sensors Monitoring blood pressure, which is essential for kidney function, is now possible thanks to pressure sensors. These sensors typically work between 0 mmHg (the equivalent of a perfect vacuum) to around 200 mmHg (a higher systolic blood pressure). Because they can accurately track pressure changes throughout the circulatory system, pressure sensors excel in this field. Due to their exceptional accuracy and precision in detecting even the smallest blood pressure variations, these sensors are essential for the early identification of hypertension and its impact on kidney function. They discuss the need of continual blood pressure monitoring since persistently high or unstable blood pressure may result in kidney damage. B. Blood glucose sensor These devices measure blood sugar levels across a predefined range, often between 20 mg/dL and 600 mg/dL or more. Their ability to properly determine blood sugar levels is what makes them special. These sensors are very sensitive and precise, allowing them to pick up even little fluctuations in blood glucose levels. They talk about how important it is for diabetics to monitor their blood glucose levels since diabetes and kidney issues are closely related. On the basis of solid information, timely medication may lessen or even prevent kidney damage. C. Heart rate sensor The typical heart rate sensor range is 30 to 240 beats per minute (bpm). Their capacity to monitor heart rate variability makes them special since it might provide details about overall cardiovascular health.

These sensors are very sensitive and precise in tracking heart rate patterns and identifying variations that can signify renal stress. Given the strong connection between renal and cardiac function, they stress the need of regular cardiovascular monitoring. 2 17 20 3 D. Temperature sensors These devices monitor the body's temperature across a certain range, often from 90° to 108°F (32° to 42 °C). These sensors can detect even little temperature variations because of their precision. They are well known for their ability to precisely and accurately identify changes in body temperature that might indicate the presence of a fever or conditions that affect kidney function. Temperature sensors aid in the early detection of diseases, enabling prompt medical intervention and the recovery of kidney function. E. Biosensors The highly specialised tools known as biosensors can measure blood markers like urea nitrogen and creatinine. They only operate within a limited range that is utilised to evaluate the biomarker. It is generally known that biosensors can detect these symptoms and determine kidney function with a very high degree of accuracy and precision. They fill the requirement for a precise and simple examination of kidney-related biomarkers, helping to identify renal failure early and assessing overall health.

4 Need for Machine Learning

It is crucial for anyone working in the healthcare sector to be able to anticipate and forecast probable emergency situations using real-time sensor data. Predicting emergency situations becomes a crucial part of starting early treatment operations, even if the integrated IoT system previously mentioned makes it easier to send patient information directly to healthcare specialists. In order to successfully accomplish this important goal, this study uses a variety of machine learning models, including Linear Regression (LR), Support Vector Machines (SVM), k-Nearest Neighbours (KNN), Artificial Neural Networks (ANN), and Naive Bayes (NB).How we analyse and interpret medical data has completely altered as a result of the usage of machine learning algorithms in the healthcare industry. These models are forecasting devices that might identify possible problems based on sensor data while keeping tabs on kidney function, eventually enabling prompt medical action. A. Linear regression Linear Regression is a foundational machine learning model widely used for predictive analysis and understanding the relationship between input variables and an output variable. In the context of healthcare and kidney health monitoring, it plays a pivotal role in forecasting potential health issues based on sensor data. The essence of Linear Regression lies in establishing a linear relationship between the input variables (sensor readings) and the output variable (kidney function and health status). This relationship is expressed mathematically as: $Y = \beta_0 + \beta_1 X_1 + \beta_2 X_2 + \ldots + \beta_n X_n$ Linear Regression endeavors to find the best-fit line that minimizes the difference between predicted values and actual observations, typically using a method called Ordinary Least Squares (OLS). This line serves as a predictive model that can be used to forecast kidney health based on sensor readings. In the context of the IoT-based healthcare system discussed earlier, Linear Regression can identify trends and associations between sensor data and potential kidney-related issues, empowering healthcare providers with valuable insights for proactive patient care. B. Support vector machine In the healthcare industry, SVMs are extensively used, including in the integrated IoT system used in this study to monitor kidney function. SVMs are trustworthy machine learning models. SVMs are excellent at classification problems because to their distinctive structural and functional characteristics. Their main goal is to build an ideal hyperplane, a multidimensional decision boundary that effectively divides data points into discrete groups. SVMs are utilised in the field of renal health to choose the best hyperplane that effectively separates patients with different health statuses based on sensor data. They stand out and ensure that various health problems may be readily detected by raising the margin, or the distance between the hyperplane and the closest data points from each class.

Additionally, SVMs use the kernel technique to handle data that may not be initially linearly separable, enabling the collection and utilisation of complicated patterns and correlations in sensor data for the early diagnosis of kidney-related illnesses. C. K- Nearest Neighbour The K-Nearest Neighbours (KNN) algorithm, which is crucial for tracking kidney health in the integrated IoT system covered in this work, has a unique character and structure. Using the instance-based learning principle, KNN memorises the whole dataset during training and relies predictions on the similarity between new and old data points. KNN is adept at identifying people working in the healthcare sector who have comparable sensor data patterns and health statuses, enabling the effective grouping of patients for the early forecasting of kidney-related issues. In order to facilitate speedier therapies and improved patient outcomes in the management of renal health, KNN's primary capability is its ability to classify patients according to their proximity in feature space. D. Artificial Neural Network The integrated IoT system under discussion makes substantial use of artificial neural networks (ANNs), a dynamic and highly adaptable family of machine learning models. These networks are designed to improve healthcare applications like the prediction and ongoing monitoring of kidney health by drawing inspiration from the intricate structure and function of the human brain. A network of interconnected nodes called neurons that have been thoughtfully arranged into different layers makes up the brain of ANNs. An input layer, one or more hidden layers, and an output layer normally make up an ANN. Every neuron in the network receives information from other neurons and transmits it using an activation function to produce an output. The adaptability and ability of ANNs to learn from data is what makes them so fantastic. These networks successfully adjust their internal parameters during training to reduce discrepancies between expected and actual results by changing the weights and biases linked to each neuron. ANNs have emerged as essential tools for processing and interpreting complicated sensor data in the healthcare industry. They are very good at seeing complex connections 1 1 2 3 4 5 6 9 11 18 26 31 4 and patterns that more conventional analytical methods can miss. ANNs are especially well-suited for the early prediction of kidney-related disorders because of this distinctive property. In order to identify minute variations and anomalies that might be signs of renal illnesses, analytical neural networks (ANNs) can scan large datasets of sensor readings and patient health information. The true power of ANNs rests in their ability to recognise intricate, non-linear data correlations. They are skilled at seeing subtle patterns that more conventional analytical techniques can miss.

ANNs are thus essential for providing precise and timely predictions on kidney health. These early alerts can improve patient care outcomes by providing proactive medical treatments and enabling healthcare professionals to take preventative measures. In this study, artificial neural networks (ANNs) serve as a fundamentally effective part of the integrated IoT system, enhancing the system's capacity to gather, analyse, and inter-pret sensor data for proactive kidney health monitoring. Their adaptability, observance of minute patterns, and aptitude for understanding complex linkages all significantly contribute to the early detection of kidney-related disorders, highlighting their crucial relevance in contemporary healthcare. E. Navie Bayes Naive Bayes, a fundamental machine learning algorithm, is utilised to monitor kidney health as a crucial component of the integrated IoT system reported in this paper. Naive Bayes is widely renowned for its simplicity and efficacy in classification issues.

The approach is based on the Bayes theorem, which calculates the likelihood of an occurrence based on previously known conditions. Naive Bayes excels in generating predictions and judgements based on the probability of specific events given the informa-tion provided by sensor data and patient health records. Despite its "naive" assumption of input feature independence, Naive Bayes has shown effectiveness in a wide range of real-world applications, including risk assessment and medical diagnosis. Given that continuous monitoring generates large amounts of data in IoT-enabled healthcare sys-tems, its efficiency in processing enormous datasets makes it particularly useful. Using Naive Bayes, healthcare workers may swiftly examine sensor data, assisting in the early prediction of kidney-related disorders and ultimately improving patient care results. Based on sensor data, these machine learning algorithms may anticipate kidney health and function. These algorithms grow adept at spotting patterns and correlations between sensor readings and kidney health outcomes after being trained with large datasets. When sensor data is sent into the algorithms, they quickly produce predictions regarding the patient's kidney health. This capacity to identify probable complications allows medical personnel to administer treatment as soon as possible, reducing the incidence of kidney-related crises. The architecture of these machine learning models is shown in Fig. 2. It generally consists of layers of neurons and connections for processing sensor input. The sensor measurements are received by the input layer, which then sends them to one or more hidden layers, each of which extracts and learns important attributes from the data. The output layer also gives a predicted evaluation of kidney function and health. Accurate predictions and rapid response are now achievable because to the enhanced sensor data processing enabled by this architectural design.

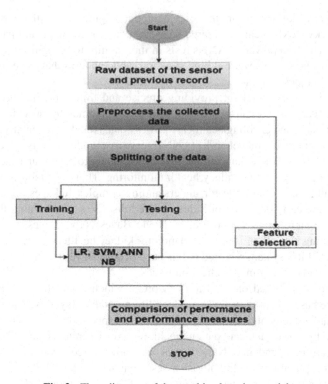

Fig. 2. Flow diagram of the machine learning model

5 Results and Simulation

This study put the suggested IoT system to the test with eight hours of continuous patient health monitoring. Complete patient monitoring was made possible by the sensors in the system, which showed astonishing precision in detecting even the smallest changes in a number of vital factors including temperature and pressure. The IoT system demonstrated its dependability and endurance throughout the course of the 8-h monitoring period by collecting and processing data in real-time. Table I displays the sample 8-h data at one-hour intervals. The patient's body temperature was efficiently monitored by the temperature sensors, which allowed for the early detection of any feverish symptoms or other temperature-related abnormalities. This skill is especially important in the healthcare sector since a high body temperature may often be an early indicator of a more severe medical condition, including renal problems. Furthermore, the device's pressure sensors demonstrated accuracy in recording changes in blood pressure over time. For a thorough evaluation of a patient's total cardiovascular health, which is directly tied to kidney function, the ability to recognise blood pressure changes is essential. Any variations 24 5 in blood pressure patterns were immediately recognised and reported to the system for study in order to keep the medical team informed of the patient's status. The IoT system's ability to provide trustworthy and ongoing health monitoring was proven by the findings of this prolonged 8-h testing session. The device provides healthcare practitioners with a crucial tool for pro-active patient care by accurately detecting and reporting minute changes in temperature, pressure, and other crucial data. As a result, renal health management and patient welfare are improved via quick treatment choices and proactive action.

Table 1. Sensor readings.

Time (hh:mm:ss)	Temperature (°C)	Pressure (mmHg)	Heart Rate (bpm)	Blood Glucose (mg/dL)
08:00:00	36.7	120.5	75	105
09:00:00	36.8	121.0	76	107
10:00:00	36.9	120.3	78	108
11:00:00	37.0	120.6	77	109
12:00:00	36.8	120.8	79	110
13:00:00	36.7	120.4	74	104
14:00:00	36.6	120.2	76	106
15:00:00	36.9	120.7	78	108

Table 2. Performance metrics

Machine Learning Model	Accuracy (%)	Precision (%)	Recall (%)	F1 Score (%)
ANN	97	96	98	99
KNN	86	95	93	91
SVM	87	91	86	89
NB	84	84	82	84
LR	79	81	79	80

The machine learning model receives these sensory inputs from Table 1 and predicts the result shown in Fig. 3. These projections are based on the training each model has received through sensor data input. Machine learning models that assess sensor data to provide projections for the patient's health rates may be used by healthcare professionals to continuously monitor the patient's state of health. The early detection of heart rate irregularities or trends may be aided by these projections, allowing for rapid medical intervention and proactive patient care.

The machine learning models were assessed throughout the research's evaluation phase utilising a dataset made up of the medical records of 100 people who had kidney-related problems. The results of this in-depth analysis showed how accurately each model predicted the consequences for health. Surprisingly, Artificial Neural Networks (ANN) outperformed the other models in terms of accuracy, scoring 96.4%, demonstrating its propensity for spotting complex data patterns. K-Nearest Neighbours (KNN), which underperformed but was still competitive, with an accuracy of 93.2%, further proving its

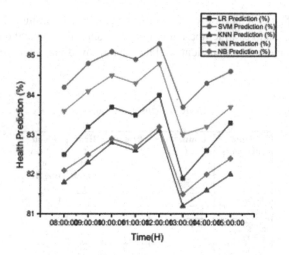

Fig. 3. Prediction from machine learning model

suitability for usage in applications for health prediction. Support Vector Machine (SVM) surpassed Linear Regression (LR) and Naive Bayes (NB), which generated accuracy ratings of 88.7% and 85.2%, respectively. These accuracy findings, which are demonstratively displayed in Fig. 4, provide insightful information on the dependability of each machine learning model in predicting health outcomes for patients with renal illnesses and provide a solid foundation for sane healthcare management decision-making.

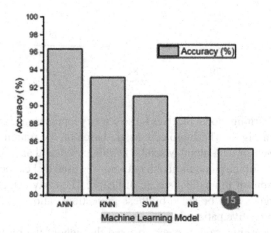

Fig. 4. Accuracy of the machine learning model

Table 2 lists important performance indicators for each machine learning model employed in the study, including accuracy, precision, recall, and F1 score. The accuracy of positive predictions is evaluated by precision, the model's capacity to identify all true positive cases is evaluated by recall, and the F1 score offers a fair evaluation that takes into account both false positives and false negatives. Accuracy is used to gauge a forecast's overall degree of accuracy. These measures show the overall accuracy of each model's predictions of kidney health outcomes. A high accuracy guarantees precise positive predictions, a high recall ensures that significant examples are not forgotten, and a balanced F1 score accounts for uneven class distribution. With a focus on delivering precise and timely patient care, these insights inform healthcare decisions made within the integrated IoT healthcare system.

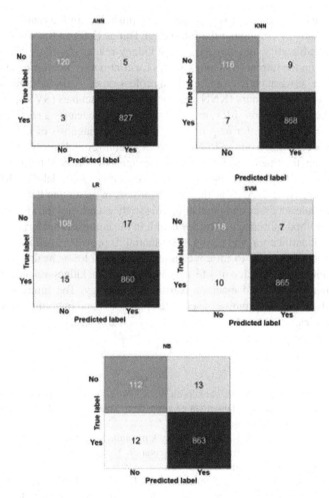

Fig. 5. Confusion matrix of the machine learning model.

Each machine learning model's performance at classifying patients' health conditions within the integrated IoT healthcare system is thoroughly evaluated by the confusion matrices. The confusion matrix for each machine learning model is shown in Fig. 5. The columns of each matrix represent the predictions made by the model, and the rows represent each patient's current health state. In the confusion matrix for the ANN model, for instance, there were 120 true positive cases where the model correctly identified patients with kidney issues, 5 false negatives where positive cases were missed, and 3 false positives where positive outcomes were incorrectly predicted. There were also 872 true negative cases where the model correctly identified patients without kidney issues.

6 Conclusion

Finally, this study represents a significant accomplishment in the realm of integrated healthcare systems by employing the Internet of Things (IoT) and machine learning to improve the identification and management of kidney-related disorders. The creation of a system based on the Internet of Things allows for continuous monitoring and real-time communication between patients and medical professionals. Artificial Neural Networks (ANN), k-Nearest Neighbours (KNN), Support Vector Machines (SVM), Naive Bayes (NB), and Linear Regression (LR) are some of the machine learning techniques used in this study. These models offer helpful data on the early diagnosis of kidney disorders when they are incorporated into an IoT framework, enabling quick interventions and individualised patient treatment. Additionally, a thorough assessment of these models using confusion matrices and performance metrics reveals their dependability. KNN, SVM, NB, and LR were close to ANN as the top performers in predicting health statuses due to their remarkable accuracy and precision. This study establishes the groundwork for a cutting-edge method of managing kidney health in the context of integrated healthcare, where prompt identification and action are essential. It provides healthcare professionals with the tools they need to improve patient outcomes, lower healthcare costs, and ultimately improve the quality of life for those at risk of kidney-related illnesses by seamlessly merging IoT and machine learning technology. The future of healthcare looks bright thanks to the promise of scalable application and ongoing improvement of these technologies.

References

1. Ahemad, M.T., Hameed, M.A., Vankdothu, R.: COVID-19 detection and classification for machine learning methods using human genomic data. Meas.: Sens. **24**(Oct), 100537 (2022). https://doi.org/10.1016/j.measen.2022.100537
2. Ahammed, M., Mamun, M.Al., Uddin, M.S.: A machine learning approach for skin disease detection and classification using image segmentation. Healthc. Anal. **2**(Oct), 100122 (2022). https://doi.org/10.1016/j.health.2022.100122
3. Gobalakrishnan, N., Pradeep, K., Raman, C.J., Ali, L.J., Gopinath, M.P.: A systematic review on image processing and machine learning techniques for detecting plant diseases. In: Proceedings of the 2020 IEEE International Conference on Communication and Signal Processing, ICCSP 2020, pp. 465–468 (2020). https://doi.org/10.1109/ICCSP48568.2020.9182046
4. Rehman, A., Abbas, S., Khan, M.A., Ghazal, T.M., Adnan, K.M., Mosavi, A.: A secure healthcare 5.0 system based on blockchain technology entangled with federated learning technique. Comput. Biol. Med. 150(Aug), 106019 (2022). https://doi.org/10.1016/j.compbiomed.2022.106019

5. Ferreira, C., Gonçalves, G.: Remaining useful life prediction and challenges: a literature review on the use of Machine Learning Methods. J. Manuf. Syst. **63**(May), 550–562 (2022). https://doi.org/10.1016/j.jmsy.2022.05.010

6. Yeh, Y.H.F., Chung, W.C., Liao, J.Y., Chung, C.L., Kuo, Y.F., Lin, T.Te.: A comparison of machine learning methods on Hyperspectral plant disease assessments. In: IFAC Proceedings Volumes (IFACPapersOnline), vol. 1, Issue PART 1. IFAC (2013). https://doi.org/10.3182/20130327-3-jp-3017.00081

7. Jiang, Y., Dai, P., Fang, P., Zhong, R. Y., Zhao, X., Cao, X.: A2-LSTM for predictive maintenance of industrial equipment based on machine learning. Comput. Ind. Eng. 172(Aug) (2022). https://doi.org/10.1016/j.cie.2022.108560

8. Qin, L.W., et al.: Precision measurement for Industry 4.0 standards towards solid waste classification through enhanced imaging 21 30 7 sensors and deep learning model. Wirel. Commun. Mob. Comput. (2021). https://doi.org/10.1155/2021/9963999

9. Amponsah, A.A., Adekoya, A.F., Weyori, B.A.: A novel fraud detection and prevention method for healthcare claim processing using machine learning and blockchain technology. Decis. Analyt. J. **4**(Aug), 100122 (2022). https://doi.org/10.1016/j.dajour.2022.100122

10. Liu, C., et al.: Probing an intelligent predictive maintenance approach with deep learning and augmented reality for machine tools in IoT-enabled manufacturing. Robot. Comput.-Integr. Manufact. **77**(Nov), 102357 (2022). https://doi.org/10.1016/j.rcim.2022.102357

11. Taheri, G., Habibi, M.: Comprehensive analysis of pathways in Coronavirus 2019 (COVID-19) using an unsupervised machine learning method. Appl. Soft Comput. **128**, 109510 (2022). https://doi.org/10.1016/j.asoc.2022.109510

12. Rajotte, J.F., Bergen, R., Buckeridge, D.L., El Emam, K., Ng, R., Strome, E.: Synthetic data as an enabler for machine learning applications in medicine. IScience **25**(11), 105331 (2022). https://doi.org/10.1016/j.isci.2022.105331

13. Zhang, X., Chen, X., Hong, H., Hu, R., Liu, J., Liu, C.: Decellularized extracellular matrix scaffolds: recent trends and emerging strategies in tissue engineering. Bioact. Mater. **10**(Aug), 15–31 (2022). https://doi.org/10.1016/j.bioactmat.2021.09.014

14. Rejeb, A., et al.: The Internet of Things (IoT) in healthcare: taking stock and moving forward. Internet Things (Netherlands) **22**(Feb), 100721 (2023). https://doi.org/10.1016/j.iot.2023.100721

15. Talukder, M.A., et al.: An efficient deep learning model to categorize brain tumor using reconstruction and fine-tuning. Expert Syst. Appl. **230**(May), 120534 (2023). https://doi.org/10.1016/j.eswa.2023.120534

16. Fayad, M., Mostefaoui, A., Chouali, S., Benbernou, S.: Toward a design model-oriented methodology to ensure QoS of a cyber-physical healthcare system. Computing **104**(7), 1615–1641 (2022). https://doi.org/10.1007/s00607-022-01058-5

17. Pandey, A., Jain, K.: A robust deep attention dense convolutional neural network for plant leaf disease identification and classification from smart phone captured real world images. Ecol. Inform. **70**(June), 101725 (2022). https://doi.org/10.1016/j.ecoinf.2022.101725

18. Alshamrani, M.: IoT and artificial intelligence implementations for remote healthcare monitoring systems: a survey. J. King Saud Univ. – Comput. Inf. Sci. **34**(8), 4687–4701 (2022). https://doi.org/10.1016/j.jksuci.2021.06.005

19. Sharathchandra, D., Ram, M.R.: ML based interactive disease prediction model. In: 2022 IEEE Delhi Section Conference, DELCON 2022 (2022). https://doi.org/10.1109/DELCON54057.2022.9752947

Efficient Characterization of Cough Sounds Using Statistical Analysis

Vodnala Naveenkumar[1](✉) ⓘ, Lankireddy Pratapreddy[2] ⓘ,
and Yarlagadda PadmaSai[1] ⓘ

[1] VNR Vignana Jyothi Institute of Engineering and Technology, Hyderabad 500090, Telangana,
India
vnaveenkumar.vnk@gmail.com
[2] Jawaharlal Nehru Technological University, Hyderabad 500090, Telangana, India

Abstract. Cough serves as a principal symptom in respiratory conditions. Variations in cough sound characteristics provide valuable diagnostic insights. There is a lack of evidence in characterizing cough sounds and misinterpretation leads to severe consequences. This paper presents the efficient characterization of cough sounds using statistical analysis; in addition, both cough sound and speech characteristics are compared. The proposed method extracts spectral and time domain attributes, further subjected to statistical and histogram analysis. The results show that the 25th percentile of spectral roll-off and spectral flux, along with the maximum and mean values of spectral flatness, are vital for characterizing cough sounds. Additionally, the maximum and 75th percentile of zero crossing rate, median of spectral bandwidth, and minimum, maximum, median, mean, standard deviation, 25th percentile, and 75th percentile of spectral centroid contribute significantly to this characterization. The distribution of features in cough sounds discloses that spectral roll-off spreads up to 7800 Hz, spectral flatness ranges from 0 to 0.22, spectral flux varies between 0.3 and 0.6, zero crossing rate extends up to 0.4, spectral centroid spans up to 4300 Hz, and spectral bandwidth varies between 1300 Hz to 3200 Hz. Using these attributes as inputs for artificial intelligence models thereby improves respiratory disease diagnosis efficiency.

Keywords: spectral features · temporal feature · statistical measurement · cough sound pattern

1 Introduction

World Health Organization states that chronic respiratory diseases disturb the function of airways and the structure of the pulmonary system. Spirometry is a traditional lung function test used to measure airflow limitation. However, children and the elderly encounter constraints in accessing this test, and equipment accessibility is inadequate in remote regions. Chest X-rays and CT scans help in the diagnosis of the lungs, but excessive exposure to X-rays is harmful [1]. The cough sounds serve as diagnostic assistance for respiratory diseases and reflect pathophysiological mechanisms of the respiratory system, but they lack efficient characterization.

© The Author(s), under exclusive license to Springer Nature Switzerland AG 2024
D. Garg et al. (Eds.): IACC 2023, CCIS 2054, pp. 272–285, 2024.
https://doi.org/10.1007/978-3-031-56703-2_22

The conventional cough sound pattern includes an initial burst of sound, a noisy interval, and a second burst of sound [2]. J. Smith et al. categorized cough sounds as cough, productive cough, wheezing cough, and wheezing productive cough, and also found that coughs with mucus have longer second phases [3]. Cough sound is initiated by sensory receptors in various locations such as the larynx and lower lung region that send signals to the brainstem [4–6]. These segmentation methods are confined to accurately describing cough sounds due to their non-stationary and continuous nature.

The respiratory diagnosis system utilizes feature vectors [7] from the time domain, frequency domain, and mixed domain to achieve high accuracy. The cough sound is analyzed using spectral analysis to identify changes in frequency bands [8]. The spectral analysis [3] is used to distinguish acoustic differences between coughs with and without mucus in voluntary cough sounds. Cough sounds are quantified using cough epochs and measured cough intensity [9] using cough sound power, peak energy, and mean energy. The study in [10] has identified two frequency bands in cough spectra based on their low-tone prominence, harmonicity, and high-frequency components. A comparison of acoustic features of cough sounds among pneumonia and non-pneumonia clusters is done [11] by analyzing time, frequency, psychoacoustics, and energy.

An investigation [12] separated cough sounds into intrinsic mode-function components using the empirical-mode decomposition method based on frequency bands. As part of an investigation in [13], the authors distinguished cough sounds from non-cough sounds but did not characterize cough sounds. However, similar cough sounds are produced by different respiratory illnesses, and co-morbidities [14] in many patients, which must be considered in real-world situations. Audio features [15] are found to help build machine-learning classifiers for cough-based diagnosis engines. Artificial Intelligence (AI)-based methods and deep learning models [16–18] are proposed for cough sound detection and differentiation of respiratory diseases. Most of the machine-learning techniques utilize automated extraction of time-frequency cough features [19, 20] for the identification of COVID-19.

R.V.Sharan et al. employed the cochleagram to extract features [21], a time-frequency representation derived from the frequency selectivity property of the human cochlea. M. You et al. captured multiple subband signals by using Mel-frequency cepstral coefficients (MFCC), and Gammatone Frequency Cepstral Coefficients feature [22] to find cough events and their exact boundaries from an audio stream.

Existing approaches segment cough sounds into initial and subsequent bursts. Respiratory diagnosis systems employ feature vectors duration, frequency, and mixed domains. Acoustic features allow comparison of cough sounds within respiratory disease clusters, aiding in constructing machine-learning classifiers. Incorporating cough sounds into models is common in existing systems. Yet, insufficiently defined characteristics can hinder effective model development.

The contribution of this research lies in the detailed characterization of cough sounds, particularly distinguishing between those with voiced content and those without. The method employs spectral roll-off, entropy, flatness, flux, zero crossing rate, centroid, and bandwidth attributes, examining their statistical measures. The distribution of features in cough sounds is also presented.

The paper is structured as follows: Sect. 1 introduces the current research, related work, and background. Section 2 details the methods and materials, including the analysis of spectral and temporal features in cough sounds with and without voiced content. Section 3 highlights the results of statistical and histogram analysis, comparing the distribution of cough sounds and speech. Finally, Sect. 4 concludes the entire research endeavor.

2 Material and Methods

Cough sounds are differentiated by the way of vibration of vocal folds and are described by extracting features related to the respiratory system, glottal information, and voice model [23, 24]. A coughing sound with content such as a grunt or a groan embedded in it is found with specific characteristics that include voiced components. In such a scenario, the cough sound is titled "cough sound with voiced content" which is presented in Fig. 1(a). A coughing sound which is produced primarily by the expulsion of air from the lungs does not possess audible vocal components, in which case, those are titled "cough sound without voiced content" and presented in Fig. 1(b).

In the present work, cough sounds are collected from healthy subjects and respiratory-diseased patients from various hospitals in a less noisy environment with the help of doctors. Zoom H5 handy recorder is used for cough sound recording. The distance between the mouth of the subject and the recorder is in the range of 30 cm to 100 cm. To do experiments on cough sounds Python programming language is used.

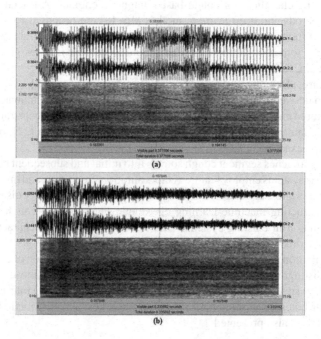

Fig. 1. A coughing sound (a) with voiced content and (b) without voiced content.

The recordings used for characterization consist of 20 recordings of coughing sounds with voiced content and coughing sounds without voiced content each type. The duration of these recordings ranges from 110 ms to 420 ms, and they are captured in noise-free environments. The statistical analysis is done using, minimum (min), maximum (max), mean, 25% of the median (med_25), median, 75% of the median (med_75), and standard deviation (std).

2.1 Spectral Roll-Off

The Spectral roll-off denotes the frequency underneath which a specific percentage of the overall spectral energy lies. It is measured using Eq. (1). The spectral roll-off of cough sounds is shifted toward higher frequencies due to their explosive nature. Cough sounds with voiced content have spectral roll-off varying from 1378 Hz to 9216 Hz, with a mean of 4451 Hz, which is presented in Fig. 2(a). The coughing sounds without voiced content have spectral roll-off varying from 1808 Hz to 9819 Hz, with a mean of 5705 Hz, which is presented in Fig. 2(b).

$$\text{Spectralroll} - \text{off} = f(i) \text{forwhich} \frac{\sum_{j=1}^{i} p(j)}{\sum_{j=1}^{N} p(j)} \geq \text{roll\_percent} \tag{1}$$

where f(i) is the center frequency of the ith frame, p(j) is the magnitude-squared of the frequency response of the jth bin, N is the number of frequency bins, and roll_percent is 85%.

2.2 Spectral Entropy

Spectral entropy is a measure of the randomness or uncertainty of the energy distribution in a signal's frequency domain. Spectral entropy is calculated using Eq. (2). Cough sounds tend to have higher spectral entropy, indicating more complexity and less tonality. The entropy values are higher in the initial burst of cough sounds, indicating high uncertainty, which is presented in Fig. 2(c) and (d).

$$H(X) = -\sum_{i=1}^{i=N} P(f_i) log2(P(f_i)) \tag{2}$$

where $H(X)$ is the spectral entropy of the signal X, N is the number of frequency bins in the signal's spectrum, and $P(f_i)$ is the energy of the ith frequency bin.

2.3 Spectral Flatness

Spectral flatness (SFT) provides information about how evenly the energy of a sound is distributed across different frequencies. The SFT is obtained as the ratio between the geometric mean and arithmetic mean of the power spectrum using Eq. (3). Figure 2(e) demonstrates that cough sounds with voiced content have spectral flatness, predominantly near '0', with a maximum value of 0.047 due to periodic vocal fold vibrations.

The cough sounds without voiced contents have SFT farther away from '0', with a maximum value of 0.22, indicating a lack of periodic vocal fold vibrations is presented in Fig. 2(f).

$$SFT = \frac{\sqrt[N]{\prod_{n=0}^{N-1} p(n)}}{\frac{1}{N}\sum_{n=0}^{N-1} p(n)} \tag{3}$$

where $p(n)$ is the magnitude-squared of the frequency response of the nth bin, N is the number of frequency bins.

2.4 Spectral Flux

Spectral flux is measured as the squared difference in normalized magnitudes between the spectra of two successive frames using Eq. (4). Spectral flux points to sudden changes in spectral magnitudes. Figure 2(g) and (h) provide the spectral flux for both forms of cough sounds having a mean value of 0.43. These findings indicate that the spectral content of cough sounds changes rapidly over time, varying significantly in terms of frequency content, and intensity.

$$SFL_{(i,i-1)} = \sum_{k=1}^{k=WL} (E_i(k) - E_{i-1}(k))^2 \tag{4}$$

where SFL is the spectral flux of ith and $(i\text{-}1)^{th}$ frames, $E_i(k)$ is the normalized magnitude of the kth bin in an ith frame, WL is the length of the frame.

2.5 Zero Crossing Rate (ZCR)

The ZCR is a measure of the amount of sign changes in a signal from positive to negative or vice versa within a specified time interval, which is given in Eq. (5). ZCR for the cough sound without voiced content is higher, with a maximum value of 0.51 and a mean of 0.22 compared to the cough sound with voiced content, with a mean of 0.1 and a maximum value of 0.23, which is demonstrated in Fig. 2(i) and (j).

$$ZCR = \frac{1}{N} \sum_{n=1}^{n=N-1} |s[n]| > \varepsilon \tag{5}$$

where N is the length of the signal, $s[n]$ is the value of the signal at time step n, ε is a small threshold, and the summation is taken over all time steps n from 1 to $N\text{-}1$.

2.6 Spectral Centroid

The spectral centroid calculates the center mass of a sound's frequency spectrum using Eq. (6). It gives the frequency band where most of the energy is concentrated. Cough sounds have a higher spectral centroid because they have more energy at higher frequencies, due to the burst of air produced during a cough, which is presented in Fig. 2(k) and (l). The spectral centroid of a cough with voiced contents has a range from 1045 Hz to 3996 Hz, with a mean of 2154 Hz, whereas the spectral centroid of a cough without voiced contents has a range from 907 Hz to 5397 Hz, with a mean of 3124 Hz.

$$Ci = \frac{\sum_{k=1}^{k=WL}(f(k)P(k))}{\sum_{k=1}^{k=WL}P(k)} \tag{6}$$

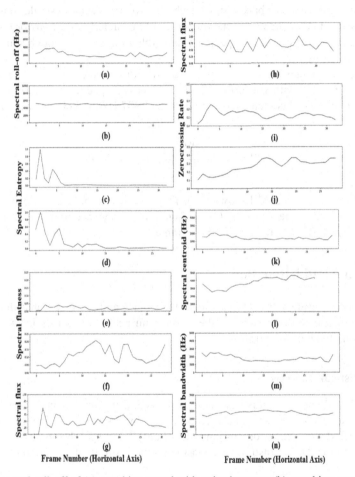

Fig. 2. Spectral roll-off of (a) coughing sound with voiced content (b) coughing sound without voiced content; Spectral entropy of (c) coughing sound with voiced content (d) coughing sound without voiced content; Spectral flatness of (e) coughing sound with voiced content (f) coughing sound without voiced content; Spectral flux of (g) coughing sound with voiced content (h) coughing sound without voiced content; Zero Crossing Rate of (i) coughing sound with voiced content (j) coughing sound without voiced content; Spectral centroid of (k) coughing sound with voiced content (l) coughing sound without voiced content; Spectral bandwidth of (m) coughing sound with voiced content (n) coughing sound without voiced content.

where C_i is the centroid of ith frame, $f(k)$ is the frequency of the kth bin in the frequency spectrum, $P(k)$ is the power of the kth bin, and WL is the length of the frame.

2.7 Spectral Bandwidth

Spectral bandwidth is used to describe the distribution of energy within a frequency band. Spectral bandwidth is measured as the spread of the power spectrum around its centroid using Eq. (7). The bandwidth will change over time within a single cough sound, which is indicative of changes in the properties of the underlying airway or lung tissue. Figure 2(m) and (n) depict the spectral bandwidth with a voiced cough sound and an unvoiced cough sound.

The spectral bandwidth of a coughing sound with voiced contents has a range from 1273 Hz to 3605 Hz, with a mean of 2286 Hz, whereas the spectral centroid of a coughing sound without voiced contents has a range from 1307 Hz to 3760 Hz, with a mean of 2348 Hz.

$$SBWi = \frac{\sum_{k=1}^{k=WL}(|f(k) - C_i|P(k))}{\sum_{k=1}^{k=WL}P(k)} \tag{7}$$

where SBW_i is the spectral bandwidth of ith frame, C_i is the spectral centroid of ith frame, $f(k)$ is the frequency of the kth bin in the frequency spectrum, $P(k)$ is the power of the kth bin, and WL is the length of the frame.

3   Results and Discussion

The results are evaluated using statistical techniques and are elaborated upon in the subsequent detailed discussion. Further, histogram analysis provides insight into the distribution of significant attributes.

3.1   Statistical Analysis

Tables 1, 2, and 3 provide statistical analyses of cough with voiced content, cough without voiced content, and speech signals, respectively. In this work, 20 speech recordings are considered along with cough sound recordings. These speech signals are randomly chosen from the "Texas Instruments Massachusetts Institute of Technology (TIMIT)" database.

The results indicate that specific attributes, including the 25th percentile, maximum, and mean values of spectral flatness, the 25th percentile of spectral flux, maximum, and 75th percentile of ZCR, as well as minimum, maximum, median, mean, standard deviation, 25th percentile, and 75th percentile of spectral centroid, along with the median of spectral bandwidth, offer a more significant characterization of cough sounds. The spectral entropy does not exhibit impact. Utilizing a combination of these attributes provides a precise and comprehensive representation of cough sound characteristics.

Table 1. Statistical analysis of cough with voiced content

Attributes	Min	Max	Mean	med_25	Median	med_75	Std
Spectral Roll-off (in Hz)	1378	9216	4451	2670	4392	5943	1949
Spectral Entropy	0	1	0.067	0.001	0.005	0.021	0.174
Spectral Flatness	0	0.04	0.012	0.003	0.01	0.018	0.011
Spectral Flux	0	1	0.409	0.293	0.402	0.551	0.225
ZCR	0.02	0.22	0.1	0.061	0.086	0.131	0.046
Spectral Centroid (Hz)	1045	3996	2154	1542	2122	2619	700
Spectral Bandwidth (Hz)	1273	3605	2286	1864	2276	2680	527

Table 2. Statistical analysis of cough with unvoiced content

Attributes	Min	max	Mean	med_25	Median	med_75	Std
Spectral Roll-off (in Hz)	1808	9819	5705	4392	5555	7321	1961
Spectral Entropy	0	1	0.079	0.003	0.023	0.076	0.15
Spectral Flatness	0	0.22	0.057	0.009	0.036	0.094	0.057
Spectral Flux	0	1	0.438	0.324	0.45	0.552	0.222
ZCR	0.035	0.51	0.222	0.144	0.230	0.305	0.097
Spectral Centroid (Hz)	907	5397	3124	2473	3229	3730	917
Spectral Bandwidth (Hz)	1307	3760	2348	1807	2470	2792	574

Table 3. Statistical analysis of speech signals

Attributes	Min	Max	Mean	med_25	Median	med_75	Std
Spectral Roll-off (in Hz)	861	3445	1770	1335	1636	2153	597
Spectral Entropy	0	1	0.062	0	0	0.01	0.18
Spectral Flatness	0	0	0	0	0	0	0
Spectral Flux	0.0	1	0.304	0.148	0.258	0.44	0.221
ZCR	0.02	0.102	0.060	0.051	0.06	0.07	0.016
Spectral Centroid (Hz)	583	1626	1019	867	994	1152	221
Spectral Bandwidth (Hz)	381	1349	745	565	719	874	218

3.2 Histogram Analysis

The histogram in Fig. 3(a) shows that frames for cough sounds with voiced content are primarily between 1550–1950 Hz and 4100–4700 Hz, but some lower-frequency values exist due to the voiced content. Figure 3(b) shows cough sounds without voiced content display spectral roll-offs mostly between 4200–5200 Hz and 7000–7800 Hz, all at high frequencies. Figure 3(c) presents, speech signals typically occur between spectral roll-off values of 1100–1500 Hz, which are lower frequencies. Increased spectral roll-off during the compression phase, indicating strong expulsion and distinguishing coughs from speech.

The statistical analysis reveals the fact that voiced cough sounds exhibit spectral flatness levels ranging from 0 to 0.047, whereas cough sounds without voiced content possess spectral flatness values ranging from 0 to 0.22. It indicates the presence of airway obstruction or turbulence caused by inflammation or mucus. The spread of spectral flatness values is presented in Fig. 4(a), (b), and (c) using a histogram. The histogram representation in Fig. 5(a), (b), and (c) shows the distribution of spectral flux values for cough sounds and speech signals. Cough sounds show spectral flux values between 0.3 and 0.6, while speech signals range between 0.05 and 0.3. It denotes fast changes in airway obstruction due to infections or physiological alterations, leading to airway narrowing and increased turbulence during coughing.

The histogram illustrated in Fig. 6(a), (b), and (c) reveals that most frames of unvoiced cough sounds are distributed over zero crossing rate values of 0.05 and 0.4, indicating that unvoiced cough sounds have higher ZCR compared to voiced cough sounds and speech signals. The spread of ZCR values for voiced cough and speech signals is between 0.05 and 0.2. The spread of spectral centroid values for speech signals between 583 Hz and 1626 Hz, which is lower than that of voiced and unvoiced cough sounds, which are between 1045 Hz and 3996 Hz, and 907 Hz and 5397 Hz, respectively. The histograms in Fig. 7(a), (b), and (c) present the distribution of the majority of frames for each sound type. Based on the histogram in Fig. 8(a) and (b), most frames in cough sounds have a wider frequency spread, ranging from 1300 Hz to 3200 Hz, compared to speech signals. The majority of frames in speech signals, presented in Fig. 8(c) have a narrow frequency spread, ranging from 400 Hz to 1000 Hz.

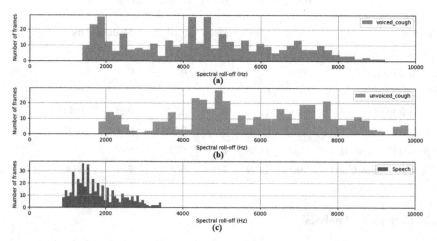

Fig. 3. Histogram of spectral roll-off of (a) coughing sounds with voiced content (b) coughing sounds without voiced content (c) speech signals.

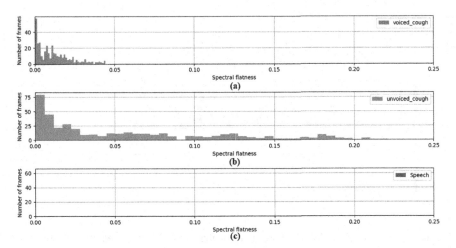

Fig. 4. Histogram of spectral flatness of (a) coughing sounds with voiced content (b) coughing sounds without voiced content (c) speech signals.

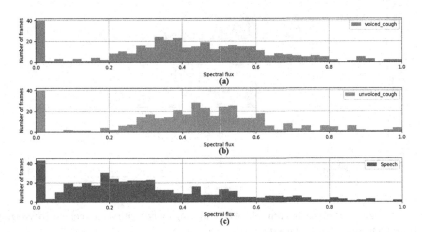

Fig. 5. Histogram of the spectral flux of (a) coughing sounds with voiced content (b) coughing sounds without voiced content (c) speech signals.

The summary of the distribution of attributes in cough sounds and speech is presented in Table 4.

Existing methods primarily concentrate on cough sound detection and classification. From traditional to advanced techniques like K-Nearest Neighbor, Support Vector Machines, and Artificial Neural Networks, the focus remains on predicting respiratory diseases or categorizing them based on cough sounds. However, without a comprehensive understanding of input data such as cough sounds, this may lead to future inaccuracies. Therefore, enhancing the reliability of AI-based models necessitates a deep comprehension of cough sound characteristics.

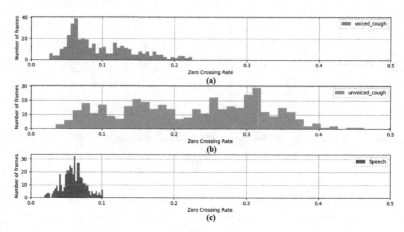

Fig. 6. Histogram of Zero Crossing Rate of (a) coughing sounds with voiced content (b) coughing sounds without voiced content (c) speech signals.

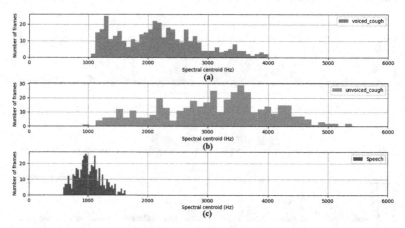

Fig. 7. Histogram of the spectral centroid of (a) coughing sounds with voiced content (b) coughing sounds without voiced content (c) speech signals.

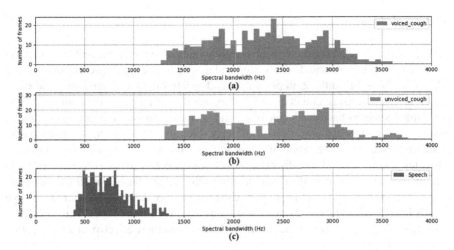

Fig. 8. Histogram of the spectral bandwidth of (a) coughing sounds with voiced content (b) coughing sounds without voiced content (c) speech signals.

Table 4. Distribution of attributes in cough sounds and speech

Attribute	Cough with voiced content	Cough without voiced content	Speech	Observations
Spectral roll-off	1550 Hz to 1950 Hz; and 4100 Hz to 4700 Hz	4200 Hz to 5200 Hz; and 7000 Hz to 7800 Hz	1100 Hz to 1500 Hz	Less overlap among the sounds
Spectral flatness	0 to 0.047	0 to 0.22	0	Cough sounds spread toward higher values; Speech is almost zero
Spectral flux	0.3 to 0.6	0.3 to 0.6	0.05 to 0.3	Very little overlap between cough sounds and speech
ZCR	0.05 to 0.2	0.05 to 0.4	0.05 to 0.1	Variation in spread towards higher values
Spectral centroid	1100 Hz to 2900 Hz	2100 Hz to 4300 Hz	580 Hz to 1460 Hz	Less overlap among the sounds
Spectral Bandwidth	1300 Hz to 3200 Hz	1300 Hz to 3200 Hz	400 Hz to 1100 Hz	No overlap between cough sounds and speech

4 Conclusion

In this paper, the characterization of cough sounds using spectral and time domain attributes has been presented. The major findings of this research present the spectral roll-off, spectral flux at the 25th percentile, and spectral flatness's maximum and mean values in characterizing cough sounds. Also, zero crossing rate (maximum and 75th percentile), spectral bandwidth (median), and spectral centroid (minimum, maximum, median, mean, standard deviation, 25th percentile, and 75th percentile) significantly contribute to the characterization of cough sounds. Histogram analysis revealed that the attributes of cough sounds are distributed in closer proximity to each other compared to speech. Further augmenting the research with additional attributes like MFCCs and Linear Prediction Cepstrum Coefficient (LPCCs) may enhance the characterization of cough sounds beyond the current significant attributes explored in this paper. Thus, it is concluded that the combination of these attributes results in a more effective characterization of cough sounds.

References

1. Rudraraju, G., et al.: Cough sound analysis and objective correlation with spirometry and clinical diagnosis. Inform. Med. Unlocked **19**, 100319 (2020). https://doi.org/10.1016/j.imu.2020.100319
2. Korpáš, J., Sadloňová, J., Vrabec, M.: Analysis of the cough sound: an overview. Pulm. Pharmacol. **9**(5–6), 261–268 (1996). https://doi.org/10.1006/pulp.1996.0034
3. Smith, J., Ashurst, H., Jack, S., Woodcock, A., Earis, J.: The description of cough sounds by healthcare professionals. Cough **2**(1), 1–9 (2006). https://doi.org/10.1186/1745-9974-2-1
4. Widdicombe, J.G.: Neurophysiology of the cough reflex. Eur. Respir. J. **8**(7), 1193–1202 (1995). https://doi.org/10.1183/09031936.95.08071193
5. Canning, B.J., Chang, A.B., Bolser, D.C., Smith, J.A., Mazzone, S.B., McGarvey, L.: Anatomy and neurophysiology of cough: CHEST guideline and expert panel report. Chest **146**(6), 1633–1648 (2014). https://doi.org/10.1378/chest.14-1481
6. Widdicombe, J., Fontana, G.: Cough: what's in a name? Eur. Respir. J. **28**(1), 10–15 (2006). https://doi.org/10.1183/09031936.06.00096905
7. Islam, R., Abdel-raheem, E., Tarique, M.: A study of using cough sounds and deep neural networks for the early detection of Covid-19, January 2020
8. Pahar, M., Klopper, M., Reeve, B., Warren, R., Theron, G., Niesler, T.: Automatic cough classification for tuberculosis screening in a real-world environment. Physiol. Meas. **42**(10) (2021) https://doi.org/10.1088/1361-6579/ac2fb8
9. Shi, Y., Liu, H., Wang, Y., Cai, M., Xu, W.: Theory and application of audio-based assessment of cough. J. Sens. **2018** (2018). https://doi.org/10.1155/2018/9845321
10. Adhi Pramono, R.X., Anas Imtiaz, S., Rodriguez-Villegas, E.: Automatic cough detection in acoustic signal using spectral features. In: Proceedings of Annual International Conference on IEEE Engineering Medicine and Biology Society EMBS, pp. 7153–7156 (2019). https://doi.org/10.1109/EMBC.2019.8857792
11. Chung, Y., et al.: Diagnosis of pneumonia by cough sounds analyzed with statistical features and AI. Sensors **21**(21) (2021). https://doi.org/10.3390/s21217036
12. Lee, K.K., et al.: Sound: a non-invasive measure of cough intensity. BMJ Open Respir. Res. **4**(1), 1–9 (2017). https://doi.org/10.1136/bmjresp-2017-000178

13. Martinek, J., Klco, P., Vrabec, M., Zatko, T., Tatar, M., Javorka, M.: Cough sound analysis. Acta Medica Martiniana **13**(Suppl.-1), 15–20 (2018). https://doi.org/10.2478/acm-2013-0002

14. Infante, C., Chamberlain, D., Fletcher, R., Thorat, Y., Kodgule, R.: Use of cough sounds for diagnosis and screening of pulmonary disease. In: GHTC 2017 - IEEE Global Humanitarian Technology Conference, vol. 2017, pp. 1–10 (2017). https://doi.org/10.1109/GHTC.2017. 8239338

15. Sharan, R.V.: Cough sound detection from raw waveform using SincNet and bidirectional GRU. Biomed. Sig. Process. Control **82**(2022), 104580 (2023). https://doi.org/10.1016/j. bspc.2023.104580

16. Soltanian, M., Borna, K.: Covid-19 recognition from cough sounds using lightweight separable-quadratic convolutional network. Biomed. Sig. Process. Control **72**(October), 2022 (2021). https://doi.org/10.1016/j.bspc.2021.103333

17. Preum, S.M., et al.: A review of cognitive assistants for healthcare: trends, prospects, and future directions. ACM Comput. Surv. **53**(6) (2021). https://doi.org/10.1145/3419368

18. Ijaz, A., et al.: Towards using cough for respiratory disease diagnosis by leveraging Artificial Intelligence: a survey. Inform. Med. Unlocked **29**, 100832 (2022). https://doi.org/10.1016/j. imu.2021.100832

19. Tena, A., Clarià, F., Solsona, F.: Automated detection of COVID-19 cough. Biomed. Signal Process. Control **71** (2022). https://doi.org/10.1016/j.bspc.2021.103175

20. Sharma, G., Umapathy, K., Krishnan, S.: Audio texture analysis of COVID-19 cough, breath, and speech sounds. Biomed. Signal Process. Control **76**, 103703 (2022). https://doi.org/10. 1016/j.bspc.2022.103703

21. Sharan, R.V., Abeyratne, U.R., Swarnkar, V.R., Porter, P.: Automatic croup diagnosis using cough sound recognition. IEEE Trans. Biomed. Eng. **66**(2), 485–495 (2019). https://doi.org/ 10.1109/TBME.2018.2849502

22. You, M., Liu, Z., Chen, C., Liu, J., Xu, X.H., Qiu, Z.M.: Cough detection by ensembling multiple frequency subband features. Biomed. Signal Process. Control **33**, 132–140 (2017). https://doi.org/10.1016/j.bspc.2016.11.005

23. Zhang, Z.: Toward real-time physically-based voice simulation: an eigenmode-based approach. Proc. Meet. Acoust. **30**(1) (2017). https://doi.org/10.1121/2.0000572

24. Zhang, Z.: Mechanics of human voice production and control. J. Acoust. Soc. Am. **140**(4), 2614–2635 (2016). https://doi.org/10.1121/1.4964509

An Efficient Method for Heart Failure Diagnosis

Ravi Kumar Sachdeva[1] , Anshika Singla[1] , Priyanka Bathla[2] ,
Anurag Jain[3(✉)] , Tanupriya Choudhury[4] , and Ketan Kotecha[5]

[1] Chitkara University Institute of Engineering and Technology, Chitkara University, Punjab,
India
{ravi.sachdeva,anshika0287.cse19}@chitkara.edu.in

[2] Chandigarh University, Gharuan, Mohali, Punjab, India
priyanka.e12005@cumail.in

[3] School of Computer Sciences, University of Petroleum and Energy Studies, Dehradun, India
dr.anuragjain14@gmail.com

[4] CSE Department, Symbiosis Institute of Technology, Symbiosis International University,
Lavale Campus, Pune, Maharashtra 412115, India
tanupriya.choudhury@sitpune.edu.in

[5] Symbiosis Centre for Applied Artificial Intelligence, Symbiosis Institute of Technology,
Symbiosis International (Deemed University), Pune 412115, India
director@sitpune.edu.in

Abstract. The primary objective of this research paper is to develop an efficient method for the early identification of heart failure. Two classification techniques—Logistic Regression (LR) and Naive Bayes (NB)—were used in a series of experiments utilizing the heart failure dataset from the UCI repository. The authors selected accuracy as the performance metric and applied the robust feature selection technique to both classifiers. The experimental approach systematically excluded each prediction attribute and calculated accuracy with the remaining features. Notably, when the Platelets feature was removed, both LR and NB obtained a remarkable 100% accuracy. This significant finding highlights the potential of the suggested model for the early detection of heart failure. This research gives priceless insights that might empower doctors in improving heart failure diagnosis and patient care by identifying critical predictors. The proposed model shows potential for medical practitioners engaged in diagnosing heart failure.

Keywords: Heart failure · Heart disease · Machine learning · Feature selection · Logistic regression · Naïve Bayes

1 Introduction

Congestive heart failure (CHF), often known as heart failure, is a medical condition brought on by a decline in the heart's ability to pump blood [1]. Fluid accumulation in the arteries and tissue can be caused by filling insufficiency and intracardiac strain. Congestion results from a collection of fluid and presents it as oedema and inflammation. Dyspnea, extreme tiredness, and leg swelling are typical symptoms. Dyspnea can cause

D. Garg et al. (Eds.): IACC 2023, CCIS 2054, pp. 286–295, 2024.
https://doi.org/10.1007/978-3-031-56703-2_23

people to wake up at night and can happen with exercise or while resting. Heart failure often does not result in chest pain; however, it might if the heart attack leads to heart failure [2]. The level of symptoms during strenuous work serves as a gauge for heart failure severity. Heart failure is when the heart either fails to pump blood to the rest of the body during systole or fails to fill with blood during diastole, lowering intracardiac pressures [3].

Identifying heart problems in a person is complex and requires various details, laboratory tests, and types of equipment [3]. Early-stage detection of heart disease also reduces cost and mortality. The most common reason for adult hospitalization is heart disease, a common and potentially fatal illness. When the heart fails, the effects on the body are frequently more severe than when other, more complicated organs, like the liver and kidneys, fail [1].

Worldwide, approximately 64.3 million individuals suffer from heart failure. Researchers foresee an upward trend in the incidence of recognized heart failure, which is currently estimated to affect 1% to 2% of the elderly population in affluent nations [4]. The mortality risk is like that of several malignancies. Around 1% of the people, or 8–10 million people, are thought to have heart failure in India.

Doctors should employ machine learning (ML) algorithms to identify heart failure in its early stages and get more effective and structured diagnosis[5]. ML has proven itself a breakthrough in critical disease diagnosis [6, 7]. The latest developments of Industry 4.0 include artificial intelligence (AI), the Internet of Things, ML, cloud computing, and big data. These innovations are essential to the healthcare sector, particularly ML and AI. ML makes it simpler to detect failing hearts as soon as feasible and can lengthen the lives of those with heart issues [8].

This paper's main contribution is a novel and precise model for the early identification of heart failure. This paper proposes a novel method for predictive modelling in cardiovascular healthcare using a comprehensive heart failure dataset and two well-known classification approaches, Logistic Regression (LR) and Naïve Bayes (NB). The authors identified crucial predictors that considerably improve early heart failure diagnosis and achieved 100% accuracy rates for both classifiers after removing the Platelets feature using a methodical feature selection approach. By giving clinicians a powerful tool for early heart failure detection, which can ultimately result in lower mortality rates and improved treatment approaches, this research has enormous promise for improving patient care.

The remainder of the research paper is divided among the subsequent sections. The study on diagnosing heart failure by various researchers is shown in Sect. 2. Section 3 depicts the data and research methodology embraced by the researchers. Section 4 discusses the result and conclusion. Section 5 talks about the conclusion of the work conducted and the long-run scope of the research.

2 Related Work

The work of researchers who have worked in similar areas and provided ML models for heart failure prediction is presented below:

Hazra et al. [1] observed that the cleaned and trimmed dataset provides superior accuracy than the unclean dataset having missing values. The authors suggested that by using knowledge from appropriate datasets, data mining could assist in choosing the course of treatment to be employed.

Garg et al. [2] used the dataset on the Kaggle website for their experiments. The dataset consists of thirteen attributes. The authors used Python as their programming language for the experiments. The authors conducted their experiments using two classifiers, K nearest neighbors (KNN) and Random Forest (RF). KNN gave an accuracy of 86.885%, and on the other hand, RF provided an accuracy of 81.967%. KNN's value of k was 12, as it provided the best results.

Alotaibi [3] emphasized that the ratio of heart patients is increasing daily, and to overcome the issue, there is a need to build a system that could predict heart failure in the early stages. So, he proposed an ML model using five different algorithms. The author used the Rapid Miner tool for his experiments. The authors obtained 93.19% accuracy using the Decision Tree (DT), 87.36% accuracy using LR, 89.14% accuracy using RF, 87.27% using NB, and 92.30% using the Support Vector Machine (SVM).

Pasha et al. [4] applied SVM, KNN, DT, and the Artificial neural network (ANN) binary model to predict heart failure and compared the accuracy levels on the heart failure dataset. The author collected the dataset from Kaggle. After experimenting with the data, they found each classifier returns different accuracies for the collected data. The obtained accuracies were 81.97% using SVM, 67.20% using KNN, 81.97% using DT, and 85.24% using ANN. The authors concluded that ANN gave the best results.

Rubini et al. [8] used the dataset available at the University of California, Irvine (UCI) repository. The authors offered a heart disease expectation framework based on ML techniques like RF, LR, SVM using the linear kernel, SVM using the radial base kernel, and NB to predict the accuracy of heart failure early. RF provided the highest accuracy at 84.81%.

Lakshmana Rao et al. [9] collected the dataset from Kaggle. The authors applied three different sampling techniques and concluded that different classifiers gave the best results for each sampling technique. For Adaptive Synthetic Sampling and Synthetic Minority Oversampling, RF and Extra-Tree gave the best results.

Shrivastava and Chaubey [10] obtained the Cleveland Heart Disease dataset from UCI, applied it to pre-process to drop the missing value data, and applied some ML techniques like KNN, DT, SVM, and RF to calculate the accuracy. The accuracy achieved for the heart failure prediction dataset using different methods is 71% using DT, 87% using KNN, 84% using SVM, and 83% using RF.

Dritsas et al. [11] used the Waikato Environment for Knowledge Analysis (WEKA) to conduct the experiments. WEKA is a free software program based on Java and has a data mining toolbox. The authors split the dataset into 30% testing data and 70% training data for the experiments. The authors used the NB, SVM, RF, and LR techniques of ML. The authors achieved 59.59% accuracy using NB, 70.61% using SVM, 70.86% using RF, and 72.06% using LR. The author concluded that LR is empowering and superior in exactness, review, and area under the curve (AUC) against the rest of the ML models.

Previous research in heart failure prediction has made progress in utilizing various ML techniques and datasets, emphasizing the need for precise predictive models. However, a noticeable research gap exists, particularly in achieving high accuracy. The suggested method outperforms existing approaches by attaining 100% accuracy. The model presented in the paper improves predictive accuracy and identifies key predictors crucial for early heart failure diagnosis. The proposed method surpasses existing models, promising improved patient care and reduced mortality rates.

3 Methodology

3.1 Dataset

The authors ran tests using the heart failure dataset accessible on UCI[12]. The dataset consists of twelve prediction traits and one result property. The resulting trait is DEATH_EVENT, representing whether the patient is deceased during the follow-up period. The number of records present in the dataset is 299. Using a bar graph, Fig. 1 shows the distribution for the result attribute, i.e., DEATH_EVENT. Fig. 1 depicts the distribution of the 'DEATH_EVENT' result attribute in the heart failure dataset. It shows the proportion of cases with the labels "0" (indicating no death) and "1" (indicating death), giving a clear picture of how these outcomes are distributed in the dataset.

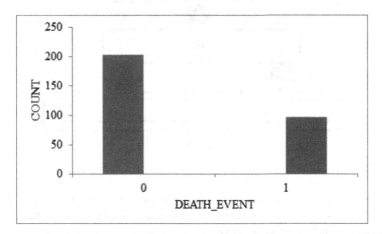

Fig. 1. Bar Graph Depicting Distribution for the Result Attribute, i.e., DEATH_EVENT

3.1.1 Research Methodology

The author used LR and NB classifiers to conduct the dataset experiments. The authors used accuracy as the performance parameter and applied the robust feature selection technique to both classifiers. The authors performed the experiments and calculated the accuracy by initially taking all prediction attributes. Afterwards, for every feature, the authors dropped it and calculated the accuracy for the remaining set of prediction attributes. Figure 2 displays the researchers' chosen research methodology. Below is the description of the classifiers used:

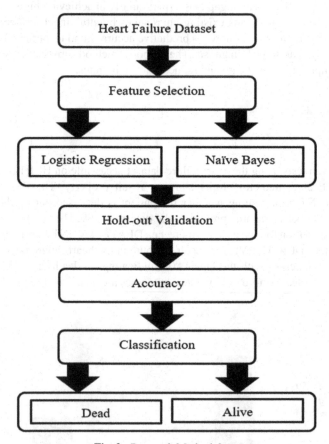

Fig. 2. Research Methodology

1. Logistic Regression (LR): An ML algorithm is used to calculate or predict the probability of a binary event occurring. LR helps in solving classification problems. The expression of LR is as follows [11]:

$$Logit(p) = \ln \frac{p}{1-p} \qquad (1)$$

2. Naïve Bayes (NB): Similar to LR, NB is also an ML technique. It is based on Bayes' theorem. It is also employed to address classification issues. It is a simple probabilistic classifier. The equation of the technique is represented below [11]:

$$P(X|Y) = \frac{P(Y|X) * P(X)}{P(Y)} \tag{2}$$

Accuracy is the percentage of samples correctly classified across all the samples [13].

4   Results and Discussion

The experiments used an HP notebook featuring an Intel Core i5 processor and 8 GB RAM. Google Colab, a cloud-based platform, was employed for Python execution. Table 1 shows the accuracy achieved for LR and NB classifiers considering all features. LR achieved 80% accuracy, and NB obtained 83% accuracy with all attributes considered. Figure 3 shows the comparison of accuracy for both classifiers.

Table 1. Accuracy Achieved by LR and NB

Classifier	Accuracy (%)
LR	80
NB	83

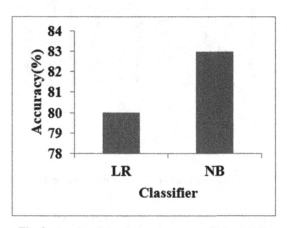

Fig. 3. Bar Graph Depicting Accuracy of LR and NB

Table 2. Accuracy Achieved by LR and NB by Dropping Different Features

Features	LR Accuracy (%)	NB Accuracy (%)
Age	96.6	93.3
Anaemia	93.3	86.6
Creatinine_phosphokinase	93.3	93.3
Diabetes	93.3	86.6
Ejection_fraction	96.6	76.6
High_blood_preasure	90	86.6
Platelets	100	100
Serum_creatinine	96.6	90
Sex	93.3	86.6
Smoking	93.3	86.6
Time	73.3	76.6

Table 2 shows the accuracy achieved when a particular feature was dropped. It displays the accuracy of dropping different features, one at a time. When a feature was omitted, Figs. 4 and 5 compare the accuracy of LR and NB classifiers.

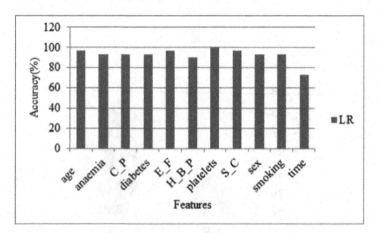

Fig. 4. Bar Graph Depicting Accuracy of LR by Dropping Different Features

When the Platelets feature was dropped, the authors achieved 100% accuracy for both classifiers. A graphical depiction known as a Receiver Operating Characteristic (ROC) explains the performance range for the classification tasks at various thresholds [13]. The value under the ROC curve for LR and NB is 1.000. Figure 6 is the ROC curve for LR, and Fig. 7 is the ROC curve for the NB classifier.

Compared to recently published articles on heart failure prediction, this study's remarkable achievement of 100% accuracy stands out as a significant breakthrough.

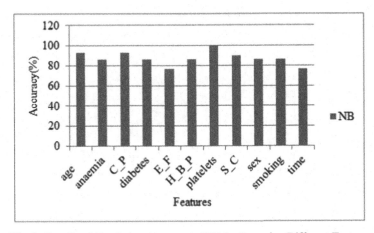

Fig. 5. Bar Graph Depicting Accuracy of NB by Dropping Different Features

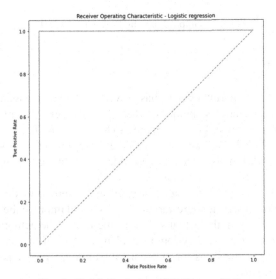

Fig. 6. Graph Depicting ROC Curve of LR

While many previous works shown in the related work section reported accuracy rates ranging from 59.59% to 93.19%, this research demonstrates a substantially higher level of accuracy, setting a new standard in the domain.

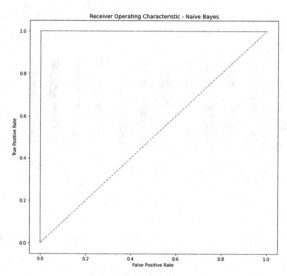

Fig. 7. Graph Depicting ROC Curve of NB

5 Conclusion

After carrying out the experiments, ML has proved to be a boon in medical science. The author used ML classification techniques, LR and NB, to diagnose heart failure at an early stage. LR had an accuracy of 80%, compared to 83% for NB. The authors noticed that both classifiers provided 100% accuracy with the remaining features when the Platelets feature was removed. Finally, it can be concluded that clinicians can successfully use the suggested model for early heart failure diagnosis.

Several possible future areas can be investigated to further this research. First and foremost, the use of larger and more varied datasets could improve the model's dependability and applicability in the actual world. In the future, the authors will implement a graphical user interface-based system to implement the model. Collaboration across various healthcare organizations for external validation can give detailed insights into the model's performance.

Acknowledgement. This research was supported by an RSF (Research Support Fund) Grant from Symbiosis International University, Pune, India.

References

1. Hazra, A., Mandal, S., Gupta, A., Mukherjee, A.P., Mukherjee, A.: Heart disease diagnosis and prediction using machine learning and data mining techniques: a review. Int. J. Adv. Comput. Sci. Technol. **10**, 2137–2159 (2017)
2. Garg, A., Sharma, B., Khan R.: Heart disease prediction using machine learning techniques. In: 1st International Conference on Computational Research and Data Analytics, pp. 1–9. IOPScience, India (2020).https://doi.org/10.1088/1757-899X/1022/1/012046

3. Alotaibi, F. S.: Implementation of machine learning model to predict heart failure disease. Int. J.Adv. Comput. Sci. Appl. (IJACSA) **10**(6), 261–268 (2019).https://doi.org/10.14569/IJA CSA.2019.0100637

4. Pasha, S.N., Ramesh, D., Mohmmad, S., Harshavardhan, A., Shabana: Cardiovascular disease prediction using deep learning techniques. In: International Conference on Recent Advancements in Engineering and Management (ICRAEM-2020), pp. 1–6. IOPScience, India (2020).https://doi.org/10.1088/1757-899X/981/2/022006

5. Sachdeva, R.K., Garg, T., Khaira, G.S., Mitrav, D., Ahuja, R.: A systematic method for Lung Cancer Classification. In: 10th International Conference on Reliability, Infocom Technologies and Optimization (Trends and Future Directions) (ICRITO), pp. 1–5. IEEE, India (2022). https://doi.org/10.1109/ICRITO56286.2022.9964778

6. Ramesh T.R., Lilhore, U.K., Poongodi, M., Simaiya, S., Kaur, A., Hamdi, M.: Predictive analysis of heart diseases with machine learning approaches. Malays. J. Comput. Sci. 132–148 (2022). https://doi.org/10.22452/mjcs.sp2022no1.10

7. Verma, K., et al.: Latest tools for data mining and machine learning. Int. J. Innov. Technol. Explor. Eng. (IJITEE) **8**(9s), 18–23 (2019). https://doi.org/10.35940/ijitee.I1003.0789S19

8. Rubini, P.E., Subasini, C.A., Katharine, A.V., Kumaresan, V., Kumar, S.G., Nithya, T.M.: A cardiovascular disease prediction using machine learning algorithms. Ann. Roman. Soc. Cell Biol. **25**(2), 904–912 (2021)

9. Lakshmanarao, A., Swathi, Y., Sundareswar, P.S.S.: Machine learning techniques for heart disease prediction. Int. J. Sci. Technol. Res. (IJSTR) **8**(11), 374–377 (2019)

10. Srivastava, K., and Choubey, D. K.: Heart disease prediction using machine learning and data mining. Int. J. Rec. Technol. Eng. (IJRTE) **9**(1), 212–219 (2020). https://doi.org/10.35940/ ijrte.F9199.059120

11. Dritsas, E., Alexiou, S., Moustakas, K.: Cardiovascular disease risk prediction with supervised machine learning techniques. In: 8th International Conference on Information and Communication Technologies for Ageing Well and e-Health, pp. 315–321. SciTePress (2022). https:// doi.org/10.5220/0011088300003188

12. Heart failure clinical records. https://archive.ics.uci.edu/ml/datasets/Heart+failure+clinical+ records

13. Sachdeva, R.K., Bathla, P., Rani, P., Solanki, V., Ahuja, R.: A systematic method for diagnosis of hepatitis disease using machine learning. Innov. Syst. Softw. Eng. **19**, 1–80 (2023). https:// doi.org/10.1007/s11334-022-00509-8

14. Rani, P., Kumar, R., Jain, A., Lamba. R., Sachdeva. RK., Choudhury, T.: PCA-DNN: a novel deep neural network oriented system for Breast Cancer classification. EAI Endors. Trans. Perv. Health Technol. **9**, 1–18 (2023). https://doi.org/10.4108/eetpht.9.3533

Novel Machine Learning Algorithms for Predicting COVID-19 Clinical Outcomes with Gender Analysis

Yogendra Narayan Prajapati[✉] [iD] and Manish Sharma[iD]

Quantum University, Roorkee, Uttarakhand, India
ynp1581@gmail.com, director@quantumeducation.in

Abstract. The COVID-19 pandemic has created a huge challenge for health-care services around the world. Understanding the factors affecting treatment outcomes in COVID-19 is important to provide personalized and effective treatment, especially taking into account gender differences. This challenge involves using machine learning to analyze patient data, identify risk factors, and develop predictive models to predict the incidence and severity of COVID-19, including the impact of gender on the disease. This will allow doctors to create treatment plans and allocate resources efficiently based on a person's gender and other health-related factors. The aim of this article is to develop and evaluate novel machine learning algorithms to predict the clinical outcome of COVID-19 in patients, including the effect of father's gender. The goal is to develop accurate predictive models that will help doctors predict the progression and severity of COVID-19 in humans, including gender-specific factors in our study I used 7 different ML model with different k fold cross validation and compare with other model to our proposed model and got 99.45 accuracy and other model like random forest accuracy is 94.34, SVM has 95.88 accuracy and other model has got accuracy bellow 95 so we conclude that our proposed model has got best accuracy.

Keywords: Machine learning model · random forest algorithms · performance parameter (AUC-ROC) · and accuracy

1 Introduction

The COVID-19 pandemic has brought unprecedented challenges to healthcare systems worldwide. Understanding the factors that influence the clinical outcomes of COVID-19 patients is of paramount importance for efficient patient care and resource allocation. In this context, machine learning has emerged as a powerful tool for predicting clinical outcomes and identifying significant variables that contribute to disease severity. This study focuses on the development and evaluation of innovative machine learning algorithms tailored to the specific task of predicting clinical outcomes in COVID-19 patients. Notably, we place a particular emphasis on the role of gender in influencing these outcomes, as emerging evidence suggests gender-based disparities in COVID-19

D. Garg et al. (Eds.): IACC 2023, CCIS 2054, pp. 296–310, 2024.
https://doi.org/10.1007/978-3-031-56703-2_24

susceptibility and disease progression. Through the development and rigorous evaluation of these algorithms, our research aims to provide valuable insights into personalized patient management strategies and contribute to a more comprehensive understanding of the impact of gender on COVID-19 clinical outcomes [13].

The emergence of COVID-19 has presented an unprecedented global health challenge, necessitating the development of effective strategies for patient care and management. One promising avenue for improving patient outcomes is the application of machine learning algorithms. In this study, we explore innovative machine learning approaches to predict the clinical outcomes of COVID-19 patients. Notably, we also investigate the influence of gender distribution on these outcomes, recognizing the importance of accounting for demographic factors in the pursuit of tailored and equitable healthcare solutions. This research aims to enhance our understanding of the disease's impact and contribute to more precise clinical decision-making in the fight against COVID-19 [14].

Worldwide, the COVID-19 pandemic has increased morbidity and mortality rates, particularly among people with pre-existing conditions such as heart disease. Patients who already have heart disease are more likely to get sick, be admitted to the intensive care unit, need ventilators, and die from COVID-19. Therefore, early detection of high-risk individuals is important for improving treatment planning and improving outcomes. [16] Machine learning algorithms show promise in predicting the likelihood of a COVID-19 outbreak in many patients. But there aren't many studies that specifically look at people with heart disease. Therefore, the aim of this study is to develop and evaluate machine learning algorithms to predict COVID-19 clinical outcomes in cardiac patients. [15] Predicting the effect of treatment accurately can help doctors identify high-risk patients and use appropriate management strategies, such as early treatment. In addition, machine learning algorithms can help allocate resources by identifying patients who need more care and attention. This project aims to supplement data on machine learning techniques to predict treatment outcomes inCOVID-19 and highlight the importance of early detection and effective management of these patients with preexisting heart disease. Patients with heart disease prior to exposure to COVID-19 can benefit from the findings of this study and use them to inform treatment decisions and improve outcomes [15].

Description of the Dataset: This dataset includes information on patient demographics, medical history, and clinical outcomes for patients with pre-existing heart disease who were hospitalized with COVID-19. The dataset can be used to train and test machine learning algorithms for predicting clinical outcomes of COVID-19 in this patient population.

1.1 Statement Regarding Data Availability

The de-identified data used in this study is currently not publicly available but is provided by Optum as part of the data licensing agreement (Table 1).

Table 1. Data set description

Variable	Description	Type
Patient ID	Unique identifier for each patient	Categorical
Age	Patient age in years	Numerical
Gender	Patient Gender (male(M = 1) or female(F = 0))	Categorical
Hypertension	Whether the patient has a history of hypertension (yes or no)	Categorical
Diabetes	Whether the patient has a history of diabetes (yes = 1 or no)	Categorical
Chronic kidney disease	Existence of a history of chronic renal disease in the patient (yes = 1 or no)	Categorical
Previous myocardial infarction	Whether the patient has a history of previous myocardial infarction (yes or no)	Categorical
COVID-19 severity	Clinical outcome of COVID-19, classified as mild, severe, or critical	Categorical
ICU admission	Whether the patient needed to be admitted to the ICU while receiving treatment for COVID-19 (yes = 1 or no = 0)	Categorical
Mechanical ventilation	Whether the COVID-19 patient required mechanical breathing while in the hospital (yes = 1 or no = 0)	Categorical
Mortality	Whether the COVID-19 patient passed away while being treated in a hospital (yes = 1 or no = 0)	Categorical

2 Literature Survey

Michał. Colleagues [1] conducted a study that included a total of 5,191 patients with 2,348 (45.2%) being women. The average age of the patients was 64 and, around 26.3% (1,364) had diabetes. It was observed that individuals with diabetes tended to be older than those without diabetes with an age of 70 years compared to 62 years in the diabetic group. Additionally both groups had a distribution in terms of gender.

Several notable differences were found between non diabetic patients;

1. Mortality; The in hospital diabetic group had a mortality rate of 15.7% compared to 26.2%.
2. Length of hospital stay; Diabetic patients stayed in the hospital for an average of 15 days while non diabetic patients had a stay of 13 days.
3. ICU admission; Patients with diabetes were frequently admitted to the care unit (ICU) at a rate of 15.7% compared to 11%, among non diabetic patients.
4. Mechanical ventilation; Diabetic patients required ventilation often than non diabetic patients at rates of 15.5% and 11.3%, respectively.

Furthermore Iaccarino G., Grassi G. And their team [2] conducted a multivariate analysis which identified some factors associated with ICU admission;

Gender; Male patients were found to have odds (OR = 1.74; CI = 95%; p < 0.0001) of being admitted to the ICU compared to females.

Obesity; obese patients have a higher chance of admission to intensive care (difference 2.88 95% confidence interval 2.03 4.07 p-value less than 0.0001).

Chronic kidney disease; Having kidney disease was associated with an increased risk of ICU admission (difference 1,588 95% confidence interval 1.036 2,434 p-value less than 0.05).

Hypertension: Patients with hypertension were more likely to go to the intensive care unit (OR 1.314, 95% CI 1.039–1.662, p < 0.05).

Further analyzes were performed based on gender results:

men: Obesity, chronic kidney disease and hypertension were associated with more intensive care unit admissions. Chapter.

Women: Onset of obesity (OR 2,564, 95% CI 1.336–4.920, p < 0.0001) and heart failure (OR 1.775, 95% CI 1,030–3,057) was associated with a higher probability of admission to ICU.

These four nations opted to ease many of the COVID-19 restrictions during the summer months, which led to a surge in cases starting in September 2020. Throughout this period, there has been a decline in public approval for these governmental measures. This shift in sentiment was primarily motivated by economic considerations taking precedence, although it's likely that reduced confidence in the government also played a role.

Anna Sagan et al. [3] all four countries had leaned heavily on their higher hospital bed capacities, which they managed to expand even further by diverting resources from elective medical procedures. However, this strategy sometimes strained their healthcare personnel's capacity.

Curiously, despite relaxing most of the measures designed to limit virus transmission since late spring, none of the four countries managed to establish effective systems for identifying, testing, tracing, isolating, and supporting individuals. This lapse in proactive measures persisted even during the summer period.

In essence, these nations initially scaled back preventive measures during the summer, leading to an uncontrollable resurgence of COVID-19 cases by September. This shift was driven by economic concerns and potentially eroded trust in the government. Additionally, these countries heavily relied on hospital bed capacity, though this came at the expense of other medical services. Furthermore, despite easing restrictions, they failed to establish robust systems for managing virus transmission throughout the summer.

Klein SL et al. [4] The ongoing COVID-19 pandemic has revealed a large disparity in the prevalence of the disease between men and women worldwide. Failed to report and identify differences between men and women in the number of COVID-19 cases, hospitalizations, and deaths in the United States. We focus on the fact that the severe consequences of COVID-19 usually occur in men, and we focus on the importance of variables such as the expression and activity of angiotensin-converting enzyme 2 (ACE2) and variation in immune response. We also want to show the impact of gender differences on the difference between non-male factors (factors that may be related to age and race) due to the COVID-19 pandemic.

Raj Bhopal et al. [5] It is recommended that information be given to younger age groups, preferably 10 years old, more precisely 5 year olds. While this situation causes confidence in parents and young people, it will cause anxiety in the elderly. These detailed data will provide more insightful results than broad and simple estimates of mortality rates of 1–2% or less. A good understanding of death, often taken from Chinese literature, can be greatly enhanced. More importantly, we strive to improve the accuracy and understanding of our analysis. Classification is done using data mining [12]. This study considers various classification rules, including KNN and Naive Bayes. This research

Dsign: Design uses machine learning and deep learning to ensure the best crop. The proposed model has been tested with product data. Select crops based on the available environment, soil and content while considering weather and structure. Deep learning is used to perform many computationally efficient tasks, such as choosing the best crop when there are many possible alternatives. How to make an accurate crop forecast? As shown in the figure, machine learning uses the SVM method, while deep learning uses LSTM and RNN algorithms1.Bibl (Table 2).

Table 2. Literature Survey

Time: Publisher	Paper	Mythology	Parameter	Result
August 2020 /Springer	Timotius Ivan Hariyanto[a], Andree Kurniawan [6]	I conducted a search, on the Google Scholar database using keywords they're relevant, to our research goal. This search was carried out until August 3rd, 2020. I collected all the articles that are related to both COVID 19 and metformin. To perform analysis I utilized Review Manager 5.4 software	The analysis encompassed a total of 5 studies involving 6,937 patients. The meta-analysis demonstrated an association between metformin usage and a	COVID-19 [relative risk (RR) 0.54, 95% confidence interval (CI) 0.32–0.90, p = 0.02, I2 = 54%, random effects model]
2021 Springer	Michał Terlecki, Wiktoria Wojciechowska [7]	We conducted an analysis of patients who were admitted to the hospital with COVID 19 from March 6th to October 15th, 2020	A total of 1,729 patients were included. Median age was 63 years (interquartile range: 50–75 years), and 48.8% were women	The overall in-hospital mortality rate was 12.9%. The most common cardiovascular diseases are hypertension (56.1%), hyperlipidemia (27.4%), and diabetes (25 7%,

(continued)

Table 2. (*continued*)

Time: Publisher	Paper	Mythology	Parameter	Result
2021/ ELSEVER	Mariusz Gujski 1ORCID,Mateusz Jankowski 2 [8]	To carry out an analysis using hospital discharge reports of individuals who were hospitalized with COVID 19 in Poland from March, to December 2020	Hospital discharge reports of 116,539 COVID-19 patients analyzed for the study	Among COVID-19 patients, 21,490 (18.4%) died during hospitalization
2021/ ELSEVER	C. Lee [a], L. Joseph [9]	We utilized random effects models to combine the hazard ratios (HRs) while considering variations, between studies by incorporating a between study variance, in the HRs	Two observers selected and reviewed relevant studies from 5425 initially screened	KVH mortality HR: 0.82, %95 CrI: 0.69–0.98 KKH mortality HR: 0.73, %95 CrI: 0

3 Data Collection

a. **Medical information**: Medical information related to COVID-19 patients, including demographic information (age, gender), medical history, co morbidities, symptoms, treatment plans, laboratory findings, and clinical outcomes (e.g., readmissions, hospitalizations, mortality rates). Get information.

b. **Gender-specific data**: Ensure data sets include patient segments by gender to facilitate gender analysis and prediction. Data should be balanced for gender representation to avoid biased samples.

c. Ethical considerations: Adhere to ethical and confidentiality principles when collecting and using patient information, ensure appropriate anonymization procedures and consent.

Preliminary information:

a. **Data cleansing**:

Remove unnecessary, inconsistent and irrelevant data.

Find missing values by assigning or deleting to ensure data is at minimum value.

b. **Selection and Design**:

Consider clinical information and data to select relevant factors important in predicting clinical outcomes.

Create new features that can improve predictions, such as gender-specific or cross-gender. Other things change. C. **Normalization and standardization:**

Normalize numerical features to a standard scale to prevent any feature from dominating the model Training due to its large scale.

Standardize features with mean 0 and standard deviation 1 for consistency and ease of comparison. D. Coding Categorical Data:

Code categorical variables (e.g., symptoms, comorbidities) as numerical values using techniques such as one-hot coding or tag coding.

e. Dealing with Imbalanced Data (Gender Distribution):

Dealing with gender imbalance in the dataset using special techniques such as over-sampling, undersampling, or SMOTE (Synthetic Minority Oversampling Technique).

f. Data classification:

To accurately measure the performance of the model, divide the data set into training set, validation set and testing set. Ensure gender balance in all groups.

g. Data Analysis (EDA):

Conduct data analysis to understand the distribution of treatment outcomes by gender and other characteristics, identifying patterns and insights that can guide model development.

This preliminary step is necessary to prepare the data for training the machine learning algorithm and ensure that the model can predict the outcome of COVID-19 treatment outcomes, given the gender distribution of the patients. Different ML model for using prediction:

4 Machine Learning Algorithms

Various machine learning algorithms can be **used** to predict **the** Clinical **outcome** of COVID19, taking **into account** gender **distution.** These algorithms **combine** patient **history information,** including gender, symptoms, comorbidities, test results, and **treatment options,** to **predict treatment** outcomes. **Some** machine learning algorithms **used** for this **purpose are:**

4.1 Logistic Regression

Logistic regression is a simple binary classification algorithm that models the probability of a binary outcome (such as rehabilitation vs. hospitalization) as a set of variables. In this case, logistic regression can be used to predict the probability of a particular event in COVID-19 patients, taking into account that gender is one of the characteristics.

4.2 Decision Tree

Decision tree is a versatile algorithm that can be used for classification and reprocessing. In this case, decision trees; It can be trained to predict different treatment outcomes based on characteristics such as symptoms, complications, diagnosis, and gender. Decision trees provide a deeper understanding of the prediction process by capturing interactions between attributes and gender.

4.3 Random Forest

Random Forest is a type of learning that creates multiple decision trees and combines their predictions to make the final prediction. Useful for improving prediction accuracy and dealing with overfitting. By capturing the relationship between features and gender, random forests can be a reliable predictor of clinical outcomes for COVID-19 patients.

4.4 Gradient Boosting Machine (GBM)

GBM is another blended learning technique that enables sequential learning of multiple weak learners (usually decision trees) in which each learner tries to correct the learner's previous mistakes. Known for its predictive accuracy, GBM can provide accurate predictions of clinical outcomes by capturing interactions between traits and gender.

4.5 Support Vector Machine (SVM)

SVM is a powerful algorithm suitable for both classification and regression. SVM can be used to predict clinical outcomes, including symptoms, complications, diagnosis, and characteristics such as gender. SVM aims to find the best visualization that best separates different classes, taking gender into account.

4.6 Neural Networks

Neural networks, especially deep learning models, are very flexible and can capture complex patterns in data. They are useful for complex, high-dimensional data and are useful in predicting treatment outcomes in COVID-19 patients using a combination of factors, including gender.

4.7 K Neighbors Network (KNN)

KNN is a simple and intuitive algorithm that predicts outcomes based on the majority of K neighbors at a given location. KNN can be used to predict clinical outcomes of COVID-19 patients, considering gender as one of the features.

5 Feature Selection: Model for This Problem

Recursive Feature Elimination (RFE): RFE is an iterative selection process that iteratively eliminates minimal features based on important features in weighted patterns (e.g., coefficients in linear models or key patterns in a tree structure). It starts with all the features and the smallest features are removed until the desired features are reached.

SelectKBest: SelectKBest is a simple and widely used method that selects the best K features based on statistical tests (e.g. chi-square, ANOVA) to evaluate the relationship. Accurate at each specific and different target [11].

5.1 Recursive Feature Addition (RFA)

RFA is a forward selection method that starts with an empty feature set and adds features one by one based on performance criteria, including gender-specific features.

5.2 Mutual Information

Mutual information measures the interdependence or information sharing between different properties and targets. Select features with shared information.

The best model selection for this problem will require testing and comparison based on the dataset characteristics and the performance of the machine learning models used for prediction. It is often useful to test different video selection methods and evaluate their impact on the model's prediction performance. Additionally, counseling professionals and healthcare providers can provide valuable information on the selection of the most important factors to predict the outcome of COVID-19 when looking at gender [10].

6 Proposed Model

Building a machine learning model to predict gender attributes involves going through steps starting from gathering and preparing the data to selecting and evaluating the model. It's important to remember that predicting gender based on attributes can be sensitive and ethically challenging as it raises privacy concerns and may reinforce any existing biases, in the data. Here's a general overview of how you could approach creating such a model (Fig. 1);

1. **Gathering Data;**
   Collect a dataset that includes attributes that could potentially indicate some ones gender along with labeled gender information. Common attributes might include things like name, age, location, occupation and so on.
2. Data Preparation;
   Cleanse. Prepare the data by handling missing values, outliers and ensuring formatting. For example when dealing with the "name" attribute you might need to extract features such as the number of vowels or consonants or even consider factors like name length.
3. Feature Engineering;
   Create features that can help your model differentiate between genders effectively. One approach could be to incorporate data to determine whether a given name is commonly associated with males or females.
4. Model Selection;
   Choose a machine learning algorithm for your task. Common options include regression, decision trees, random forests, support vector machines (SVM) or more advanced models, like neural networks.

Step 5; Begin by dividing your dataset into two sets. One, for training and the other, for testing. This will help you assess how well your model performs. Proceed to train your selected model using the training set.

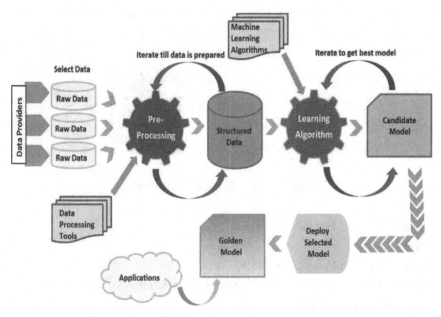

Fig. 1. Proposed Model

5. Model Evaluation:

Evaluate the performance of the test model's model using appropriate indicators such as accuracy, precision, recall, F1 score, and ROCAUC. Recognize biases and inconsistencies in prediction models.

6. Delivery: If you decide to ship your model, carefully monitor its performance in real situations and prepare to troubleshoot any issues that arise.

6.1 Gender Distribution of Normal Patient with Heart Patient

To compare the sex of normal patients and patients with heart disease, you usually analyze two databases: one contains data on normal patients and the other contains data on cardiac patients. You can then compare the gender distribution in each database for each variable. Here's how you can make this comparison:

1. Gender Report Analysis: Calculate the percentage or **number** of male and female patients in each **condition.** This will give you an initial idea of **the** gender distribution **in** each group.

2. Statistical comparison:

Perform a test such as the chiquare test to determine if there is a gender difference between the two groups. The chisquare test can help you determine whether the difference between variables is significant or simply due to risk.

3. Visualization:

Crete visualizations such as tables or graphs to show the gender distribution comparison for the two groups (Fig. 2).

Normal Patients:

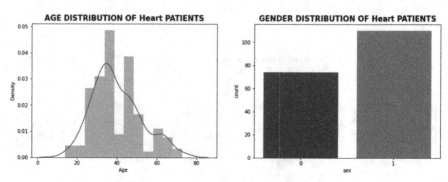

Fig. 2. Age and gender Distribution

Male: 300 (40%), Female: 450 (60%)

Heart Patients:

Male: 500 (55%), Female: 400 (45%)

Statistical test result: p-value <0.05 (significant difference)

Gender-Based Analysis:

Calculate the following metrics separately for each gender:

Total number of patients

Number of patients diagnosed with heart disease

Percentage of patients with heart disease within each gender

Visualizations: Create visualizations to represent the distribution of heart disease cases by gender. Bar charts or pie charts can effectively convey this information (Fig. 3).

Total Patients:

Male: 800, Female: 700

Patients with Heart Disease:

Male: 150, Female: 120

Percentage of Patients with Heart Disease:

Male: 18.75%, Female: 17.14%

Statistical test result: p-value > 0.05 (no significant difference)

2. Statistical Comparison:

Perform statistical tests, such as a chi-squared test or a z-test, to determine if there is a significant difference in the prevalence of heart disease between genders.

6.2 Evolution and System Performance

Performance parameters in machine learning models are metrics and metrics used to measure how well the model is performing on a task. These metrics give you information

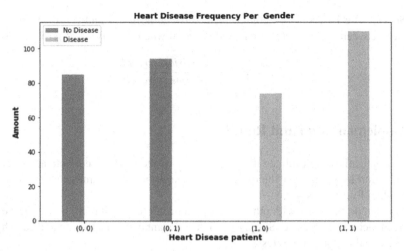

Fig. 3. Gender Frequency with heart disease

about the model's accuracy, precision, memorability, and overall performance. Some of the worst-case scenarios used in machine learning are [13]:

Accuracy: This metric calculates the number of correct prediction samples for all events in the data. It is an overall measure of how well the model predicts across all classes. However, it can be a mistake if the classes are not equal.

$$Accuracy = \frac{Number\ of\ correct\ prediction}{Total\ number\ of\ prediction}$$

$$Accuracy = \frac{(TP + TN)}{(TP + TN + FP + FN)}$$

Precision: Precision measures the percentage of correct predictions among all good predictions made by the model. It is especially important that counterfeit products are not expensive.

$$Precision = \frac{TP}{(TP + FN)}$$

Return (For Proportional or Good Quality): Returns the ratio of predicted actual quality to good. This is important when the value of false positives is high because it shows how good the model actually is.

Specificity (True Negative Ratio): Specificity measures the ratio of true negative estimates to true negative odds.

It is particularly important where counterfeit goods are of high value.

$$Specificity = \frac{TN}{(TN + FP)}$$

F1 Score: The F1 score is a compromise between accuracy and recall. It provides a balance between accuracy and recall and is useful when classifying different classes.

$$F1Score = \frac{2*Precision*recall}{Precision + recall}$$

7   Implementation and Result

In this application, we evaluate the performance of the model used, data accuracy and classification by going over the difference between the sex parameter (forest trees) of the random forest classifier.

You can do the same with other hyper parameters (e.g. jailbreak) to see their effect on the model's performance. Simply wrap the relevant code in a loop to add each hyper parameter value you want to test.

Tuning hyper parameters should balance training performance and avoid over fitting. For more complex variables, techniques such as grid search or random search can be applied.

Accuracy comparison with different model and our proposed model as given below in table (Table 3):

Table 3. Model performance

S.No	ML Model	No. of K -fold	Precession	Accuracy
1	Rando Random forest	8	94	94.34
2	SVM	8	95.23	95.88
3	Desion Tree	8	94.12	94.45
4	GB Bost	8	87.45	88.45
5	MLP classifier	10	88.88	89.56
6	Gradient Boosting	10	97	97.34
7	Proposed Model	8	99	99.45

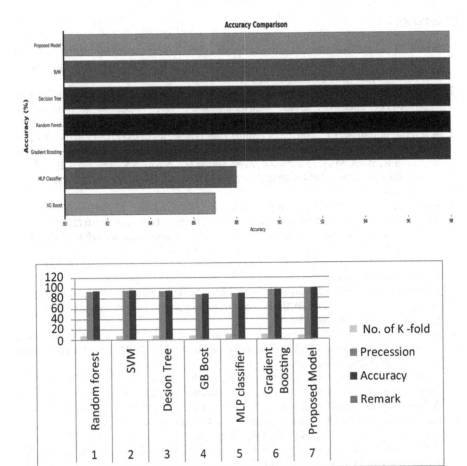

8 Conclusion

The overall aim of this study is to improve our understanding of how gender-specific factors affect COVID-19 patients. Through this research, researchers contribute to treatment using machine learning. Using these algorithms, the study aims to generate estimates of an individual's potential for exposure to COVID-19, including specific characteristics associated with each gender. The study aims to gain a more comprehensive and comprehensive understanding of the emergence and development of COVID-19 in different patients by integrating the gender distribution into the analysis. This approach recognizes the potential impact of sexual intercourse and the transmission of diseases. The significance of this study is that it can offer more accurate and predictive plans for COVID-19 patients, helping doctors to effectively allocate resources and plan therapeutic treatments for people. Using advanced machine learning techniques and recognizing the impact of gender, this research aims to improve our predictive ability to manage the COVID-19 situation and ultimately help improve patient care and outcomes.

References

1. Kania, M., et al.: Characteristics, mortality, and clinical outcomes of hospitalized patients with COVID-19 and diabetes: a reference single-center cohort study from Poland. Int. J. Endocrinol. **2023**, Article ID 8700302, 11 (2023)
2. Iaccarino, G., Grassi, G., Borghi, C., Carugo, S., Fallo, F., Ferri, C., et al.: Gender differences in predictors of intensive care units admission among COVID-19 patients: the results of the SARS-RAS study of the Italian society of hypertension. PLoS ONE **15**(10), e0237297 (2020)
3. A reversal of fortune: Comparison of health system responses to COVID-19 in the Visegrad group during the early phases of the pandemicAnna Sagan 1, Lucie Bryndova 2, Iwona Kowalska-Bobko 3, Martin Smatana 4, Anne Spranger 5, Viktoria Szerencses 6, Erin Webb 5, Peter Gaal 6PMID: 34789401 PMCID: PMC8527640. https://doi.org/10.1016/j.healthpol. 2021.10.009
4. Klein, S.L., Dhakal, S., Ursin, R.L., Deshpande, S., Sandberg, K., Mauvais-Jarvis, F.: Biological sex impacts COVID-19 outcomes. PLoS Pathog. **16**(6), e1008570 (2020)
5. Covid-19 worldwide: we need precise data by age group and sex urgentlyBMJ 2020; 369. https://doi.org/10.1136/bmj.m1366. Accessed 03 Apr 2020
6. Metformin use is associated with reduced mortality rate from coronavirus disease 2019 (COVID-19) infection
7. Association between cardiovascular disease, cardiovascular drug therapy, and in-hospital outcomes in patients with COVID-19: data from a large single-center registry in Poland. https://doi.org/10.33963/KP.15990
8. Gujski, M., Jankowski, M., Rabczenko, D., Goryński, P., Juszczyk Viruses, G.: Characteristics and clinical outcomes of 116,539 patients hospitalized with COVID-19—Poland, march–december 2020 (2021). mdpi.com
9. Mortality in diabetes compared with previous cardiovascular disease: A gender-specific meta-analysisComparaison du risque de mortalité chez les diabétiques et les patients non-diabétiques avec antécédent de malade cardiovasculaire : méta-analyse selon le sexe Author links open overlay panelC. Lee a, L. Joseph b, A. Colosimo c, K. Dasgupta a
10. Prajapati, Y.N., Sesadri, U., Mahesh, T.R., Shreyanth, S., Oberoi, A., Jayant, K.P.: Machine learning algorithms in big data analytics for social media data based sentimental analysis. Int. J. Intell. Syst. Appl. Eng. **10**(2s), 264 (2022)
11. Prajapati, Y.N., Sharma, M.: Analysis and Application of a Novel Model to Predict COVID-19 Virus's Impact on Human Heart Disease
12. Prajapati, Y.N., Kumar, M.: A review paper on cause of heart disease using machine learning algorithms. J. Pharm. Negative Results, 9250–9259 (2022). https://doi.org/10.47750/pnr. 2022.13.S09.1082
13. Upadhyay, S.K., Kumar, A.: A novel approach for rice plant diseases classification with deep convolutional neural network. Int. J. Inf. Tecnol. **14**, 185–199 (2022). https://doi.org/10.1007/ s41870-021-00817-5
14. Upadhyay, S.K., Kumar, A.: Early-stage brown spot disease recognition in paddy using image processing and deep learning techniques. Traitement du Signal **38**(6), 1755–1766 (2021). https://doi.org/10.18280/ts.380619
15. Upadhyay, S.K.: Deep transfer learning-based rice leaves disease diagnosis and classification model using InceptionV3. In: 2022 International Conference on Computational Intelligence and Sustainable Engineering Solutions (CISES), Greater Noida, India, pp. 493–499 (2022). https://doi.org/10.1109/CISES54857.2022.9844374
16. Upadhyay, S.K., Kumar, A.: An accurate and automated plant disease detection system using transfer learning based Inception V3Model. In: 2022 2nd International Conference on Advance Computing and Innovative Technologies in Engineering (ICACITE), Greater Noida, India, pp. 1144–1151 (2022). https://doi.org/10.1109/ICACITE53722.2022.9823559

A Genetic Algorithm-Enhanced Deep Neural Network for Efficient and Optimized Brain Tumour Detection

Arun Kumar[✉], Mohit Agarwal, and Mohd Aquib

Bennett University, Greater Noida, India
{e23soep0013,mohit.agarwal,mohd.aquib}@bennett.edu.in

Abstract. One of the most critical neurological disorders is a brain tumour, characterized by the uncontrolled proliferation of abnormal cells within the brain. The incorporation of cutting-edge automated technology is crucial to enhance the accurancy of tumour detection. Glioma, meningioma, pituitary, and normal brain are the four groups targeted for classification in MRI scans of the brain. Convolution neural networks that have been extensively trained, including AlexNet and VGG19, are frequently utilized for image categorization utilizing transfer learning. However, due to the significant storage space needs, they cannot be used successfully on edge devices to build robotic devices. Therefore, the classification procedure was carried out using a genetic algorithm, which takes up around 30–40% less space than the original model and reduces inference time by about 50%. Before compression, the accuracy given by AlexNet and VGG19 was 86.12% and 94.78%, respectively, and the accuracy after compression for AlexNet and VGG19 was 87.12% and 92.04%, respectively.

Keywords: Genetic Algorithm · Transfer learning · AlexNet · Brain tumour classification · VGG19

1 Introduction

Brain cancer is a common life-threatening disease, with the most aggressive form being brain tumours. Despite advancements in medical diagnosis and treatment, survival rates are low. Brain tumours can be benign or malignant, which is life-threatening and requires accurate and fast diagnosis. They can be detected using scanning techniques like MRI, PET, and CT. The research focuses on three common types of brain tumours: Glioma, Meningioma, and Pituitary Tumor. Gliomas are the most common type with the highest mortality rate, while Meningioma is a benign tumour found under the skull. Pituitary tumours are associated with the pituitary gland. Computer-aided diagnosis (CAD) systems, particularly deep learning networks, are essential for supporting healthcare. Magnetic resonance imaging (MRI) has been effectively used to analyze, monitor, diagnose, and treat brain tumours [1]. Various methods for brain tumour classification based on MRI images have been developed, including combining statistical features and neural networks, local smoothing and nonlocal means procedures, and hybrid feature extraction using principal component analysis and regularized extreme learning machines.

D. Garg et al. (Eds.): IACC 2023, CCIS 2054, pp. 311–321, 2024.
https://doi.org/10.1007/978-3-031-56703-2_25

Brain tumour detection and segmentation involve separating tumour portions from normal tissues like grey matter, white matter, and cerebrospinal fluid. Traditional techniques for image processing include threshold, edge-based, region-based, clustering, and watershed methods. Recent studies show that Machine Learning and Deep Learning can identify regions of interest in data more effectively than traditional algorithms. Deep neural networks, such as Convolutional Neural Networks (CNN), work efficiently on images, producing remarkable results in image classification, object detection, and segmentation [2].

Imaging segmentation is crucial in medical diagnosis, as it divides images into distinct sections for analysis. However, medical images often contain modest differences, noise, and missing barriers, making it difficult to solve. Computerized tomography (CT) and magnetic resonance imaging (MRI) are used to investigate the brain's internal structures, but they are more comfortable and do not use radiation. Brain tumours are devastating disorders affecting body functioning and causing symptoms like hearing or speech issues, headaches, memory loss, vision loss, and personality changes. MRI is a widely used non-intrusive imaging design that provides sensitive contrast between tumours. Accurate tumour classification and volume estimation are essential in radiation and medicine, as tumour location helps identify factors impacting normal functioning.

Researchers have used Convolution Neural Networks (CNN) and other deep learning techniques extensively, as seen by the research that is currently available [3, 4]. Certain studies additionally demonstrate the segmentation of illnesses using certain CNN models, such as SegNet, UNet, and so forth. Analogously, several research studies demonstrate the application of Artificial Intelligence (AI) methods for medical image classification and diagnosis. In more recent studies, deep learning techniques and compression with meta-heuristic approaches are used for image categorization across many domains [1, 2, 5]. A six-convolution layer CNN has been proposed by Sadoon and Ali [6] for the categorization of brain tumours into one of three classifications (glioma, meningioma, and pituitary). More recent studies demonstrate the application of compression with meta heuristic techniques and deep learning techniques for image categorization across several domains and thus motivates for further studies in this domain.

The major contribution of the article are:

- This study aids in the diagnosis of brain tumours using patient MRI scans.
- After reviewing the existing studies, we have presented a survey using MRI scans of the patients to detect brain tumours.
- The paper uses a Genetic Algorithm to condense pre-trained models.
- The paper proposed a multi-classification approach used a combination of deep feature algorithms to achieve good performance.

The remainder of the paper is structured as follows: A brief description of the different studies is discussed along with the dataset in Sect. 2. Section 3 describes the methods used and Sect. 4 describes the model compression and results. Section 5 finally covers the conclusion method.

2 Related Work

An AI-based CAD system can be simply integrated into an IoT healthcare system to diagnose and treat patients with brain tumours. Brain MRI images can be easily understood compared to medical professionals using a CAD diagnosis system. Thus, medical personnel employ CAD diagnosis systems for brain MRI image interpretation to diagnose brain tumours accurately and quickly. Different researchers and medical professionals have developed brain tumour diagnosis systems in the literature because of the significance of AI-based CAD systems. Our study focused on examining and assessing the AI-based tools and techniques that have recently been proposed for the diagnosis of brain tumour detection. In this work, we investigated cutting-edge AI systems created for the diagnosis of brain tumour detection.

In this direction, the study by Abd El-Wahab et al. [7] presents a deep learning-based system called BTC-f CNN, designed to classify brain tumours efficiently using MRI images. The system, which consists of 13 layers and uses transfer learning and cross-validation, achieved 98.63% average accuracy and 98.86% using retrained five-fold cross-validation. The proposed model outperforms state-of-the-art convolution neural networks (CNN) regarding precision, F-score, recall, specificity, and confusion matrix, making it a valuable tool for healthcare professionals. Another study by Agarwal et al. [8] used a Genetic Algorithm (GA) to optimize deep learning models, reducing storage space and improving inference time. Pre-trained CNN models are famous for image classification but require large storage capacity, making them difficult to deploy on mobile or edge devices. Extensive computer simulations are conducted on popular models. Computer simulations using popular models like ResNet50, AlexNet, VGG16, and SqueezeNet showed significant performance improvements. Alex Net's storage space decreased by 87.5%, while VGG16, ResNet50, and SqueezeNet compressed by 91%, 78%, and 38%, resulting in a 35% reduction in inference time.

Similarly, in another study, deep learning methods improved medical diagnoses using medical images like X-rays, CT scans, and MRI scans. Transfer learning-based pre-trained models like VGG19, MobileNet, and AlexNet are proposed by Agarwal et al. [9]. Traditional machine learning methods like Logistic Regression and k-nearest Neighbours are also used. With robot-based devices, pre-trained models need less space, so they're compressed using the Differential Evolution algorithm for similar accuracy. Various other studies have been presented in this direction, such as Vankdothu et al. [10], which proposed an automated brain tumour detection and classification system. The system includes MRI image preprocessing, segmentation, feature extraction, and classification. The method uses an adaptive filter to remove noise, an IKMC algorithm for segmentation, and GLCM for feature extraction. Deep learning models classify images into gliomas, meningiomas, non-tumors, and pituitary tumors. The RCNN method performs better than previous methods, with a 95.17% accuracy in classifying brain tumour tissues from MRI images.

Similarly, Afshar et al. [11] proposed a method for classifying brain tumours using a capsule network that incorporated brain MRI images with coarse tumour borders with 90.89% accuracy. Using transfer learning techniques (CNN Transfer learning), Swati et al. [12] classified brain cancers with 94.82% accuracy.

Now a days, deep learning is extensively used for the cancer treatment as they help in classifying real-time patient data.

Since the existing deep learning models needs significant resources (storage and computation), we need such deep learning models where the resource requirement is significantly lesser compared to existing deep learning models. The possible way to solve this problem is to go for compress deep learning models where the unwanted layers and filters of existing deep learning models are removed. Such models require considerably less resources and therefore suited for IoT devices. One of the first kind of model compression technique is given by Anwar et al. [6] where the number of deep neural parameters are reduced as in DNN several parameters are redundant and their participation is very less. Model Pruning can be done either during training or after the training. There are following four ways through the model can be pruned such as 1) Weight Pruning, 2) Neuron Pruning, 3) Filter Pruning and 4) Layer Pruning. However, in some case Pruning does not perform better compared to the original model. Another Breast cancer detection technique of model compression is quantization where the number of bits required to represent the weight are reduced. Similar to previous discussed pruning model, this model can also apply before and after training operation.

3 Material and Methods

3.1 Brain Tumour Disease Image Dataset

The brain tumour dataset which is used in this study is taken from the Kaggle Repository and comprises a total of 7023 images for four categories, out of which 1621 are of Glioma tumour, 1645 are of Meningioma tumour, 1757 are of Pituitary tumour, and 2000 belongs to normal brain MRI scan images. The sample images from the used dataset are shown in Fig. 1.

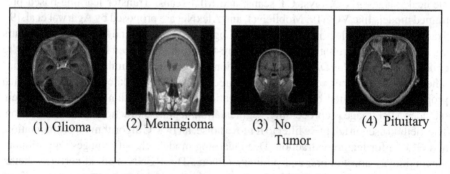

Fig. 1. Image samples from the dataset used in the study.

3.2   Deep Learning Architecture

3.2.1   AlexNet Architecture

AlexNet (Fig. 2) is a renowned convolutional neural network (CNN) structure that gained recognition following its success in the ImageNet Large Scale Visual Recognition Challenge (ILSVRC) in 2012.

This technology, developed by Alex Krizhevsky, Ilya Sutskever, and Geoffrey Hinton, represented a notable breakthrough in computer vision. The Architecture of AlexNet comprises eight layers, consisting of five convolutional layers and three fully linked layers. The architecture incorporates the utilization of ReLU (Rectified Linear Unit) as the activation function, effectively mitigating the issue of vanishing gradient and expediting the training process. The architecture comprises Convolutional layers whose primary function is to acquire hierarchical features from the input images [13]. Subsequently, max-pooling layers are employed to diminish spatial dimensions and computational complexity. Local Response Normalisation (LRN) is a technique used in AlexNet to normalize the output of the activation function in the initial layers. It is normalizing the responses across neighbouring channels aids in enhancing generalization.

Further, dropout is employed in the fully linked layers of AlexNet to mitigate over-fitting. During training, dropout randomly deactivates a specific proportion of neurons, forcing the network to acquire more resilient characteristics. The last layer employs a SoftMax activation function to facilitate multi-class classification, yielding probabilities for each class. AlexNet showed a substantial enhancement in the accuracy of picture classification compared to earlier methods, and it played a pivotal role in promoting the adoption of deep learning, particularly convolutional neural networks, throughout the computer vision field [14]. Subsequently, alternative architectures have been suggested, yet AlexNet continues to be a pivotal model in the chronicles of deep learning.

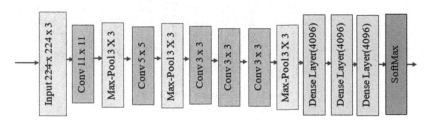

Fig. 2. Architecture of AlexNet

3.2.2   VGG19 Architecture

VGG-19 (Fig. 3) is a convolutional neural network architecture part of the VGG family. It stands for Visual Geometry Group 19. The Visual Geometry Group at the University of Oxford developed it, and it is well-known for its simplicity and success in image categorization tasks. The numerical value "19" in VGG-19 represents the overall count of layers in the network. The VGG-19 structure consists of an initial layer comprising an input layer that receives a predetermined RGB image of a consistent size, usually measuring 224 × 224 pixels. Convolutional Blocks then follow it. The architecture consists of 16 convolutional layers, each being succeeded by a Rectified Linear Unit (ReLU) activation function to incorporate non-linearity. Convolutional layers employ small receptive fields measuring 3 × 3 pixels while maintaining a stride of 1 pixel. This design decision facilitates the maintenance of a wide receptive field while simultaneously controlling the number of parameters [15]. At regular intervals, max-pooling layers are added to reduce the size of the feature maps in terms of spatial dimensions.

VGG-19 employs max pooling with a window size of 2 × 2 and a stride of 2. The last levels of VGG-19 consist of fully connected layers. These neural network layers are conventional, with each neuron being linked to every neuron in the previous layer. The VGG-19 model contains completely linked layers of 4096 neurons activated using the Rectified Linear Unit (ReLU) function. The output layer comprises the ultimate SoftMax layer utilized for categorization. The number of neurons in this layer is directly proportional to the number of classes in the classification task [16]. It is essential to mention that although VGG-19 is a robust architecture, its extensive depth and large number of parameters result in high computing costs.

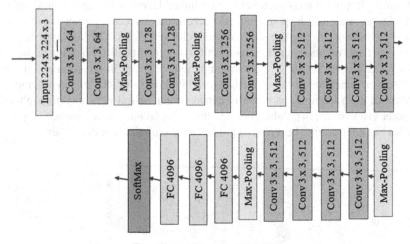

Fig. 3. Architecture of VGG19

3.2.3 Experimentation Setup

The studies were conducted exclusively on an NVIDIA supercomputer. The model's training and testing involved utilising two pre-trained models, AlexNet and VGG19. These models were equipped with pre-trained weights from the ImageNet dataset and then fine-tuned using transfer learning techniques on a dataset specifically focused on brain tumours. The suggested genetic-based models demonstrated superior performance in terms of space requirement.

4   Model Compression

4.1   Genetic Algorithm

Genetic algorithms are a promising method for optimizing machine learning model efficiency. They act as a virtual evolution simulator, replicating natural selection principles. The algorithm refines potential model architectures through crossover and mutation operations, evaluating their performance and complexity. This approach enhances the scalability and deployment of machine learning models by balancing performance and resource efficiency, thereby enhancing the overall model compression process.

The genetic algorithm (GA) is developed from humans' natural process of evolution. The scenario assumes an initial population of humans, each distinguished by a unique chromosome. The formation of these chromosomes in the CNN involves the random assignment of either 1 or 0 to each hidden neuron. For example, VGG19 reveals distinct hidden layers using various colours. The value of 1 indicates that a neuron will be kept, while 0 signifies that it will be discarded [17]. During the next stage, chromosomes engage in the exchange of genetic information with chromosomes from other persons. The resulting chromosomes are referred to as offspring chromosomes. The child chromosomes undergo a process of mutation, where a random selection of 110th of the chromosomes have their bits flipped from 1 to 0. Ultimately, a fitness function is formulated to evaluate the fitness value of both parent and child chromosomes. The chromosome with superior fitness is preserved in the population pool, while those with lower fitness values are discarded [18]. A chromosome with the highest fitness values can be acquired after multiple iterations. The iterations cease when the difference in fitness values is less than 0.00001.

The fitness function is a multivalued objective function contingent upon the model's accuracy and area under the curve (AUC). The accuracy of a model is often helpful for assessing its performance. However, the AUC (Area Under the Curve) is also valuable for evaluating performance, mainly when the dataset is balanced [19].

Genetic Algorithm (GA) is a search heuristic that simulates natural selection to find near-optimal solutions to complex problems. GAs function by keeping an individual population of potential solutions, each encoding binary digits (0 and 1) as potential solutions. The fitness function is a key element of GA, assessing the effectiveness of each solution. The initial population is the set of chromosomes chosen at random, and the three genetic operators selection, crossover, and mutation are applied iteratively to improve the population. Selection involves choosing chromosomes to be parents, crossover involves combining parent and child individuals, and mutation modifies each chromosome gene at random to add diversity. Figure 4 illustrates the procedure of the Genetic Algorithm.

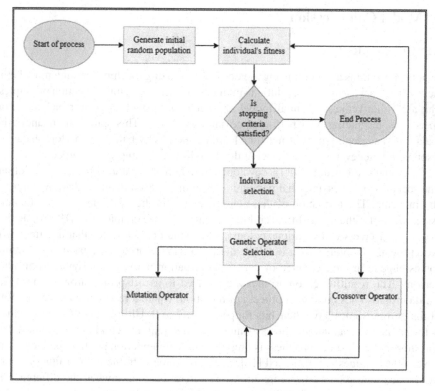

Fig. 4. A typical genetic algorithm architecture

4.2 Compression Process

The genetic algorithm, which is discussed in Sect. 4, aids in the removal of unnecessary neurons. It was discovered that in the compressed model, the dominant neurons remained but a number of redundant neurons were eliminated. The best neurons are kept in this phase so they can transport the needed information to the final output SoftMax layer, and the accuracy does not decrease because the fitness function depends on the performance parameters.

4.3 Compression Results

Model compression reduces the size of a deep learning model while maintaining its predictive performance. It is crucial for resource-constrained devices and improving memory usage and inference speed [20]. A genetic algorithm is used to achieve this, iteratively evolving a population of potential compressed models through selection, crossover, and mutation [21]. The algorithm aims to find an optimal or near-optimal compressed representation of the original model, ensuring efficient size and predictive power [22]. Table 1 shows the original accuracy achieved by the deep learning models using the transfer learning approach and the final accuracy achieved after compressing the model using a genetic algorithm [23]. The inference time before and after compressing the model is depicted in Table 2.

The Genetic Algorithm was crucial for removing unnecessary neurons. Activation images from both the original and compressed models were methodically generated and then subjected to a comparison study. The findings revealed a clear pattern: many unnecessary neurons were successfully eliminated, resulting in a condensed model where dominating neurons remained prominent. Even with the decrease in neurons, the model's accuracy remained strong. The accuracy of this resilience can be due to the complexities of the fitness function, which delicately integrates performance characteristics. Therefore, the Genetic Algorithm guarantees the preservation of the most efficient neurons, which possess the capacity to transmit crucial information to the final output SoftMax layer. A comparative analysis was performed on the activation images of the 2nd and 3rd block convolution layers of AlexNet and VGG19 to demonstrate the genetic algorithm procedure.

Table 1. Performance of deep learning models

Model	Original Size (KB)	Compressed Size (KB)	Original accuracy (%)	Final accuracy (%)
AlexNet	281,161	73,279	86.12	87.12
VGG19	211,421	92,206	94.78	92.04

Table 2. Inference time of deep learning models

Model	Original inference time (S)	Final inference time (S)
AlexNet	39.49	21.06
VGG19	116.43	24.78

5 Conclusion

Brain tumours significantly threaten human health, and early diagnosis and intervention are crucial. This research uses advanced technologies like deep transfer and machine learning to diagnose brain tumours from MRI images. Transfer learning achieved a remarkable accuracy of 94.78% using VGG19, while the genetic algorithm achieved 92.04% accuracy. Regarding inference time, AlexNet takes only 21.06 s, less than the original 39.49 s. The research also focuses on model deployment on edge devices, ensuring widespread accessibility to these life-saving technologies. The methodologies developed can be applied to other human diseases, laying the groundwork for future efforts. This research represents a significant stride towards revolutionizing medical diagnostics, particularly brain tumour detection.

References

1. Yar, H., Hussain, T., Agarwal, M., Khan, Z.A., Gupta, S. K., Baik, S.W.: Optimized dual fire attention network and medium-scale fire classification benchmark. IEEE Trans. Image Process. **31**, 6331–6343 (2022)
2. Skandha, S.S., Agarwal, M., Utkarsh, K., Gupta, S.K., Koppula, V.K., Suri, J.S.: A novel genetic algorithm-based approach for compression and acceleration of deep learning convolution neural network: an application in computer tomography lung cancer data. Neural Comput. Appl. **34**(23), 20915–20937 (2022)
3. Agarwal, M., Singh, A., Arjaria, S., Sinha, A., Gupta, S.: Toled: tomato leaf disease detection using convolution neural network. Procedia Comput. Sci. **167** 293–301 (2020)
4. Agarwal, M., Gupta, S.K., Biswas, K.K.: Grape disease identification using convolution neural network. In: 2019 23rd International Computer Science and Engineering Conference (ICSEC), pp. 224–229. IEEE (2019)
5. Agarwal, M., Kaliyar, R.K., Gupta, S.K.: Differential evolution based compression of CNN for apple fruit disease classification. In: 2022 International Conference on Inventive Computation Technologies (ICICT), pp. 76–82. IEEE (2022)
6. Sadoon, T.A., Ali, M.H.: Deep learning model for glioma, meningioma and pituitary classification. Int. J. Adv. Appl. Sci. ISSN **2252**(8814), 8814 (2021)
7. Abd El-Wahab, B.S., Nasr, M.E., Khamis, S., Ashour, A.S.: BTC-FCNN: fast convolution neural network for multi-class brain tumor classification. Health Inf. Sci. Syst. **11**(1), 3 (2023). https://doi.org/10.1007/s13755-022-00203-w
8. Agarwal, M., Gupta, S.K., Biswas, M., Garg, D.: Compression and acceleration of convolution neural network: a Genetic Algorithm based approach. J. Ambient. Intell. Humaniz. Comput. **14**(10), 13387–13397 (2023). https://doi.org/10.1007/s12652-022-03793-1
9. Agarwal, M., Kaliyar, R.K., Gupta, S.K.: An efficient and optimized convolution neural network for Covid and lung disease detection. In: 2023 8th International Conference on Communication and Electronics Systems (ICCES), pp. 735–740 (2023). https://doi.org/10.1109/ICCES57224.2023.10192708
10. Vankdothu, R., Hameed, M.A.: Brain tumour MRI image identification and classification based on the recurrent convolutional neural network. Meas.: Sens. **24**, 100412 (2022). https://doi.org/10.1016/j.measen.2022.100412
11. Afshar, P., Plataniotis, K.N., Mohammadi, A.: Capsule networks for brain tumor classification based on MRI images and coarse tumor boundaries. In: ICASSP 2019-2019 IEEE International Conference on Acoustics, Speech and Signal Processing (ICASSP), pp. 1368–1372 (2019). https://doi.org/10.1109/ICASSP.2019.8683759
12. Swati, Z.N.K., et al.: Brain tumour classification for MR images using transfer learning and fine-tuning. Comput. Med. Imaging Graph. **75**, 34–46 (2019). https://doi.org/10.1016/j.compmedimag.2019.05.001
13. Luca, S., et al.: Six artificial intelligence paradigms for tissue characterization and classification of non-covid-19 pneumonia against covid-19 pneumonia in computed tomography lungs. Int. J. Comput.-Assist. Radiol. Surg. **16**(3), 423–434 (2021)
14. Badrinarayanan, V., Kendall, A., Cipolla, R.: Segnet: a deep convolutional encoder-decoder architecture for image segmentation. IEEE Trans. Pattern Anal. Mach. Intell. **39**(12), 2481–2495 (2017)
15. Balzer, W., Takahashi, M., Ohta, J., Kyuma, K.: Weight quantization in Boltzmann machines. Neural Networks **4**(3), 405–409 (1991). Barrios, C.H.: Global challenges in breast cancer detection and treatment. Breast **62**, S3–S6 (2022)
16. Bucilu˘a, C., Caruana, R., Niculescu-Mizil, A.: Model compression. In: Proceedings of the 12th ACM SIGKDD International Conference on Knowledge Discovery and Data Mining, pp. 535–541 (2006)

17. Dar, R.A., Rasool, M., Assad, A., et al.: Breast cancer detection using deep learning: datasets, methods, and challenges ahead. Comput. Biol. Med. 106073 (2022)
18. Gen, M., Lin, L.: Genetic algorithms and their applications. In: Springer Handbook of Engineering Statistics, pp. 635–674. Springer (2023). https://doi.org/10.1007/978-1-4471-7503-2_33
19. Huang, H., et al.: Unet 3+: a full-scale connected unet for medical image segmentation(2020)
20. Li, X.B., Sweigart, J., Teng, J., Donohue, J., Thombs, L.: A dynamic programming based pruning method for decision trees. INFORMS J. Comput. 13(4),332–344 (2001)
21. Lipowski, A., Lipowska, D.: Roulette-wheel selection via stochastic acceptance. Physica A: Stat. Mech. Appl. 391(6), 2193–2196 (2012)
22. Nassif, A.B., Talib, M.A., Nasir, Q., Afadar, Y., Elgendy, O.: Breast cancer detection using artificial intelligence techniques: a systematic literature review. Artif. Intell. Med. 127, 102276 (2022)
23. Ronndetectioneberger, O., Fischer, P., Brox, T.: U-net: convolutional networks for biomedical image segmentation. In: Medical Image Computing and Computer-Assisted Intervention–MICCAI 2015: 18th International Conference, Munich, Germany, 5–9 October 2015, Proceedings, Part III 18, pp. 234–241. Springer (2015). https://doi.org/10.1007/978-3-319-24574-4_28

Diabetes Prediction Using Ensemble Learning

Amol Dhumane$^{(\boxtimes)}$, Shwetambari Chiwhane , Sudhanshu Thakur ,
Utkarsh Khatter , Manas Gogna , and Ameysingh Bayas

Symbiosis Institute of Technology, Affiliated to Symbiosis International University, Pune, India
amol.dhumane@sitpune.edu.in

Abstract. Using ensemble learning toward medical diagnostics as a response to diabetes on a global scale. The data set is composed of medical and demographic information collected from survey questionnaire forms filled out by patients; medical charts; and lab samples from diagnosed or at-risk subjects during patient clinic visits and hospitalizations. For instance, variables include age, sex, obesity, hypertension, ischemic heart disease, prior smoking status, post-prandial test blood, and random blood sugar levels in non-diabetic subjects. Rigorous data processing ensures reliability. Ensemble learning emphasizes the potential of predicting diabetes, thus, giving a more accurate forecast on the same and advanced prevention techniques. The approach is also useful in detailed research on the origins of diabetes and providing guidelines for prevention and treatment campaigns worldwide. The study reveals a highly accurate classification model with an overall accuracy of 95%. Precision is notable, with 95% for class 0 and 93% for class 1, while class 0 exhibits outstanding recall at 99%, whereas class 1 has a lower recall at 61%.

Keywords: Diabetes · Prediction · Ensemble Learning · Machine Learning · Random Forrest · KNN · Decision Tree · Naïve Bayes · Logistic Regression · Custom Voting Classifier

1 Introduction

Diabetes is a serious and growing chronic disease challenge to public health worldwide in the modern era. Another important endocrine disorder that affects large sections of the world's population is diabetes which involves low or inconsistent insulin generation and use. It can cause serious health problems if not properly treated. Thence, early diagnosis and correct prognosis of diabetes will allow prevention activities, individual treatment approaches and positive results to patients with this disease. Machine learning, especially ensemble learning has seen tremendous potential in the field of medical diagnosis and the case of predicting diabetes outcomes which presents an appealing alternative for much improved forecasts. In our paper, we have drawn upon the insights and findings from several notable machine learning research papers to support and enrich our research. These references serve as a foundation for our work and contribute to its credibility and depth [1–7]. Most conventional methods in formulating prediction models rely on

D. Garg et al. (Eds.): IACC 2023, CCIS 2054, pp. 322–332, 2024.
https://doi.org/10.1007/978-3-031-56703-2_26

analyses that employ only a single machine-learning algorithm for data analysis as well as interpretation. Nevertheless, some of these individual models have a tendency to provide a poor performance [8–11] because they have inherent biases, fit poorly, and show difficulties in generalization. An alternative is ensemble learning that integrates multiple separate models to produce a combined predictive system. When we combine ensemble techniques involving different algorithms under an umbrella of collective intelligence, the strength of each algorithm is utilized, and any shortcomings are negated. As a result, they provide strong and valid predictions.

When it comes to medical diagnostics which need accuracy, machine learning is a point of light in the world of computers. Diabetes prediction in its particular domain stands out for this technique of ensemble learning. As such, it calls for a new dawn for improved prognostics and approaches to fighting chronic disease burden. However, traditional approaches have their limitations in that they involve single machine learning algorithm, where the biases and over fitting can arise. Ensemble learning makes its entrance as an appealing substitute, harmonizing a multitude of models into one melodic predicting scheme [12, 13].

One advantage that ensemble leaning has to offer is that it supersedes the limitations of individual models. It is a collective intelligence created by combining several different algorithms. This type of intelligence benefits from the strengths and minimizes the shortcomings of various components. It is a strategic synergy in which the whole becomes more than the addition of all its components. The combined efforts provide reliable and informed prediction based on futuristic perspective in which prediction is an art rather than work [14-16]. However, ensemble learning for diabetes marks the beginning of a revolution in medical predictions whose impacts will reverberate across all diabetic patients worldwide and their living conditions.

Before delving into the specifics, it's essential to acknowledge the diverse contributions that have shaped this discourse. This article draws upon the collective expertise of renowned researchers, industry leaders, and practitioners in data science and machine learning [17-21]. Their insights and experiences form the backbone of our exploration, ensuring a well-rounded and informed perspective.

To guide readers seamlessly through this multifaceted journey, the article is structured as follows. The first section provides an overview of all the literature and research studies we have referenced for our project on Diabetes Prediction using Ensemble Learning. Following that, we delve into the dataset and its various attributes. The next section entails the methodology applied, then the steps taken in the implementation of the project. The Results section discusses the outcomes of our research and implementation, i.e., the results of our diabetes prediction model. Finally, the concluding remarks encapsulate key takeaways and outline avenues for further exploration.

2 Literature Review

While traversing the vast corpus of writing, we discover both achievement and impediments in application of ensemble learning to predict diabetes. Literature here is not just a writing but rather a discussion between researchers on issues such as the model diversity, feature selectivity, and the sensitive-specific equation. The refinements of ensemble learning and its efficiency as far as diabetes are concerned emerge in such scholarly communications.

Rather than simply describing prior studies, this literature review will engage critically with both the methodological approaches and substantive findings that led us into this research. This essay will untangle the complicated dance between ensemble learning algorithms and diabetes dataset, revealing the role played by this medical-machine prediction in the need of better, faster and individualized prognoses (Table 1.).

Although machine-learning based literatures on diabetes prediction bring forth important findings, each study has its own weaknesses. However, other studies like Cahn et al. (2020) [8], Thenappan et al. (2020) [9] and Hasan et al. (2020) [16] do not succeed not only in accuracy but also practicality due to some reasons; for instance, their dataset is in The application of an ensemble learning approach in our study not only gives more accurate predictions than individual models considered, but it also helps overcome shortcomings that have been observed with the use of the considered individual models.

3   About the Dataset

The Diabetes prediction dataset comprises medical as well as demographic information on patients including their diabetes status (Diabetic/Non-Diabetic). These factors include age, gender, BMI, hypertension, heart disease, smoking profile, hemoglobin A1C, and blood glucose level. Such data can be used for construction of machine-learning oriented prediction tools for estimation of diabetes risk considering individual's medical records and age. This is important for healthcare professionals to identify such patients who are likely to develop diabetes and develop specific treatment approaches. The dataset may also assist the researchers in understanding the link between other medical as well as demographic factors and diabetes (Table 2.).

3.1   Sources

The Diabetes Prediction dataset is based on electronic Health Records (EHRs). Electronic Health Records (EHRs) is a name given to digital forms of patient health records with the history of patients' disease progression, treatment plan, as well as the results. Healthcare providers, like hospitals or clinics, collect and store data in electronic health records (EHRs) during a routine examination of patients.

A number of different healthcare providers' EHRs were collated into one data set in order to make the Diabetes Prediction dataset [15]. The cleansing of data involved checking for inconsistencies, as well as eliminating all unnecessary information that was not relevant to the topic.

There are numerous benefits of using EHRs as the source of data for the Diabetes prediction dataset. In other words, EHRs comprise massive amounts of patients' data such as their demographic information and clinical facts that can improve precise machine learning models. Additionally, EHR provide a long-term perspective regarding a patient's health that might reveal some patterns of the latter's health state. Lastly, use of EHR is very common in clinical practice; hence, the Diabetes Prediction dataset is quite relevant for today's actual health care environments.

Table 1. Literature Survey

Paper	Techniques used	Features	Shortcomings
Cahn et al. (2020) [8]	These machine learning algorithms include logistic regression, random forest, and gradient boosting machines	Build and verify a machine learning model which will correctly classify transition from pre-diabetes to diabetes	The model was constructed with a limited pool of data sets, which needs further validation with large and more representative ones
Thenappan et al. (2020) [9]	Modified support vector machine	Developing an improved, accurate, and secured modified support vector machine algorithm for diabetes prediction against the common support vector machine techniques	This algorithm is very sophisticated and might be hard to implement in actual scenarios
Islam et al. (2020) [10]	Random forest algorithm	Built a random forest modeling algorithm for predicting diabetes that outperforms other machine learning models like logistic regression and decision trees	This leads to high computational cost, and it can also take longer to train on bulk data sets
Talha Mahboob Alam et al. (2019) [11]	Among others are support vector machine (SSV), random forest (RFR), and logistic regression	Proposed a model for early detection of Diabetes based on combinations logistic regression, support vector machine, and random forest algorithms	This model was devised and tested using one dataset; thus, its performance in other databases remains unclear
Kahramanli Örnek et al. (2008) [12]	Hybrid intelligent system combining artificial neural networks and fuzzy logic	Proposed a hybrid intelligent system for diabetes prediction that is more accurate than traditional machine learning algorithms	The system is complex and may be difficult to interpret

(continued)

Table 1. (*continued*)

Paper	Techniques used	Features	Shortcomings
Rajesh and Sangeetha (2012) [13]	Data mining methods and techniques, such as decision trees, association rules, and clustering	Applied data mining methods and techniques to diabetes diagnosis and identified a number of important risk factors for diabetes	The study was conducted on a relatively small dataset, and the findings need to be validated on larger and more diverse datasets
Iyer et al. (2015) [14]	Classification mining techniques, such as support vector machine, decision trees, and naive Bayes	Applied classification mining techniques to diabetes diagnosis and achieved high accuracy	The study was conducted on a relatively small dataset, and the findings need to be validated on larger and more diverse datasets

Table 2. Dataset Description

#	Column	Non-Null Count	Dtype
0	gender	100000 non-null	object
1	age	100000 non-null	float64
2	hypertension	100000 non-null	int64
3	heart_disease	100000 non-null	int64
4	smoking_history	100000 non-null	object
5	bmi	100000 non-null	float64
6	HbA1c_level	100000 non-null	float64
7	blood_glucsose_level	100000 non-null	int64
8	diabetes	100000 non-null	int64

3.2 Collection Methodology

Medical and demographic information on diagnosed or high-risk patients for diabetes constitutes the collection methodology for the diabetes prediction dataset. Data may be obtained from questionnaires, medical charts, or laboratory specimens. These data contain information on age, sex, BMI, hypertension, ischemic heart disease, smoking history, HbA1c, and fasting plasma glucose. Thereafter, they are processed and filtered to get rid of any misinformation. It can also form basis of different studies which will help in identifying possible causes of diabetes as well providing appropriate preventive and treatment measures.

4 Methodology

1. The Urgency of Predictive Modeling in Diabetes

Diabetes, which is known as diabetes mellitus, consists of various diseases involving continuous hyperglycaemia. Type 1 diabetes (T1D) and type 2 diabetes (T2D) are the two major forms of diabetes. There are various forms of diabetes including an autoimmune disease referred to as type 1 diabetes (T1D) whereby an individual's immune system targets and kills insulin-secreting pancreatic beta-cells. However, type 2 diabetes or T2D constitutes the bulk of the disease cases, and its characteristic is insulin resistance, wherein insulin does not adequately respond to insulin, resulting in high blood sugar concentration.

A quarter of a billion individuals have diabetes throughout the globe, according to WHO estimates. It is expected that this figure will grow up to 578 million people by the year 2030, which speaks in favor of developing efficient approaches against expansion of the disease's influence. In addition, diabetes has many complication risks such as cardiovascular diseases, kidney failure, nerve and eye problems, heart attack, stroke and blindness, which makes early diagnosis of this disease helps to take necessary measures towards such possible troubles.

2. Machine Learning and Medical Diagnosis

The advancement of machine learning in the medical arena is among the recent breakthroughs that significantly transform disease diagnosis and treatment. It is able to teach patterns and relationships from big data sets, making it very useful for clinicians and researchers. Support vector machines, decision trees and neural networks are also machine learning algorithms that could be used in analyzing patient data, medical records, genetic information, and lifestyle factors for making accurate predictions and offering custom healthcare guidance.

Building one machine learning model that will manage the complications and unpredictability of predicting diabetes is not easy at all. Diabetes is a complex disease that results from multiple risk factors, including genetics, environment, and lifestyle. Lastly, they indicate that there is need for a sophisticated methodology that can cover such challenges with regard to heterogeneous patients' populations and mutability aspects of the disease development.

3. Ensemble learning and its power in diabetes prediction

Using ensemble learning can help solve this problem and improve the precision and resilience of diabetes forecasting systems. Ensemble Learning entails using more than one model so as to arrive at a decision using their different perspectives, hopefully leading to a better estimation or prediction for that decision.

Ensemble methods encompass a variety of techniques, including but not limited to:

a. Bagging: However, bootstrapping is also known as bootstrap aggregation (Bagging) and entails training several copies of the same algorithm on different slices of the data, all selected randomly with replacement. Finally, the prediction is calculated as an average of individual predictions for each model in order to decrease variance and avoid over-fitting.

b. Boosting: Boosting is a stepwise technique whereby weak models are trained iteratively such that each model builds on and corrects defects observed on the previous one. The final prediction is simply an averaged combination of the different individual model predictions with greater weights assigned to the more accurate forecasts.

c. Random Forest: As noted, Random Forest is a bagging approach in which decision trees are employed. This is achieved through growing multiple trees whose votes will be combined to give the final prediction hence improving accuracy of the ensemble model.

d. Stacking: The other technique is stacking. This involves training several heterogeneous models and meta-model (mostly, an ordinary linear regression or artificial neural network). It trains the meta-model how best it should combine the outputs of the base models and predict the most accurate outcome.

Wisdom of the crowd principle refers to situations whereby the group comprises different people, each with a distinct point of view. In the same manner, an ensemble of different models can understand better the underlying patterns in diabetes prediction so that accurate predictions are possible, and misdiagnosis is avoided.

4.1 Working Steps

1. **Data Loading and Preprocessing**
   a. Include essential libraries like pandas, numpy, matplotlib, and scikit-learn.
   b. Read diabetic prediction from CSV and store it in Pandas Dataframe (df).
2. **Data Encoding**
   a. Define custom encoding functions for categorical features 'smoking_history' and 'gender'.
   b. Transform categorical data to numbers using these encoding operations on the corresponding columns of the DataFrame.
3. **Data Splitting**
   a. Separate the DataFrame into the feature matrix (X) and the target variable (y).
   b. Split the data into the training set (80%) and testing set (20%) using the train_test_split function of scikit-learn. To enable reproducibility, set a random seed.
4. **Model Building and Evaluation**

   We implemented the following models.

a. K-Nearest Neighbors (KNN
   I. Create an instance of KNN classifier with selected features (n_neighbors, metric, and p).
   II. The model should be fitted to the training data.
   III. Report the prediction results on the test data using metrics like confusion matrix, classification report, and accuracy.
b. Decision Tree
   I. Initialize a DecisionTreeClassifier.
   II. Use the training data to fit the model.
   III. Forecast upon the test data and compute the metrics.
c. Naive Bayes (GaussianNB)
   I. Initialize a GaussianNB classifier.

II. Fit the model to the training data.

III. Make predictions upon the test data and calculate the values of metrics such as RMSE, MAE.

d. Logistic Regression

  I. Initialize a LogisticRegression classifier.

  II. Estimate parameters of the model from these data.

  III. Calculate the prediction for the test data and compute metrics.

e. Random Forest

  I. Create/Initialize a RandomForestClassifier with specified parameters (i.e., n_estimators, max_depth).

  II. Adapt the model to the training data.

  III. Use your model to predict on the test data and compute some metrics.

f. Ensemble Method (Voting Classifier

  5. Combine predictions from the individual models (KNN, Decision Tree, Naive Bayes, Logistic Regression, and Random Forest) in a VotingClassifier.

  II. II.Moreover, "hard" and "soft" voting are alternative options that can be adopted as dictated by the specific models.

  III. III.Convert the training data into VotingClassifier.

  IV. IV.Determining model accuracy, predictions on the test data, and assessing ensemble metrics.

6. Cross-Validation:

  I. Use k-fold cross validation where $k = 10$ for evaluating the random forest model's performance on the entire dataset and its multiple subsets.

  II. Calculate the mean accuracy score from the cross-validation results.

5 Implementation

This study suggests a design of a new voting classifier for diabetes prediction based on a combination of several classification algorithms in order to increase the precision and stability. The process can be broken down into the following steps:

1. **Data Gathering and Processing:** Gather an exhaustive database that has different patients' profiles ranging in age, gender, family history of diseases if any, their lifestyles, and the relevant markers. Carefully pre-process your data in order to deal with the missing values, outliers, as well as normalize the features.

2. **Algorithmic Selection:** Start with fundamental models based on Decision Tress, Support Vector Machines, Random Forests, and Logistics Regression. In this respect, each of these algorithms provides its take on distinguishing patterns inherent in the data at hand.

3. **Ensemble Model Construction:** Process the selected dataset for trainings and generate individual predictions (Y1, Y2, ..., Yn) for each base learner. The probabilities predict the occurrence of specific events or constitute class labels which also depend on the algorithm used.

4. **Voting Mechanism Enhancement:** Consider incorporating a sophisticated polling system, which averages out the highest rated classifiers in terms of accuracy. A more sophisticated method makes for sounder and truer collective vote.

5. **Model Assessment:** Use different measures like accuracy, precision, recall, F1-score and AU-ROC in evaluation of the ensemble model on a validation set. Tweak hyperparameters and ensembles for best results.
6. **Interpretability and Transparency Focus:** Use complex methods of decoding the data derived from the ensemble model. Transparency and reliability depend heavily on interpretability which aims at winning doctors' trust.
7. **Deployment Streamlining:** Design a user-friendly web application that provides dynamic glucose tolerance tests. This software easily inputs the data and employs a specialized voting classifier for overall and instantaneous outcomes.

6 Results

The findings demonstrate excellent classification in which the entire accuracy for a dataset was 95%. The precision, which showed that the model hit the spot regarding relevant instances, was quite impressive. For example, the precision for class 0 was 95% meaning the model misclassified a few negatives as positives in this class. Just like that, the precision of class one was 93%, showing how accurate model identifies true positives of category one.

In addition, its recall (ability to recover all relevant instances) was highly effective especially for class 0, with an accuracy of 99%. This means that, for class 0, the model included almost all real positives. On the other hand, the recall for Class 1 was 61% showing that some major percentage of real positive instances of this category were missed out by the model.

For instance, the F1-score of 97% for class 0 and 74% for class1 proved the general capability of the mode to appropriately predict both classes. Overall performance was indicated through the macro average precision and recall of 94% and 80%, respectively. Finally, the weighted average precision and recall was 95% which showed that the performance of the model remained balanced in each class thereby confirming their capability of prediction with accuracy (Figs. 1 and 2).

The accuracy for Logistic Regression and AdaBoost Classifier is as follows –

	Model	Precision_Neg	Precision_Pos	Recall_Neg	Recall_Pos	F1_Score_Neg	F1_Score_Pos	Accuracy
0	LogisiticRegression	0.948	0.929	0.924	0.952	0.936	0.941	0.938
1	AdaBoostClassifier	0.966	0.963	0.961	0.968	0.964	0.966	0.965

Fig. 1. Accuracy of the models

The confusion matrix for the two methodologies –

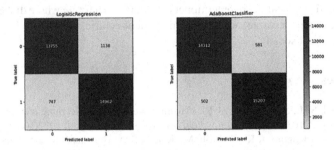

Fig. 2. Logistic Regression vs AdaBoost Classifier

Upon applying the Ensemble Method, we observed the highest accuracy to come out to be 0.97025.

Although machine-learning diabetes predictions are currently the best ones, they all have their drawbacks. The papers do not present accurate and interpretable results due to low data sizes, computation inefficiencies, and complicated algorithms that impede practical applications. On the other hand, our technique builds on the advantages of ensemble learning while surmounting the shortcomings. This approach leads to a more reliable and comprehensible model for improving the prediction methods for diabetes.

Our evaluation of the predictive abilities of Logistic Regression and AdaBoost Classifier models also yields separate accuracies. The Logistic Regression method has an accuracy of 0.97025 and serves as a gauge to measure its predictability. Additionally, the AdaBoost Classifier proves its effectiveness having an accuracy of 0.970258. We further examined the confusion matrices for each model employed in these two methodologies. The matrices provide detailed insight into the models' capacities to appropriately categorize cases and possible zones of incorrect classification.

There is an improvement in predictive accuracy after using the Ensemble Method on the combination of these methodologies. For a more reliable predictive model, the Ensemble Method results in an astounding prediction accuracy figure as high as 0.97025. It therefore points to the strength in using ensemble learning and integrating diverse systems in outdoing other methods. Among the various approaches, the ensemble approach becomes a key element leading to greater precision and stronger reliability of our diabetes prediction model.

7   Conclusion

Diabetes prediction is a critical aspect of preventive healthcare that can significantly impact patient outcomes and reduce the burden of diabetes-related complications. In this project, we aim to explore the power of ensemble learning in diabetes prediction, leveraging the collective intelligence of diverse models to achieve superior accuracy and robustness.

Through the development of an ensemble-based predictive system, we aspire to provide a valuable tool for medical professionals in making well-informed decisions, identifying high-risk individuals, and initiating proactive interventions to manage and control diabetes effectively. By combining the potential of machine learning with the domain expertise of healthcare practitioners, we envision a future where diabetes prediction becomes more accurate, accessible, and patient-centric, contributing to a healthier and more resilient society.

References

1. Ahammad, S.H., et al.:Phishing URL detection using machine learning methods. Adv. Eng. Software **173**, 103288 (2022). https://doi.org/10.1016/j.advengsoft.2022.103288
2. Ambala, S., Mangore, A.K., Tamboli, M., Rajput, S.D., Chiwhane, S., Dhumane, A. Design and implementation of machine learning-based network intrusion detection. Int. J. Intell. Syst. Appl. Eng. **12**(2s), 120–131 (2024)
3. Meshram, V., Choudhary, C., Kale, A., Rajput, J., Meshram, V., Dhumane, A.: Dry fruit image dataset for machine learning applications, Data in Brief **49**, 109325 (2023). https://doi.org/10.1016/j.dib.2023.109325
4. Dhumane, A.V., Sanas, P., Shelke, A., Kasbe, P., Salunkhe, S.: Anomaly detection at ATM center using machine learning algorithm. Int. J. Adv. Res. Sci. Commun. Technol. (IJARSCT) **6**(01)
5. Dhumane, A.V., Kaldate, P., Sawant, A., Kadam, P., Chopade, V.: Efficient prediction of cardiovascular disease using machine learning algorithms with relief and lasso feature selection techniques. In: Hassanien, A.E., Castillo, O., Anand, S., Jaiswal, A. (eds) International Conference on Innovative Computing and Communications. ICICC 2023. Lecture Notes in Networks and Systems, vol. 703. Springer, Singapore (2023). https://doi.org/10.1007/978-981-99-3315-0_52
6. Prasad, J.R., Prasad, R.S., Dhumane, A., Ranjan, N., Tamboli, M.: Gradient bald vulture optimization enabled multi-objective Unet++ with DCNN for prostate cancer segmentation and detection. Biomed. Signal Process. Control **87**, Part A (2024). ISSN 1746-8094
7. Dongare, Y., Shende, A., Dhumane, A., Tamboli, M., Rajput, S.D., Wadne, V.S.: Enhanced rainfall prediction with weighted linear units using advanced recurrent neural network. Int. J. Intell. Syst. Appl. Eng. **12**(1s), 549–556 (2023)
8. Cahn, A., Shoshan, A., Sagiv, T., Yesharim, R., Goshen, R., Shalev, V., et al.: Prediction of progression from pre-diabetes to diabetes: development and validation of a machine learning model. Diabetes Metab. Res. Rev. **36**(2), e3252 (2020). https://doi.org/10.1002/dmrr.3252
9. Thenappan, S., Rajkumar, M.V., Manoharan, P.S.: Predicting diabetes mellitus using modified support vector machine with cloud security. IETE J. Res. **68**(6), 3940–3950 (2020). https://doi.org/10.1080/03772063.2020.1782781.(inpress)
10. Islam, M.T., Raihan, M., Farzana, F., Aktar, N., Ghosh, P., Kabiraj, S.: Typical and non-typical diabetes disease prediction using random forest algorithm. In: Abstracts of the 11th International Conference on Computing, Communication and Networking Technologies, IEEE, Kharagpur, 1–3 July 2020. https://doi.org/10.1109/ICCCNT49239.2020.9225430
11. Alam, T.M., et al.: A model for early prediction of diabetes (2019). https://doi.org/10.1016/j.imu.2019.100204
12. Kahramanli, H., Allahverdi, N.:Design of a hybrid system for the diabetes and heart diseases. Expert Syst. Appl. **35**. 82–89 (2008).https://doi.org/10.1016/j.eswa.2007.06.004
13. Rajesh, K., Sangeetha, V.: Application of data mining methods and techniques for diabetes diagnosis. Int. J. Eng. Innov. Technol. **2**, 224–229 (2012)
14. Mustafa, M.: Diabetes prediction dataset, A Comprehensive Dataset for Predicting Diabetes with Medical & Demographic Data (2023)

Cancer Detection Using AI

A Predictive Deep Learning Ensemble-Based Approach for Advanced Cancer Classification

Kanika Kansal[✉] and Sanjiv Sharma

KIET Group of Institutions, Ghaziabad, India
kanika.kansal2000@gmail.com

Abstract. Breast cancer is a significant contributor to the death rate of women in developing and underdeveloped nations. Timely identification and categorization of breast cancer can facilitate the administration of the most optimal therapy to patients. Using ensemble learning, we presented a novel deep-learning architecture for breast cancer detection and classification in breast ultrasound images. In the proposed work, image features are extracted using three pre-trained CNN architectures, DenseNet121, DenseNet169, and DenseNet201, which are then averaged to form an ensemble model. Experiments are conducted using Kaggle's publicly available data set to evaluate the performance of the proposed architecture. Regarding accuracy in detecting and classifying breast cancer in ultrasound images, it has been visible that the proposed ensemble architecture outperforms other pre-defined deep learning architectures with an accuracy of 99.62%.

Keywords: Deep Learning · Breast Cancer · Ensemble Method · DenseNet · CNN

1 Introduction and Related Work

Breast cancer is one of the primary contributors to the high female death rate [1]. According to WHO, early detection is essential for facilitating treatment and enhancing survival chances [2]. In addition to skin irritation, redness, pain, and swelling, the initial stage is marked by the deterioration of nipples or an abrupt secretion of water from the nipples [3]. Diagnostic procedures such as mammography, MRI, ultrasound, thermography, and surgical incision are techniques utilized in detecting and monitoring breast cancer [4–6]. Because of comparable medical symptoms of various forms of cancer, it is extremely challenging to decode the data derived from these techniques, which makes additional examination of the data even more challenging. Examining the data is a lengthy and laborious procedure but a crucial phase in the differential diagnosis process. Hence, it has become imperative to mechanize a segment of the diagnostic procedure to mitigate the workload of the radiologist and pathologist.

In this direction, various Machine learning (ML) and Deep Learning (DL) methods have surfaced as a dominant paradigm that provides efficient ways and can intelligently perform certain diagnostic tasks automatically [7]. Deep neural networks are gaining

© The Author(s), under exclusive license to Springer Nature Switzerland AG 2024
D. Garg et al. (Eds.): IACC 2023, CCIS 2054, pp. 335–346, 2024.
https://doi.org/10.1007/978-3-031-56703-2_27

significant attention among the various ML and DL techniques due to their capacity for effortless discovery of features and learning of representations [8, 9].

A deep neural network, known as a Convolution Neural Network (CNN), is widely used in computer vision tasks because of its advantageous weight distribution and few interaction traits [10, 11]. Because of these two characteristics, CNNs can be used as regional filters to identify globally consistent patterns in images while still requiring a very small number of trainable parameters.

To generate the image class label, CNN uses its representation learning power to combine simple qualities into more complex ones gradually [11]. Transfer learning can be used as a replacement for initial instruction. The term "transfer learning" refers to the process of adapting a network that has been trained on one activity to perform another, unrelated activity [12–14].

Several research studies have made significant contributions to the field of ensemble learning for the diagnosis of breast cancer. Research in the field of literature demonstrates that shape and texture-based characteristics play a significant role in the thorough examination of medical images. Prior studies have suggested a range of machine learning and deep learning methods for the identification of breast cancer. In this direction, Aditya Golatkar et al. [15] proposed a deep learning-based method to classify H&E-stained breast tissue images for the primary diagnosis of breast cancer. The method uses an Inception-v3 convolutional neural network to extract patches based on nuclear density, discarding non-epithelial regions. The overall classification of the image is chosen by employing a majority vote across nuclear classifications. The approach attained an average accuracy of 85% across the four classifications and 93% for distinguishing between non-cancerous and malignant categories. Similarly, S. Karthik et al. [13] devised a computer-aided diagnosis (CAD) system that utilizes a deep neural network (DNN) and recursive feature elimination (RFE) to carry out automated diagnosis. The approach outperformed prior state-of-the-art methods with a 98.62% accuracy rate when tested on the Wisconsin Breast Cancer Dataset (WBCD). By utilising this cutting-edge method for early disease detection and treatment, healthcare providers may contribute to better public health. Abhishek Das et al. [16] focuses on breast cancer detection in a separate study. They use a deep learning model to transform one-dimensional data into pictures. To transform the one-dimensional input into images, the model employs a stacked ensemble approach, drawing on techniques such as the Convex Hull algorithm and t-t-distributed Stochastic Neighbour embedding. The model learns to classify and train using Convolutional Neural Networks and decomposition techniques with both the original and decomposed datasets. The model's efficacy is proven by its improved performance on synthetic datasets and breast histopathology images. Not only that, but CAD technologies are used to identify photos of breast cancer, which is a common ailment in women, according to Alireza Maleki and colleagues [17].Achieving an accuracy rate of 85%, recent research has made advancements in using deep learning techniques for diagnosing breast cancer. The Wisconsin Breast Cancer Dataset has been analyzed using computer-aided diagnosis methods, resulting in an accuracy rate of 98.62%. The utilization of CAD technologies has resulted in enhanced results when applied to both synthetic datasets and real breast histopathology pictures. These technological break-throughs play a role in identifying and treating medical conditions at an early stage, hence improving overall health and wellness.

This research presents approaches aimed at enhancing the velocity and accuracy of histopathology image categorization. The approach employs transfer learning on the histopathology breast image dataset. The BreakHis dataset exhibits accuracies of 93.6%, 91.3%, 93.8%, and 89.1%. The ultimate approach involves utilizing the DenseNet201 model as a feature extractor in conjunction with XGBoost as a classifier.

In the proposed framework, ensemble learning is used to overcome the shortcomings of extant cancer tumor detection and classification systems. This paper's primary contribution can be summed up as follows:

- To provide an approach for the detection and classification of breast cancer based on deep learning.
- To examine ensemble learning across three distinct deep learning architectures.
- To provide a comparative analysis of the accuracy of each deep learning architecture in the context of ensemble learning.

The subsequent sections are structured in the following manner: The second section offers a thorough examination of the suggested methodology, encompassing subsections such as data pre-processing and data augmentation, pre-trained Convolutional Neural Network (CNN) designs, and ensemble learning. Section 3 presents the experimental outcomes achieved through the implementation of the suggested approach, together with an assessment of its effectiveness. The work is concluded in Sect. 4, which also outlines potential avenues for future research.

2 Methodology

2.1 Data Pre-processing and Augmentation Processing

In the proposed method, ultrasound images are normalized and to expand the dataset size for CNN to enhance its accuracy, it must collect massive data sets. Moreover, CNN's effectiveness decreases with tiny data sets due to overfitting. It suggests that the network exhibits exceptional performance when trained with data but performs poorly when tested with different data. Data augmentation is employed in the proposed system to expand the dataset and mitigate overfitting problems [18]. The data augmentation method utilizes basic image processing techniques and geometric changes on picture data sets to effectively enhance the number of samples. The image data collection undergoes pre-processing through color manipulation, transformation (including translation, scaling, and rotation), inversion, and noise perturbation.

2.2 Pre-trained CNN Architecture

DenseNet 121

The CNN architecture DenseNet-121 was proposed in 2016 by Gao Huang. While conventional DL designs have many parameters and suffer from the vanishing gradient problem, a new family of models called Dense Nets aims to solve both issues. DenseNet-121 connects all layers directly, unlike standard CNNs, which sequentially pass information from one layer to the next layer. Each layer takes input from the previous layer and all preceding layers in the network [19].

Thus, DenseNet-121 fosters feature reuse and information flow throughout the network, making data representation learning more efficient and effective. DenseNet-121's architecture has four dense blocks with each block containing some layers. The output feature maps of all preceding layers are concatenated to generate the input to the following layers in each dense block [20]. This approach decreases the number of parameters, preventing overfitting and memory usage. DenseNet-121 also uses bottleneck layers to reduce computational load while retaining representational power.

DenseNet-121 excels at computer vision tasks like image classification, object recognition, and segmentation using semantics. DenseNet-121 may generalize well with fewer training samples due to its dense connection and effective parameter usage (Fig. 1).

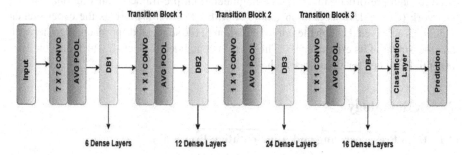

Fig. 1. DenseNet 121 Architecture

DenseNet 169

DenseNet-169 proposed by Gao Huang in 2016 is a CNN architecture that extends DenseNet-12. DenseNet-169 adds layers and parameters while preserving dense connections to improve the model's representational power [21]. Like DenseNet-121, DenseNet-169 uses dense connectivity, where each layer in a dense block receives input from all preceding levels. This dense connectivity improves feature reuse and efficient information flow via the network, improving gradient propagation and reducing the vanishing gradient problem. DenseNet-169 has four dense blocks like DenseNet-121, but each block has more convolutional layers [22]. The model may capture more complicated and abstract properties from incoming data due to this deeper architecture's more parameters. Before the 3 × 3 convolutions, DenseNet-169 used bottleneck layers to reduce feature map dimensionality. DenseNet-169 performs better due to its more complex architecture. This increases memory and computing requirements during training and inference. DenseNet-169 is generally preferred when computational resources are not a concern, and the task requires a more powerful model.

DenseNet-169 excels at image classification, object recognition, and segmentation using semantics. In tasks with a lot of training data, its extensive connectivity promotes robust feature learning without overfitting [23]. DenseNet-169 has extensive use in both theoretical and applied theories, specifically in transfer learning and DL solutions for image-related problems (Fig. 2).

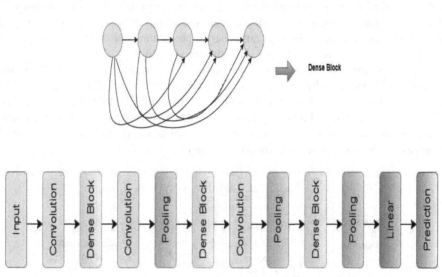

Fig. 2. (a) Dense block (b) Complete structure of DenseNet169

DenseNet 201

DenseNet-169 was extended by Gao Huang in 2016 to propose a sophisticated CNN architecture from the DenseNet family, DenseNet-201, which deepens the architecture to learn complex features from input data. DenseNet-201 uses dense connectivity like other DenseNet models [24]. Dense blocks get direct input from all preceding layers. A dense connection improves feature reuse and information flow, enabling gradient propagation and solving the vanishing gradient problem. DenseNet-201 is larger than DenseNet-169 and DenseNet-121. Like DenseNet-169, it has four dense blocks with extra convolutional layers. DenseNet-201's depth allows it to adapt more complicated and abstract data patterns, making it more effective for challenging tasks. Like other DenseNet variations, DenseNet-201 uses bottleneck layers to reduce computing complexity [25]. These bottleneck layers lower the feature map dimensionality before executing computationally costly 3 × 3 convolutions, balancing model size and efficiency. DenseNet-201's capacity and depth require more memory and processing resources during training and inference. Thus, it is employed when computational resources are abundant, and tasks require a stronger model.

DenseNet-201 excels at image classification, object identification, and semantic segmentation. Its extensive connection allows robust feature learning without overfitting tasks with large amounts of training data.

2.3 Ensemble Learning

Ensemble learning is a significant technique that improves overall performance by combining the predictions of multiple models. Ensemble learning operates on the premise that by combining the results of multiple models, each possessing unique strengths and limitations, the resultant ensemble can generate predictions that are more precise and resilient than those generated by any individual model [26].

By employing this methodology, the potential for overfitting is reduced, and the model's ability to generalize is improved. Ensemble methods, including bagging, boosting, and stacking, have demonstrated efficacy across diverse domains such as classification, regression, and anomaly detection. Their implementation has significantly enhanced the precision of predictions and decision-making processes in the realm of complex machine-learning endeavors (Figs. 3 and 4).

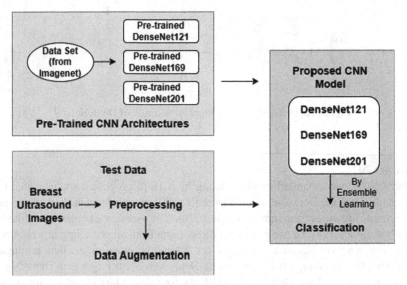

Fig. 3. The Working Flow of the Proposed Framework

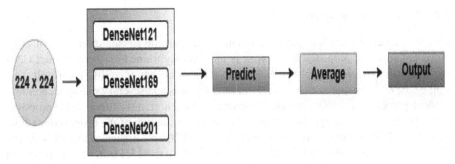

Fig. 4. Proposed Ensemble Model

3 Results and Discussions

3.1 Dataset

The Kaggle breast ultrasound dataset [27] is utilized to assess the efficacy of the proposed framework. The first technique of augmenting the dataset consists of rotating and magnifying one thousand images. During the execution of the proposed structure, eighty percent of the dataset is utilized for training purposes. In comparison, twenty percent of the dataset is utilized for verifying the accuracy of the proposed architecture, i.e., 800 images are used to train the architecture. In contrast, the remaining 200 images are used to assess the trained model (Fig. 5).

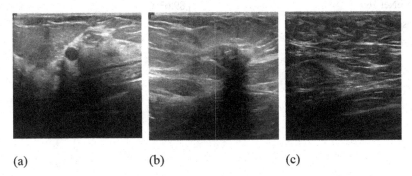

(a)   (b)   (c)

Fig. 5. (a) Benign image (b) Malignant image (c) Normal image

3.2 Results and Analysis

Before transferring the learning data to ensemble learning for the extraction of combined features, the proposed framework is individually trained on three distinct CNN architectures, namely DenseNet121, DenseNet169, and DenseNet201. The results of a single CNN are compared to a set of combined features and several existing techniques. Table 1 presents both the individual outcomes of each architecture and the proposed ensemble learning strategy. In addition, during the evaluation of the proposed method, training and testing data sets are separated. The 80/20 split indicates that 80% of the data is used for training CNN architectures and 20% is used for testing. The proposed framework provides a more accurate classification of cancer cells in breast ultrasound images than individual architectures.

As demonstrated in Table 1, the classification accuracy of DenseNet121, DenseNet169, and DenseNet201 architectures is 89.50%, 89.63%, and 91.62%, respectively, whereas the proposed framework achieves an accuracy of 99.62%. These results demonstrate that the proposed framework of the ensemble method outperforms the other three breast cancer tumor detection and classification architectures in terms of accuracy (Fig. 6).

Table 1. Accuracy comparison of the models used in the study.

Models	Accuracy
DenseNet 121	89.50%
DenseNet 169	89.63%
DenseNet 201	91.62%
Ensemble Model	99.62%

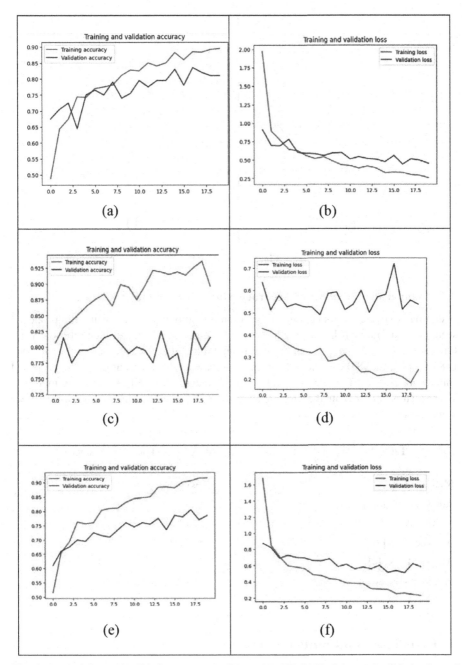

Fig. 6. (a) Training and validation accuracy of DenseNet121 (b) Training and validation loss of DenseNet121 (c) Training and validation accuracy of DenseNet169 (d) Training and validation loss of DenseNet169 (e) Training and validation accuracy of DenseNet201 (f) Training and validation loss of DenseNet201 (g) Training and validation accuracy of DenseNet Ensemble (h) Training and validation loss of DenseNet Ensemble

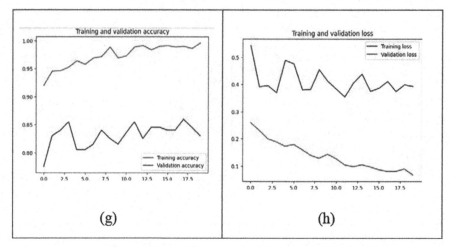

Fig. 6. (*continued*)

3.3 Comparative Analysis of Accuracy with Existing Studies

A comparative analysis is conducted between the outputs obtained using the proposed structure and four well-known methods to determine the efficacy of the proposed structure, as shown in Table 2. It can be seen from Table 2 that the accuracy of the methods is 85%, 98.62%, 98.08%, and 92%, respectively, whereas the accuracy of the proposed framework is 99.62%, which is greater than the accuracy of all four existing methods. These results demonstrate the superior accuracy of the proposed method relative to other comparable approaches.

Table 2. Comparison of various existing studies based on their accuracies

Methods	Accuracy
Aditya Golatkar [1]	85%
S. Karthik [2]	98.62%
Abhishek Das [3]	98.08%
Alireza Maleki [4]	92%
Proposed Framework	99.62%

4   Conclusion and Future Work

In this study, we proposed a novel deep-learning structure for the detection and classification of breast cancer using the concept of ensemble learning. In this framework, breast image features are extracted using three distinct CNN architectures (DenseNet121, DenseNet169, and DenseNet201) that are combined using the concept of ensemble learning to enhance classification accuracy.

Similarly, we also proposed a data augmentation technique to increase the size of a data set to enhance the efficacy of the CNN structure. Lastly, the performance of the proposed structure is compared to that of distinct CNN architectures as well as other existing methodologies. It has been visible that the proposed structure gives accurate output without initial training, thereby improving classification efficiency. The development and validation of a deep learning structure for breast cancer detection and classification, utilizing ensemble learning and multiple CNN architectures, presents promising opportunities for future research in medical image analysis. The model could be enhanced by incorporating advanced CNN architectures and integrating multi-modal data. Transfer learning techniques could expedite the development of new diagnostic tools. Future research should focus on optimizing data augmentation and ensemble learning methods and adapting to emerging deep learning methodologies.

References

1. Siegel, R.L., et al.: Colorectal cancer statistics, 2017. CA Cancer J. Clin. **67**(3) (2017). https://doi.org/10.3322/caac.21395
2. Early detection: A long road ahead. Nat. Rev. Cancer **18**(7) (2018). https://doi.org/10.1038/s41568-018-0021-8
3. Ganesan, K., Acharya, U.R., Chua, C.K., Min, L.C., Abraham, K.T., Ng, K.H.: Computer-aided breast cancer detection using mammograms: a review. IEEE Rev. Biomed. Eng. **6**, 77–98 (2013). https://doi.org/10.1109/RBME.2012.2232289
4. Zheng, Y.: Breast cancer detection with Gabor features from digital Mammograms. Algorithms **3**(1) (2010). https://doi.org/10.3390/a3010044
5. Fleet, B.D., Yan, J., Knoester, D.B., Yao, M., Deller, J.R., Goodman, E.D.: Breast cancer detection using haralick features of images reconstructed from ultra wideband microwave scans. In: Linguraru, M.G., et al. (eds.) CLIP 2014. LNCS, vol. 8680, pp. 9–16. Springer, Cham (2014). https://doi.org/10.1007/978-3-319-13909-8_2
6. Tan, M., Zheng, B., Leader, J.K., Gur, D.: Association between changes in mammographic image features and risk for near-term breast cancer development. IEEE Trans. Med. Imaging **35**(7), 1719–1728 (2016). https://doi.org/10.1109/TMI.2016.2527619
7. Shen, D., Wu, G., Suk, H.I.: Deep learning in medical image analysis. Ann. Rev. Biomed. Eng. **19**, 221–248 (2017). https://doi.org/10.1146/annurev-bioeng-071516-044442
8. LeCun, Y., Hinton, G., Bengio, Y.: Deep learning. Nature **521** (2015)
9. Hoffer, E., Ailon, N.: Deep metric learning using triplet network. In: Feragen, A., Pelillo, M., Loog, M. (eds.) SIMBAD 2015. LNCS, vol. 9370, pp. 84–92. Springer, Cham (2015). https://doi.org/10.1007/978-3-319-24261-3_7
10. Astani, M., Hasheminejad, M., Vaghefi, M.: A diverse ensemble classifier for tomato disease recognition. Comput. Electron. Agric. **198**, 107054 (2022). https://doi.org/10.1016/j.compag.2022.107054
11. Javed, M.S., Majeed, H., Mujtaba, H., Beg, M.O.: Fake reviews classification using deep learning ensemble of shallow convolutions. J. Comput. Soc. Sci. **4**(2), (2021). https://doi.org/10.1007/s42001-021-00114-y
12. Qummar, S., et al.: A deep learning ensemble approach for diabetic retinopathy detection. IEEE Access **7** (2019). https://doi.org/10.1109/ACCESS.2019.2947484
13. Karthik, S., Srinivasa Perumal, R., Chandra Mouli, P.V.S.S.R.: Breast cancer classification using deep neural networks. Knowl. Comput. Appl.: Knowl. Manipulation Process. Techn.: Volume 1 (2018). https://doi.org/10.1007/978-981-10-6680-1_12

14. Mohammed, A., Kora, R.: An effective ensemble deep learning framework for text classification. J. King Saud Univ.-Comput. Inf. Sci. **34**(10) (2022). https://doi.org/10.1016/j.jksuci.2021.11.001

15. Golatkar, A., Anand, D., Sethi, A.: Classification of breast cancer histology using deep learning. In: Campilho, A., Karray, F., ter Haar Romeny, B. (eds.) ICIAR 2018. LNCS, vol. 10882, pp. 837–844. Springer, Cham (2018). https://doi.org/10.1007/978-3-319-93000-8_95

16. Das, A., Mohanty, M.N., Mallick, P.K., Tiwari, P., Muhammad, K., Zhu, H.: Breast cancer detection using an ensemble deep learning method. Biomed. Signal Process. Control **70** (2021). https://doi.org/10.1016/j.bspc.2021.103009

17. Maleki, A., Raahemi, M., Nasiri, H.: Breast cancer diagnosis from histopathology images using deep neural network and XGBoost Biomed. Signal Process. Control **86** (2023). https://doi.org/10.1016/j.bspc.2023.105152

18. Krizhevsky, A., Sutskever, I., Hinton, G.E.: ImageNet classification with deep convolutional neural networks. Commun. ACM **60**(6) (2017). https://doi.org/10.1145/3065386

19. Solano-Rojas, B., Villalón-Fonseca, R., Marín-Raventós, G.: Alzheimer's disease early detection using a low cost three-dimensional densenet-121 architecture. In: Jmaiel, M., Mokhtari, M., Abdulrazak, B., Aloulou, H., Kallel, S. (eds.) ICOST 2020. LNCS, vol. 12157, pp. 3–15. Springer, Cham (2020). https://doi.org/10.1007/978-3-030-51517-1_1

20. Chhabra, M., Kumar, R.: A smart healthcare system based on classifier DenseNet 121 model to detect multiple diseases. In: Marriwala, N., Tripathi, C.C., Jain, S., Kumar, D. (eds.) Mobile Radio Communications and 5G Networks. LNNS, vol. 339, pp. 297–312. Springer, Singapore (2022). https://doi.org/10.1007/978-981-16-7018-3_23

21. Dalvi, P.P., Edla, D.R., Purushothama, B.R.: Diagnosis of coronavirus disease from chest X-Ray images using DenseNet-169 Architecture. SN Comput. Sci. **4**(3) (2023). https://doi.org/10.1007/s42979-022-01627-7

22. Rahman, M.T., Dola, A.: Automated grading of diabetic retinopathy using DenseNet-169 architecture. In: 2021 5th International Conference on Electrical Information and Communication Technology, EICT 2021 (2021). https://doi.org/10.1109/EICT54103.2021.9733431

23. Ashwini, A., Purushothaman, K.E., Rosi, A., Vaishnavi, T.: Artificial Intelligence based real-time automatic detection and classification of skin lesion in dermoscopic samples using DenseNet-169 architecture. J. Intell. Fuzzy Syst. (2023). https://doi.org/10.3233/jifs-233024

24. Lu, T., Han, B., Chen, L., Yu, F., Xue, C.: A generic intelligent tomato classification system for practical applications using DenseNet-201 with transfer learning. Sci. Rep. **11**(1) (2021). https://doi.org/10.1038/s41598-021-95218-w

25. Jaiswal, A., Gianchandani, N., Singh, D., Kumar, V., Kaur, M.: Classification of the COVID-19 infected patients using DenseNet201 based deep transfer learning. J. Biomol. Struct. Dyn. **39**(15) (2021). https://doi.org/10.1080/07391102.2020.1788642

26. Zeng, T., Wu, L., Peduto, D., Glade, T., Hayakawa, Y.S., Yin, K.: Ensemble learning framework for landslide susceptibility mapping: different basic classifier and ensemble strategy. Geosci. Front. **14**(6) (2023). https://doi.org/10.1016/j.gsf.2023.101645

27. "Kaggle ultrasound" (2023). Accessed on 20 Aug 2023. https://www.kaggle.com/datasets/aryashah2k/breast-ultrasound-images-dataset

Predictive Deep Learning: An Analysis of Inception V3, VGG16, and VGG19 Models for Breast Cancer Detection

Kanika Kansal[✉] and Sanjiv Sharma

KIET Group of Institutions, Ghaziabad, India
kanika.kansal2000@gmail.com

Abstract. Breast cancer is a major contributor to cancer-related death in women. A higher likelihood of survival could result from early detection if the patient could receive the appropriate medicine while it is still in its early stages. Most often, a medical professional will use medical imaging or manual physical analysis to make a diagnosis. These efforts might be drastically cut with an automated approach. Using deep learning approaches, this paper proposes a system for autonomously analyzing ultrasound pictures. Using data obtained from the web repository Kaggle, three deep learning models—InceptionV3, VGG16, and VGG19—are applied to validate the suggested method. With the help of a confusion matrix and accuracy metrics, we compare the outcomes produced by these three deep learning methods. With an accuracy rate of 99.75%, the InceptionV3 model proved to be the most effective.

Keywords: Breast cancer · Deep Learning · VGG16 · VGG19 · InceptionV3

1 Introduction

Clinical imaging and detection have made a huge stride forward with the use of deep learning for breast cancer classification [1]. Medical imaging of benign or malignant breast lesions may now be detected with remarkable accuracy by researchers and doctors using CNNs and other deep-learning architectures [2]. Early and accurate diagnosis of malignant anomalies can be achieved by using deep learning algorithms that can extract complicated patterns and features from imaging modalities like mammograms, ultrasounds, MRI, and histopathology slides [3]. Deep learning in breast cancer categorization improves diagnostic accuracy and facilitates early interventions and better patient outcomes by streamlining the decision-making process for healthcare providers [4]. Deep learning promises to improve our ability to successfully combat breast cancer as research and development in this area continue to grow. Figure 1 shows the working of a deep learning model.

In this study, a comparative analysis of deep learning models like Inception V3, VGG 16, and VGG 19 for breast cancer classification and detection using the pre-trained models and the publicly available Kaggle dataset of ultrasound images is performed.

D. Garg et al. (Eds.): IACC 2023, CCIS 2054, pp. 347–357, 2024.
https://doi.org/10.1007/978-3-031-56703-2_28

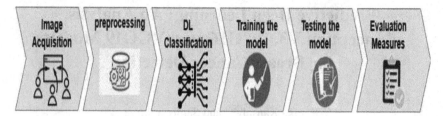

Fig. 1. Working Flow of a Deep Learning Model

This paper will proceed as described below. The associated work is detailed in Sect. 2. In Sect. 3, a set of approaches and procedures for detecting and classifying breast cancer is presented. Section 4 shows the results, followed by a conclusion in Sect. 5.

2   Related Work

Throughout the world, breast cancer is a highly common and well-researched form of cancer among women. The scope of study on breast cancer extends over several decades, covering a broad range of subjects such as its epidemiology, etiology, molecular biology, and therapy approaches [5]. Scientists have made notable advancements in identifying various risk factors. Moreover, the implementation of sophisticated imaging techniques and the identification of biomarkers have enhanced the ability to detect and predict the outcome of a disease at an early stage [6]. This study has resulted in the creation of targeted therapies such as Herceptin and advanced immunotherapies. The abundance of publications in this domain emphasizes the significance of ongoing investigation and cooperation to gain a deeper comprehension of and counteract this intricate and destructive ailment, consequently enhancing the well-being of numerous persons impacted by breast cancer.

In this direction, various research work has been proposed such as Surbhi et al. [7] explores the potential of using deep learning approaches for analyzing breast cancer patient's chances of survival following surgery. All deep learning methods were shown to be effective at predicting survival rates, with the Restricted Boltzmann Machine showing the greatest accuracy (0.97) in the study. The best accuracy was found using Deep Autoencoders (0.96) and CNN (92%). However, more study is required to ascertain the optimal layout for maximum precision. Similarly, yadavendra et al. [8] classified breast cancer tumors using a variety of algorithms, including the Xception model, a hybrid of logistic regression and a random forest classifier, the AdaBoost classifier, the bagging classifier, the voting classifier, and the Xception model on a standard dataset of breast Histopathology images.

When compared to other approaches, the Xception model achieved the highest levels of accuracy, recall, and F1 scores. This study intends to speed up the process of cor-rectly classifying tumors, hence raising awareness and decreasing anxiety about the disease. Furthermore, faezehsadat et al. [9] employed breast cancer histopathology images to test several deep-learning models for the classification of breast cancer, it determines the most precise models for binary, four, and eight classifications. Newer models that haven't been studied before are also investigated here, such as NASNet, SENet, ResNeXt, and Dual Path Net. Similarly, ghada hamed et al. [10] achieved a 91% accurate diagnosis using machine learning techniques and suggested the best model as RetinaNet using the concept of "You Only Look Once". In addition, farjana et al. [11] compare the results of the BreakHis dataset trained with the Inceptionvl, LeNet-5, AlexNet, VGG-16, ResNet-50, and LeNet-5 CNN architectures. Test accuracy, AUC, precision, recall, and f1-score were all best for the Inceptionvl network at 40X, 100X, 200X, and 400X magnification levels, respectively.

Advancements in breast cancer research have been achieved by identifying risk factors, developing imaging techniques, and discovering biomarkers. These advancements have paved the way for the development of targeted medicines and immunotherapies.

Deep learning techniques have been employed in the analysis of breast cancer, namely in the prediction of survival rates and the classification of tumors. This emphasizes the necessity for continuous collaboration to have a deeper comprehension of and counteract this intricate ailment.

3 Research Methodology

3.1 CNN

CNN is a type of Deep Neural Network commonly employed for image analysis. CNN closely resembles conventional Neural Networks [12]. It consists of neurons that have been trained on the data beforehand. Each neuron receives nearly inputs in a nonlinear manner, as indicated by the dot product function [13]. The entire network serves a singular, distinct purpose. Class scores are on one end and raw image pixels are on the other. The model is further implemented followed by the deployment of a completely interconnected dense layer [14].

3.2 Dataset Used

The dataset was collected through a free and publicly available digital repository, Kaggle [15]. The 1000-image Dataset was collected which contained benign, malignant, and normal cases. The Utilization of three distinct deep learning algorithms for statistical evaluation of the selected dataset is represented in Fig. 2. The baseline data comprises breast ultrasound images of females ranging in age from 25 to 75 years. The information was gathered in 2018. There are 600 female patients in the patient population. The dataset comprises 780 images, each of which has an average dimension of 500 by 500 pixels. The format of the images is PNG.

3.3 Inception V3

Inception V3 (Fig. 3), a deep CNN architecture developed by Google's Deep Learning team, is renowned for its effectiveness and precision in image classification and object recognition tasks. It employs modules with varying filter diameters, batch normalization, and factorized convolution to decrease computational complexity [16].

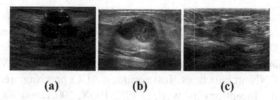

(a)   **(b)**   **(c)**

Fig. 2. (a) Benign case (b) malignant case (c) normal case

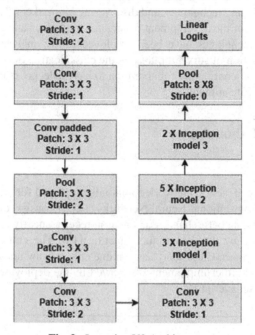

Fig. 3. Inception V3 Architecture

3.4 VGG16

VGG16 (Fig. 4), is a deep CNN architecture devised by the Visual Geometry Group at the University of Oxford. It has 16 weight layers, 13 convolutional layers, and 3 fully connected layers, making it an effective model for image classification [17]. The uncomplicated architecture of VGG16 has contributed to advanced image recognition results despite the size of its parameters [18].

3.5 VGG19

VGG19 (Fig. 5), is a deep CNN used for computer vision tasks. It comprises 16 convolutional layers and 3 fully connected layers for a total of 19 layers, making it an effective model for image classification and feature extraction. VGG19 is extensively employed in image-related tasks for transfer learning and fine-tuning [19].

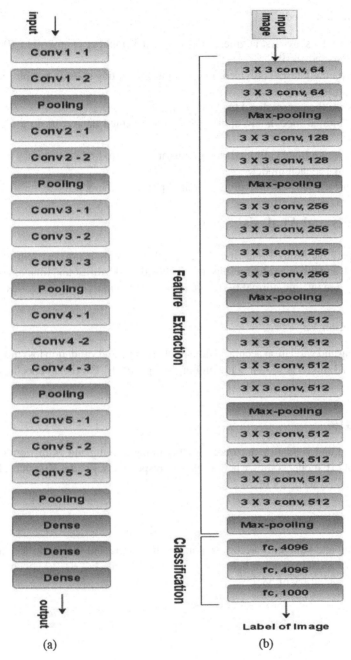

Fig. 4. (a)VGG16 Architecture (b) VGG19 Architecture

3.6 Algorithm Used

- Dataset images are first augmented to make their number from 780 to 1000 for the comparative analysis.
- The prepared dataset is divided into training and testing subsets by splitting it in an 80:20 ratio.
- Images are then normalized for further processing.
- All pre-trained models are applied to this augmented dataset to do a comparative analysis.
- All three models are compiled, and graphs are drawn to find the accuracy by applying 30 epochs for each model.
- A confusion matrix is then drawn for all 3 pre-trained models.

4 Results and Analysis

The Comparative Analysis for Breast Cancer Classification using deep learning models is executed, and the individual results are displayed. 1000 ultrasound images comprising benign, malignant, and normal tissue are classified into individual categories.

4.1 Inception V3

The training and validation accuracy along with training and validation loss model for the Inception V3 model is shown below in Fig. 6 respectively. For the 30 epochs, Inception V3 achieved an accuracy of 99.37%.

4.2 VGG16

The training and validation accuracy along with the training and validation loss model for the VGG 16 model is shown below in Fig. 7 respectively. For the 30 epochs, Inception V3 achieved an accuracy of 56.25%.

4.3 VGG19

The training and validation accuracy along with training and validation loss model for the VGG 19 model is shown below in Fig. 8 respectively. For the 30 epochs, VGG 19 achieved an accuracy of 58.25%.

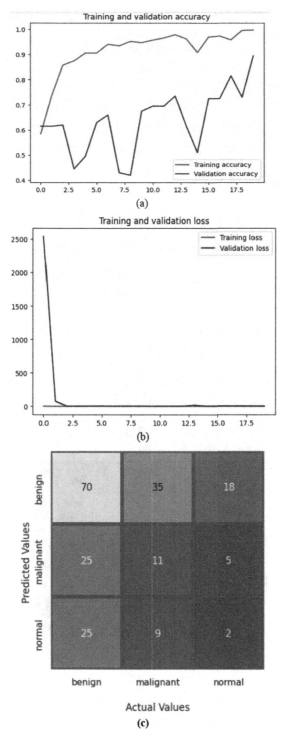

Fig. 5. (a) Training and validation accuracy (b) training and validation loss (c) Confusion matrix for Inception V3 model.

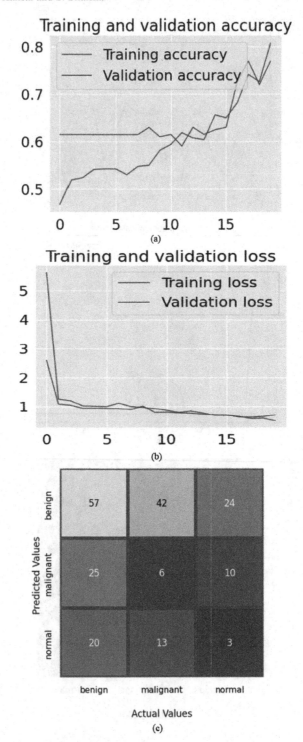

Fig. 6. (a) Training and validation accuracy (b) training and validation loss (c) Confusion matrix for VGG 16 model.

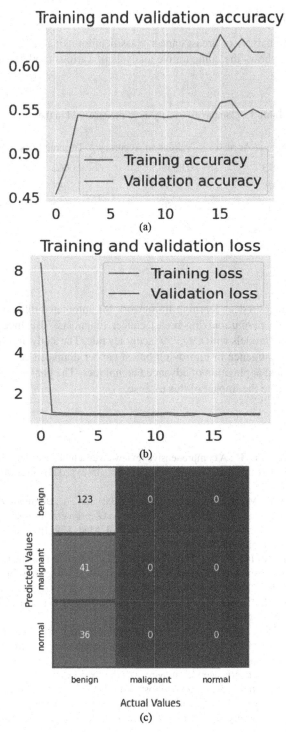

Fig. 7. (a) Training and validation accuracy (b) training and validation loss (c) Confusion matrix for VGG 16 model.

4.4 Comparative Analysis

The comparative analysis of breast cancer classification using various deep models is shown in Table 1 shows the comparative analysis of various models employed in this study.

Table 1. Comparative analysis of models used in the study.

Model	Training Accuracy	Validation Accuracy	Training Loss	Validation Loss
InceptionV3	0.9975	0.8950	0.0062	0.6366
VGG16	0.8075	0.7700	0.5055	0.7037
VGG19	0.5437	0.6150	0.9963	0.9362

5 Conclusion

This study introduces a deep learning framework for automated ultrasound image processing, potentially revolutionizing breast cancer diagnosis. The InceptionV3 model outperformed other models with a 99.75% accuracy rate. The study highlights the potential of artificial intelligence in improving breast cancer diagnosis and calls for further research and clinical application of advanced techniques. The goal is to improve patient outcomes and reduce the impact of this disease.

References

1. Mohammed, A., Kora, R.: A comprehensive review on ensemble deep learning: opportunities and challenges. J. King Saud Univ.-Comput. Inf. Sci. 35(2) (2023). https://doi.org/10.1016/j.jksuci.2023.01.014
2. Marrón-Esquivel, J.M., Duran-Lopez, L., Linares-Barranco, A., Dominguez-Morales, J.P.: A comparative study of the inter-observer variability on Gleason grading against Deep Learning-based approaches for prostate cancer. Comput. Biol. Med. 159, 106856 (2023). https://doi.org/10.1016/j.compbiomed.2023.106856
3. Khan, S., Islam, N., Jan, Z., Din, I.U., Rodrigues, J.J.C.: A novel deep learning based framework for the detection and classification of breast cancer using transfer learning. Pattern Recognit. Lett. 125 (2019). https://doi.org/10.1016/j.patrec.2019.03.022
4. Aslani, S., Jacob, J.: Utilisation of deep learning for COVID-19 diagnosis. Clin. Radiol. 78(2) (2023). https://doi.org/10.1016/j.crad.2022.11.006
5. Maleki, A., Raahemi, M., Nasiri, H.: Breast cancer diagnosis from histopathology images using deep neural network and XGBoost. Biomed. Signal Process. Control 86 (2023). https://doi.org/10.1016/j.bspc.2023.105152
6. Pineda, J., et al.: Geometric deep learning reveals the spatiotemporal features of microscopic motion. Nat. Mach. Intell. 5(1) (2023). https://doi.org/10.1038/s42256-022-00595-0
7. Gupta, S., Gupta, M.K.: A comparative analysis of deep learning approaches for predicting breast cancer survivability. Arch. Comput. Meth. Eng. 29(5) (2022). https://doi.org/10.1007/s11831-021-09679-3

8. Yadavendra, S.C.: A comparative study of breast cancer tumor classification by classical machine learning methods and deep learning method. Mach. Vis. Appl. **31**(6) (2020). https://doi.org/10.1007/s00138-020-01094-1

9. Shahidi, F., Daud, S.M., Abas, H., Ahmad, N.A., Maarop, N.: Breast cancer classification using deep learning approaches and histopathology image: a comparison study. IEEE Access **8** (2020). https://doi.org/10.1109/ACCESS.2020.3029881

10. Hamed, G., Marey, M.A.E.R., Amin, S.E. S., Tolba, M.F.: Deep learning in breast cancer detection and classification Adv. Intell. Syst. Comput. (2020)https://doi.org/10.1007/978-3-030-44289-7_30

11. Parvin, F., Al Mehedi Hasan, M.: A comparative study of different types of convolutional neural networks for breast cancer histopathological image classification. In: 2020 IEEE Region 10 Symposium, TENSYMP 2020 (2020).https://doi.org/10.1109/TENSYMP50017.2020.9230787

12. Li, Z., Liu, F., Yang, W., Peng, S., Zhou, J.: A survey of convolutional neural networks: analysis, applications, and prospects. IEEE Trans. Neural Netw. Learn. Syst. **33**(12) (2022). https://doi.org/10.1109/TNNLS.2021.3084827

13. Yamashita, R., Nishio, M., Do, R.K.G., Togashi, K.: Convolutional neural networks: an overview and application in radiology. Insights into Imaging 9(4) (2018). https://doi.org/10.1007/s13244-018-0639-9

14. Acharya, U.R., et al.: A deep convolutional neural network model to classify heartbeats. Comput. Biol. Med. **89** (2017). https://doi.org/10.1016/j.compbiomed.2017.08.022

15. "kaggle ultrasound" (2023) Accessed on 20 Aug 2023. https://www.kaggle.com/datasets/aryashah2k/breast-ultrasound-images-dataset

16. Wang, C., et al.: Pulmonary image classification based on inception-v3 transfer learning model. IEEE Access **7** (2019). https://doi.org/10.1109/ACCESS.2019.2946000

17. Mascarenhas, S., Agarwal, M.: A comparison between VGG16, VGG19 and ResNet50 architecture frameworks for Image Classification. In: Proceedings of IEEE International Conference on Disruptive Technologies for Multi-Disciplinary Research and Applications, CENTCON 2021 (2021). https://doi.org/10.1109/CENTCON52345.2021.9687944

18. Qassim, H., Verma, A., Feinzimer, D.: Compressed residual-VGG16 CNN model for big data places image recognition. In: 2018 IEEE 8th Annual Computing and Communication Workshop and Conference, CCWC 2018 (2018).https://doi.org/10.1109/CCWC.2018.8301729

19. Dey, N., Zhang, Y.D., Rajinikanth, V., Pugalenthi, R., Raja, N.S.M.: Customized VGG19 architecture for pneumonia detection in chest X-Rays. Pattern Recognit. Lett. **143** (2021). https://doi.org/10.1016/j.patrec.2020.12.010

Innovation in the Field of Oncology: Early Lung Cancer Detection and Classification Using AI

Kapila Moon[✉] and Ashok Jethawat

Pacific Academy of Higher Education and Research University, Udaipur, India
kapila.moon@gmail.com

Abstract. Human society has confronted numerous threats throughout its history, ranging from the Bubonic Plague to the recent COVID-19 pandemic. Despite the challenges, solutions have been developed for most issues, often at an affordable cost. However, one persistently expensive and life-threatening problem remains: cancer. Cancer acts like a societal curse, impacting individuals on mental, physical, and financial fronts. While remedies exist, they come at a significant cost, and survival rates, particularly for lung cancer, are often discouraging. Early detection is crucial, but human error in interpreting CT scans and MRI scans can lead to catastrophic consequences. To address accuracy concerns, an AI-based approach has been devised, aiming to minimize errors. This innovation significantly increases the likelihood of early problem detection, enabling prompt initiation of life-saving treatments. The current tested algorithms show promising results, empowering medical professionals, especially oncologists, to identify lung cancer in its early stages. This advancement holds the potential to substantially improve patients' chances of survival.

Keywords: Cancer · CT scan · Lung Cancer · MRI · Oncologists

1 Introduction

Lung cancer is a prevalent type of cancer that originates in the cells of the lungs. It is the second most common cancer globally, affecting both men and women, with an estimated 2.2 million new cases diagnosed in 2020, accounting for 11.4% of all cancer diagnoses. In terms of cancer-related deaths, lung cancer is the leading cause and accounted for approximately 18.0% of all cancer deaths in 2020, with an estimated 1.8 million deaths. The two main types of lung cancer are non-small cell lung cancer (NSCLC) and small cell lung cancer (SCLC), with NSCLC accounting for about 84% of all cases [2]. Lung cancer rates vary significantly by geography, with the highest rates in North America, Europe, and East Asia. Tobacco smoking is the primary cause of lung cancer, with up to 90% of all cases being attributed to smoking. Other risk factors for lung cancer include exposure to radon gas, air pollution, and occupational exposure to carcinogens. The symptoms of lung cancer vary depending on the type and stage of the cancer and may include cough, chest pain, and shortness of breath. Screening for lung cancer is recommended for people at high risk, and treatment options depend on the type and stage of the cancer, as well as the person's overall health. Treatment methods may include surgery, radiation therapy, chemotherapy, targeted therapy, and immunotherapy.

D. Garg et al. (Eds.): IACC 2023, CCIS 2054, pp. 358–375, 2024.
https://doi.org/10.1007/978-3-031-56703-2_29

Despite recent advances in treatment options for lung cancer, the overall prognosis for the disease remains poor, with a five-year survival rate of around 19% for all stages combined. Early detection and treatment of lung cancer can significantly improve the prognosis, highlighting the importance of timely diagnosis and treatment [4]. Lung cancer research has made several exciting developments in recent years, including the identification of new genetic mutations that can be targeted with precision medicine and the creation of new immunotherapies that use the body's immune system to fight cancer. These advances have improved treatment options and outcomes for people with lung cancer. Efforts to reduce the incidence of lung cancer continue, with a focus on decreasing tobacco smoking, promoting healthy air quality, and raising awareness about the risks associated with lung cancer. Smoking cessation remains the most effective way to reduce the risk of lung cancer, as well as other smoking-related diseases such as heart disease and chronic obstructive pulmonary disease (COPD). In summary, lung cancer is a significant public health concern, with high rates of incidence and mortality worldwide. Treatment options for lung cancer include surgery, radiation therapy, chemotherapy, targeted therapy, and immunotherapy, and the choice of treatment depends on several factors, including tumour size and location, cancer stage, and the individual's overall health [5]. In Sect. 1.1, the fundamental concepts of lung cancer and related studies are elucidated. Sections 1.2 and 1.3 offer insights into the existing cancer detection processes and their durations, respectively. Section 2 presents an overview of the research conducted in this field over the past few decades. Section 3 delineates the problem statement, providing a detailed description of the issue. Section 4 focuses on an AI-based methodology, detailing the architecture and datasets employed for the early detection of lung cancer. Section 5 showcases promising results obtained from real-time datasets. The final section presents concluding remarks.

1.1 Lung Cancer and Its Study

Lung cancer is a prevalent form of cancer that originates in the lungs, and it is responsible for a large number of cancer-related deaths worldwide. It can be categorized into two main types: small cell lung cancer (SCLC) and non-small cell lung cancer (NSCLC), with NSCLC being the most common, accounting for about 85% of cases. The primary risk factor for lung cancer is smoking, whether it is through cigarettes, pipes, or cigars. Other factors that can increase the risk of lung cancer include exposure to second-hand smoke, asbestos, radon, and air pollution. Symptoms of lung cancer can vary but may include persistent cough, chest pain, shortness of breath, hoarseness, unexplained weight loss, and fatigue. The treatment for lung cancer depends on the cancer's type and stage and may involve surgery, chemotherapy, radiation therapy, targeted therapy, and immunotherapy. Early detection is critical to improving outcomes, and lung cancer screening is recommended for high-risk groups such as current or former smokers.

1.2 Current Lung Cancer Detection Process

Detecting lung cancer involves considering various factors, including the patient's medical history, risk factors, and symptoms. However, there are some standard methods used for diagnosing lung cancer, which may include:

- Imaging tests: Imaging tests, such as chest X-rays, CT scans, and PET scans, are used to detect abnormalities in the lungs that may indicate lung cancer.
- Sputum cytology: This test involves examining mucus or phlegm expelled from the lungs to detect the presence of cancer cells.
- Biopsy: A biopsy involves removing a small piece of tissue from the lung and examining it under a microscope to detect the presence of cancer cells.
- Bronchoscopy: This procedure involves using a thin tube with a camera at the end to look inside the lungs and take tissue samples for biopsy.
- Needle aspiration: This process involves inserting a thin needle into the lung to remove a small sample of tissue for biopsy.
- Once lung cancer is diagnosed, additional tests, such as an MRI or bone scan, can be performed to determine the extent to which the cancer has spread to other parts of the body. These tests help doctors determine the most effective treatment options for patients.

1.3 Current Problems with Lung Cancer Detection Processes

The process of detecting and diagnosing lung cancer has certain limitations and challenges. One of the main challenges is the possibility of false positive or false negative results, which may lead to unnecessary additional testing or missed diagnoses. Invasive procedures such as lung biopsy and bronchoscopy carry risks and complications, and may not always yield accurate results. Lung cancer screening is currently recommended only for high-risk groups, leaving other populations at risk of missed opportunities for early detection. Additionally, access to screening and diagnostic programs may be limited in certain areas, particularly in rural or low-income areas. Finally, there is a limited number of biomarkers available for early detection of lung cancer, which underscores the need for more sensitive and specific biomarkers. Addressing these challenges and improving lung cancer detection and diagnosis will require further research and development of new technologies and approaches, as well as improving access to screening and diagnostic programs for all populations.

2 Literature Survey

The authors in their study [1], medical imaging is crucial in detecting and monitoring lung cancer in its early stages. Several imaging modalities, including X-rays, MRI, PET, CT, and molecular imaging, have been extensively studied for lung cancer detection. However, these techniques have limitations, such as the inability to classify cancer images automatically, making them unsuitable for patients with other pathologies. Thus, there is an urgent need for a sensitive and accurate approach to diagnosing lung cancer early. Deep learning is a rapidly growing field in medical imaging, with emerging applications in medical image-based and textural data modalities. Deep learning-based medical imaging tools can aid clinicians in accurately and quickly detecting and classifying lung nodules. This paper presents recent advances in deep learning-based imaging techniques for early lung cancer detection.

The scientists in their paper said [2], Lung cancer is currently the primary cause of cancer-related fatalities, and early detection and treatment are critical to a patient's survival. One of the primary obstacles to overcome is the need for an accurate diagnosis in a short period, without requiring extensive computing power. A proposed solution to this challenge is the SqueezeNodule-Net, a lightweight and precise convolutional neural network (CNN) that can quickly differentiate between benign and malignant nodules, while only needing a mid-range computing system. The model is based on the SqueezeNet, a compact CNN model, and its Fire Module, which underwent modifications in two ways and compared with other state-of-the-art models. The team utilized 888 CT scans from the LUNA16 public dataset, generating 2D 50 × 50 images of malignant and benign nodules following appropriate preprocessing. Additionally, they also created 3D images to demonstrate that the models could handle more spatial information without requiring more computing power. The SqueezeNodule-Net V1 obtained 93.2% accuracy, 94.6% specificity, and 89.2% sensitivity for 2D images, while SqueezeNodule-Net V2 achieved 94.3% accuracy, 95.3% specificity, and 91.3% sensitivity. In 3D space, SqueezeNodule-Net V1 produced 94.3% accuracy, 96.0% specificity, and 87.4% sensitivity, while SqueezeNodule-Net V2 obtained 95.8% accuracy, 96.2% specificity, and 90.2% sensitivity. Overall, the SqueezeNodule-Net V1 is 1.2–1.06 times smaller, 1.31–1.5 times faster, and has 0.8–2.5 better classification performance compared to Squeeze-Net, while SqueezeNodule-Net V2 is 1.4–1.5 times larger, 0.04–1.5 times faster, and has 0.1–2.7 times better classification performance. The innovators stated that [3] Cancer is a significant cause of human mortality worldwide, and medical professionals and researchers are actively combating the disease. According to the 2019 report from the American Cancer Society, skin cancers, lung cancers, breast cancers, prostate cancers, and brain cancers are among the leading causes of cancer-related deaths. Early detection of cancer is crucial for improving survival rates. To this end, a study proposes using deep learning algorithms based on the VEE NET architecture for detecting lung cancer. This project aims to reduce the time and error rate involved in visually examining medical images and interpreting the results manually. By implementing deep learning techniques, the proposed approach can identify the presence of lung cancer without requiring multiple consultations from different physicians. This can facilitate earlier diagnosis and prompt action to prevent further consequences in a cost-effective manner. A web application has been developed to enable hospitals to detect lung cancer from input x-ray images.

The researchers said [4] that Cancer is a disease characterized by uncontrollable cell division of abnormal cells that can spread to other organs of the body. It falls under the category of non-communicable diseases (NCDs), accounting for 71% of total deaths globally, with lung cancer being the second most commonly diagnosed cancer after breast cancer in women. The survival rate for lung cancer is just 19%. Different methods such as X-ray, CT scan, PET-CT scan, bronchoscopy, and biopsy are used for lung cancer diagnosis. However, to determine the subtype of lung cancer, histology based on tissue type H and E staining is widely used, which is done on tissue aspirated from a biopsy. Studies have revealed that the type of histology is associated with prognosis and treatment in lung cancer, highlighting the urgent need for early and accurate detection of lung cancer histology. As the treatment is dependent on the type of histology, molecular profile, and disease stage, analysing the histopathology images of lung cancer is essential. Deep learning techniques have been employed to speed up the diagnosis of lung cancer and reduce the burden on pathologists. Several studies have reported the efficacy of convolutional neural networks (CNN) in the classification of histopathological images of various cancer types, including brain, skin, breast, lung, and colorectal cancer. This study employs ResNet 50, VGG-19, Inception_ResNet_V2, and DenseNet for feature extraction and triplet loss to guide the CNN, thereby increasing inter-cluster distance and reducing intra-cluster distance in the tri-category classification of lung cancer images (normal, adenocarcinoma, and squamous cell carcinoma).

3   Problem Statement

Detecting and treating lung cancer early is critical for improving patient outcomes and reducing mortality rates. However, traditional methods of diagnosis such as chest X-rays and CT scans are time-consuming and require high levels of expertise to interpret accurately. AI-based lung cancer detection processes can play an important role in this regard. These processes use machine learning algorithms to analyse medical images of the lungs and identify suspicious areas that may be indicative of lung cancer. The algorithms can learn from vast amounts of data, making them capable of detecting patterns and features that may be difficult for human experts to identify. By utilizing AI-based lung cancer detection processes, clinicians can quickly and accurately identify areas of concern and make informed decisions about the best course of treatment. This can lead to earlier detection of lung cancer, improving patient outcomes and reducing mortality rates.

Moreover, AI-based lung cancer detection processes can reduce the workload of radiologists and other medical professionals by automating the process of identifying and analysing medical images. This can free up time for these professionals to focus on other areas of their work, such as patient care and treatment planning. Additionally, AI-based lung cancer detection processes can be more cost-effective than traditional methods of diagnosis, as they reduce the need for expensive diagnostic tests such as biopsies and invasive procedures.

In summary, AI-based lung cancer detection processes have the potential to transform the way lung cancer is diagnosed and treated. By improving the accuracy and efficiency of diagnosis, these processes can save lives and improve patient outcomes.

4   Methodologies and Its Details

Early lung cancer detection using Vgg16, Vgg19, ResNet38, and SqueezeNet methodologies involves training convolutional neural networks (CNNs) on a dataset of lung images to classify them as either cancerous or non-cancerous.

1. Dataset Preparation:

   – Collect a dataset of lung images that includes both cancerous and non-cancerous cases.

– Split the dataset into training and testing sets, ensuring a balanced distribution of cancerous and non-cancerous images.

2. Preprocessing:

– Prepare the images by resizing them to a specific input size required by the CNN architecture (e.g., 224 × 224 pixels).
– Normalize the image pixel values to a range suitable for training neural networks (usually rescaling them between 0 and 1).

3. Model Architecture:

– Vgg16 and Vgg19 are deep CNN architectures that [consist of multiple convolutional layers followed by fully connected layers.
– ResNet38 is a deeper network architecture that utilizes skip connections to alleviate the vanishing gradient problem.
– SqueezeNet is a lightweight CNN architecture designed to reduce model size and computational complexity.

4. Model Training:

– Initialize the specified CNN architecture (Vgg16, Vgg19, ResNet38, or SqueezeNet) with random weights.
– Train the model on the training dataset using a supervised learning approach.
– During training, the model learns to extract relevant features from lung images and classify them as cancerous or non-cancerous.
– The weights of the model are adjusted iteratively using an optimization algorithm like Stochastic Gradient Descent (SGD).

5. Evaluation and Testing:

– After training, evaluate the trained model's performance on the testing dataset.
– Compute evaluation metrics such as accuracy, precision, recall, and F1-score to assess the model's performance.
– Compare the performance of different models (Vgg16, Vgg19, ResNet38, SqueezeNet) to determine the most effective methodology for early lung cancer detection.

6. Hyperparameter Tuning:

– Experiment with different hyperparameters (learning rate, batch size, optimizer, etc.) to optimize model performance.
– Use techniques like cross-validation and grid search to find the best combination of hyperparameters.

7. Deployment:

– Once the model achieves satisfactory performance, it can be deployed in a real-world scenario for early lung cancer detection.
– Input lung images can be fed into the trained model, and the model will output the probability of the image being cancerous or non-cancerous.

– Medical professionals can utilize this information to aid in the diagnosis and treatment planning for lung cancer patients.

The detailed implementation of each methodology (Vgg16, Vgg19, ResNet38, SqueezeNet) may involve specific optimizations and fine-tuning steps, which could be beyond the scope of this detailed explanation.

The process of detecting and classifying lung cancer using an AI-based approach typically involves several steps. First, a dataset of lung CT images from patients with both malignant and benign nodules is collected. The images are then pre-processed to enhance the features of the nodules and ensure the accuracy of the model. Next, an AI model such as a deep convolutional neural network (CNN) is trained using the pre-processed images, adjusting the model parameters to minimize the error and evaluating its performance. Once the model is trained, it can be used to detect and classify lung nodules in new CT images by predicting the likelihood of a nodule being malignant or benign. The ultimate goal of this approach is to improve the accuracy and efficiency of lung cancer diagnosis, leading to better patient outcomes.

There are two primary types of lung cancer: non-small cell lung cancer (NSCLC) and small cell lung cancer (SCLC). Below is an in-depth explanation of each type:

- Non-Small Cell Lung Cancer (NSCLC):
  NSCLC is the most common type of lung cancer, accounting for approximately 84% of all cases. It has several subtypes, including:

  This subtype is the most prevalent and accounts for around 40% of all cases. It develops from cells that produce mucus in the airway lining. Adenocarcinoma typically grows slowly and is frequently found in the outer regions of the lungs. It's more common in non-smokers and women (Fig. 1).

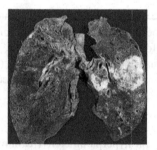

Fig. 1. Lung Situation in Adenocarcinoma

- Squamous cell carcinoma
  Squamous cell carcinoma accounts for approximately 25–30% of all lung cancers. It develops from cells that line the airways and is typically found in the central region of the lungs, near the primary bronchial tubes. Squamous cell carcinoma usually grows faster than Adenocarcinoma and is often linked to a smoking history (Fig. 2).

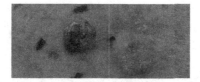

Fig. 2. Squamous Cell Carcinoma Cancer Cells

- Large cell carcinoma
  This subtype accounts for around 10–15% of all lung cancers. It can develop in any part of the lungs and grows quickly. Large cell carcinoma is more difficult to treat than adenocarcinoma or squamous cell carcinoma because it often spreads quickly and is resistant to chemotherapy (Fig. 3).

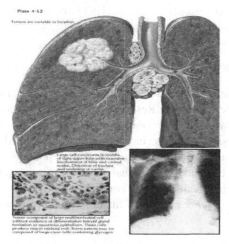

Fig. 3. Presence of Large Cell Carcinoma in Lungs

- Other rare subtypes of NSCLC include Adenosquamous Carcinoma, Pleomorphic Carcinoma, and Sarcomatoid Carcinoma. Less common types of lung cancer include small cell carcinoma, carcinoid tumour, and mesothelioma.Treatment options for NSCLC depend on the subtype and stage of cancer. Treatment may involve surgery, radiation therapy, chemotherapy, targeted therapy, or immunotherapy.
- Small Cell Lung Cancer (SCLC)
  SCLC is less common than NSCLC, accounting for about 13% of all lung cancer cases. It is an aggressive form of lung cancer that spreads quickly. SCLC is usually divided into two stages: limited stage (cancer is only in one lung) and extensive stage (cancer has spread beyond one lung). Treatment options for SCLC typically involve chemotherapy and radiation therapy. Surgery is typically not an option because the cancer has often spread beyond one lung by the time it is diagnosed (Fig. 4).

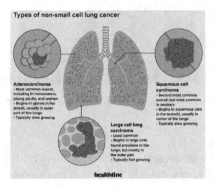

Fig. 4. Lung Situation in Small Cell Lung Cancer

In summary, lung cancer is a complex disease with multiple subtypes, each with unique characteristics and treatment options. Early detection and treatment are critical for improving patient outcomes and reducing mortality rates.

4.1 Architecture Used

Microsoft Research introduced ResNet34 in 2015 as a deep convolutional neural network architecture. It belongs to the ResNet family of models known for their ability to train much deeper networks than previous architectures without the problem of vanishing gradients. The ResNet34 architecture has 34 layers arranged into four stages. The first stage comprises a convolutional layer and a max pooling layer. The second and third stages consist of two and three residual blocks, respectively, each having two convolutional layers and an identity shortcut connection. The fourth stage comprises three residual blocks, with a higher number of filters in each layer than the previous stages (Fig. 5).

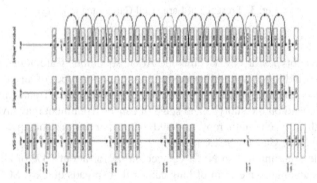

Fig. 5. ResNet34 Architecture

The primary characteristic of ResNet34 and other ResNet architectures is the use of residual connections. These connections allow the network to skip one or more layers and connect directly to a deeper layer, avoiding the problem of vanishing gradients and enabling efficient training of very deep networks. In ResNet34, identity shortcuts implement residual connections by simply adding the input of a block to its output.

The final convolutional layer's output in ResNet34 is fed into a global average pooling layer, followed by a fully connected layer with two outputs for binary classification, such as malignant vs. benign, or multiple outputs for multi-class classification, such as adenocarcinoma, squamous cell carcinoma, etc.

ResNet34 is a powerful architecture that achieves state-of-the-art performance on various image classification tasks, including lung cancer detection from CT images (Fig. 6).

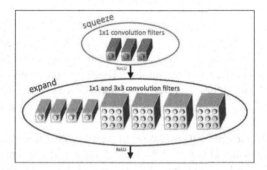

Fig. 6. SqueezeNet Architecture

SqueezeNet is an architecture for deep neural networks that was introduced by UC Berkeley researchers in 2016. Its main goal is to maintain high accuracy while being computationally efficient, which makes it well-suited for deployment on devices with limited resources, such as embedded systems or smartphones.

SqueezeNet is composed of "fire modules" that consist of a squeeze layer followed by an expand layer. The squeeze layer reduces the number of input channels using 1×1 convolutional filters, while the expand layer increases the number of output channels using a combination of 1×1 and 3×3 convolutional filters. SqueezeNet also has several pooling layers and a final convolutional layer.

One of the key innovations of SqueezeNet is the use of "bottleneck" layers, which are designed to reduce the number of parameters in the network. These layers consist of a 1×1 convolutional layer followed by a 3×3 convolutional layer, which reduces the number of input channels and then expands them again. This allows the network to use fewer parameters without sacrificing accuracy.

Overall, SqueezeNet is highly efficient, requiring fewer parameters and computations than many other deep neural network architectures. It has been shown to achieve competitive accuracy on various image classification tasks, including lung cancer detection from CT images (Fig. 7).

The VGG16 architecture was proposed by the Visual Geometry Group at the University of Oxford in 2014, and it has since become one of the most widely used and popular deep convolutional neural network architectures for image classification. It comprises 16 layers, including 13 convolutional layers and 3 fully connected layers, organized into

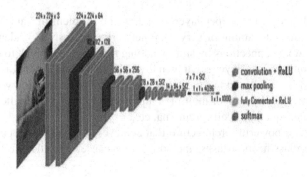

Fig. 7. VGG16 Architecture

five blocks. The first two blocks contain two convolutional layers each, while the last three blocks contain three convolutional layers each. All convolutional layers use 3 × 3 filters with a stride of 1 and same padding. The fully connected layers are arranged in two blocks, with one fully connected layer and a ReLU activation function in each block. The final fully connected layer has a SoftMax activation function and produces the network's output.

VGG16 is characterized by its use of small convolutional filters, enabling it to learn complex features from input images while maintaining a relatively low number of parameters. It also employs a large number of filters in each layer, enhancing the network's representational power. While VGG16 has achieved state-of-the-art results on numerous image classification tasks, including lung cancer detection from CT images, it is computationally expensive compared to other architectures, which may limit its utility for resource-constrained devices.

VGG19 is a deep convolutional neural network architecture that was introduced by researchers from the Visual Geometry Group (VGG) at the University of Oxford in 2014. It is very similar to VGG16, but has a slightly deeper architecture (Fig. 8).

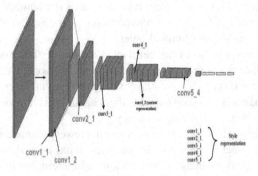

Fig. 8. VGG19 Architecture

The VGG19 architecture consists of 19 layers, including 16 convolutional layers and 3 fully connected layers. The convolutional layers are arranged in five blocks with multiple convolutional layers in each block, followed by a max pooling layer. The number of convolutional layers in each block is slightly larger than in VGG16, with the first two blocks having two convolutional layers each and the last three blocks having four convolutional layers each.

Similar to VGG16, VGG19 employs small convolutional filters to learn complex features from the input images while keeping the number of parameters relatively small. It also uses a large number of filters in each layer to increase the representational power of the network.

The fully connected layers of VGG19 are arranged in a similar way to VGG16, with two blocks of fully connected layers, each followed by a ReLU activation function. The final fully connected layer has a SoftMax activation function and produces the output of the network.

Overall, VGG19 is a robust architecture that has demonstrated state-of-the-art performance on a wide range of image classification tasks, including the detection of lung cancer from CT images. However, like VGG16, it is computationally expensive compared to some other architectures.

Dataset used to test proposed approach:
The "Lung and Colon Cancer Histopathological Images" dataset, is utilized for the detection and classification of lung cancer through AI-based methods. This dataset includes 15,000 histopathological images of lung tissue samples, with 5000 images allocated to each of the three classes: lung benign tissue, lung adenocarcinoma, and lung squamous cell carcinoma.

Each image in the dataset is an RGB image with dimensions of 512×512 pixels, representing a microscopic view of lung tissue. The images are labelled based on the tissue type, with lung benign tissue labelled as class 0, lung adenocarcinoma labelled as class 1, and lung squamous cell carcinoma labelled as class 2.

This dataset is highly suitable for the training and testing of AI-based approaches to lung cancer detection and classification, due to the large number of high-quality images that accurately represent the different types of lung tissue. Additionally, the equal distribution of samples among the three classes prevents the model from being biased towards any particular class, which is critical for precise classification.

Through the utilization of this dataset, researchers and developers can employ various AI-based approaches, such as convolutional neural networks (CNNs), to achieve accurate classification of lung tissue samples and improve the precision of lung cancer detection and diagnosis.

5   Results and Discussion

Discussed methodology is tested on Lung and Colon Cancer Histopathological Images using various methods by fine tuning their hidden layers and hyper parameters mentioned in Sect. 4. Successfully tested these methods and shown results in Figs. 9, 10, 11, 12. First part of image gives confusion matrix and second part shows top losses.

In conclusion, the analysis of confusion matrices and examination of images with the highest losses for ResNet34, SqueezeNet, VGG16, and VGG19 reveal valuable insights into the performance of these models. By scrutinizing the patterns of misclassifications

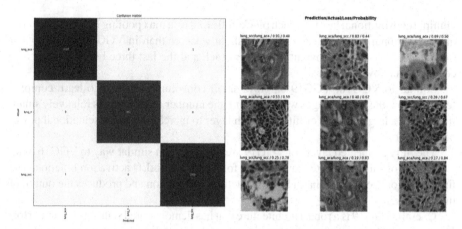

Fig. 9. Confusion Matrix and Images with top losses for ResNet34

and understanding the specific instances where the models struggle, we gain a deeper understanding of their strengths and limitations.

The confusion matrix provides a comprehensive summary of the model's predictive accuracy across different classes, highlighting areas of potential improvement. Meanwhile, exploring images with top losses allows us to pinpoint challenging cases where the models face difficulties in accurate classification.

In essence, the findings from these evaluations contribute to a more nuanced understanding of the strengths and weaknesses of ResNet34, SqueezeNet, VGG16, and VGG19. This knowledge can guide further refinement of these models, ultimately enhancing their performance and reliability in real-world applications (Fig. 13).

From the results it is evident that the developed model of ResNet34 outperformed both the works of the authors of the paper [1] where their accuracy performed at 82.74% against the developed model accuracy of 99.93%. The current improvement is by 17.19% compared to the previous referred work. Also, the developed model of SqueezeNet has also outperformed the referred papers [2] where the accuracy is at 93.2%. The currently developed accuracy stands at 96.6% which increases the previous work accuracy by 3.4% which is very significant as well. VGG16 model is working at an accuracy of 99.43% against 100% but the developed model by the author seems overfitted [3] and VGG19 works at an accuracy of 98.9% against an accuracy of 92.1%. A significant analysis is also done to observe that the best performing model developed is of ResNet34 followed by VGG16, VGG19 and SqueezeNet although the performance is much better than the current developed algorithms (Table 1).

Software used to develop prototypes are as python as programming language, GPU enabled machine to clean data, train model, test model.

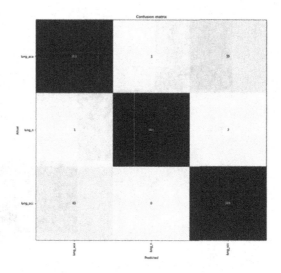

Prediction/Actual/Loss/Probability

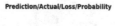

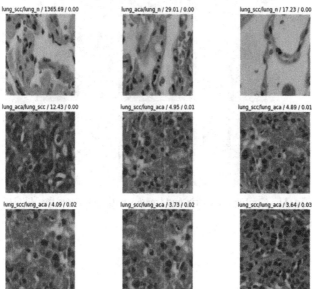

Fig. 10. Confusion Matrix and Images with top losses for SqueezeNet

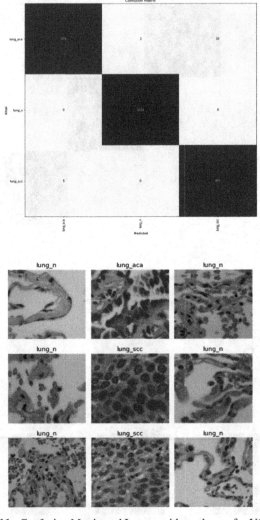

Fig. 11. Confusion Matrix and Images with top losses for VGG16

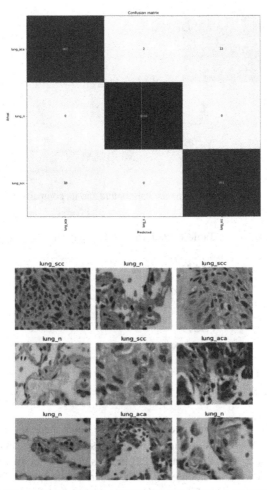

Fig. 12. Confusion Matrix and Images with top losses for VGG19

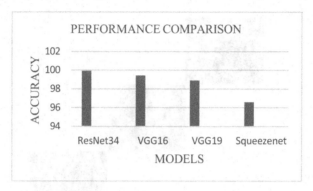

Fig. 13. Performance Parameters and its comparison

Table 1. Performance Comparison

Sr. No	Model	Accuracy
1	Resnet34	99.93%
2	VGG16	99.43%
3	VGG19	98.9%
4	SqueezeNet	96.6%

6   Conclusion

From the results, it is pretty much evident that the developed algorithms have outperformed the current used state of the art algorithms. This proves another fact that use of AI in Lung Cancer on CT scan and MRI images can provide much higher yields in early detection and without much error. This enhances the speed of the detection and also enables the doctors with the opportunity to start the medication early for a patient and help the patients save their lives.

References

1. Wang, L.: Deep learning techniques to diagnose lung cancer. Cancers **14**(22), 5569 (2022)
2. Tsivgoulis, M., Papastergiou, T., Megalooikonomou, V.: An improved SqueezeNet model for the diagnosis of lung cancer in CT scans. Mach. Learn. Appl. **10**, 100399 (2022)
3. Sheriff, S.T.M., Kumar, J.V., Vigneshwaran, S., Jones, A., Anand, J.: Lung cancer detection using VGG NET 16 architecture. In: International Conference on Physics and Energy (ICPAE 2021) (2021)
4. Baranwal, N., Doravari, P., Kachhoria, R.: Classification of histopathology images of lung cancer using convolutional neural network (CNN). arXiv:2112.13553 [eess.IV]. Desseroit, M.C., et al.: Development of a nomogram combining clinical staging with 18 F-FDG PET/CT image features in non-small-cell lung cancer stage I–III. Eur. J. Nucl. Med. Mol. Imaging **43**(8), 1477–1485 (2016)

5. van Gómez López, O., et al.: Heterogeneity in [^{18}F] Fluorodeoxyglucose positron emission tomography/computed tomography of non-small cell lung carcinoma and its relationship to metabolic parameters and pathologic staging. Mol. Imaging **13**(9), 7290 (2014)

6. Rebouças Filho, P.P., Cortez, P.C., da Silva Barros, A.C., Albuquerque, V.H.C., Tavares, J.M.R.: Novel and powerful 3D adaptive crisp active contour method applied in the segmentation of CT lung images. Med. Image Anal. **35**, 503–516 (2017)

7. Yin, P., Zhang, S., Lyu, J., Osher, S., Qi, Y., Xin, J.: Blended coarse gradient descent for full quantization of deep neural networks. Res. Math. Sci. **6**, 1–23 (2019)

8. Zhang, G., Lin, L., Wang, J.: Lung nodule classification in CT images using 3D DenseNet. J. Phys. Conf. Ser. **1827**(1), 012155 (2021). IOP Publishing

9. Zhou, S., Wu, Y., Ni, Z., Zhou, X., Wen, H., Zou, Y.: Dorefa-net: Training low bitwidth convolutional neural networks with low bitwidth gradients (2016). arXiv preprint arXiv: 1606.06160

10. Manafi-Farid, R., et al.: [18F] FDG-PET/CT Radiomics and artificial intelligence in lung cancer: technical aspects and potential clinical applications. Semin. Nucl. Med. **52**(6), 759–780 (2022). WB Saunders

11. Sajja, T., Devarapalli, R., Kalluri, H.: Lung cancer detection based on CT scan images by using deep transfer learning. Traitement du Signal **36**(4), 339–344 (2019). https://doi.org/10.18280/ts.360406

Colon Cancer Nuclei Classification with Convolutional Neural Networks

Kancharagunta Kishan Babu⬚, Bhavanam Santhosh Reddy$^{(\boxtimes)}$ ⬚, Akhil Chimma⬚, Paruchuri Pranav⬚, and Kamatam Santhosh Kumar⬚

Department of Computer Science and Engineering – AIML and IOT, Vallurupalli Nageswara Rao Vignana Jyothi Institute of Engineering and Technology, Hyderabad 500090, India
bhavanamsanthoshreddy@gmail.com
https://vnrvjiet.ac.in/

Abstract. CRC or Colorectal Cancer also called as bowel cancer is the development of cancer from colon or rectum. Detection of CRC can be very essential that can help the diagnosed with effectual treatment preventing potential loss of life. Conventional methods can be challenging because of its excessive dependence on the expert to detect accurately. This paper aims to compare results obtained from popular deep learning models such as AlexNet, GoogleNet, MobileNet, by performing on the "CRCHistoPhenotypes" dataset furthermore, inter-comparison of the same is done by applying Data Augmentation methods. Comparison is done on the basis of training time, accuracy, weighted f1 score, specificity and sensitivity. An enhancement in testing accuracy was observed, even in the case of the state-of-the-art network, GoogLeNet. It exhibited an increase of around 2.3%, achieving an impressive 80% accuracy following the utilization of data augmentation methods.

Keywords: Colon cancer classification · Deep Convolutional Neural Networks · Data Augmentation · Deep Learning

1 Introduction

Colorectal cancer is the third most common cancer in The United States. In 2023 alone, 153, 020 were diagnosed with the malady. It is the most diagnosed cancer worldwide. In 2020, about 1,880,025 people were diagnosed with CRC. It is estimated that around 52,550 deaths will result in 2023 from the US. Additionally, CRC occupies the second position in fatality standings [1]. An estimated 153,020 new CRC cases are believed to be diagnosed [2]. To overcome these fatal deities, research is needed to be performed for the most required detection in the earliest stages.

Machine learning models have been applied to detect colon cancer before. Since the study shows that one of the papers [3] is proposed for improving polyp classification based on physical examination of data. It uses an ensemble approach to model a data driven approach to improve two-way classification of colorectal cancer using logistic regression, classification trees and random forest. Since Machine learning algorithms require a proficiency in the domain it is being applied to, they aren't usually adapted and resorted to Deep learning.

© The Author(s), under exclusive license to Springer Nature Switzerland AG 2024
D. Garg et al. (Eds.): IACC 2023, CCIS 2054, pp. 376–385, 2024.
https://doi.org/10.1007/978-3-031-56703-2_30

Deep learning has much potential to make contributions in the medical field of CRC research. This can help pathologists identify and prevent loss of life in early stages. Deep learning can change the approach usually taken towards CRC research. It has been applied to CRC overtime continuing till date [4, 5]. CNN has shown a promising performance in this field.

Xu et al. [13] introduced an innovative technique employing unsupervised deep learning with autoencoders to classify cell nuclei, utilizing a softmax classifier to categorize higher-level features. Bychkov et al. [14] proposed a novel classifier that cleverly integrates convolutional and recurrent neural network architectures to enhance the classification of Colorectal cancer. Shao et al. [15] presented an alternative approach for interactive cell nuclei classification called DAPC (deep active learning with pairwise constraints). Ali Hamad's research [16] introduced a two-stage deep learning approach that combines the Fully Convolutional Regression Network (FCRN) for nuclei localization with a Convolutional Neural Network (CNN) for nuclei classification. Other models have been applied to Routine colon cancer images like GoogLeNet [7], AlexNet [8], ResNet-50 [9], MobileNet [10], RCCNet [11], SoftMax [12]. These Convolutional Neural Networks are extended deeper further by deep feature extraction and by extending the width and depth of the network [6].

The main objective of this paper is to find the deep learning model that is best suited for the Colon cancer classification on the dataset. To achieve the same, different models (AlexNet, GoogLeNet, MobileNet, RCCNet, ResNet, SoftMax) are trained on the dataset "CRCHistoPhenotypes" containing 22,444 images of four classes. Additionally, Data Augmentation is used on the dataset to train the models again to reduce the overfit percentage and improve the performance of the models. Training time, Accuracy, F1 score, Specificity, and Sensitivity are employed in comparison of models' performance and from the final results GoogLeNet is observed to have the most promising performance than the rest.

The following sections of this paper are outlined below: In Sect. 2, a thorough investigation of diverse deep convolutional architectures is presented. Section 3 provides an intricate description of the experimental setup, encompassing details about the dataset, metrics, and the application of data augmentation techniques. Section 4 is devoted to the exposition of results and an extensive analysis. Lastly, in Sect. 5, the paper concludes by summarizing the pivotal findings and insights.

2 Proposed System

Deep Learning is more often than not employed in performing classification tasks. Deep Learning models can achieve state-of-the-art accuracy bettering sometimes that of human possibility. It has a role to play in Colon Cancer Classification. Normally, there are many models to choose from for the vocation of classification. It poses a problem in choosing a model that is able to classify precisely.

In 2012, the introduction of AlexNet [8] by Krizhevsky marked a significant leap in deep learning and computer vision. It featured a 16-layer architecture with eight trainable layers, including three fully connected (FC) layers and five convolutional layers, totaling approximately sixty million trainable parameters. Notably, AlexNet introduced innovations like the ReLU activation function and dropout regularization.

To address vanishing gradient issues in deep neural networks, ResNet emerged as a solution, using residual connections. ResNet, including the popular ResNet-50 [9], had 50 layers combining convolutional and fully connected layers. While deep neural networks like ResNet were effective but resource-intensive, MobileNet [10] introduced in 2017, provided faster inference and lower memory usage, particularly suitable for resource-constrained environments. MobileNet employed depth-wise separable convolutions, featuring 30 layers for real-time applications. Additionally, SoftMax CNN IN27 [12] was introduced for histology image classification, but concerns arose about its depth for handling complex datasets.

RCCNet [11], a convolutional neural network, achieved success in colon cancer classification with over 1.5 million parameters and seven trainable layers. GoogLeNet [7] introduced inception models, using parallel convolutional filters of varying sizes efficiently within a 22-layer depth, maintaining computational efficiency and superior accuracy.

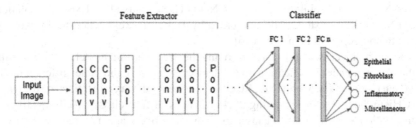

Fig. 1. CNN Architecture for Classification of Images

Figure 1 shows the CNN Architecture for classification of images, A CNN models consist of input, convolutional layers for feature extraction, pooling layers for down sampling, and fully connected layers for prediction. The specific CNN model determines the number of layers. Convolutional layers perform the essential convolution operation with kernel weight updates through backpropagation. Pooling layers reduce the output size by taking maximum, minimum, or average values. This combination identifies important image features. Fully connected layers convert the output into a 1D numerical vector for training and prediction. Predictions are compared to labels to calculate loss, updating weights in both the fully connected and convolutional layers.

During testing, CNN models process images to determine the most likely class label based on the highest probability. This paper assesses various CNN models like AlexNet [8], GoogLeNet [7], ResNet50 [9], MobileNet [10] and RCCNet [11] using metrics such as accuracy, F1 score, sensitivity, and specificity. Data augmentation techniques, including shearing, zoom transformations, and flips, are used to enhance model performance.

This study focuses on tackling this problem to identify the model that works best. All the models (AlexNet, GoogLeNet, MobileNet, RCCNet, ResNet, SoftMax) are evaluated under the same conditions and their performance is ranked based on metrics (Accuracy, F1 score, Sensitivity and Specificity). The Dataset contained nuclei patches belonging to four classes. The models are evaluated again using Data Augmentation methods on Dataset which are in turn evaluated based on their scores.

3 Experimental Setup

This section is reserved for the description of dataset, explanation of metrics used for comparison of the models and the results obtained.

In our experimental configuration, we employed TensorFlow version 2.12.0, Python version 3.8 and nVIDIA GPU K40. The image dataset is divided into a ratio of 8:2, with an 80–20 split for training and testing respectively.

3.1 Dataset

The research utilises publicly available dataset "**CRCHistoPhenotypes**", consisting of histological routine colon cancer nuclei patches [13], is used for comparison of the models. "CRCHistoPhenotypes" dataset contains 22,444 images of four classes, each represented by unique set of nuclei patches. Each image patch in the dataset has the dimensions of 32 × 32 × 3, allowing detailed analysis and classification. Four classes: Epithelial containing 7722 images, Fibroblast contains 5712 images, Inflammatory containing 6971 images and Miscellaneous 2019 images showcasing diversity and composition of the dataset. Figure 2 shows sample data where each column represent the Epithelial (7722), Fibroblast (5712), Inflammatory (6971) and Miscellaneous (2019) respectively.

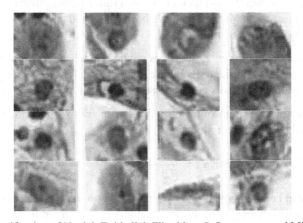

Fig. 2. Classification of Nuclei: Epithelial. Fibroblast, Inflammatory and Miscellaneous

3.2 Data Augmentation

Data augmentation comprises a range of approaches to expand a dataset by either modifying existing data instances or generating entirely new ones based on the original dataset.

During the training of machine learning models, data augmentation functions as a regularization method to counteract overfitting. The techniques which we have employed are as follows

Shear Operations. Shear operations entail altering an image by displacing or distorting its content along a specific direction, typically the x or y axis. This transformation changes the orientation of objects in the image without altering their size. It introduces variations that can help the model become more robust to different perspectives.

Zoom Transformations. Zoom transformations modify the scale or magnification of the image. They can either magnify or reduce the content of the image. Zooming helps the model by allowing a detailed learning to recognize objects at variable scales, making it more robust to variations in object size.

Horizontal and Vertical Flips. A horizontal flip creates a mirrored version of the original image, as if it were viewed in a mirror, effectively swapping the positions of objects on the left and right. A vertical flip inverts the top and bottom sections of the image. Flips help the model become invariant to changes in object orientation.

To enhance the model's performance, data augmentation techniques are applied, including shear operations with a variability range of 0.2, zoom transformations within a 0.2 range, as well as the implementation of both horizontal and vertical flips.

3.3 Metrics

Performance of the models are compared based on the following metrics: accuracy, weighted F1 score, sensitivity and specificity furthermore training time is also considered for the evaluation criteria. Metrics that have been calculated and used for the evaluation of models in this paper are as follows

Training Time. Though training time does not hold much significance in evaluating a model it is nonetheless considered a metric in this paper for the special cases where a model's other evaluation factors are high in estimation but takes much training time.

Accuracy. Accuracy in simple terms is defined as the ratio of classifications correctly done to the total number of classifications made i.e.,

$$Accuracy = \frac{TP + TN}{TP + TN + FP + FN} \tag{1}$$

Accuracy can be maintained high by placing the prediction always in the majority class label. Since, accuracy can't be practically depended upon in most of the cases, more sophisticated metrics like f1 score, precision, and recall need to be employed.

F measure. F-measure is the harmonic mean of the recall and precision. F1 score gives importance to both. F1 Score is maximum when Precision becomes equal to Recall and is used in combination with the aforementioned metrics to give a detailed picture.

$$F1Score = 2 \times \frac{precision \times Recall}{Precision + Recall} \tag{2}$$

Specificity. Specificity also called as True Negative Ratio (TNR) is the ratio of True Negatives to the total actual Negatives i.e., number of correct negative predictions. Specificity should be as high as possible.

$$TNR = \frac{TN}{TN + FP} \tag{3}$$

Sensitivity or Recall. Sensitivity also called as True Positive Ratio (TPR) is the ratio of True Positives to the total actual Positives i.e., number of correct positive predictions. Recall should be as high as possible

$$TPR = \frac{TP}{TP + FN} \tag{4}$$

4 Result Analysis

We have conducted an experiment to compare the performance of various Deep learning models like AlexNet, GoogleNet, MobileNet, RCCNet, ResNet, and Softmax whose results are tabulated below in Table 1 and Table 2. Table 2 results having been obtained by applying Data Augmentation techniques such as Flipping, Shear and Zoom transformation of images to improve the total count thereupon increasing Accuracy score (Figs. 3 and 4).

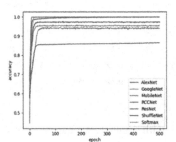 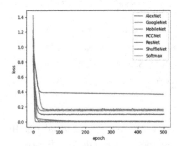

Fig. 3. Accuracy graph against Epochs   **Fig. 4.** Loss Graph against Epochs

After examining the data in Table 1, several notable conclusions can be drawn. GoogLeNet excels in terms of testing accuracy, achieving an impressive 77.7%, closely followed by AlexNet at 76.78%. Subsequently, SoftmaxCNN, RCCNet, MobileNet, and ResNet achieve accuracies of 74.27%, 73.2%, 73.56%, and 69.56%, respectively.

When considering the F1 score, GoogleNet stands out with a remarkable maximum value of 0.775, with AlexNet as a close runner-up at 0.767. GoogleNet also exhibits exceptional performance in Specificity and Sensitivity, with values of 0.927 and 0.77, surpassing the performance of the other models. In terms of training time, RCCNet emerges as the fastest, completing training in just 1363 s, with SoftmaxCNN and AlexNet following closely behind.

Table 1. Depicts the comparison of the models without implementing Data Augmentation techniques. Best scores in each field are highlighted

Model	Without Data Augmentation											
	Time (in sec)	Accuracy (in percent)			Loss		F1 Score (for unit %)		Specificity (for unit %)		Sensitivity (for unit %)	
		Train	Test	Overfit	Train	Test	Train	Test	Train	Test	Train	Test
ResNet	3456.75	**99.98%**	69.56%	30.42%	0.0004	2.83	**0.9998**	0.694	**0.9999**	0.898	**0.9998**	0.69
MobileNet	4406.86	93.93%	72.56%	21.37%	0.1635	1.02	0.9389	0.725	0.9826	0.916	0.931	0.71
RCCNet	**1363.4**	97.1%	73.2%	23.9%	0.101	0.9	0.971	0.731	0.991	0.918	0.968	0.71
SoftMax CNN	1404.75	95.61%	74.27%	**21.34%**	0.146	0.87	0.9552	0.739	0.9879	0.923	0.9474	0.72
AlexNet	1652.35	99.95%	76.78%	23.16%	0.002	2.12	0.9994	0.767	0.9998	0.923	0.9994	0.76
GoogLeNet	2663.91	99.94%	**77.7%**	22.24%	0.007	1.12	0.9995	**0.775**	0.999	**0.927**	0.9994	**0.77**

Table 2. Depicts the comparison of the models by implementing Data Augmentation techniques. Best scores in each field are highlighted

Model	With Data Augmentation											
	Time (in sec)	Accuracy (in percent)			Loss		F1 Score (for unit %)		Specificity (for unit %)		Sensitivity (for unit %)	
		Train	Test	Overfit	Train	Test	Train	Test	Train	Test	Train	Test
ResNet	10485	80.54%	75.51%	5.03%	0.497	0.65	0.8041	0.753	0.9504	0.935	0.7726	0.72
SoftMax CNN	**5575.58**	80.25%	78.14%	**2.11%**	0.523	0.58	0.7985	0.775	0.949	0.941	0.7666	0.74
RCCNet	5843.89	81.27%	79.12%	2.15%	0.496	0.56	0.8086	0.787	0.951	0.943	0.776	0.75
AlexNet	17560.9	**85.98%**	79.67%	6.31%	0.377	0.68	**0.8577**	0.795	**0.962**	0.940	**0.8367**	**0.778**
MobileNet	8331.92	83.95%	79.71%	4.24%	0.408	0.55	0.837	0.795	0.9572	**0.946**	0.8124	0.76
GoogLeNet	6571.45	84.6%	**80%**	4.6%	0.408	0.54	0.844	**0.796**	0.959	0.944	0.819	0.773

Upon comparing the final results in Table 2 with Table 1, we can discern notable improvements. GoogleNet demonstrates a testing accuracy increase of approximately 2.3%, reaching an impressive 80% accuracy. MobileNet exhibits a substantial boost in testing accuracy, surging by about 7.1% to reach 79.71%, closely followed by AlexNet, RCCNet, SoftMaxCNN, and ResNet, respectively. There is a noticeable reduction in overfitting across all models. The high sensitivity and specificity scores of the models indicate their proficiency in accurate classification across all classes.

An increase of 0.02 is observed in the sensitivity and specificity scores for GoogleNet when compared to the previous results obtained without data augmentation. GoogleNet achieves the highest F1 Score of 0.796 among the models, closely followed by MobileNet and AlexNet, both with a score of 0.795. In terms of training time, SoftMaxCNN stands out with the shortest duration, taking only 5575 s, followed by RCCNet and GoogleNet (Figs. 5 and 6).

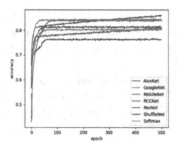

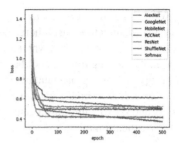

Fig. 5. Accuracy graph against Epochs   **Fig. 6.** Loss Graph against Epochs

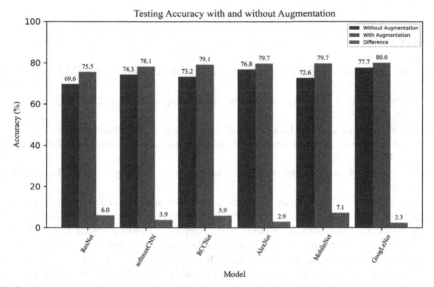

Fig. 7. Comparison of Accuracies for all models with and without Data Augmentation along with respective Overfit.

Figure 7 shows each model's testing accuracies and their respective overfit percentages. It can be seen that the difference in overfit ranges from [2.3–7.1]. Additionally, it can be observed that the testing accuracies are more when implemented by using Data Augmentation techniques than their counterparts.

5 Conclusions and Future Scope

In this paper, we have done a comparative study on a number of Convolutional Neural Network models in classification of Colon Cancer. All the models' performances are evaluated in Nuclei patches on "CRCHistoPhentotypes". This study is not only focused on comparison between different models but also between same models implemented with and without Data Augmentation. The initial phase of comparing results by traditional ways led to huge overfit which pressed us to use Data Augmentation techniques that reduced the overfit percentage drastically. Through this study it is made clear that among the architectures used here for experiment GoogleNet has the higher accuracy closely followed by AlexNet which has both next best in accuracy standings and higher F1 score, its training time cannot be overlooked.

Our upcoming approach entails leveraging GANs to create synthetic images, which we aim to utilize in image classification tasks. This strategy seeks to expand both the diversity and size of our training dataset, with the prospect of improving the performance of our classification models.

Acknowledgements. We thank Department of AIML & IOT for their generosity in providing for nVIDIA GPU K40 that was used in this specific research.

References

1. Siegel, R.L., Miller, K.D., Wagle, N.S., Jemal, A.: Cancer statistics, 2023. CA Cancer J. Clin. **73**(1), 17–48 (2023)
2. Miller, K.D., et al.: Cancer treatment and survivorship statistics, 2022. CA Cancer J. Clin. **72**(5), 409–436 (2022)
3. Xie, X., Xing, J., Kong, N., Li, C., Li, J., Zhang, S.: Improving colorectal polyp classification based on physical examination data—an ensemble learning approach. IEEE Robot. Autom. Lett. **3**(1), 434–441 (2017)
4. Xu, L., et al.: Colorectal cancer detection based on deep learning. J. Pathol. Inform. **11**(1), 28 (2020)
5. Hasan, M.I., Ali, M.S., Rahman, M.H., Islam, M.K.: Automated detection and characterization of colon cancer with deep convolutional neural networks. J. Healthc. Eng. **2022** (2022)
6. Sarwinda, D., Bustamam, A., Paradisa, R.H., Argyadiva, T., Mangunwardoyo, W.: Analysis of deep feature extraction for colorectal cancer detection. In: 4th International Conference on Informatics and Computational Sciences (ICICoS 2020), pp. 1–5. IEEE (2020)
7. Szegedy, C., et al.: Going deeper with convolutions. In: Proceedings of the IEEE Conference on Computer Vision and Pattern Recognition 2015, pp. 1–9 (2015)
8. Krizhevsky, A., Sutskever, I., Hinton, G.E: ImageNet classification with deep convolutional neural networks. Adv. Neural Inf. Process. **25** (2012)
9. He, K., Zhang, X., Ren, S., Sun, J.: Deep residual learning for image recognition. In: Proceedings of the IEEE Conference on Computer Vision and Pattern Recognition, pp. 770–778 (2016)
10. Howard, A.G., et al.: MobileNets: efficient convolutional neural networks for mobile vision applications. arXiv preprint arXiv, 1704.04861 (2017)
11. Basha, S.S., Ghosh, S., Babu, K.K., Dubey, S.R., Pulabaigari, V., Mukherjee, S.: RCCNet: an efficient convolutional neural network for histological routine colon cancer nuclei classification. In: 15th International Conference on Control, Automation, Robotics and Vision (ICARCV), pp. 1222–1227. IEEE (2018)
12. Sirinukunwattana, K., Raza, S.E.A., Tsang, Y.W., Snead, D.R., Cree, I.A., Rajpoot, N.M.: Locality sensitive deep learning for detection and classification of nuclei in routine colon cancer histology images. IEEE Trans. Med. Imaging **35**(5), 1196–1206 (2016)
13. Xu, J., et al.: Stacked sparse autoencoder (SSAE) for nuclei detection on breast cancer histopathology images. IEEE Trans. Med. Imaging **35**(1), 119–130 (2015)
14. Bychkov, D., et al.: Deep learning based tissue analysis predicts outcome in colorectal cancer. Sci. Rep. **8**(1), 3395 (2018)

15. Shao, W., Sun, L., Zhang, D.: Deep active learning for nucleus classification in pathology images. In: 15th International Symposium on Biomedical Imaging (ISBI 2018), pp. 199–202. IEEE (2018)
16. Hamad, A., Ersoy, I., Bunyak, F.: Improving nuclei classification performance in H&E stained tissue images using fully convolutional regression network and convolutional neural network. In: IEEE Applied Imagery Pattern Recognition Workshop (AIPR 2018), pp. 1–6. IEEE (2018)

Genetic Algorithm-Based Optimization of UNet for Breast Cancer Classification: A Lightweight and Efficient Approach for IoT Devices

Mohit Agarwal[1]([⊠])(iD), Amit Kumar Dwivedi[1](iD), Suneet Kr. Gupta[1](iD), Mohammad Najafzadeh[2], and Mani Jindal[3]

[1] Bennett University, Greater Noida, India
{mohit.agarwal,amit.dwivedi,suneet.gupta}@bennett.edu.in
[2] Department of Water Engineering, Graduate University of Advanced Technology, Kerman, Iran
m.najafzadeh@kgut.ac.ir
[3] CHRIST (Deemed to be University), Bangalore, India

Abstract. IoT devices are widely used in medical domain for detection of high blood sugar and life threatening disease such as cancer. Breast cancer is one of the most challenging type of cancer which not only affects women but in some cases men also. Deep learning is one of the widely used technology which provides efficient classification of cancerous lumps but it is not useful for IoT devices as the devices lack resources such as storage and computation. For the suitability in IoT devices, in this work, we are compressing UNet, the popular semantic segmentation technique, for the pixel-wise classification of breast cancer. For compressing the deep learning model, we use genetic algorithm which removes the unwanted layers and hidden units in the existing UNet model. We have evaluated the proposed model and compared with the existing model(s) and found that the proposed compression technique suppresses the storage requirement to 77.1%. Additionally, it also improves the inference time by 3.82× without compromising the accuracy. We conclude that the primary reason of inference time improvement is the requirement of less number of weight and bias by the proposed model.

Keywords: Deep Learning · UNet · Genetic Algorithm · Compression & Acceleration · Semantic Segmentation

1 Introduction

Breast cancer is the most commonly diagnosed cancer among women. In USA about 30 % of newly diagnosed cancer is Breast cancer. It is estimated in 2023 that 297,790 new cases of invasive breast cancer are expected to be diagnosed in U.S. women along with 2,800 new cases of invasive breast cancer in men [1,17].

Breast cancer can be cured easily and the chances of survival of the patient enhances, if it is detected early. Detection of the Breast cancer is done through

D. Garg et al. (Eds.): IACC 2023, CCIS 2054, pp. 386–396, 2024.
https://doi.org/10.1007/978-3-031-56703-2_31

the Breast Mammogram images. Generally, it appears in the breast in form of lump. Since number of cases of breast cancer is high, the detection of Breast cancer incurs huge load at the radiologist [10,12].

Deep learning and machine learning based approaches suppresses the overall load at the radiologist as it provides automatic detection of breast cancer cases through analysis of mammogram images. Since deep learning based approaches (Such as UNet [20], SegNet [8]) need significant computation requirement, for IoT devices it may not be suitable as the devices are small and may contain less resources. Traditional Machine Learning methods such as SVM, Random Forest, etc. are hard to be trained for image segmentation as it cannot be trained on pixel level values and need handcrafted features which are feasible for only classification purposes.

Compressed deep learning such as Compressed UNet [3] is an efficient solution for IoT devices where the redundant and hidden units are removed as their effect is insignificant on the result. Since UNet is popular method of image segmentation, we chose UNet for our work. In the proposed work, we have applied the Genetic Algorithm to compress the UNet architecture where we ensured that the performance of model is similar to original model. The meta heuristics based approach of Genetic Algorithm was chosen so that a difficult problem of choosing which filters should be eliminated can be simplified. It is done with a usage of a fitness function which helps in moving in right direction in each iteration step in case of neurons removal from the model. The contribution of our work is as follows:

- We emphasize the importance of compressed deep learning model and its applicability in IoT devices.
- We highlight that genetic algorithm is useful for compressing the existing deep learning model (For example UNet).
- We evaluate the performance of the proposed compression technique over UNet architecture.
- We create a productive method for representing the chromosome with the fitness function in a way that maximizes the compressed model's performance.

In what follows, Sect. 2, discusses the existing literature supporting this work. Section 3, discusses the proposed methodology. Section 4, discusses the experimental evaluation of this work followed by conclusion in Sect. 5.

2 Related Work

Deep learning is widely used for data classification purposes in current scenario. For the life-threatening diseases such as cancer, data classification plays a major role as it efficiently identifies the cancerous lumps and helps the doctors to start the adequate treatment of the patient.

Now a days, IoT devices are extensively used for the cancer treatment [6] as they help in classifying real-time patient data. Since the existing deep learning models needs significant resources (storage and computation) and IoT devices are often resource scarce, we need such deep learning models where the resource requirement is significantly lesser compared to existing deep learning models.

The possible way to solve this problem is to go for compress deep learning models where the unwanted layers and filters of existing deep learning models are removed. Such models require considerably less resources and therefore suited for IoT devices.

One of the first kind of model compression technique is given by Anwar et al. [7] where the number of deep neural parameters are reduced as in DNN several parameters are redundant and their participation is very less. Model Pruning [15] can be done either during training or after the training. There are following four ways through the model can be pruned such as 1) Weight Pruning, 2) Neuron Pruning, 3) Filter Pruning and 4) Layer Pruning [25]. However, in some case Pruning does not perform better compared to the original model. Another technique of model compression is quantization [9] where the number of bits required to represent the weight are reduced. Similar to previous discussed pruning model, this model can also apply before and after training operation. Another popular technique of model compression is knowledge distillation [11] where the teacher student framework is used. Teacher represents a model trained on the large data set whose knowledge is transferred for the training of smaller student dataset. However, applicability of this model only for the classification purpose limits the use of this model. In order to reduce the model storage requirement, rank based factorization model [23] is given where large size model matrix is reduced to smaller size matrix. Besides of the storage requirement, factorization of the convolution layer improves the speed of the inference process. However, as compared to previous discussed model, low rank factorization can also apply before and after training.

Some meta-heuristic based compression techniques are also used in the existing literature where genetic algorithm is used for the compression of the deep learning model. Skanda et al. [21], has classified the lung disease using compressed deep learning model using genetic algorithm. The authors tested the compressed model on Lung dataset LIDC-IDRI and found the model size is reduced by 90.3% while the performance of the model is intact. Another meta heuristic technique, Differential Evolution is used by Yar et al. [24] for attention based InceptionV3 where the author has classified the Fire images.

Ogundokun et al. [18] have proposed a IoT based diagnosis of breast cancer by sending the annotated histopathological cell images to a cloud server where they are classified using a trained CNN and results are relayed back and displayed on doctor's device for finalizing and medical recommendation.

De et al. [19] have written a systematic review of usage of IoT devices in field of breast cancer treatment. Authors have proposed usage of wearable IoT devices for the careful monitoring of mental calm state, physical activity, sleep pattern, calories burnt etc. This can help in preventing any deterioration in patient's health condition suddenly.

As seen in this section various techniques related to IoT and deep learning are prevalent these days for detection of breast cancer. Several existing model compression techniques were also discussed in this section. The following section describes the usage of deep segmentation models and its compression using GA along with its results.

3 Proposed Methodology

In this section, we will discuss about the considered deep learning model (UNet). Additionally, a discussion of Genetic Algorithm is done to compress the UNet for its suitability in IoT devices.

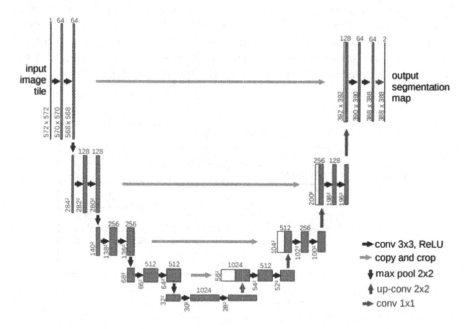

Fig. 1. U-Net [20]

U-Net [20] is well accepted technique for fast and precise medical image segmentation where a U-shaped structure (as depicted in Fig. 1) is made to optimize the network performance. There are several variants of UNet in literature (for example UNet+ [26], UNet++ [27] and UNet3+ [14] etc.,) which depend upon the U shaped structure of the U-Net. However, they still lack in performance due to higher number of parameters and unsupported floating-point operation. In addition to this, doubled feature channel in each downsampling step of UNet3+, increases the complexity of the model. There are few more techniques such as SegNet [8] have advantages over UNet as it solves the vanishing gradient problem. However, it increases the complexity and may lead to overfitting. Therefore, the above techniques are not suitable for the IoT devices as it requires considerable computing and storage resources.

For the sake of less resource requirement in IoT devices, we compress U-Net [3] architecture. For the compression purpose, we have used genetic algorithm which removes the redundant/ useless hidden units from UNet.

Introduction to Genetic Algorithm (GA) is a type of search heuristic that attempts to find near-optimal or ideal solutions to complex problems by simulating the process of natural selection. GAs are frequently employed to produce excellent answers for search and optimization problems [13,22].

GAs function by keeping an individual population of potential solutions. Every chromosome is a potential solution to the issue being resolved. Character strings, usually binary digits (0 and 1), are used to encode the chromosomes. The step by step description of Genetic Algorithm is given in the Fig. 2 which mainly comprises three operations: 1) Selection, 2) Crossover and 3) Mutation. In what follows, the genetic algorithm is described. The randomly generated chromosomes are presented in Fig. 3. In the proposed work, the length of the chromosome is constant which is equal to the number of hidden units in UNet architecture.

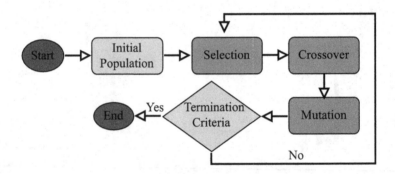

Fig. 2. Genetic Algorithm

Fitness function is a key element of genetic algorithm (GA), a class of evolutionary algorithms applied to optimization and search problems. A candidate's or individual's possible solution's effectiveness in resolving the issue at hand is assessed using the fitness function. The primary goal of fitness function is to give each potential solution a numerical value, also referred to as the fitness score or fitness value. In the proposed fitness function, there are two objective 1) minimization of hidden units in UNet 2) accuracy of the UNet. By comprising these two objectives with weighted sum approach is described as follows (refer Eq. 1):

$$\text{Fitness score} = W_1 \left(1 - \frac{\Psi}{\Phi}\right) + W_2 \times \text{Accuracy} \tag{1}$$

where $\Psi \leq \Phi$ and $\sum_{i=1}^{2} W_i = 1$.

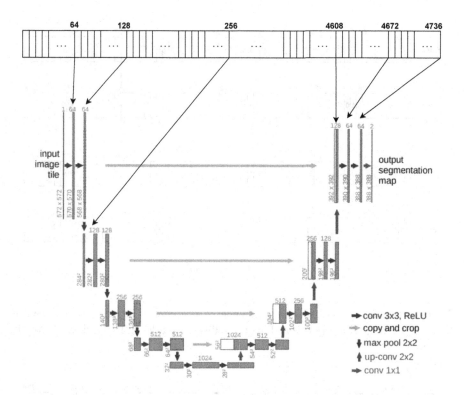

Fig. 3. Chromosome representation

Here Ψ is the number of hidden neurons in compressed model and Φ is the number of hidden neurons in the original UNet model. W_1 and W_2 are weight-age given to two objectives of model compression and accuracy measures.

Initial Population is the set of chromosomes chosen at random is the starting point for the GA. The three genetic operators selection, crossover, and mutation are then applied iteratively to improve the population.

Selection is the process of choosing chromosome who want to be parents by the selection operator from the current population. The most physically fit people are more likely to be selected as parents. In the proposed study we have selected Roulette Wheel algorithm [16] for selection.

Crossover is the process where two parent individuals are combined to make two kid individuals using the crossover operator. To accomplish this, portions of the parents' chromosomes are switched as shown in Fig. 4.

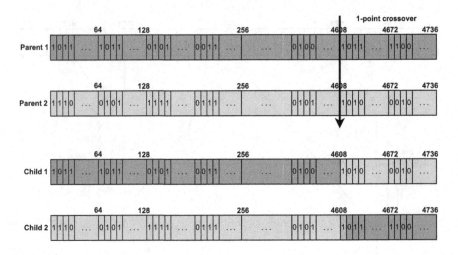

Fig. 4. Crossover

Mutation is the process of modifies each chromo genes at random as shown in Fig. 5 using mutation operator. This contributes to adding fresh diversity to the populace.

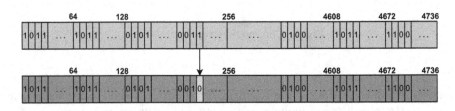

Fig. 5. Mutation

4   Results and Discussions

Utilizing the Python programming language, UNet training and compression tests were conducted on an NVIDIA DGX v100 processor. For comparison, we also took Mini SegNet [2] model. Breast ultrasound image dataset is utilized to test the compressed UNet using the genetic algorithm.

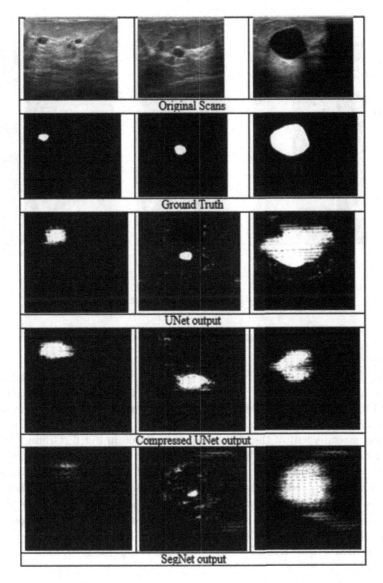

Fig. 6. Comparison among various segmentation techniques (a) Original ultrasound images, (b) ground truth, (c) output by UNet, (d) Output by compressed UNet (proposed method), and (e) Output by SegNet

It is well known that analysis of ultrasound image(s) of patients are the possible way for Breast cancer detection. So, we have collected the breast ultrasound image dataset for the experiments [5]. The dataset consists ultrasound images of 600 female patients with age range from 25 to 75 years old.

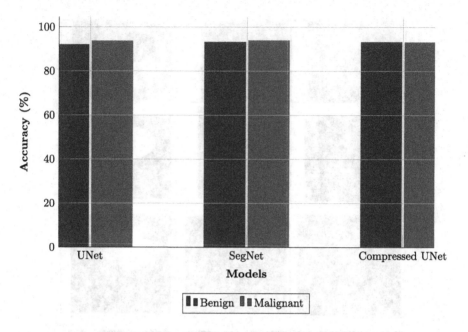

Fig. 7. Model vs. Accuracy

The dataset was developed in the year 2018 which consists of 780 mono-chrome images of an average size of 500 * 500 pixels and the images are cate-gorized into three classes, 1) normal, 2) benign, and 3) malignant. The sample images of different classes are presented in Fig. 6 (Original Scans). The more accurate measurement of the above classes are given in Fig. 6 (Ground Truth).

For experimental work, the dataset is divided into train and test with the ratio 80:20. During the experiment, we found that the Compressed UNet model outperforms compared to existing models such as UNet and MiniSegnet [4] as shown in Table 1. Inference time is the time taken by the model to produce the segmented output of 10 test images. Compared to UNet, the considered compressed model takes 93489 KB less storage space. In addition to this, the proposed model takes 8.15 s less inference time compared to UNet.

Table 1. Comparison of storage space and inference time

Model	Size (in KB)	Inference Time (in sec)
UNet	121311	11.03
Mini SegNet	21433	8.91
Compressed UNet	27822	2.88

The performance of the proposed compressed model and models used in comparison is shown in the Fig. 6. Using this figure, we can see that even after the compressing of the UNet model by 4.36x (from Table 1), the segmentation results are similar. From the Fig. 7, it is clear that the proposed model gives similar accuracy even after compressing the existing UNet Model.

5 Conclusions

Deep learning is an efficient way to detect Breast cancer from the Mamogram images. However, it is not suitable for IoT devices as it requires significant computing and storage resources. In this work, we have given an efficient model for Breast cancer detection using IoT devices. We have shown that the proposed model is efficient compared to existing models through experiments. In the proposed work, we have used UNet architecture for classification and applied genetic algorithm for compression of UNet architecture. From the obtained results, it has been observed that 78% compression has been achieved with 3.82x improvement in the inference time without compromising the accuracy. As a future work, the same methodology can be applied for compression and acceleration of deep neural network architecture.

References

1. Breast cancer statistics. https://www.breastcancer.org/facts-statistics. Accessed 01 Nov 2023
2. GitHub - imlab-uiip/keras-segnet: SegNet model implemented using keras framework – github.com. https://github.com/imlab-uiip/keras-segnet. Accessed 08 Nov 2023
3. Agarwal, M., Gupta, S.K., Biswas, K.K.: Plant leaf disease segmentation using compressed UNet architecture. In: Gupta, M., Ramakrishnan, G. (eds.) PAKDD 2021. LNCS (LNAI), vol. 12705, pp. 9–14. Springer, Cham (2021). https://doi.org/10.1007/978-3-030-75015-2_2
4. Agarwal, M., Gupta, S.K., Biswas, K.K.: A compressed and accelerated SegNet for plant leaf disease segmentation: a differential evolution based approach. In: Karlapalem, K., et al. (eds.) PAKDD 2021. LNCS (LNAI), vol. 12714, pp. 272–284. Springer, Cham (2021). https://doi.org/10.1007/978-3-030-75768-7_22
5. Al-Dhabyani, W., Gomaa, M., Khaled, H., Fahmy, A.: Dataset of breast ultrasound images. https://www.kaggle.com/datasets/aryashah2k/breast-ultrasound-images-dataset/data, https://doi.org/10.1016/j.dib.2019.104863
6. Albino de Queiroz, D., André da Costa, C., Aparecida Isquierdo Fonseca de Queiroz, E., Folchini da Silveira, E., da Rosa Righi, R.: Internet of things in active cancer treatment: a systematic review. J. Biomed. Inform. **118**, 103814 (2021). https://doi.org/10.1016/j.jbi.2021.103814, https://www.sciencedirect.com/science/article/pii/S153204642100143X
7. Anwar, S., Hwang, K., Sung, W.: Structured pruning of deep convolutional neural networks. ACM J. Emerg. Technol. Comput. Syst. (JETC) **13**(3), 1–18 (2017)
8. Badrinarayanan, V., Kendall, A., Cipolla, R.: SegNet: a deep convolutional encoder-decoder architecture for image segmentation. IEEE Trans. Pattern Anal. Mach. Intell. **39**(12), 2481–2495 (2017)

9. Balzer, W., Takahashi, M., Ohta, J., Kyuma, K.: Weight quantization in Boltzmann machines. Neural Netw. **4**(3), 405–409 (1991)
10. Barrios, C.H.: Global challenges in breast cancer detection and treatment. Breast **62**, S3–S6 (2022)
11. Buciluă, C., Caruana, R., Niculescu-Mizil, A.: Model compression. In: Proceedings of the 12th ACM SIGKDD International Conference on Knowledge Discovery and Data Mining, pp. 535–541 (2006)
12. Dar, R.A., Rasool, M., Assad, A., et al.: Breast cancer detection using deep learning: datasets, methods, and challenges ahead. Comput. Biol. Med. 106073 (2022)
13. Gen, M., Lin, L.: Genetic algorithms and their applications. In: Pham, H. (ed.) Springer Handbook of Engineering Statistics, pp. 635–674. Springer, London (2023). https://doi.org/10.1007/978-1-4471-7503-2_33
14. Huang, H., et al.: UNet 3+: a full-scale connected UNet for medical image segmentation (2020)
15. Li, X.B., Sweigart, J., Teng, J., Donohue, J., Thombs, L.: A dynamic programming based pruning method for decision trees. INFORMS J. Comput. **13**(4), 332–344 (2001)
16. Lipowski, A., Lipowska, D.: Roulette-wheel selection via stochastic acceptance. Phys. A **391**(6), 2193–2196 (2012)
17. Nassif, A.B., Talib, M.A., Nasir, Q., Afadar, Y., Elgendy, O.: Breast cancer detection using artificial intelligence techniques: a systematic literature review. Artif. Intell. Med. **127**, 102276 (2022)
18. Ogundokun, R.O., Misra, S., Douglas, M., Damaševičius, R., Maskeliūnas, R.: Medical internet-of-things based breast cancer diagnosis using hyperparameter-optimized neural networks. Future Internet **14**(5), 153 (2022)
19. de Queiroz, D.A., da Costa, C.A., de Queiroz, E.A.I.F., da Silveira, E.F., da Rosa Righi, R.: Internet of things in active cancer treatment: a systematic review. J. Biomed. Inform. **118**, 103814 (2021)
20. Ronneberger, O., Fischer, P., Brox, T.: U-net: convolutional networks for biomedical image segmentation. In: Navab, N., Hornegger, J., Wells, W.M., Frangi, A.F. (eds.) MICCAI 2015, Part III. LNCS, vol. 9351, pp. 234–241. Springer, Cham (2015). https://doi.org/10.1007/978-3-319-24574-4_28
21. Skandha, S.S., Agarwal, M., Utkarsh, K., Gupta, S.K., Koppula, V.K., Suri, J.S.: A novel genetic algorithm-based approach for compression and acceleration of deep learning convolution neural network: an application in computer tomography lung cancer data. Neural Comput. Appl. **34**(23), 20915–20937 (2022)
22. Sohail, A.: Genetic algorithms in the fields of artificial intelligence and data sciences. Ann. Data Sci. **10**(4), 1007–1018 (2023)
23. Tan, H., Cheng, B., Wang, W., Zhang, Y.J., Ran, B.: Tensor completion via a multi-linear low-n-rank factorization model. Neurocomputing **133**, 161–169 (2014)
24. Yar, H., Hussain, T., Agarwal, M., Khan, Z.A., Gupta, S.K., Baik, S.W.: Optimized dual fire attention network and medium-scale fire classification benchmark. IEEE Trans. Image Process. **31**, 6331–6343 (2022)
25. Yeom, S.K., et al.: Pruning by explaining: a novel criterion for deep neural network pruning. Pattern Recogn. **115**, 107899 (2021)
26. Zhang, T.T., Jin, P.J.: Segmentation is tracking: Spatial-temporal map vehicle trajectory reconstruction and validation. IEEE Trans. Intell. Transp. Syst. (2023)
27. Zhou, Z., Siddiquee, M.M.R., Tajbakhsh, N., Liang, J.: UNet++: redesigning skip connections to exploit multiscale features in image segmentation. IEEE Trans. Med. Imaging **39**(6), 1856–1867 (2019)

Classification of Colorectal Cancer Tissue Utilizing Machine Learning Algorithms

N. Sai Satwik Reddy⬥, A. Venkata Siva Manoj(✉)⬥, and V. Sowmya⬥

Amrita School of Artificial Intelligence, Amrita Vishwa Vidyapeetham,
Coimbatore, India
addalavenmanoj@gmail.com, v_sowmya@cb.amrita.edu

Abstract. In this study, we propose a cost-effective computer-aided detection system based on machine learning for the classification of colorectal cancer tissues. Colorectal cancer stands as the third most prevalent cancer globally and is the second leading cause of malignancy-related deaths. The proposed computer-aided detection system involves partitioning each image out of 7180 histopathological images into 16 equal-sized blocks. Subsequently, features are extracted from each block of image in RGB (red, green, blue), HSV (hue, saturation, value), and L*a*b* color spaces. The extracted features include regional and gray-level co-occurrence matrix features. Following the extraction, these features undergo scaling to eliminate outliers before being input into a machine learning classifier. The performance of the machine learning models is enhanced by optimizing the hyperparameters of the models. Notably, CatBoost outperformed all other models, achieving an exceptional accuracy of 95.19%. This remarkable accuracy indicates CatBoost as a promising model for the task of colorectal cancer tissue classification.

Keywords: Colorectal cancer · Histopathological images · Gray level co-ocurrence matrix · Feature extraction · Machine learning · Image processing

1 Introduction

Colorectal cancer (CRC), one of the most formidable types of malignancy, originates in the colon or rectum, components of the digestive system responsible for processing and expelling waste [1]. According to the World Health Organization (WHO), it is reported as the third most prevalent form of cancer globally, constituting around 10% of total cancer diagnoses and ranking as the second primary contributor to cancer-related fatalities across the globe [2]. People with certain hereditary syndromes, like familial adenomatous polyposis or lynch syndrome, are associated with a higher risk of developing this disorder [3]. It is primarily diagnosed in the elderly population, with most instances occurring in subjects aged 50 and older [4].

A few commonly observed signs of CRC include rectal bleeding, constipation, persistent diarrhea, anemia, cramps, and discomfort in the abdomen [5]. The

D. Garg et al. (Eds.): IACC 2023, CCIS 2054, pp. 397–409, 2024.
https://doi.org/10.1007/978-3-031-56703-2_32

probability of developing CRC is elevated with smoking and alcohol consumption [6]. Colorectal cancer progresses through five stages, each indicating the extent of the disease. In Stage 0, abnormal cells are only in the innermost lining of the colon or rectum. Stage I marks the invasion into the deeper layers of the colon or rectal wall. As the cancer advances to Stage II, it may involve further growth into nearby tissues. In Stage III, the cancer reaches the lymph nodes, while Stage IV is characterized by the spread to distant organs such as the liver or lungs [7]. Timely detection and appropriate intervention become increasingly critical as the cancer progresses through these stages [8].

Various methods are employed to diagnose CRC, ranging from non-invasive stool tests such as the guaiac fecal occult blood test (gFOBT), fecal immuno-chemical test (FIT), and FIT-DNA, to visual examinations such as sigmoi-doscopy and colonoscopy. Stool tests can detect blood or DNA markers, prompt-ing further investigation if positive. Sigmoidoscopy, which focuses on the lower colon, is recommended every 5 or 10 years. Colonoscopy, which examines the entire colon, is advised every 10 years and has proven effective in reducing CRC risks. Virtual colonoscopy, utilizing computed tomography (CT) scans, provides detailed images but may miss small polyps [9].

The above mentioned diagnostic methods can be expensive, hence there is a need for a more cost-effective computer-aided detection (CAD) system for detecting CRC [10]. In a CAD system for CRC, various appropriate features can be extracted from histopathological images and then input into machine learning (ML) models for the classification of CRC. This approach is highly beneficial for the early detection of CRC and is also economic.

In this work, we propose an effective CAD system for the precise classifi-cation of tissue classes of CRC. It involves filtering histopathological images to reduce noise. Subsequently, these images undergo conversion into two distinct color spaces and are partitioned into 16 blocks of equal size to facilitate fea-ture extraction. Breaking histopathological images into equal-sized blocks for feature extraction is crucial for localized analysis, as it allows for the extraction of features in distinct regions of interest. In histopathological images, certain structures or anomalies may only be present in specific regions, and analyzing these regions separately can provide more accurate information.

This approach improves computational efficiency through parallel process-ing, adapts to image variability, enhances sensitivity to local changes, and boosts accuracy in feature localization. Following this, region properties and gray-level co-occurrence matrix (GLCM) features are extracted from the filtered histopathological images and input into ML algorithms for CRC tissue classifi-cation. The identification of the most suitable ML model for this classification task is determined through a comprehensive comparative analysis.

The rest of the paper is organized as follows: Sect. 2 provides a concise review of the related works. Section 3 gives a brief description of the dataset used, and Sect. 4 provides a detailed overview of the proposed approach. Section 5 illustrates the results, followed by the conclusion and future scope in Sect. 6.

2   Literature Survey

Very few works have proposed ML-based methods integrated with image datasets for CRC classification, but most of the works have utilized deep learning techniques for this task. Three-dimensional GLCM features are extracted and fed into ML algorithms for detecting CRC in [11]. In [12], differential-box-counting method is utilized to extract features from the histopathological features and ML models are employed for the classification task. HSV color space and multi-layer perceptron are employed for image processing and detection of CRC [13]. The method proposed in [14] automates colorectal cancer detection and grading by segmenting regions of interest, extracting features normalized with Z scores, and using an SVM classifier to detect cancer. This method resulted in an accuracy of 81%. A dataset containing 5000 histopathological images is employed and six distinct sets of features are extracted from the images for the CRC classification task [15]. Histogram of oriented gradients, statistical moments based on color components, and haralick features are extracted and fed into an ensemble voting classifier comprising different variants of support vector machines as base models [16]. In [17], multiple texture based features are extracted from the histopathological images and fed into ML classifier to classify into three types of tissue classes. Pre-processing of biomedical data is a crucial step before classifying the disorder [18].

The histopathological images are extracted from 420 subjects and fed into the Visual Geometry Group-16 (VGG-16) deep neural network model to predict the presence or absence of CRC [19]. [20] provides a comprehensive overview of deep learning methods utilized for CRC classification. Inception V3 deep neural network is employed to distinguish between healthy and CRC positive subjects in [21]. ResNet-50 model is utilized to distinguish between 8 tissue classes of CRC in [22]. Four convolutional neural networks (CNNs), namely ResNet-101, Inception-v3, DenseNet-161, and ResNeXt-50, are employed in [23]. Additionally, two ensemble deep learning models are created using the four mentioned CNNs to classify CRC tissues. [24] investigated a transfer learning approach that integrates DenseNet169 with SVM (Radial Basis Function kernel) for the classification of 8 tissue classes in CRC. [25] also employed VGG-16 model for classification of CRC tissues. [26] focusses on the integration of K-Means based morphological segmentation for effective image segmentation and VGGNet-16 for accurate classification of the tissue classes. Capsule network model is employed to classify different types of breast cancer in [27]. U-Net, proposed in [28], achieved better accuracy compared to SegAN and SegNet for both skin and brain tumor classification. In [29], an unsupervised deep learning method is utilized to extract features from biomedical images, and K-means clustering is employed for the classification of various diseases.

Understanding the internal decision-making process of the deep learning models is challenging due to their black box nature. The exploration of region properties extracted from histopathological images for colorectal cancer (CRC) tissue classification has hitherto been unexplored in existing methodologies. This study explores the potential of region properties in conjunction with GLCM features to capture patterns and trends in images for the classification task. Localized image analysis is beneficial in capturing underlying patterns within image blocks, enhancing their utility for classification purposes.

3   Dataset

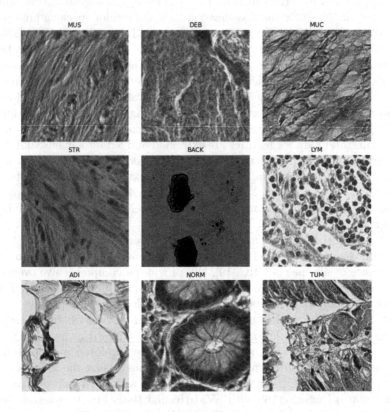

Fig. 1. Sample images of the 9 tissue classes.

CRC-VAL-HE-7K [30] is the publicly accessible dataset used in this study. This dataset comprises 7180 image patches obtained from 50 subjects suffering from CRC of type adenocarcinoma. These image patches are extracted from hematoxylin and eosin-stained histological images of human colorectal cancer (CRC) and normal tissue. All these histopathological images are provided by the tissue bank of the National Center for Tumor Diseases (NCT, Heidelberg, Germany). The dimensions of each image are 224 pixels by 224 pixels, with a spatial resolution of 0.5 microns per pixel. These images exist in the RGB color space. The tissue classes and the corresponding number of image patches in the dataset for each class are illustrated in the Table 1. Sample images of each tissue class are depicted in the Fig. 1.

Table 1. Description of Tissue Classes

S.No	Tissue Class Name	Number of image patches
1	Adipose (ADI)	1338
2	Background (BACK)	847
3	Debris (DEB)	339
4	Lymphocytes (LYM)	634
5	Mucus (MUC)	1035
6	Muscle (MUS)	592
7	Normal colon mucosa (NORM)	741
8	Cancer-associated stroma (STR)	421
9	Colorectal adenocarcinoma epithelium (TUM)	1233

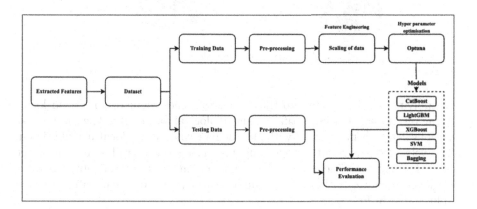

Fig. 2. Proposed pipeline for the classification of nine tissue classes.

4   Methodology

RGB images are converted into HSV and L*a*b* color spaces. Subsequently, these converted images are segmented into 16 blocks of equal size. The features are then extracted from these image blocks and fed into the ML classifiers, followed by the performance assessment of the models to find the best ML classifier for this classification task. A schematic block diagram of the proposed methodology is presented in the Fig. 2.

4.1   Filtering

The image patches in the dataset likely exhibit noise due to inherent histological variations in tissue composition, potential staining artifacts, biological variability within tissues, differences in the imaging process, and the extraction of image patches from larger histological images. The spatial resolution of 0.5 microns per pixel and the microscopic nature of the images may also contribute to fine-scale noise.

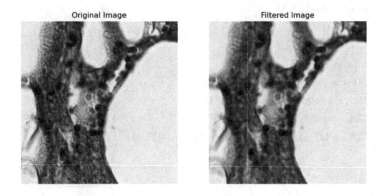

Fig. 3. Illustration of a sample filtered image.

Applying a median filter to these image patches reduces noise from histological variations, staining artifacts, and biological variability. The filter works by replacing each pixel value with the median value in its local neighborhood, effectively smoothing out outliers and preserving the overall structure of the image. It smoothens fine-scale noise, enhancing image clarity for robust analysis of colorectal cancer pathology. A sample histopathological image after filtering is illustrated in Fig. 3.

4.2   Feature Extraction

The image patches undergo conversion into the HSV and L*a*b* color spaces before the extraction of features. Fig. 4 represents the sample image in all three color spaces. Each image patch in every color space, initially sized at 224 pixels by 224 pixels, is subsequently partitioned into 16 blocks of uniform size. This partitioning is helpful in capturing the pattern more accurately. The process of feature extraction is explicitly demonstrated in the Fig. 5.

The two sets of features extracted from these image blocks are outlined below:

– **GLCM features**: GLCM features quantify spatial relationships within an image, offering insights into texture patterns through parameters such as contrast, homogeneity, dissimilarity, and energy. These four GLCM features are extracted from the images.
– **Region features**: Region features are distinctive characteristics, such as rectangularity, elongation, convexity, compactness, and solidity from specific areas of an image. These five region features are extracted from the image blocks for the further classification tasks.

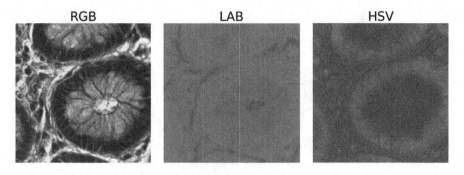

Fig. 4. Illustration of the histopathological image patch in RGB, L*a*b*, and HSV color spaces.

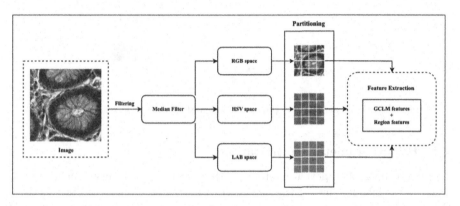

Fig. 5. Illustration of flow diagram for feature extraction.

4.3 Feature Scaling

The standard scaler is a crucial tool in data preprocessing for ML, facilitating feature scaling by transforming the data to have a mean of 0 and a standard deviation of 1. This ensures that features with different scales contribute equally to the model training process, preventing undue influence from variables with larger magnitudes. The formula for standard scaling is expressed as:

$$\text{Standardized Value}(x') = \frac{x - \mu}{\sigma}$$

where x is the original value, μ is the mean of the feature, and σ is its standard deviation.

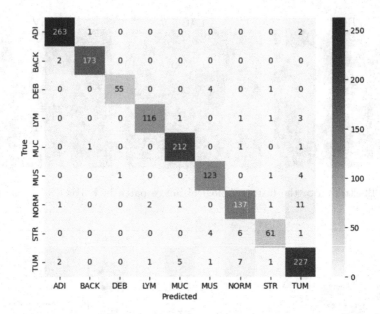

Fig. 6. Illustration of the confusion matrix of CatBoost model.

4.4 Hyperparameter Optimization

The fine-tuning of hyperparameters of ML classifiers is a very crucial step to enhance the effectiveness of the models for the classification tasks. In this work, Optuna library is employed to find the best set of hyperparameters for each ML model. Optuna finds the best hyperparameters for ML classifiers via an optimization process that systematically searches the hyperparameter space, aiming to minimize or maximize a predefined objective function that indicates the model's performance.

4.5 Classification

The ML models considered in this study for this multi-class classification problem are as follows:

- Categorical Boosting Classifier (CatBoost)
- Light gradient-boosting machine (LightGBM)
- Extreme Gradient Boosting Classifier (XGBoost)
- Support Vector Machines (SVM)
- Bootstrap Aggregation Classifier (Bagging)

CatBoost is specifically designed to handle categorical features effectively, making it robust and efficient. XGBoost and LightGBM are gradient boosting algorithms that excel in handling complex datasets, with XGBoost known for its scalability and LightGBM for its efficient training speed. SVMs are powerful classifiers that separate data points in a hyperplane, maximizing the margin between different classes. Bagging classifier is an ensemble technique that combines predictions from multiple models, reducing variance and improving overall performance. The test data and training data are in a 20:80 proportion.

4.6   Evaluation Metrics

The error metrics used in this work to evaluate the performance of the ML models are illustrated in the Table 2.

Table 2. Error Metrics for performance assessment of the ML models

S.No	Error metric	Formula
1	Accuracy	$\dfrac{TP + TN}{TN + FP + TP + FN}$
2	Precision	$\dfrac{TP}{TP + FP}$
3	Recall	$\dfrac{TP}{TP + FN}$
4	F1 score	$\dfrac{2 \times \text{Precision} \times \text{Recall}}{\text{Precision} + \text{Recall}}$

where TP denotes true positives, TN represents true negatives, FP is false positives, and FN denotes false negatives.

5   Results and Discussions

The optimal set of hyperparameters obtained using Optuna for each model is presented in Table 3. These optimized hyperparameters are utilized to improve the classification performance of the ML models. Various evaluation metrics computed for the performance assessment of ML models are presented in Table 4. The CatBoost model outperformed the other ML models achieving an impressive accuracy of 95.19%. The performance of LightGBM, XGBoost, and SVM is satisfactory. The Bagging classifier performed poorly and resulted in the lowest accuracy of 87.33%.

The number of true positives and true negatives is very high in the confusion matrix presented in Fig. 6, indicating the exceptional performance of CatBoost in classifying the types of CRC tissues. The performance of CatBoost is highlighted by correctly classifying 1367 out of 1436 test samples. The performance comparison of the ML models is depicted in Fig. 7.

A significant separation among the classes is observed in the t-Distributed Stochastic Neighbor Embedding (t-SNE) plot in the Fig. 8. Receiver operating characteristic (ROC) curves are presented in the Fig. 9. Steeper ROC curves with an area under the curve (AUC) equal to 1 indicate that the CatBoost model is exceptional at distinguishing between classes.

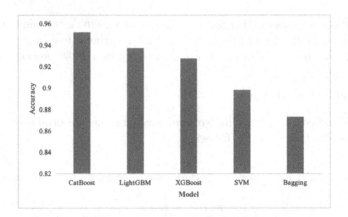

Fig. 7. Illustration of the performance comparison of models.

Table 3. Illustration of optimized hyperparameters used to enhance the performance of the ML models.

Model	Hyperparameters	Constants
CatBoost	'auto_class_weights': 'None'	'border_count': 55, 'l2_leaf_reg': 3.56, 'depth': 6, 'learning_rate': 0.09
LightGBM	-	'lambda_l1': 0.005, 'lambda_l2': 5.43e-05, 'num_leaves': 189, 'feature_fraction': 0.5, 'bagging_fraction': 0.84, 'bagging_freq': 3, 'min_child_samples': 79, 'n_estimators': 165, 'max_depth': 5, 'learning_rate': 0.18
XGBoost	'booster': 'gbtree'	'gamma': 0.193, 'subsample': 0.70, 'colsample_bytree': 0.95, 'max_depth': 3, 'learning_rate': 0.27
SVM	'kernel': 'poly'	'C': 3.55, 'degree': 2, 'gamma': 6.57
Bagging	-	'n_estimators': 230, 'max_samples': 0.95, 'max_features': 0.35

The exceptional results obtained indicate that GLCM and regional features, extracted through localized analysis of histopathological images, can accurately identify latent trends within the images and effectively distinguish between different colorectal tissue classes using machine learning algorithms.

The performance of the proposed approach can be further improved by conducting a deeper localized analysis of the histopathological images to capture the underlying patterns more effectively. Additionally, exploring the potential of other features, such as Hu moments, can enhance the robustness of the methodology presented in this work.

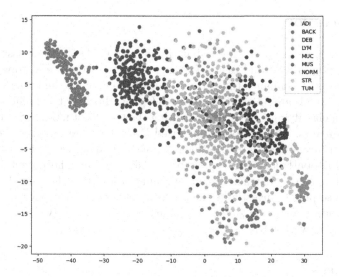

Fig. 8. The t-SNE visualization of the test data.

Table 4. Performance Evaluation of the ML models

Model	Evaluation Metrics			
	Accuracy	Precision	Recall	F1 score
CatBoost	**0.9519**	**0.9520**	**0.9519**	**0.9518**
LightGBM	0.9373	0.9371	0.9373	0.9362
XGBoost	0.9276	0.9271	0.9276	0.9266
SVM	0.8983	0.8992	0.8983	0.8985
Bagging	0.8733	0.8833	0.8733	0.8684

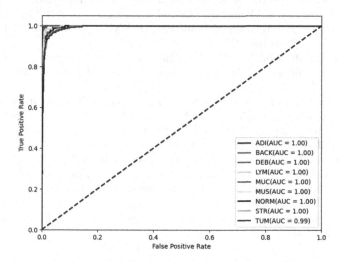

Fig. 9. Illustration of the ROC-AUC plot of CatBoost model.

6   Conclusion

In this paper, we propose an ML-based, effective CAD for the classification of CRC, utilizing GLCM and region features extracted from the histopathological image records. To enhance the performance of the models, the hyperparameters of the ML models are fine-tuned using the Optuna library. The highest accuracy achieved in classifying CRC is 95.19% using the CatBoost model with fine-tuned hyperparameters. The proposed ML-based CAD is accurate and cost-effective.

In the future, we can enhance this research by expanding the dataset, acquiring more histopathological image records, and exploring the potential of other features that can be extracted from the images and used for the classification task. We also plan to investigate the potential of advanced deep learning models, such as vision transformers, convolutional neural networks (CNNs), and recurrent neural networks (RNNs).

References

1. Ajay, M., Manvjeet, K., et al.: Computer-aided-diagnosis in colorectal cancer: a survey of state of the art techniques. In: 2016 International Conference on Inventive Computation Technologies (ICICT), vol. 1, pp. 1–6. IEEE (2016)
2. Marmol, I., Sanchez-de-Diego, C., Pradilla Dieste, A., Cerrada, E., Rodriguez Yoldi, M.J.: Colorectal carcinoma: a general overview and future perspectives in colorectal cancer. Int. J. Mol. Sci. **18**(1), 197 (2017)
3. Galiatsatos, P., Foulkes, W.D.: Familial adenomatous polyposis. Off. J. Am. Coll. Gastroenterol. ACG **101**(2), 385–398 (2006)
4. Haraldsdottir, S., Einarsdottir, H.M., Smaradottir, A., Gunnlaugsson, A., Halfda-narson, T.R.: Colorectal cancer-review. Laeknabladid **100**(2), 75–82 (2014)
5. John, S.K.P., George, S., Primrose, J.N., Fozard, J.B.J.: Symptoms and signs in patients with colorectal cancer. Colorectal Dis. **13**(1), 17–25 (2011)
6. Zheng, L., Eniola, E., Wang, J.: Machine learning for colorectal cancer risk prediction. In: 2021 International Conference on Cyber-Physical Social Intelligence (ICCSI), pp. 1–6. IEEE (2021)
7. Rathore, S., Hussain, M., Ali, A., Khan, A.: A recent survey on colon cancer detection techniques. IEEE/ACM Trans. Comput. Biol. Bioinf. **10**(3), 545–563 (2013)
8. Marcuello, M., et al.: Circulating biomarkers for early detection and clinical management of colorectal cancer. Mol. Aspects of Med. **69**, 107–122 (2019)
9. Biller, L.H., Schrag, D.: Diagnosis and treatment of metastatic colorectal cancer: a review. Jama **325**(7), 669–685 (2021)
10. Shaban, M., Awan, R., Fraz, M.M., Azam, A., Tsang, Y.W., Snead, D., Rajpoot, N.M.: Context-aware convolutional neural network for grading of colorectal cancer histology images. IEEE Trans. Med. Imaging **39**(7), 2395–2405 (2020)
11. Alqudah, A.M., Alqudah, A.: Improving machine learning recognition of colorectal cancer using 3D GLCM applied to different color spaces. Multimed. Tools Appl. **81**(8), 10839–10860 (2022)
12. Tripathi, A., Kumar, K., Misra, A., Chaurasia, B.K.: Colon cancer tissue classification using ml. In: 2023 6th International Conference on Information Systems and Computer Networks (ISCON), pp. 1–6. IEEE (2023)

13. Ahmad, M.Y., Mohamed, A., Yusof, Y.A.M., Ali, S.A.M.: Colorectal cancer image classification using image pre-processing and multilayer perceptron. In: 2012 International Conference on Computer & Information Science (ICCIS), vol. 1, pp. 275–280. IEEE (2012)

14. Sengar, N., Mishra, N., Dutta, M.K., Prinosil, J., Burget, R.: Grading of colorectal cancer using histology images. In: 2016 39th International Conference on Telecommunications and Signal Processing (TSP), pp. 529–532. IEEE (2016)

15. Kather, J.N., et al.: Multi-class texture analysis in colorectal cancer histology. Sci. Rep. **6**(1), 27988 (2016)

16. Rathore, S., Hussain, M., Iftikhar, M.A., Jalil, A.: Ensemble classification of colon biopsy images based on information rich hybrid features. Comput. Biol. Med. **47**, 76–92 (2014)

17. Chaddad, A., Desrosiers, C., Bouridane, A., Toews, M., Hassan, L., Tanougast, C.: Multi texture analysis of colorectal cancer continuum using multispectral imagery. PLoS ONE **11**(2), e0149893 (2016)

18. Reddy, N.S.S., Reddy, V.P.M.S., Mohan, N., Kumar, S., Soman, K.P., et al.: A fast iterative filtering method for efficient denoising of phonocardiogram signals. In: 2023 3rd International Conference on Intelligent Technologies (CONIT), pp. 1–6. IEEE (2023)

19. Bychkov, D., et al.: Deep learning based tissue analysis predicts outcome in colorectal cancer. Sci. Rep. **8**(1), 3395 (2018)

20. Tamang, L.D., Kim, B.W.: Deep learning approaches to colorectal cancer diagnosis: a review. Appl. Sci. **11**(22), 10982 (2021)

21. Xu, L., et al.: Colorectal cancer detection based on deep learning. J. Pathol. Inform. **11**(1), 28 (2020)

22. Tsai, M.-J., Tao, Y.-H.: Deep learning techniques for the classification of colorectal cancer tissue. Electronics **10**(14), 1662 (2021)

23. Paladini, E., Vantaggiato, E., Bougourzi, F., Distante, C., Hadid, A., Taleb-Ahmed, A.: Two ensemble-CNN approaches for colorectal cancer tissue type classification. J. Imaging **7**(3), 51 (2021)

24. Ohata, E.F., Chagas, J.V.S.D., Bezerra, G.M., Hassan, M.M., de Albuquerque, V.H.C., Filho, P.P.R.: A novel transfer learning approach for the classification of histological images of colorectal cancer. J. Supercomput. 1–26 (2021)

25. Damkliang, K., Wongsirichot, T., Thongsuksai, P.: Tissue classification for colorectal cancer utilizing techniques of deep learning and machine learning. Biomed. Eng. Appl. Basis Commun. **33**(03), 2150022 (2021)

26. Vidhya, S., Shijitha, M.R.: Deep learning based approach for efficient segmentation and classification using VGGNet 16 for tissue analysis to predict colorectal cancer. Ann. Rom. Soc. Cell Biol. 4002–4013 (2021)

27. Anupama, M.A., Sowmya, V., Soman, K.P.: Breast cancer classification using capsule network with preprocessed histology images. In: 2019 International Conference on Communication and Signal Processing (ICCSP), pp. 0143–0147. IEEE (2019)

28. Sachin, T.S., Sowmya, V., Soman, K.P.: Performance analysis of deep learning models for biomedical image segmentation. In: Deep Learning for Biomedical Applications, pp. 83–100. CRC Press (2021)

29. Ganeshkumar, M., Sowmya, V., Gopalakrishnan, E.A., Soman, K.P.: Unsupervised deep learning-based disease diagnosis using medical images. In: Cognitive and Soft Computing Techniques for the Analysis of Healthcare Data, pp. 203–220. Elsevier (2022)

30. Kather, J.N., Halama, N., Marx, A.: 100,000 histological images of human colorectal cancer and healthy tissue, April 2018

Prediction of Breast Cancer Using Machine Learning Technique

Madhav P. Namdev[1] ⓘ, Sakil Ahmad Ansari[2] ⓘ, Arjun Singh[3(✉)] ⓘ,
Pushpa Choudhary[4] ⓘ, Arun Kumar Singh[3] ⓘ, and Jaideep Kumar[2]

[1] GL Bajaj Institute of Technology and Management, Greater Noida 201306, India
[2] Raj Kumar Goel Institute of Technology, Ghaziabad 201003, India
[3] Greater Noida Institute of Technology, Greater Noida 201310, India
innovativearjunsingh@gmail.com
[4] Galgotias University, Greater Noida 203201, India

Abstract. The prognosis and survival chances for people with breast cancer can be significantly improved by an early diagnosis. Therefore, it is crucial to accurately identify malignant tumors nowadays, it has become a frequent health problem and its occurrence is also increased and has high morality. It is also increased due to unawareness and change in the lifestyle of women. It is quite difficult to detect it in the early stage. It is also the deadliest disease after lung cancer. The most optimal machine learning technique to utilize to diagnose a certain disease is still a debate because different things can affect how accurate the results are. Hence, it is mandatory to devote effort in building up a strategy that produces fewer mistakes while improving precision. The research compares four algorithms SVM, Logistic Regression, Random Forest, and KNN—that prognosis the course of breast cancer using various datasets. Following a precise comparison of our models, we discovered that KNN outperformed all other algorithms and had a better efficiency of 97.8%. And, KNN has proven to be effective in predicting and diagnosing breast cancer and gives the best results in terms of accuracy and precision. Improved accuracy by using a variety of algorithms on the basis of the data set and model's predictions also did a fantastic statistical analysis.

Keywords: Breast Cancer · logistic regression · K-NN · SVM · Random Forest · Decision Tree

1 Introduction

It is the subsequent occurring cancer in the world after lung cancer. Invasive breast cancer in women is anticipated to cause 246660 new diagnoses and 40450 new cases of death in the US in the year 2016. In this cancer cells starts growing exceedingly and quickly from the breast creating bump like structure [1]. Cancer arises due to multiple generation of cells which occurs widely, breast cancer cells usually grouped together to form bump or a tumor which can be detected using the X-RAY images. This cancer spreads when malignant cells enter the bloodstream or lymphatic system and are transported to other

D. Garg et al. (Eds.): IACC 2023, CCIS 2054, pp. 410–420, 2024.
https://doi.org/10.1007/978-3-031-56703-2_33

bodily areas. Genetic change or mutation is one of the major factors of breast cancer. Breast cancers are in two main forms: invasive carcinoma and ductal carcinoma in situ (DCIS) [2]. One including "phyllodes tumors" and angiosarcoma, are uncommon. For breast cancer outcomes, there are several classification schemes. Few symptoms of breast cancer are headaches, tiredness, discomfort and immobility, reduction in bone mass and osteoporosis. For this, there are various methods available for categorizing and result calculating systems. This may be medically identified at early stage from mammography during a screening test or a transportable cancer detection kit. Breast cancer stage is highly correlated with the malignant transformation of breast tissues as the disease progresses. Breast cancer is classified into four stages (I–IV), each of which describes how far along the illness is [3]. These characteristics include the size of the tumor, lymph node metastasis, and distant metastases. In order to limit the spread of the disease, patients undergo various treatments such as breast cancer surgery, chemotherapy, radiation, and endocrine therapies [4, 5]. To accurately differentiate between benign and malignant patients and develop effective classification algorithms, we are analyzing various datasets and exploring machine learning applications. Our ultimate goal is to increase accuracy while minimizing error rates. With the help of the Jupiter platform and the 10-fold cross authentication test, we are evaluating and analyzing the data. We strive to ensure the accuracy and efficiency of our analysis and to minimize any potential errors. Therefore, we are committed to producing plagiarism-free work, adhering to the highest standards of academic integrity.

1.1 Exiting System

In the view current systems there are various ways to predict whether a person is having cancer or not. But these methods are costly and require a lot of time no doubt these methods are accurate but at the same time with more and more data prevailing in the medical field we can use the capabilities of machine learning to predict whether a person having benign and malignant. Since the existing systems are very slow time taking but at the same time very much accurate. So, we can try to avoid using of slow and traditional systems for non-serious patients who are not sure of cancer they can be detected and classified and they can opt for the complete test.

2 Literature Survey

Genetic changes that result in unchecked cell growth can be the cause of breast cancer. Breast cancer cells typically develop a lump or tumor that may be seen on x-rays. Invasive carcinoma and ductal carcinoma in situ (DCIS) are the two main subtypes of breast cancer. Less frequent subtypes include angiosarcoma and phyllodes tumors. Wang et al. (2018) used logistic regression and got 96.4% of their predictions right. Using the use of KNN and SVM (Akbuday et al. (2018)) 96.85% of the time, the Breast Cancer Dataset was correctly categorized. Random Forest was utilized in Kaya Keles et al. (2018) study, Breast Cancer prediction and recognition Using Data Mining which had a 92.2% accuracy rate. 'Vikas Chaurasia' and 'Saurabh Pal' (2019) evaluated the performance of a variety of supervised learning classifiers, including Naive Bayes, SVM-RBF kernel,

RBF neural networks, Decision trees (J48), and basic CART, in order to discover the best classifier for breast cancer datasets. In comparison to Random Forest, Dalen et al. (2019) found that using ADABOOST significantly improved research accuracy. The accuracy attained by Kavitha et al. (2020) was 96.3%, which was lower than that of earlier research that used ensemble techniques and neural networks.Sinthia et al. found a back propagation technique accuracy rate of 94.2%. In the Wisconsin Breast Cancer datasets, the SVM-RBF kernel outperformed other classifiers with an accuracy score of 96.84%.Support vector machine, K-NN, Random Forest, Naïve-Bayes, and Artificial Neural Network were some of the classification techniques used. The three primary areas of focus in cancer development prediction and prognosis are risk analysis or cancer perceptivity prediction, cancer recurrence prediction, and cancer survival rate prediction. The goal of cancer diagnosis and treatment is to stop recurrence. This is the second issue in cancer development prediction and prognosis [6]. The Anaconda machine learning environment's libraries were used to test the classifiers described in this study. To test and assess our classifiers we employed the 10fold cross-validation method which involves dividing the original dataset into a training sample and a test set for model training and evaluation, respectively. In this study evaluated each classifier's performance using a number of parameters-including model construction time, properly classified cases, mistakenly classified instances, and accuracy. If the infection has spread to other areas of the body, the side effects of breast cancer may change [7]. Although it is possible to have touch-insensitive melanoma lymph centers, the lymphatic veins under the arm are often the first areas of the cancer that are visible. Cancerous cells have the capacity to assault and spread to nearby organs and tissues. When they do, further warning signs of the threat, such as pain and stiffness or headaches, may appear. Here are a few early indicators of breast cancer that should be noted.

2.1 Lumps Under the Armpit or on the Breast that Lately Emerged

A. A thickening or augmentation of one or both breasts.
   b. Breast dimples, redness, or irritation.

2.2 Redness and/or Flakiness in the Breasts and/or Breasts

A. Sensation of tightness or pain surrounding the genitalia (nipple).

2.3 Breast Milk May Be Replaced with Blood or Other Materials Oozing from the Diaper Rash

A. An obvious change in the shape or size of the breasts.
   b. Any type of soreness in the breasts.
   Describe in Fig. 1. Alteration of the breast's size, form, or appearance; dimples, redness, or pitting; modification of the nipple's appearance or the skin around it (areola); and/or unusual discharge from the nipple.

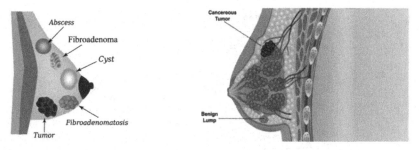

Fig. 1. Symptoms of Breast Cancer

2.4 Breast Cancer Data Set

The Breast Cancer Wisconsin (Diagnostic) Data set was used to train and evaluate the models (BCWD). The dataset consists of one classification label and thirty characteristics. These are the features of the breast cell nuclei that were captured on camera. The class label can have just two possible values: 0 and 1. Write a 0 or a 1, with 0 denoting benign and 1 malignant breast cancer, to indicate if the cancer is benign or malignant (Table 1).

Table 1. Existing Related Work

Researchers	Method	Finding	Dataset
Arpit et al., 2015	Genetically optimized neural Network (GONN)	Accuracy is good, but data set is small	WBCD
Hiba et al., 2016	Support Vector Machine	High Learning time	WBCD
Hiba et al., 2016	K-Nearest Neighbor (KNN)	Computationally expensive	WBCD
Hiba et al., 2016	Naïve Bayes (NB)	Feature independence Assumptions	WBCD
Teresa et al., 2017	Convolution Neural Network (CNN)	Data-efficient learning	Image Dataset

3 Proposed Methodology

Initially collect the data that will be practiced by the classification and regression algorithms before pre-processing. Real-world data is frequently inaccurate, unreliable, and incomplete. Preprocessing data offers a dependable solution to these problems. The UCI dataset was pre-processed using the standardization method. Discuss in below Fig. 2. This phase is essential because the caliber and volume of data you gather will have a direct bearing on how well your prediction model performs [7, 8].

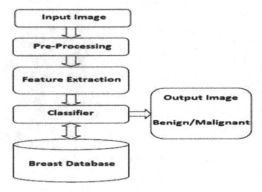

Fig. 2. Data Processing Graph

For our training data in this situation-we gathered breast cancer samples from both benign and aggressive types. It entails moving our data to the right place and getting it ready for use in our machine learning training. The ordering will then be randomized when we have accumulated all of our data [11, 12]. The goal of feature projection is to reduce the number of dimensions in the data while retaining all the essential information needed to make accurate predictions. By doing this, it can decrease the computational complexity and processing time required for data analysis while increasing the efficacy and efficiency of machine learning [8, 9] algorithms. With feature projection, data from a high-dimensional space is converted into a lower-dimensional space (with fewer attributes). Both linear and nonlinear reduction procedures may be used, depending on the type of correlations between the features in the dataset. Features having different magnitudes, units, and ranges are frequently found in datasets [12, 13]. All features must be scaled to the same magnitude level, though, because the Euclidean distance between two data points is calculated by the majority of machine learning algorithms [14]. Scaling can support this. Before training the system on the data, supervised learning includes labeling the input and output of the data. The model may predict the future by analyzing fresh data after being trained on existing data. Regression and classification are the two primary categories of machine learning issues, each of which is further subdivided into approaches. Regressions concerns are because of a real or none discrete variables such as 'Salary' or 'Weight'. While screening emails, the result of categorization issues is a category like "spam" or "not spam," in contrast. On the other hand, unsupervised learning is a method where the computer is given unlabeled or unclassified material and permitted to analyze it without being given any specific instructions. Using this strategy, tagged data are not necessary, and the system may function without clear instructions.

3.1 Pre-processing Data

We initially collect the data that will be practiced by the classification and regression algorithms before pre-processing. Real-world data is frequently inaccurate, unreliable, and incomplete. Preprocessing data offers a dependable solution to these problems. The UCI dataset was pre-processed using the standardization method. This phase is essential because the caliber and volume of data you gather will have a direct bearing on how well your prediction model performs [7]. For our training data in this situation-we gathered breast cancer samples from both benign and aggressive types.

3.2 Features Selection

The goal of feature projection is to reduce the number of dimensions in the data while retaining all the essential information needed to make accurate predictions. By doing this, it can decrease the computational complexity and processing time required for data analysis while increasing the efficacy and efficiency of machine learning algorithms [8].

3.3 Feature Scaling

Features having different magnitudes, units, and ranges are frequently found in datasets. All features must be scaled to the same magnitude level, though, because the Euclidean distance between two data points is calculated by the majority of machine learning algorithms. Scaling can support this [15].

3.4 Model Selection

Before training the system on the data, supervised learning includes labeling the input and output of the data. The model may predict the future by analyzing fresh data after being trained on existing data. Regression and classification are the two primary categories of machine learning issues, each of which is further subdivided into approaches. Regression concerns are because of a real or none discrete variables: - such as 'Salary' or 'Weight'. While screening emails, the result of categorization issues is a category like "spam" or "not spam," in contrast. On the other hand, unsupervised learning is a method where the computer is given unlabeled or unclassified material and permitted to analyze it without being given any specific instructions. Using this strategy, tagged data are not necessary, and the system may function without clear instructions [16].

3.5 Prediction

The prediction or inference stage is essential in machine learning because it uses data to provide answers to queries. The ultimate benefit of machine learning is found here, where all of our efforts have culminated.

In this dataset there are only two potential values for the outcome variable, or dependent variable, Y: M (Malign) or B. (Benign) As a result, we will classify data using supervised learning. We may begin with a straightforward linear model because we have chosen three major areas of machine learning categorization techniques. It is essential to scale the dataset's characteristics since they frequently have varying magnitudes, units, and ranges. To understand more clearly here is Fig. 3. Scaling enables all characteristics to be at the same magnitude level as most machine learning algorithms determine the Euclidean distance between 2 data points [9]. The prediction or inference stage is essential in machine learning because it uses data to provide answers to queries. The ultimate benefit of machine learning is found here, where all of our efforts have culminated.

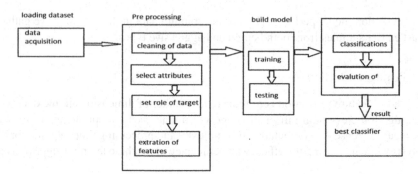

Fig. 3. Working model diagram

4 Algorithm Used

4.1 Logistic Regression

Professionals across industries use logistic regression algorithms for data mining, predictive analytics and modeling, and data classification. Professionals ranging from bankers and medical researchers to statisticians and universities find logistic regression helpful to predict future trends. Logistic regression enables scientists, researchers, and institutions to predict the future even before actual data is available. In order to predict binary outcomes based on independent factors, logistic regression is frequently utilized. Logistic regression development predates the field of machine learning.

4.2 K-Nearest Neighbor (KNN)

A supervised machine learning method called K-Nearest Neighbor (KNN) depends on labeled data. It is a nonparametric technique that categorizes test data points according to how far they are from the closest training data points without taking the dataset's dimensions into account. KNN is unique in that it does not presume any underlying distribution of the data and does not require the data to be linearly separable.

4.3 Support Vector Machine (SVM)

A supervised machine learning method called K-Nearest Neighbor (KNN) depends on labeled data. It is a nonparametric technique that categorizes test data points according to how far they are from the closest training data points without taking the dataset's dimensions into account. KNN is unique in that it does not presume any underlying distribution of the data and does not require the data to be linearly separable [17].

4.4 Random Forest

A random forest is an ensemble learning technique that blends many decision trees to generate predictions. The algorithm produces a "forest" of decision trees, as the name suggests. Each tree forecasts the class of each observation independently, and the final prediction is formed by taking the average vote of all the trees. Each decision tree in a random forest is trained using a unique collection of data and characteristics. As a result, the model's accuracy is increased and over fitting is decreased.

4.5 Decision Tree

The principles of decision trees, related algorithms, templates, samples, and best practices for creating a decision tree in 2022 are explained in this article. Regression and classification problems are frequently solved using decision trees. In classification issues, target variables holding discrete values are used by tree models to label or classify an entity. However, in regression issues, the objective variable has continuous values (actual numbers), and tree models are employed to predict results for unobserved data [18].

5 Experimental Results

A. Collecting data from Kaggle.
B. Cleaning the data which wasn't necessary because the data was already cleaned.
C. Exploratory data analysis of the data so as to remove outliers and biases.
D. Building models.
E. Inferential data analysis as to assess the accuracy and judge the need of a perfect algorithm.

We have used SVM, Random Forest, and K-NN among other algorithms to compute, compare, and assess their outcomes on the WBCD dataset for the detection of breast cancer [10]. After careful analysis, we discovered that KNN was the most effective algorithm, outperforming all others with an accuracy of 97.8%. In conclusion, KNN has proven to be useful in predicting and diagnosing breast cancer, and it outperformed all other algorithms we examined in terms of accuracy and precision shown in Table 2 and its percentage graph Fig. 4. In this model used a machine learning classifier since the major target of this problem is to create an accurate and predictive breast cancer detection system [6]. As we discuss in Fig. 5. By using Wisconsin Breast Cancer Diagnostics dataset models that assists support vector machines (SVMs), random forests, neural networks, and K-Nearest Neighbors (KNN) are evaluated for improved accuracy. Training and Testing: The algorithms for Logistic Regression, SVC, Decision Tree, and Random Forest were next trained and evaluated using the scaled dataset [18].

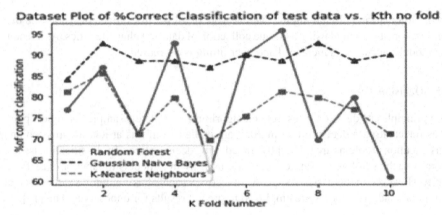

Fig. 4. Percentage Classification Graph

Table 2. Comparison analysis.

Method Used	Accuracy Percentage
Random Forest	95.5%
Neural network	94.3%
SVM	96.84%
Back propagation	94.2%
KNN	97.85%

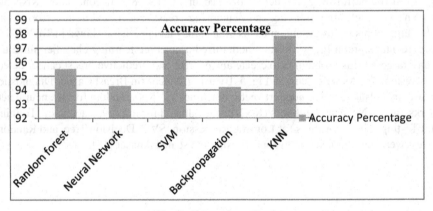

Fig. 5. Comparison Graph

6 Conclusion

In our experimental experiments, we divided the data using a 70:30 ratio into training and testing sets. Used Jupiter's support for a variety of machine learning methods to tackle real-world issues, including data pre-processing, classification, regression, clustering, and association rules. Used the 10fold cross-validation method, which divides the original dataset into a training sample and a test set for model training and assessment, respectively, to test and evaluate our classifiers. In this study, we assessed the effectiveness of each classifier using a variety of metrics, such as model creation time, the proportion of correctly classified cases to the proportion of incorrectly classified cases, and accuracy. To analyse the data set and began developing a model. I then tested the model's correctness by performing exploratory and inferential data analyses on it. I then tweaked and occasionally modified the model to increase its accuracy. To test and assess our classifiers, we used the 10-fold cross-validation technique, which divides the original dataset into a training sample and a test set.

References

1. Rani, A., Sharma, N.: Comparative analysis and visualization of breast cancer using machine learning models. In: 2022 10th International Conference on Reliability, Infocom Technologies and Optimization (Trends and Future Directions) (ICRITO), pp. 1–5. IEEE (2022)
2. Fotouhi, H., Čaušević, A., Lundqvist, K., et al.: Proceedings - International Computer Software and Applications Conference, Atlanta, United States, IEEE Computer Society, pp. 1–11 (2016)
3. Kavitha, R.K., Rangasamy, D.D.: Breast cancer survivability using adaptive voting ensemble machine learning algorithm Adaboost and CART algorithm, vol. 3, Special Issue 1, February 2014 (2014)
4. Reddy, C.S., Singh, R., Bhavani, R., Dasgupta, S., Singh, Y., Singh, S.P.: Using machine learning techniques for cancer classification. In: 2022 International Conference on Innovative Computing, Intelligent Communication and Smart Electrical Systems (ICSES), pp. 1–4. IEEE (2022)
5. Huang, R., et al.: Joint-phase attention network for breast cancer segmentation in DCE-MRI. Expert Syst. Appl. **224**, 119962 (2023)
6. Salian, P., Murthy, A., Salian, S.: Analysis of telecom churn using machine learning techniques. In: 2022 International Conference on Artificial Intelligence and Data Engineering (AIDE), pp. 58–63. IEEE (2022)
7. Shankar, J.R., Nithish, S., Babu, M.N., Karthik, R., Afridi, A.S.: Breast cancer prediction using decision tree. J. Phys. Conf. Ser. **1916**(1), 012069 (2021). IOP Publishing
8. Asif, S., Wenhui, Y., Jinhai, S., Tao, Y., Waheed, Z., Amjad, K.: A novel one-dimensional convolutional neural network for breast cancer classification. In: 2021 7th International Conference on Computer and Communications (ICCC), pp. 847–852. IEEE (2021)
9. Fatima, N., Liu, L., Hong, S., Ahmed, H.: Prediction of breast cancer, comparative review of machine learning techniques, and their analysis. IEEE Access **8**, 150360–150376 (2020)
10. Wang, H., Yoon, S.W.: Breast cancer prediction using data mining method. In: IIE Annual Conference. Proceedings, p. 818. Institute of Industrial and Systems Engineers (IISE) (2015)
11. Savalia, M.R., Verma, J.V.: Classifying malignant and benign tumors of breast cancer: a comparative investigation using machine learning techniques. Int. J. Reliab. Qual. E-Healthc. **12**(1), 1–19 (2023)

12. Vikas, C., Saurabh, P.: A novel approach for breast cancer detection using data mining techniques. Int. J. Innov. Res. Comput. Commun. Eng. **2**(1), 2456–2465 (2014)
13. Bhardwaj, A., Tiwari, A.: Breast cancer diagnosis using genetically optimized neural network model. Expert Syst. Appl. **42**(10), 4611–4620 (2015)
14. Ashraf, O.I., Siti, M.S.: Intelligent breast cancer diagnosis based on enhanced Pareto optimal and multilayer perceptron neural network. Int. J. Comput. Aided Eng. Technol. **10**(5), 543–556 (2018)
15. Liu, N., Qi, E.S., Xu, M., Gao, B., Liu, G.Q.: A novel intelligent classification model for breast cancer diagnosis. Inf. Process. Manage. **56**(3), 609–623 (2019)
16. Saleh, H., Alyami, H., Alosaimi, W.: Predicting breast cancer based on optimized deep learning approach. Comput. Intell. Neurosci. **2022** (2022)
17. Naji, M.A., El Filali, S., Aarika, K., Benlahmar, E.H., Abdelouhahid, R.A., Debauche, O.: Machine learning algorithms for breast cancer prediction and diagnosis. Procedia Comput. Sci. **191**, 487–492 (2021)
18. Amethiya, Y., Pipariya, P., Patel, S., Shah, M.: Comparative analysis of breast cancer detection using machine learning and biosensors. Intell. Med. **2**(2), 69–81 (2022)

Author Index

Printed in the United States
by Baker & Taylor Publisher Services